The World Turned
Right Side Up

The World Turned Right Side Up

A History of the Conservative Ascendancy in America

GODFREY HODGSON

HOUGHTON MIFFLIN COMPANY

BOSTON   NEW YORK   1996

For information about permission to reproduce selections from
this book, write to Permissions, Houghton Mifflin Company,
215 Park Avenue South, New York, New York 10003.

For information about this and other Houghton Mifflin
trade and reference books and multimedia products, visit
The Bookstore at Houghton Mifflin on the World Wide Web
at http://www.hmco.com/trade/.

Library of Congress Cataloging-in-Publication Data
Hodgson, Godfrey.
The world turned right side up : a history of the conservative
ascendancy in America / by Godfrey Hodgson.
p.   cm.
Includes bibliographical references and index.
ISBN 0-395-82294-7
1. Conservatism — United States. 2. United States —
Politics and government — 1945–1989. 3. United States —
Politics and government — 1989–   I. Title.
JC573.2.U6H63   1996
320.5'2'0973 — dc20   96-21744   CIP

Printed in the United States of America

QUM 10 9 8 7 6 5 4 3 2 1

Book design by Melodie Wertelet

JUNK BOOK

THE STATE OUGHT NOT to be considered as nothing better than a partnership agreement in a trade of pepper and coffee, calico or tobacco, or some other such low concern, to be taken up for a little temporary interest, and to be dissolved by the fancy of the parties . . . As the ends of such a partnership can be obtained in many generations, it becomes a partnership not only between those who are living, but between those who are living, those who are dead, and those who are to be born.

— *Edmund Burke, Reflections on the Revolution in France*

Acknowledgments

I CANNOT ADEQUATELY THANK all those who have helped me to write this book. They include those writers from whom I learned about conservative ideas and the conservative movement. Where would I have been, for example, without Martin Anderson's *Revolution*, or John Judis's biography of William F. Buckley, or George H. Nash's *The Conservative Intellectual Movement in America*? My thanks, too, to all those who agreed to be interviewed.

My work was greatly facilitated by the generosity of Charles Blitzer, the director of the Woodrow Wilson International Center for Scholars in Washington, where I spent three months reading in the pleasantest possible circumstances, and to everyone in the sandstone castle, and especially to my helpful research assistant, David Eiswert. Thanks, too, to all my friends in Washington, and especially to Tricia and Harry McPherson for their unfailing kindness.

I am grateful as always to my debonair literary agent, Robert Ducas, for his counsel and encouragement, and to everyone at Houghton Mifflin Company who has worked so hard to get this book ready in so short a time. I am particularly indebted to Frances Apt, a brilliant manuscript editor. The most special debt of gratitude is to Steven Fraser, who had the faith in me to propose that I write a book about conservatism, the patience to wait until I was free to write it, and the skill to carry it through.

Thank you, too, to Stephen Somerville, Rosemary Allan, and the Fellows of the Reuter Foundation Program at Green College, Oxford, who showed such understanding. Thank you, as always, to my children, Pierre and Francis, Jessica and Laura, for your patience, and above all to my beloved wife, Hilary.

Contents

Preface

JaNK   BooK

THE USUAL POLITICAL PROGRESSION in individual lives is from left to right. When people are young, they are impatient with the old and the established. As they get older, most of them are not so keen to change things. They have acquired a certain stake in things as they are. So, with the passing years, they become, as we used to say, more conservative.

The drift in my own life has been in the opposite direction. I began as a conservative, and I have become — well, perhaps the best expression for my peculiar personal jigsaw of political attitudes, which emphasizes public and private liberty, respect for tradition, and skepticism about organized self-interest, is a deeply out-of-date word. I fear I may be a Whig.

I grew up, you might say, in the Middle Ages. Out of my window as a child I could see the medieval towers of York Minster. I was educated in quiet British places — Oxford, York, Winchester, and Oxford again — and in the ancient classical tradition. At the time, I found the aura of the past both benign and protective. Long-founded institutions seemed more civilized and society fairer than I can now see they were.

I grew up, too, in the generation — I was eleven years old when World War II ended — that feared and utterly rejected communism. Although some of my contemporaries embraced something they called "socialism," for a long time I could never quite rid myself of the suspicion that the word was a euphemism for various essentially unconstructive resentments.

I have since come to have great respect for some people who call themselves socialists, though I have never been convinced that public ownership is sensible for most kinds of enterprise. But it was not until I went to the United States as a graduate student in the 1950s, and more especially not until I started work as a Washington reporter in the 1960s and 1970s, that I ceased to think of myself as a conservative.

I covered the civil rights movement in the South, the Kennedy and Johnson years, and the critical presidential election of 1968. In the process, I became aware of what I saw at the time as a certain emotional impoverishment as well as thinly veiled self-interest in traditional conservatism. I could see how it had acted as a shield for racism, class and money privilege, and sometimes for tyranny. At the same time, I was aware quite early of the hubris and the failure of the liberalism of the Kennedy-Johnson years. Indeed, in 1976 I published a book in which I tried to anatomize the assumptions made by what I called, rather loosely, "the liberal consensus," which I saw as "hardly to be distinguished from a more sophisticated and less resolute conservatism."

Of course I was also aware that a new yeast was at work in American conservatism. At the University of Pennsylvania I had been taught by a brilliant conservative, Robert Strausz-Hupé. I had read Russell Kirk and James Burnham, Peter Viereck and William F. Buckley. I had covered the Goldwater campaign and interviewed Senator Goldwater. In 1968, when I and a group of colleagues from the London *Sunday Times* wrote a book about the presidential election, we gave a good deal of attention to Nixon's "Southern strategy." At different times I reported on several arms of the swelling conservative movement, and eventually I spent most of a year making a television biography about Ronald Reagan.

Even so, when Margaret Thatcher became prime minister in Britain in 1979, and even more when Ronald Reagan won the presidential election in 1980, I found myself bewildered. It was not the fact of conservative victory. That seemed to be inevitable after the failures of British Labour and American liberals. What puzzled me was the incoherent cocktail of ideas that were being melded together and offered under the marketing label "conservative." In particular, I was baffled by excited proclamations that conservatism — passionately advocated by Wall Street arbitrageurs and tenured professors in large graduate schools — had somehow become a radical philosophy, while liberalism — a set of beliefs I had heard articulated by industrial workers in Detroit and by black schoolteachers in Alabama — was seen as the doctrine of the elite. There was something fishy here, I thought, and I wanted to understand how these improbably associated ideas had been fitted together.

As the years went by, I was sometimes irritated by a certain cliquishness about conservative intellectual life. Conservatives seemed forever to be demanding, "Are you one of us?" There was a propagandistic tone — "We're taking over!" — to so much of what they wrote. Still, I was more seriously annoyed by the failure of those who did not accept conservative oracles uncritically to take conservative arguments seriously. And I longed for someone to ask even the most basic questions about the Emperor's wardrobe.

So when, seven years ago, I was asked to write what turned into this book, I was delighted at the opportunity to attempt what I had already tried to do with the world of liberalism: to trace how ideas and events were plaited together to make a political tradition. There were to be delays and obstacles, most of them of my own making; but here at last is my best attempt to understand what has been, after all, a serious effort to transform the world.

I am not a political philosopher. Although I was trained as a historian, I am essentially a reporter. So in the first nine chapters of this book I have tried to report as clearly as I can how modern American conservatism grew from the despised and unfashionable set of ideas it was in 1945 until it captured the seats of power. The last two chapters describe what happened to the high hopes of 1981 in the course of the Reagan and Bush years. They pose what I think are the most insistent questions about this process: Was there a Reagan revolution? And how permanent have the changes been that were made in the name of conservatism? By implication, they also ask: How has it all turned out? I leave it to the reader to see how much he agrees with my verdict.

Washington D.C.—Oxford
1993–1996

The World Turned
Right Side Up

JUNK BOOK

❧ 1 ❧

The World Turned
Right Side Up

I am a conservative because I'm for change.
— *Senator Roger Jepsen, Republican of Iowa*[1]

"THE WORLD TURNED UPSIDE DOWN" was the name of the tune
— a popular song of the day in London — that the band of the victorious American army is said to have played as Lord Cornwallis's Redcoats
stacked their arms and surrendered at Yorktown.[2] "Bliss was it in that
dawn to be alive," wrote the young William Wordsworth of another
revolution, only eight years later, when he read of the fall of the Bastille,
"but to be young was very heaven." And from time to time since then
other events have been inscribed in letters of red in the political calen-
dar, not least among them the ten days of the Russian Revolution in St.
Petersburg in 1917, which certainly did shake the world.

A conservative revolution sounds like a contradiction in terms. And
certainly the arrival of Ronald Reagan in the White House in January
1981 was not revolutionary in style. No tumbrils carried white-faced
aristocrats along Pennsylvania Avenue to their execution; there was no
guillotine in Lafayette Square. If anything, it was the newcomers accompanying the Reagans to Washington who belonged to an American
aristocracy of talent and money. At the six inaugural balls held to accom-
modate all the celebrants who had flocked to town, many observers
commented on the pervasive smell of money lavished, for example, on
dresses designed by the new First Lady's favorite and friend, Oscar de la
Renta, and on the elaborate coiffures worn by both husbands and wives.
Stretch limos, not tumbrils, were the vehicles of choice in Washington
in January 1981.

Yet the day of President Reagan's inauguration, January 21, 1981, was generally understood to be a turning point in American political history. The language of revolution was freely applied to it, both by those who dreaded and by those who eagerly awaited the changes the new Republican administration was expected to introduce.

The purpose of this book is twofold: to show how conservatism, a despised and impotent political philosophy at the end of World War II, proved to be a spectacular ideological "comeback kid"; and to inquire why, fifteen years after the triumph and triumphalism of the Reagan years, as the Republicans confront President Clinton, conservatism has proved, on the whole, so confusing and disappointing as a guiding star for political action.

The margin of Reagan's election victory surprised the pundits and was not predicted by the polls.[3] In May the journalist Morton Kondracke wrote in *The New Republic*, which then still regarded itself as a liberal magazine, "Anyone betting on the outcome of the Carter-Reagan election would be foolish to wager very much, because the race gives every promise of being hard and close."[4] In the event, Reagan carried every region of the country, including the industrial Northeast and the South, the two sections to which Jimmy Carter had owed his victory in 1976. In the popular vote, Reagan won a lead of eight million votes, or 7 percent, overall. Experts noticed, in particular, the inroads he had made into the blue-collar, working-class neighborhoods, traditional heartland of the Democratic electorate. From the start, this was interpreted as an event of more than electoral significance. American presidential elections, after all, have always had two functions. They are obviously an opportunity to choose a president and some thousands of other office holders, but they are also a time to reflect on the nation's agenda and, if the majority of the electorate wants, to change it. Conservatives were quick to claim that this was indeed what the voters were saying: that they rejected liberalism and embraced conservatism as the public philosophy of America. "Reagan's victory in the 1980 elections completed the conservative ascent," wrote one historian.[5] "Gone were the dour tones and long looks of 1974." This was "the greatest victory for conservatism since the American Revolution" for Howard Phillips, leader of the Conservative Caucus. For John T. Dolan, of the National Conservative Political Action Committee, it was "the most massive political victory in the history of conservatism." "Conservatives don't have to be ashamed of what they profess in order to win elections," rejoiced Paul Weyrich, of the Committee for the Survival of a Free Congress.[6]

Was Reagan's triumph in fact a true turning point, an irreversible break in the American political mood? Perhaps. That is precisely one of the questions this book will try to answer. But whether it was or not, it is worth recalling that it was not seen as inevitable or even especially likely at the time. Although public opinion surveys picked up a shift to Reagan in the last week of the campaign, virtually all of them predicted that the result would be close. Carter may have been damaged by Reagan's effective performance in the candidates' only debate, less than a week before the poll. He was certainly hurt by the presence in the race of a relatively liberal third-party candidate, John B. Anderson, of Illinois; and especially by the protracted agony of the Tehran hostage crisis. If the Iranians had released the American hostages before Election Day, then there might have been a conservative revolution — but it would not have been symbolized by a Reagan victory in 1980.

Reagan, however, conducted himself as though he did indeed carry the mandate of heaven. From the start, wrote the young conservative journalist Burton Yale Pines, the incoming president "behaved as if he was ushering in a new era."[7] The *Washington Post* spoke of a "tidal wave" and, even more vaguely, expressed its editorial conviction that "something of gigantic proportions" had occurred.

The paper's highly respected political expert, David Broder, said Reagan's inauguration was "the start of a new era" and "the biggest power shift in Washington since 1952." Within weeks, Broder's conservative rivals, Robert Novak and Rowland Evans, were at work on a book they called *The Reagan Revolution*.[8]

Memory, to be sure, foreshortens historical processes. In retrospect, it is easy to say that between November 5, 1980, when Ronald Reagan was elected president of the United States, and January 23, 1981, the world was turned upside down. Conservatives, indeed, would prefer to say that the world, upended by decades of liberal error, was turned right side up.

In reality, those hectic weeks were simply the moment when changes which had been maturing for decades, and had acquired immense momentum over the preceding five years, were finally fulfilled. It was to be many years more before the full implication of Reagan's victory became plain. Fifteen years later, it is still possible to disagree on how deep and lasting the changes Reagan symbolized have been. Ironically, those who most want a conservative revolution to take place are those most likely to deny that there was anything that can seriously be called a Reagan revolution. Even today, there is no more important or urgent issue than whether the American people want the changes symbolized by Reagan's occupation of the White House to continue. The 1996 presidential election is, among other things, a national referendum on the conservative agenda which Reagan brought with him to Washington.

Yet unmistakably, 1980 is remembered as one of those rare electoral realignments that shake the American political system as a child shakes a kaleidoscope, so that the existing elements are juggled into a totally new pattern.[9] Indeed, political mythology has already cast Reagan as the spearhead of an international ideological upheaval comparable with those of 1789 and 1917, and as the catalytic agent for ideas that would transform politics and society in the United States and far beyond. Like all myths, that idea contains elements of truth; it is also a gross oversimplification.

In the very month of Reagan's victory, George Gilder, one of the more excited prophets of a new conservative era, published his best-known book, *Wealth and Poverty*. Its first sentence pronounced that "the most important event in the recent history of ideas is the demise of the socialist dream."[10] Yet it was almost nine years before the communist regimes of Eastern Europe crumbled after the Soviet Union withdrew its support, and another two years before communism collapsed in the Soviet Union itself. In many parts of Eastern Europe and the former Soviet Union, communists of one stamp or another are already back in power, and the same may well happen in Russia. Close to a quarter of the human race still lives under communist rule in China. Socialism as a dream may be dead; socialism as a political system has proved surprisingly durable.

On a close look, the idea of a worldwide conservative revolution in 1980 does not hold water.[11] Even in the United States, what happened was complex and more gradual than is often remembered. The ideas Reagan embodied had been spreading and gathering strength for close to half a century when he became president. Equally, his own impact on the political process did not happen all at once. "There is a tidal wave coming," wrote Republican Representative Jack Kemp in 1979, "equivalent to the one that hit in 1932, when an era of Republican dominance gave way to the New Deal. It's going to happen again, and we'll find millions upon millions of Americans surprising themselves by voting Republican . . . because they see in the GOP a better shot at the American Dream." In 1980, surprised at themselves or not, millions of Americans did just that. At long last the sixty-nine-year-old Ronald Reagan, who had seriously considered running for president in 1968 and had come close to winning the Republican nomination in 1976, finally swept into the White House, with an overwhelming majority. Even then, though, some of the shrewdest political observers, while sensing that Reagan was a phenomenon and a portent, were not ready to concede conservative claims that the world had indeed been turned right side up.

On December 6, 1980, for example, a month after Reagan's victory, TRB, the veteran columnist in *The New Republic*, greeted the supposed conservative revolution in coolly dismissive terms:

> The fact is there are real questions these days, with accelerating and intensifying foreign and domestic problems, whether the fragmented system of divided government invented by the founding fathers hasn't reached the limit of tolerance . . . So the country elects an affable Hollywood actor whose whole art is communicating . . . How he will boost defense, cut taxes, end inflation, and balance the budget all at once nobody knows.[12]

That was an extremely pertinent question, as we shall see. TRB, however, went on to give Ronald Reagan, almost contemptuously, "a free ride for about six months." Not much different was the measured judgment of the *New York Times*'s bureau chief in Washington, Hedrick Smith, writing on Inauguration Day itself.[13]

> The nation today arrived at a fascinating and quite remarkable moment in its political history: A 69-year-old citizen-politician who spent most of his working life in another profession, has entered the White House and won the opportunity to lead a conservative political revolution.
>
> Or more precisely to lead a conservative reformation that seeks to redirect the role of government in American life and perhaps to reshape the national political landscape for the rest of the century.
>
> For Ronald Wilson Reagan . . . is a crusader, the first missionary conservative to be elected with the aim of reversing the liberal New Deal revolution of governmental activism and Democratic party dominance established by Franklin D. Roosevelt almost half a century ago.

Some Republicans, Smith conceded, went further and believed that an irresistible tide of conservatism had swept the land, and that the mood of the country had shifted irreversibly to the right. He quoted the irrepressible Kemp as interpreting the election as an opportunity for the conservative Republicans to stay in power "for two generations." Yet Smith was not yet ready to concede as much as that. For the time being, the *New York Times* was ready to accept a Republican victory; it would not yet accept that a great historical transformation had taken place. Even two months later, the Gallup Poll, so far from recording evidence of a landslide for conservatism, found that only 59 percent of those questioned said they approved of Reagan's handling of the presidency, as against 65 percent for Nixon, 73 percent for Kennedy, and 75 percent for the recently humiliated Carter at the same stage of their respective presidencies.[14]

Less than two weeks after that, President Reagan was shot by a young man named John W. Hinckley as he left a meeting with labor leaders at the Washington Hilton Hotel.[15] Absurd and gratuitous as the shooting was, it touched a sore nerve in American sensibility, the one bared by the assassination of John F. Kennedy eighteen years earlier. Reagan himself, in the most natural and spontaneous way, set his sails to this warm wind. Close to his seventieth birthday, he behaved with a courage and grace that won over all but his bitterest opponents. Quipping like the debonair heroes of those classic Hollywood comedies he was old enough to have acted in, he brought back memories of a golden age not only for Hollywood but for the country.

Lyndon Johnson had enjoyed a vicarious political honeymoon after Kennedy's assassination. Reagan was fortunate enough to enjoy the reaction to his own shooting. Congress had gone along with Johnson when he asked it to pass a civil rights bill as a monument to Kennedy. Now the congressmen fell in behind Reagan's economic proposals. For only the second time in almost thirty years, a president found a favorable climate for his legislative proposals on Capitol Hill, and Reagan took full advantage. He persuaded Congress to pass the biggest spending and tax cuts in history; it slashed domestic social programs by over $130 billion while at the same time approving most of Reagan's increased military spending requests.[16]

It would no doubt be too much to say that Ronald Reagan owed his political successes in 1981 to John Hinckley. He earned them for himself. Still, the transformation of his political fortunes after the shooting was undeniably dramatic. People admired the way Reagan had confronted his trauma. You could say that Reagan had made his own luck. Politicians — and journalists — were quick to pick up the idea that to be critical of this pleasant man in his convalescence would not be clever.

For a few crucial months, the habitual rigor of Washington's scrutiny was abated. By late July even the doubting Hedrick Smith was converted to admiration. In six months, he said, Reagan had wrought not only a dramatic shift in economic policies; he had also "swept to a political mastery of the Congress not seen since LBJ."[17] Though Reagan's personal ratings in the polls were to fluctuate for years to come, and though his personal shortcomings were analyzed with painful honesty in many a profile and editorial, after the shooting no politician and few journalists dared to ignore his popularity. In spite of ups and downs, his reelection by a landslide in 1984 was a foregone conclusion. By July 1986 *Time* magazine could say, in unusually unrestrained language:

> Ronald Reagan has found the American sweet spot. The 75-year-old man is hitting home runs . . . Reagan is a sort of masterpiece of American magic — apparently one of the simplest, most uncomplicated creatures alive, and yet a character of rich meanings, of complexities that connect him with the myths and powers of his country in an unprecedented way.[18]

In a study written for the Brookings Institution and published in 1985, John Chubb and Paul Peterson wrote:

> The American political system, during the presidency of Ronald Reagan, has been transformed to an extent unknown since the days of Franklin Roosevelt. The terms of political debate, the course of domestic and foreign policy, and the dominant line of political cleavage have all been fundamentally changed.[19]

So if it took some time for the idea to take hold that Reagan represented a revolutionary break with the course of American politics over the last half century, after his reelection the idea of a "Reagan revolution" became widely accepted. It became a cliché of political journalism. And it was perhaps the sincerest flattery that liberals, brows furrowed with anxiety, began to take seriously the idea that the country was embarked for the foreseeable future on a conservative course. Not a few of them, indeed, paid to conservatives a form of flattery even more sincere than imitation by crossing the ideological divide and joining them.

No one expounded the idea that a conservative revolution was taking place more consistently or with greater conviction than Martin Anderson, the Republican economist who had worked for the Nixon administration as well as Reagan's. Anderson did not make the mistake of suggesting that Reagan brought a conservative revolution to Washington with him overnight. The change came, he wrote in his book *Revolu-*

tion, "like a rising tide — silently, inexorably, gently lapping forward."[20] Only the political waves were noticeable, and they rushed in, then receded, each time reaching higher up the beach, first with Barry Goldwater in 1964, then with Richard Nixon in 1968, and finally, decisively, with Ronald Reagan in 1980. Anderson made a distinction that is vital for understanding what has happened in the United States in the past forty years: he pointed out the relation between political events and an underlying change in the world of ideas.

> The election of Ronald Reagan in 1980 and many of the events that followed were the political results of an intellectual movement building [in the United States] for many years and to a lesser extent throughout the world . . . That movement was no accident, but rather the logical outgrowth of policy ideas and political forces set in motion during the 1950s and 1960s, ideas and forces that gathered strength and speed during the 1970s, then achieved power in the 1980s, and promise to dominate national policy in the United States for the remainder of the twentieth century.[21]

In an interview in his office at the Hoover Institution at Stanford University, Anderson expanded that idea. "There has been an intellectual revolution," he told me, "moving with the power and speed of a glacier." Glaciers move very slowly, but they move with irresistible force. "Every now and then the glacier comes up against a tree. As it gets closer and closer to fifty percent, everyone says there has been a sudden change. But in fact, underneath, the intellectual change is smooth and unstoppable. Ideas do move the world."[22]

"IDEAS," TO QUOTE the title of a book by the conservative philosopher Richard Weaver, "have consequences."[23] Ideas cause people to behave as they do, and the events they cause in turn change people's ideas. One of the purposes of this book is to illustrate this reciprocal relationship between ideas and events, and in particular to show how they interacted over the past fifty years to transform conservatism from a defeated, proscribed, and unpopular set of beliefs in America into a powerful operating ideology.

But it is hard to separate ideas from words, and words in political discourse have a way of shifting their meanings to meet the needs of politicians whose desire to persuade is stronger than their passion to explain. "With words," it is said, "we rule men." Three words, in particular, are critical to understanding what has happened in America since

1945: *republican, liberal,* and above all *conservative.* This is, after all, to put it at its simplest, the story of how liberal ideas were discredited and conservatives took over the Republican Party.

Each of those three words, as it happens, has had an unusually checkered and confused history. Each has changed its meaning over the years. Each has come to mean something close to the opposite of what it meant at an earlier period. The Republicans were once what we now call Democrats. Liberals were once believers in a kind of modern conservatism. And modern conservatives hold some of the views that conservatives once abominated. So it is worth looking back at how each of those three portmanteau words came to carry its modern baggage.

Republicanism had always been associated with the struggle against monarchy. Since the best-known republics in eighteenth-century Europe — Holland and Geneva — were also Protestant, and the Catholic Church was associated with absolute monarchy, it was natural for the leaders of the American Revolution, Protestants brought up on classical culture in the Age of the Enlightenment, to call the state they were forging out of thirteen rebellious colonies a "republic."

It was even more natural for Thomas Jefferson, who, with Governor Clinton of New York, was the founder of what was to become the Democratic Party, to call it the Republican Party, and so it remained until 1828.[24] The modern Republican Party did not come into existence until 1854; its origins are usually traced to a protest meeting convened by a certain Alvin E. Bovay in the Congregational church in Ripon, Wisconsin. It grew out of the outraged opposition to the Kansas-Nebraska bill by Free Soil men. The bill tore up thirty years of compromise between North and South by allowing slavery to enter the territories, and so shattered the existing party system. Instead of two national parties, the Democrats and the Whigs, each with a Northern and a Southern wing, half a dozen parties, embryo parties and political alliances — Whigs, Democrats, Know-Nothings, Free Soilers, Abolitionists, and "fusionists" — came into existence, and the politicians milled about among them. Out of this political cauldron the Republicans emerged as the party of Lincoln, champions of the Union, and emancipators of the slaves.

The Republican Party dominated Northern politics from 1868 until 1896. Like all great political parties, it was a coalition, reflecting the elements that had created it. As the party of Lincoln and of the Radical Republicans who had tried to reconstruct the South, it embodied both victory and emancipation. As the heir of the Know-Nothings, horrified at the mass immigration of Catholic Germans and Irish, it was the party of Northern Protestants. As the heir of (some) Whigs, it was the party of big business, and the natural home of the respectable monied and educated class.

By the 1880s, the radical legacy had been largely forgotten, at least outside the South. Nationally, at least, the Republican Party had become a conservative party in the old-fashioned sense of the word. It was dedicated to the preservation of the dominant white Anglo-Saxon Protestant culture and the interests of big business, as interpreted by the bosses who drove the business machine of the Gilded Age.[25]

The social conflicts of the Progressive Era broke this mold. Many of the most high-minded Republicans enrolled with Theodore Roosevelt under the insurgent banner of the Bull Moose, and the split in Republican ranks allowed the Democrats to take power under Woodrow Wilson. But after 1919, Republican hegemony settled over the political landscape again. A new nativism responded to the crest of immigration in the first decade of the century. A new prosperity revived the prestige of businessmen. A new intolerance saw a tough crackdown on labor unions and radicals and the rise of the second Klan. A new Americanism, fortified by the dominant position in which the United States had emerged from World War I, might have carried on the aggressive nationalism of Teddy Roosevelt. Instead, it took the form of isolationism.

Only the dramatic crack-up of the Republican system, with the onset of the Great Depression in 1929, ended more than two generations in which the Republicans were the natural ruling party and the natural ruling class were Republicans. No doubt they were overblamed for the collapse of the world economic system in 1929. Still, by the end of World War II, a mere decade and a half after the 1929 disaster — that is, an interval no longer than that separating the election of Ronald Reagan to the presidency in 1980 from the election of 1996 — the Republicans were still discredited, divided, and demoralized. Most of all, they were in the market for a new creed.

POLITICAL PHILOSOPHERS argue about the precise implications of the word "liberal,"[26] but the most interesting point about its history is that it has come to have almost exactly opposite meanings in Europe and in the United States. Originally, the liberals in politics were those who favored freedom in the sense of toleration. A liberal in Italy, for example, was one who opposed the pope's temporal rule. In Britain, around the middle of the nineteenth century, it acquired a new meaning. A "Manchester liberal," typically a businessman, was a believer in free markets and free trade. That meaning caught on in continental Europe, where to this day "liberal" in its various translations describes a believer in free-market economics. The great Austrian apostles of free market economics, F. A. Hayek and Ludwig von Mises, called themselves "liberals," not conservatives.[27] European liberals were on the right of the political spectrum.

In Britain, the Liberal Party replaced the Whigs as the main opposition to the Tories, as W. S. Gilbert's Sergeant Willis understood:

> That every boy and every gal
> That's born into this world, alive
> Is either a little Liberal,
> Or else a little Conservative!

By the beginning of the nineteenth century the liberal party was something of a hybrid. It provided a political home for both liberal businessmen and for their discontented "Lib-Lab" employees. After 1906 the labor unions and most working-class voters transferred their loyalty to the new Labour Party. The Liberal Party became, and has remained, a permanent third party, to the left of the Conservatives but not a party of the left.

In the United States, with neither an established church nor (outside the South) a landlord class, there were too few Tories to need a whole party to combat them. So the word "liberal" was not used to denote a particular political party until the birth in 1944 of the New York Liberal Party. The word came to be widely used in its modern sense only in the later New Deal years. After 1945, it became a euphemism for a man or woman of the left. In the late 1930s even the Communist Party had substantial influence in the big industrial unions and among some intellectuals.[28] With the coming of the Cold War, assorted leftists, radicals, and moderate socialists took to using the word "liberal" to describe themselves.

On January 4, 1947, a number of prominent liberals met at the Willard Hotel in Washington and founded Americans for Democratic Action as a pressure group on the left of the Democratic Party. (They included Eleanor Roosevelt, Hubert H. Humphrey, the theologian Reinhold Niebuhr, and the historian Arthur M. Schlesinger, Jr.) At that first meeting, the economist John Kenneth Galbraith urged his friends to call it the Liberal Union, but without success. It is perhaps a pity, because one not present at the Willard meeting, though he joined ADA not long afterward, was the president of the Screen Actors Guild in Hollywood, a certain Ronald W. Reagan.[29]

In the 1950s and 1960s, liberals supported government action of all kinds: a government health care program was high on their list of priorities. At the same time, they were strongly anticommunist and strongly supportive of American policy in the Cold War. "Liberal," in fact, had come to be a euphemism for a position that in other countries would have been called "social democrat" or "democratic socialist."

With John Kennedy, and even more with Lyndon Johnson, American liberalism triumphed. ("Kennedy promised," said Arthur Schlesinger; "Johnson delivered."[30]) Johnson himself said in his first address to Congress that he was going to build "the kind of nation that President Roosevelt hoped for, President Truman worked for, and President Kennedy died for." But Johnson's own policies exposed the liberals to a deadly crossfire. On the one hand, they were derided by the radicals of the New Left as cowardly servants of "the system," which they saw as oppressing black people in Mississippi and killing brown people in Vietnam. From the other flank, they were being denounced by all those who wanted to sweep away the massive machinery with which liberals had tried to deliver a New Deal and build a Great Society — those, in fact, who called themselves "conservatives."

IN ONE OF the most noisome depths of Dante's Inferno there stood a miscreant, up to his throat in filth, who complained that the ordure was "not as thick and black as it was wont to be." He was temperamentally, in the old sense of the word, a conservative. As long as men and women have debated proposed innovations, some have opposed them on principle. But philosophical conservatism means something more than a general suspicion of change. The deeply conservative British writer Lord Hugh Cecil,[31] son of the great Tory prime minister the Marquess of Salisbury, was right when he said that modern conservatism was born of the opposition to the French Revolution.[32] "Conservatism did not become part of political speech until about 1830 in England," the conservative philosopher Robert Nisbet agreed. "But its philosophical substance was brought into being by Edmund Burke in his *Reflections on the Revolution in France.*"[33]

Conservatism has always been reactive, a response to political movements which the conservative feared and wanted to halt. Samuel Huntington, of Harvard, called it a "situational ideology."[34] He meant that it has always responded to specific challenges to the *status quo*, rather than committing itself to defend any particular philosophy. The career of the first and one of the greatest conservative thinkers, Edmund Burke, illustrates the point.[35] Burke started out in life as a Whig. That is to say, he belonged to that one of the two historic parties in eighteenth-century England which preserved a revolutionary tradition. Whigs defended "the good old cause for which Hampden died in the field and Sidney on the scaffold"[36]: the cause, that is, of the English Revolution. What is more, in the 1770s Burke was also a supporter of the American Revolution. It was only after the French Revolution, with his brilliant pamphlet *Thoughts on the Recent Revolution in France*, published in October 1790, just sixteen months after the fall of the Bastille, that he placed himself firmly in the conservative camp.

Of course conservatives have almost always detested the expropriation of private property, whether carried out directly by revolutionary regimes or gradually through taxation. So conservatism has always been, among other things, the doctrine of those who have much to lose and are afraid to lose it. But quite often in history those who had most to lose felt they could afford to hold, or to affect, egalitarian attitudes. Philippe duc d'Orléans, who liked to be called Philippe Égalité, was the richest man in pre-Revolutionary France. Burke's patrons, the Whig lords, with their revolutionary memories, included the wealthiest landlords in England and Ireland.[37]

Traditional European conservatives, in any case, were interested in defending not just their own and their order's property, but the whole legal and social system that protected and guaranteed the rights of property: king, nobility, landowning, parliament, courts of law, magistrates, army, navy, and the whole parallel spiritual hierarchy of the church, from the archbishops with their princely landed estates down to the parish clergy.

Conservative principles sprang not just from vested interests, though these played their part, nor from political theory, though men like Burke and Benjamin Disraeli in England, John Adams and Alexander Hamilton in the United States, well knew how to erect imposing edifices of theory. They sprang most of all from instincts, and in particular from three: a suspicion of utopian thinking and of the characteristic desire of much modern thought to rebuild human society; a respect for tradition and a tendency to believe that it embodies greater wisdom than any individual; and a reverence for institutions, and especially for the nation, the church, and the family.[38]

The conservative characteristically thinks other matters more important than politics. Quentin Hogg, for example, the British Conservative lawyer-politician, wrote that "the man who puts politics first is not fit to be called a civilized human being, let alone a Christian."[39] Although there have always been religious radicals, conservatism does seem to come naturally to those who put religion ahead of politics, and more generally to those who emphasize the nonrational and the transcendental dimensions of life, as opposed to the practical and the rational.

By the time the wreckage of World War II had been cleared away, in most Western democracies a parliamentary political system was dominated by peaceful struggle between one or more parties of change and one or more parties of order. Only in the United States was there no obvious equivalent of this politics of economic class, no conservative party like the British Tories. This was hardly because conservatism did not exist as a political force in the United States, however. There is a ripe native American conservative tradition stretching back to the Revolutionary War and beyond. This book is not the story of the invention of American conservatism. It is the story of how many indigenous conservative traditions came together as a united political movement and, incidentally, of how serious divisions still split that movement.

In the South, of course, conservatism was well established. Southern conservatives had defended slavery, and in the twentieth century they rallied behind the defense of segregation. Even as late as the 1940s virtually all Southern politicians were conservative on racial, social, and constitutional issues. The only radicalism was economic. The South's representation in Congress may have embraced fairly radical propositions about many economic questions, but Southern Democrats in Congress voted solidly as conservatives. Not only that; they frequently voted together with Republican conservatives to form a block that actually controlled Congress as a whole, on many important issues, including racial issues, until the 1960s.

There were many other conservative traditions, too, in the America of 1945 besides that of the South. Corporate business might have decided to make a temporary truce with big government in the Roosevelt years, an accommodation that would last until the 1970s but not beyond them, but few corporate executives truly welcomed government intervention, government regulation, or the taxation needed to pay for them. Nor did the possessors of wealth, earned or inherited. As for the trade unions, corporate management in the 1940s and 1950s accepted the advantages of industrial peace and partnership. But management never really gave up on a conservative model of economic relations, one in which managers would be free to manage and the market would be free from the interference of either government or labor. Farmers, too, while not immune to waves of radicalism and happy enough (like many businessmen) to be massively subsidized by government, remained deeply conservative on most political and social issues. The squatter and homesteader in the West, Robert Nisbet has pointed out, "could fight against government and financial speculator as determinedly as the owner of vast cattle ranges."[40]

Strong religious traditions inclined many Americans to conservative ways of thought. In the 1940s the Roman Catholic Church in the urban Northeast and Middle West was still predominantly conservative. The Mormon Church in Utah was a bastion of traditionalism. Conservative Protestants in many parts of the country, not least in New England, still shared many of the cautious instincts of classic conservatives; the influence of ecumenical and liberal theology had not yet permeated the mainstream Protestant denominations. Evangelical, fundamentalist, and pentecostal Protestants, growing in numbers and also achieving the social and financial advancement that had previously eluded them as groups, were not yet involved in politics.

Religion was to provide the link between two traditions that may at first seem diametrically opposed: the conservatism of the elites and the populism of the excluded. Throughout their history, Americans have discussed politics in terms of "images of conflict between the powerful and the powerless," as one recent history puts it.[41]

> The haughty financier wraps chains of debt around small farmers . . . The stout industrialist — top hat on his fleshy head and diamond stickpin gleaming from his silk tie — clashes with the working man dressed in overalls . . . The federal bureaucrat, overeducated and amoral, scoffs at the God-fearing nuclear family in its modest home.[42]

This contrast between rich and poor, powerful and powerless, elite and common people, has zigzagged through American history from left to right. (It is not always possible to draw a line between left and right.) Like a creature of mythology or dreams, American populism has changed its shape. Classically, it was a movement of agrarian radicalism, and so theoretically on the left, as in the rising of the impoverished farmers of the South and the Great Plains from the late 1870s to the 1890s. But was the movement for Prohibition a movement of left or right? It was certainly populist. The Ku Klux Klan was on the right, but it too reflected some of the impulses — racist and nativist, anti-Catholic and anti-Semitic, but also antimetropolitan and antielitist — that went to make up populism. In the 1930s the new industrial trade unionism captured something of the moral élan of American populism, but by the 1960s at least a piece of the tattered mantle had passed to George Wallace, who fought equality for working black people in the name of "this average man in the street, this man in the textile mill, this man in the steel mill, this barber, the beautician, the policeman on the beat."[43]

By the 1970s, the eagles of populism, fickle birds, had flown into the camp of the conservatives; how that came about will be another theme of this book. It was in large measure the alliance between the economic conservatism of the business culture and the social conservatism of religious populists that created a new coalition and armed it with the big battalions it needed to make Reagan's victory possible.

For a majority of Americans in the 1940s, the Great Depression seemed to have brought permanent discredit to traditional Republican conservatism. But there was always a substantial minority who never bought that proposition, never accepted discredit. In many parts of the country there was a sense of outrage that traditional American attitudes to property, like attitudes to religion, social order, and the family, were under threat. These attitudes were as old as the Republic; indeed, much older. They had traveled across the Atlantic in fragile sailing craft. They were reinforced by the reaction to successive movements for radical change, by successive waves of alarming modernity. In the 1880s and 1890s, it was rural populism and urban anarchism that were the threat. In the early 1900s, it was the Progressive movement and immigrant socialism. Most of all, in the panic engendered by the economic collapse, it was the New Deal. Conservatism in the United States has never been a mere static opposition to change. Historically, it has been dynamic: the moving force of a series of reactions to change.

The South and the West; the wealthy and respectable upper middle classes; corporate management; populism — at the end of World War II these vast, potentially conservative forces in American life were latent. Their strength was still hobbled by three circumstances. Conservative leaders, such as Herbert Hoover, were blamed for the Great Depression. Conservative electoral support was split between two rival political parties. And those who were potentially conservatives did not possess, at the end of World War II, any set of beliefs coherent enough to be called an ideology.

THE RISE OF conservatism is, among other things, the story of how those latent conservative forces in American life came to exert themselves. It is also the narrative of how American conservatives came to commit their fortunes to those of the Republican Party; how they came to see themselves as involved in a war to the knife against liberalism; and how they hammered out a working ideology, only to watch it crack along the lines of its internal inconsistencies and contradictions.

The paradox at the center of the claim made by Ronald Reagan and the conservative movement that swept him to power was this: they were conservatives in most of the traditional meanings of the word; at the same time what they proposed was consciously radical, even revolutionary. "I am a conservative," said Roger Jepsen, one of the conservatives elected to the Senate on Reagan's coattails in 1980, "because I'm for change."

This apparent paradox can be partially explained away as the normal tidal swing of democratic politics. Many of the things the Reagan conservatives wanted to change were in reality things they wanted to *un-change*. They wanted to undo some of the things that liberals had done since the New Deal. More especially, they wanted to cancel some of the policies Democratic administrations had brought in under Presidents John F. Kennedy and Lyndon B. Johnson.

One of the themes of this book will certainly be the spreading reaction, both among the leaders of American politics and opinion and among ordinary, unpolitical Americans, against what was seen as the excessive, misconceived, and unsuccessful activism of liberal government. A subtheme is the way conservatives succeeded in identifying liberalism, understandably but not fairly, as merely the political doctrine of the privileged and the supercilious. This was the bridge over which populism passed from the liberal left to the conservative right.

FROM THE START, the revived American conservatism[44] after 1945 embraced two radically different traditions and tried uneasily to reconcile them.[45] One was that strand of political ideas that goes back to Edmund Burke. It stresses tradition, order, community, religion, and the organic model of society Burke had in mind when he said that society should be "a partnership not only between those who are living but between those who are living, those who are dead, and those who are to be born."[46] That is the traditionalist and authoritarian strand of conservative thinking.

The other was an ideology of individualism which sought to tear away all restraints that might prevent a free man from seeking his own ends in a free market of goods and ideas. This is the ideology of the pioneer, the entrepreneur, the capitalist, the philosophy of the economic libertarian.[47] It is also, in America, the populist tradition.

There is a fundamental conflict between those traditions. In the intellectual sphere, William F. Buckley, Jr., and his friends were successful, at least for a time, in marrying them together. They did so in part because a third strand of conservatism, the angry anticommunism of the 1950s, overlapped the traditionalist-authoritarian and the libertarian-capitalist kinds of conservatism. In the political arena Ronald Reagan did his best to suppress or at least distract attention from their differences. But they are different. And there are other cross-cutting divisions, too, such as those which separate a traditionalist populist like Pat Buchanan from an elitist economic libertarian like Malcolm (Steve) Forbes.

By 1986 Robert Nisbet could write:

> Reagan's victory in 1980 was widely hailed as a conservative triumph, and in a considerable degree it was. For a quarter of a century he had been widely known in America as an apostle of full-blown political and economic conservatism. If there was also a noticeable streak of populism . . . it harmonized well with conservative dogma . . . Reagan's triumph, though, was one of a coalition of persuasions.[48]

Nisbet went on to mention some of these "polyglot" persuasions in the Reagan coalition: conservative, populist, far right, evangelical, libertarian, nationalist, militarist, and so on. We shall see how each of these tributaries brought its water to what became a Nile or an Amazon, or rather a conservative Mississippi, flowing quietly but with irresistible impetus through the American heartland. In later chapters I will try to estimate what will be the lasting effects of this major episode in American political history, unpicking the interaction of ideas and events.

It will not be enough, though, to trace the evolution of the ideas that seemed to promise a Reagan revolution. We shall see how those ideas worked out in practice. And we will have to acknowledge that, for all the success they achieved, a high price was paid in inequality and division. Fifteen years after Reagan's triumph, it may look as if conservatism is still the dominant ideology in America. Far fewer people than twenty years ago admit to being liberals. Some doctrines of the new conservatism, especially in the economic sphere, have become received wisdom. Conservative orthodoxy dominates much of the discourse in newspapers, on television, especially on radio. Corporate conservatism subsidizes scholars, writers, and publicists who defend conservative doctrine, and tries to marginalize any who try to question it. Conservative politicians control both Houses of Congress. It takes a certain courage to avow liberal ideas. And many conservative ideas have certainly swept their challengers from the field.

And yet . . . conservatism has not wholly triumphed. If the heralds of conservative triumphalism in 1981 had been right, Bill Clinton would not now be the president of the United States. The moderate Colin Powell would not have shown such immense and widely distributed political appeal. And Senator Bob Dole would not now be the Republican candidate. For Dole is not the candidate of the conservatives who were supposed to have triumphed in 1981, but of an older and far less ideological Republicanism. If conservatism had truly been the youth of the world rediscovered, as its partisans told us, surely it would have found some more dynamic champion than Senator Dole or some less dark and angry prophet than Patrick Buchanan. Whatever the successes of conservatism, and as we shall see there have been brilliant and very significant successes, the record of the years since 1981 is not the record of national redemption, religious revival, and economic bonanza the heralds of conservative revolution foretold.

The next five chapters tell the story of the rise of the new conservatism, trying to unravel the relationship between conservative ideas and political events. Then, in Chapters 7, 8, and 9, I will describe the crucial phase that made possible the triumph of Reaganism: the rejection of liberal assumptions in the 1970s in relation to religious and social issues, to economics, and to the position of the United States in the world. The last two chapters will look at what has happened to the hopes of a Reagan revolution, first under George Bush, and then after the Democrats recaptured the White House.

In practice, conservative doctrines have led to two unexpected and (for many) unwanted transformations. The first is the partial "Southernization" of American politics. When, in the aftermath of the Supreme Court's 1954 decision in the *Brown* case, the federal government, reluctantly and gingerly, set out to bring Southern racial mores into line with the national norm, the assumption was that the South was a vestigial region. Its destiny, it seemed in 1963, must be to become more like the rest of the country. In some respects, including the adoption of formal and legal social equality for African Americans, that is more or less what has happened. In other ways, however, the rest of the country has become more like the South. There are, as we shall see, many aspects of this reverse takeover. But both political parties are now heavily Southernized. It is quite fitting that Democrats, led by a president from Arkansas, are locked in political battle with Republicans led by a speaker of the House from Georgia, and that a clean sweep of many of the states of the former Confederacy on Super Tuesday delivered the Republican nomination to Senator Dole. To a disquieting degree, national politics in the 1990s are "about" race, in a profound and pervasive sense, as Southern politics were in the past.

If American politics seem, as a result of the conservative insurgency, to be becoming more "Southern," they are also, paradoxically and as a result of the workings of the law of unintended consequences, becoming more "European." They are now, that is, ideological politics as they never were before. And that is because they are now class politics as they have not been since the Progressive Era, and perhaps even more than they were then. The reason is simple. The consequences of Republican conservative economic and social policies have been to increase inequality, sharply and against the historic trend in America.

The Great Depression ended with the Great Rearmament in 1940–1941. For more than a generation after that, Americans not only enjoyed rising incomes, they enjoyed more *equal* incomes. That period of growing prosperity and growing equality admittedly ended before the triumph of Reaganism. The fading of the postwar prosperity in the 1970s, indeed, was one of the factors that favored the conservative triumph. But inequality and divisiveness have been among the consequences, intended or otherwise, of conservatism. Inevitably they have had as their result, in turn, a new style of party politics. Its rationale no longer lies buried in half-forgotten issues dating back to the Civil War. Its style is sharp, contemporary, and bitter. The alignments may be confused. The policies are often subordinated to the politics. The tone is raucous, and the attention span is that of the soundbite. These are populist politics in the age of a money power beyond the dreaming of a Mark Hanna or a J. P. Morgan: the collective economic power of the media industry. But the difference is unmistakable. The word "class" is not much used outside the academy. Most Americans cling to the idea that class divisions are part of the bad old folkways of Europe. But the fact is that fifteen years of conservative dominance have brought back to American soil the politics of class.

Before we go down into the political marketplace to analyze how that has happened, we must go back to the places, high on the bare mountainside, where the tiny springs of fragile new tributaries first appeared to feed the rivers of conservatism. As American forces won the decisive battles of World War II, the new conservative ideas, in all the innocence of hope, first saw the light. Surprisingly, perhaps, they appeared first not in Congress or in newspapers or on the electoral stump, but in a number of notably ill-assorted books.

⚑ 2 ⚑

Headwaters

Ideas Have Consequences
— *Title of book by Richard Weaver (1948)*

IT WAS EARLY IN 1963 that I first interviewed Robert Kennedy, then attorney general in his brother's administration. I was shown into a cavernous office, ornamented with murals in the New Deal socialist-realist style. A handsome, unexplained young woman walked in with a shambling, bearlike black dog. Who was she? A dog walker, GS10? K9 handler to the Rat Pack? The dog, I recognized. This must be Brumas, a celebrity in his own right.

Kennedy was then at the center of the storm over desegregation in the South, a story I had been covering for the past year. Indignant black leaders from the Eastern Shore of Maryland to the Gulf of Mexico, and their outraged liberal supporters from New York and Los Angeles, were urging him to action. Conservatives in small Southern towns and in the Capitol of the United States were bringing every pressure to bear on him to go slow on the enforcement of the Supreme Court's *Brown* decision. The Kennedy administration's cautious drive for civil rights legislation was stalled by what was known as the conservative majority in Congress, an alliance between Republicans and the Southern Democrats (a hundred-odd of the latter in the House, more than twenty in the Senate, including most of the leaders of the club of committee chairmen, the so-called "whales"), who always voted with them on racial issues. But there was a further complication. A significant minority of urban and suburban Republican liberals and moderates, men like John V. Lindsay of New York and Peter Frelinghuysen of New Jersey in the House, Edward Brooke of Massachusetts and Jacob Javits of New York in the Senate, regularly voted with the Democratic liberals on civil rights.

Wouldn't it be better, I asked Kennedy, if, instead of this jungle of party loyalties, which made sense only in terms of political traditions going back to the Civil War and beyond, there were a clear division between a liberal party and a conservative party? That, after all, I argued, was the real fault line in American politics. No, he argued with some vehemence, the country was already sharply divided vertically, between sections, races, and ethnic groups. It would be dangerous to split it horizontally, too, between liberals and conservatives. That way, he said, lay the rift between haves and have-nots, and the ideological politics of Europe. I remember being surprised that a politician usually represented in the Washington press as a hard-nosed political operative should feel so strongly about such a theoretical issue. I was even more surprised when he dived into the deep drawer of his imposing desk, the drawer where traditional politicians kept their whiskey bottle, and fished out a shoebox full of five-by-eight cards on which he had scribbled notes on what sundry pundits had to say on the question.

THE POINT IS not that Robert Kennedy was right or wrong to fear a political system polarized ideologically between conservatives and liberals, right and left. The point is that, thirty years later, it is precisely what has happened. Whether or not Americans individually are truly polarized in that way, politics are now a conflict between liberals of various shades and different tribes of conservatives. The old party allegiance of Democrats and Republicans, rooted in forgotten nineteenth-century quarrels about the abolition of slavery, states' rights, free silver, immigration, and the tariff, means little or nothing today. The new ideological commitments to conservatism in one form or another, or to the liberal persuasion, have come to dominate the political discourse and the political battlefields. It is on the whole the conservatives who have been winning those arguments, the liberals who are on the defensive.

As the slow shifts of ideological hegemony go, the transformation has been surprisingly swift. A third of a century ago, when I had that conversation with Robert Kennedy, conservatism still seemed a residual faith, a holdover from an older world. It was widely associated in the public mind with the South and so, perhaps unfairly, with racism; with isolationism, and so with reluctance to fight Nazism, even, unfairly in most cases, with anti-Semitism; with the self-interested economic nostrums of big business and of the coupon-clipping rich. Twenty years farther back, in the last years of World War II, as the United States stepped onto the summit of its glory as the victorious leader of a world coalition led by a liberal Democratic administration, dedicated to converting the world to the American liberal creed, conservatives seemed even more marginal to American politics. American conservatives, in 1945, were obsolete, impotent, even quaint.

Pick up four books written by conservatives in those war years, and you get a strong sense of how lonely, despised, even proscribed, the conservatives of the 1940s felt. They tramped, more in hope than confidence, and more in defiance than in hope, through what seemed to them a boundless wilderness of collectivism. Most of those who deigned to notice them at all were sure that they were marching defiantly under the banners of the past.

LET US LOOK a little closer at those four books. They have little in common except that they were all to number among the holy scriptures of the new conservatism. They are milestones that measure how far conservatism has come since its nadir at the height of World War II. They are often profoundly in conflict with one another, and their authors were even more diverse than their books. Three of the four titles were finished in 1943: Ayn Rand's spectacular best seller *The Fountainhead*; Albert Jay Nock's eccentric but brilliant autobiography, *Memoirs of a Superfluous Man*; and Friedrich August von Hayek's *The Road to Serfdom*.[1] Russell Kirk's *The Conservative Mind*, a dazzling work of intellectual history, appeared ten years later.

This is not to say that these were the only four books to be counted among the foundation stones of the new conservatism. For one thing, three of their four authors were to produce other books with comparable influence. (The exception was Nock, who died in 1945.) Other writers were consciously swimming against the powerful intellectual tide that was running toward more or less democratic versions of collectivism, liberalism, and social democracy. One of them, Ludwig von Mises, eighteen years older than Hayek, and, like him, an old-fashioned Austrian liberal (in the European sense of that word), actually published two powerful tracts in that same year, 1944: *Omnipotent Government* and *Bureaucracy*.[2] Von Mises had left Austria in 1934 to teach in Geneva, and in 1940 he emigrated to America. In 1945 he was found a visiting chair at New York University, and in 1949 he published his *summa*, a "capitalist manifesto," almost a thousand pages long, called *Human Action*. He was logical, lucid, intransigent. His passionate hostility to the State and all its works, and especially to the men who served it, had been hardened by his generation's experience of what the overmighty state had wrought in Europe. He was also tactless, dogmatic, an awkwardly uncompromising champion of the pure doctrine of *laissez-faire*. In *Omnipotent Government* he spelled out the kernel of his creed:

> The essential teaching of liberalism is that social cooperation and the division of labor can only be achieved in a system of market ownership of the means of production, i.e. within a market society, or capitalism. All the other principles of liberalism — democracy, personal freedom of the individual, freedom of speech and of the press, religious tolerance, peace among the nations — are consequences of this basic postulate.[3]

It is doubtful whether Ludwig von Mises could have maintained quite so stark an identification of civilization with capitalism had he been writing a quarter of a century later. By then, in every country of Western Europe, not to mention the United States and all other developed countries, mixed economic systems of various kinds — Christian democracy in West Germany and Italy, social democracy in Scandinavia, governments of the center left and center right in both France and Britain — had demonstrated their ability to deliver precisely those "principles" of liberalism. Like Hayek, it can be argued, von Mises drew overgeneralized conclusions from the tragic experience of his own life. Most of us do.

While the world was at war, Friedrich von Hayek was teaching in London and von Mises in New York, and a young sergeant in the Chemical Warfare Service named Russell Kirk was reading to keep boredom at arm's length in Utah, a North Carolinian named Richard Weaver was seeking a basis for a new conservative philosophy, not in the practices of Victorian *laissez-faire* capitalism but in the Middle Ages.[4] Like so many other conservative intellectuals, Weaver started out as a socialist; he was actually the secretary of a local branch of the Socialist Party of America for two years at the University of Kentucky. Then in 1933 he went to do doctoral work at Vanderbilt University in Tennessee, where he came under the influence of that attractive group of nostalgic reactionaries who called themselves the Southern Agrarians.

By 1939, after teaching at Texas A and M and being depressed by what he saw as the "meaningless" and "stultifying" orthodoxy of liberalism and the optimistic Whig view of history, Weaver quit his teaching job and immersed himself in a study of the American Civil War. He came to the conclusion that the Old South, with its feudal organization of society, its uncomplicated religious faith, its concept of the gentleman, and its code of chivalry, had been "right without realizing the grounds of its rightness." It was "the last nonmaterial civilization in the Western world."[5] Weaver was specially drawn to the idea of chivalry, which he saw as a device for creating a spiritual value that "stood above war itself." Eventually he came to the conclusion that Western man had made an "evil decision" as long ago as the fourteenth century.[6] That was when philosophers abandoned the belief of Thomas Aquinas and his contemporaries in universal values and, under the English philosopher William of Occam, chose the path of "nominalism" instead.

Behind the dry arguments of the medieval Schoolmen, Weaver argued in *Ideas Have Consequences*, published in 1948, lay a fateful decision: to abandon the belief that there is a source of truth higher than human experience. As far back as that, Weaver argued, Europeans and therefore, later, Americans set out on a long road that would lead to the rejection of God and so to the "dissolution of the West." This strange, powerful book, born of the painfully radical search of a provincial scholar in remote arguments for the keys to what he believed had gone profoundly wrong, was to have immense influence. It has been called the "*fons et origo* of the contemporary American conservative movement," or, you might say, its fountainhead.

Both Ludwig von Mises and Richard Weaver, the Austrian refugee and the unreconstructed Southerner, torn from their intellectual and cultural roots, as they saw, by war, belonged to what Albert Jay Nock celebrated as "the Remnant." Nock was so convinced of his own obsolescence that he saw himself as a "superfluous man,"[7] member of a powerless remnant of cultivated, philosophical men, pushed to one side by the trampling, trough-bound horde of submen. Nock quoted with approval the answer proposed by the architect Ralph Cram Adams to the question: "Why we do not behave like human beings?" Adams's answer was: "Because the great majority of us, the masses of mankind, are not human beings [and] consequently we have all along been putting expectations upon the masses of *homo sapiens* which they are utterly incapable of meeting."[8] He also liked Flaubert's dictum that "the only way to stay calm in your plate is to regard the human race as a vast association of cretins and rabble."[9]

"One has great affection for one's dogs," Nock commented, "even when one sees them reveling in tastes and smells which to us are unspeakably odious. That is the way dogs are; one does not try to change their peculiar *penchant*." Nature, Nock consoled himself in the strangely noble concluding paragraphs of his *Memoirs*, leaving the reader even more in doubt than usual how far his tongue was into his cheek, had abruptly ended production of the great saurians. Therefore nature could, with equal suddenness, stop turning out "the neolithic psychically anthropoid variety of *homo sapiens*, which now exists in an overwhelming majority," and replace it with the psychically human variety, which seems to appear only sporadically. Improbable, Nock grants you, but then so was the fate of the saurians; it could happen.

Where did Albert Jay Nock acquire this aggressively contemptuous elitism, this violent distaste for the great majority of his fellow humans? Not in the steam-heated luxury of a millionaire's palace, nor in the ivy-covered cloisters of academic privilege. His ancestors were English and French, but neither Tory squires nor monarchist aristocrats. His English grandfather, a Methodist from Staffordshire, had come to America to manage a steel mill; two uncles worked, respectively, as the head of a locomotive works and the superintendent of a rolling mill.[10] His mother's family were French. They had fled the persecution of Protestants in the late seventeenth century. His father was an Episcopalian clergyman in what was then the leafy suburb of Brooklyn, where he lived until his father moved to Alpena, Michigan, a remote logging town, full of rural democracy and home music-making, and altogether "a standing advertisement for Mr. Jefferson's notion that the virtues which he regarded as distinctively American thrive best in the absence of government."[11] At St. Stephen's (later Bard College) in Illinois, a small college with fewer than a hundred students, "three miles by clay road from the railway," he studied "the grand old fortifying classical curriculum" of Latin and Greek.[12] French and German he seems to have picked up in the polyglot backyards of Brooklyn.

Nock tried a number of ways of earning his living, including the unlikely trade of semiprofessional baseball. Then, after attending divinity school in Middletown, Connecticut, he became an Episcopalian minister and served in parishes in Pennsylvania, rural Virginia, and Detroit. After ten years he left the ministry and his wife and two children and became a journalist. He worked on *The American Magazine* with the muckrakers Lincoln Steffens, Ida Tarbell, and John Reed, later author of *Ten Days That Shook the World*, the classic admiring account of the Russian Revolution. Nock himself became a "single taxer" and an admirer of Henry George. After 1914 he made four visits to Europe, possibly as a secret agent for his friend William Jennings Bryan, Wilson's secretary of state. He visited England, Italy, Belgium, Russia, and Germany. He briefly joined the staff of Oswald Garrison Villard's *Nation*, and in 1920, with the British liberal Francis Nicolson, he founded *The Freeman*.

Always he read, widely and deeply, and his reading told him that Western society, and especially the booming, boosting American society of the Progressive Era, was fatally given over to what he called "economism." (Characteristically, he explained that to him the word meant what most people understood by "materialism," which was "ambiguous and inexact.") "Its God was its belly . . . American society had the morale of an army on the march . . . the morale of the looter, the plunderer . . . 'Go and get it!' was the sum of the practical philosophy presented to America's young manhood by all the voices of the age."

In his thirties, Nock tells us, he dismissed any interest in politics, which he claims to have regarded for the rest of his life "as a mere spectacle, mostly a comedy, rather squalid, rather hackneyed, whereof I already knew the plot from beginning to end." And so at forty-four he emigrated to Europe. "I had nothing against America or American society, nothing whatever . . . I was like a man who had landed in Greenland with a cargo of straw hats. There was nothing wrong with Greenland or with the hats . . . but there was not the faintest chance of a market for his line of goods." In Europe, too, he found economism rampant, but it had not yet made a clean sweep. In Belgium — of all places, a Frenchman might say — he found the civilized life, the lost paradise, he had sought in vain in America.

> Its pleasures and diversions were amiable, unmechanized, satisfying. They gave the sense of being taken as a wholesome and regular part of life. One was as much at home in the museums, the concert hall, the theater, the opera, as in one's own house . . . I would get a light, unhurried dinner at the Trois Suisses or the Pourquoi Pas, and then when the bell rang I would leave my hat and overcoat in the restaurant, walk twenty paces to the Monnaie's side entrance, and join in a performance of high professional excellence pervaded by the spirit of the highly gifted, highly cultivated amateur . . . When the performance was over, I would retrieve my hat and coat, stroll over to some nearby resort for a taste of steamed mussels and Spätenbrau beer, while I listened to some energetic discussion, perhaps of the opera, perhaps of any other subject under the sun.[13]

Alas! Even in Belgium, this amiable, unmechanized way of life was under threat. Even before the war Nock watched the slow suffocation of life's amenities. He returned to America. There, the only virtues that were glorified were "the barbaric virtues, the virtues of the jazz artist and the cinema hero, tempered on occasion by the virtues of Jenghiz

Khan, Attila, Brennus," the Gaul who threw his sword into the scales, crying "*Vae victis!*" (Woe to the vanquished!) The only ideals inculcated were those of "the psychopath . . . the homicidal maniac." In this uncongenial environment, Nock founded *The Freeman*, and he proved a brilliant editor. He was, said Lewis Mumford, the architectural critic, "the very model of the old-fashioned gentleman, American style: quiet-spoken, fond of good food, punctilious in little matters of courtesy." Others were irritated by his habit of sprinkling his conversation with quotations in half a dozen languages. Brooks Adams said he had the "testy and obstinate look of a Tintoretto Doge."[14] After four years, what with mounting losses and poor health, he felt obliged to resign, then headed back to Europe. There, he watched horrified society "floundering toward collectivism," the plague of modernism, the illusion that equality could be achieved by "the very worst and most incompetent agency for the purpose — political action."

Nock was more fortunate than many unemployed journalists. Three rich Philadelphians, two ladies and the husband of one of them, came to him and offered to keep *The Freeman* going. When he said that it was too late, they gave him financial support to write lives of his great heroes, Jefferson and the bawdy French Renaissance humanist Rabelais. In point of fact, his friend and former colleague, Suzanne La Follette, tried to restart *The Freeman* in 1930, but it collapsed with the onset of the Depression, and Nock was left writing his books.

He traced many of the faults — the vices he saw in America between the two wars — to the transformation of American education. He wrote a book, *The Theory of Education in the United States*, which the educationists hated, but which was taken up by the Jesuits, "the only body of men in America who have the faintest notion of what education means." He traced the source of decadence in American education to the import from Germany, by Charles W. Eliot of Harvard, Daniel Coit Gilman of Johns Hopkins, and others, of the elective system in education, first at the graduate level, then the undergraduate, the secondary, and eventually the primary and even the kindergarten levels. The revolution began by guillotining the classical curriculum. But even worse, in Nock's eyes, was the principle of the new educationist, which he expressed with characteristic waspishness: "The regime perceived that while very few can be educated, everyone who is not actually imbecile or idiotic can be trained in some way or another, as soldiers can be trained in military routine, or monkeys are trained to pick fruit."

In one sense, Nock was a classic conservative. He did think that things had once been better. He always preserved a regard for the America of his early years, the Currier and Ives America of robust boys' games in the leafy Brooklyn backyards, the men's choirs, *Liederkranz* and *Gesangverein* of rustic Michigan, the "fortifying" classical learning of the little school that lay three miles of clay, muddy in winter, dusty in summer, from the newly laid railroad, in the days when the cars that made Detroit famous were horse-drawn.

In those days, he grudgingly allowed, the impulse of the reformers and the progressives was understandable. That early America was redeemable. "One could think of American society," he wrote, "as Bishop Warburton thought of the English Church, that like the ark of Noah it is 'worth saving, not for the sake of the unclean beasts that almost filled it and probably made most noise and clamour in it, but for the little corner of rationality that was as much distressed by the stink within as by the tempest without.'"

That, in a sentence, is the Nockian doctrine of the Remnant, inherited from Isaiah by way of Matthew Arnold, and expounded by him in many articles. His fundamental idea was that if society itself is doomed by the ruthless gluttony of the many, the survival of the elect few is imperative.

Nock's conservative instinct, though, was shrunk by his pessimism, as it was to be dishonored at the end of his life by his growing anti-Semitism. He thought the values of an older America might have been worth saving, but he doubted whether there was any hope of saving them. He was so horrified by the greed and vulgarity he saw around him that he convinced himself that the majority of human beings were in fact subhuman, animals. American life, in particular, he saw as specially dominated by the values of the "looters and plunderers, the plug-ugly and the thug." In one of his most characteristic passages, he described a New York bar where forty-two of the great American business leaders of the Gilded Age were commemorated by photographs. If they were not human beings, wrote Nock of these heroes of the American way of life, these captains of industry, princes of philanthropy and culture, Henry Ford and Thomas Alva Edison among them, you couldn't hate them for not behaving like human beings. "The mass-men who are princes, presidents, politicians, legislators, can no more transcend their psychical capacities than any wolf, fox, or polecat in the land. How then is one to hate them, notwithstanding the appalling evil that they do?"

AT THE TIME Albert Jay Nock was slipping out of the opera in Brussels to munch a dish of mussels and listen to the civilized conversation of the Bruxellois, a girl named Alice Rosenbaum was growing up in a comfortable apartment in St. Petersburg.[15] Her father, Fronz Rosenbaum, was a science graduate who owned a pharmacy. It was a happy, modestly prosperous home; one of Alice's friends when she was growing up was the sister of the novelist Vladimir Nabokov.[16] Later in life, although she grew to hate Russia, she never mentioned that she had experienced anti-Semitism; what she loathed was the Russian pessimism and the way Russians glorified the tragic. Alice loved what she had read of the confident, upbeat West: at first England and then America. She was a dreamy child who loved to read romantic novels and fall in love with their heroes, especially with Cyrus, the hero of an otherwise unremembered novel called *The Mysterious Valley*, by the forgotten French writer Maurice Champagne.[17]

Then came the Revolution. It was horrifying enough in itself for a sensitive girl of twelve. The funeral of the delegates to the constitutional assembly who had been murdered by the Bolsheviks stayed vivid in her memory all her life. She could not forget the sound of muffled drums and the salute of cannon as the bodies rolled slowly under the windows of her parents' apartment, and the open coffin of a beautiful woman delegate was frozen in her mind's eye, the white face and black hair vivid against a scarlet pillow.[18] Her imagination was never anything but vivid.

She also never forgot the day she stood in her father's shop as her father gathered up his personal belongings and hid them in the apartment. When he returned, armed soldiers burst in and stamped a red seal on the door.[19] The shop had been nationalized. Communism had made an implacable and in the end spectacularly effective enemy. At first, it is true, she did not show any great interest in politics. She fled Petrograd (as St. Petersburg had been renamed) with her family when they moved to the Crimea. Then she returned and went to the university, where she studied philosophy and read Schiller, Nietzsche, Dostoevsky.[20] She graduated with high honors and dreamed of becoming a writer, if possible a writer for the romantic, wonderful movies. But the best job she could get was as a guide to the Peter and Paul fortress. Such a woman — intelligent, passionate, profoundly out of sympathy with communism, and Jewish into the bargain — would almost certainly have ended up in the *gulag* sooner or later. If she had survived there until 1942, she would even more certainly have been gunned down by an SS Einsatszkommando or taken to Auschwitz to be gassed.

Instead, there came the letter from America. From a cousin in Chicago, to be precise, named Sarah Lipsky, *née* Portnoy.[21] After a long, careful correspondence and a long, painful wait, the Russian passport arrived and, following some dangerous misunderstandings, the American consul in Riga gave her a visa. In 1926, aged twenty-one, she landed in New York in a snowstorm, and with a new name: she decided to call herself Ayn Rosenbaum, after a Finnish writer she had never read.[22] Her new surname she took from the typewriter at her aunt's house in Chicago. It was a Remington-Rand. She wrote down names that began with an R. Ayn Remington. No . . . Ayn Rand![23]

Chicago could not hold her. She went to Hollywood, stayed at the Studio Club, where Kim Novak and Marilyn Monroe later lived as their fame struck, got a job as an extra, fell in love, lost her job, worked as a waitress, almost starved.[24] Finally she realized that it was as a writer, not as an actress (though she was certainly good-looking enough for that, with her wide-spaced dark eyes and the cool elegance of her features), that she was going to make her name and fortune. Even so, it was a long, bitter struggle. Universal bought her scenario for *Red Pawn*, a romantic tale of a passionate woman who sleeps with a communist jailer to free her lover; it was traded to Paramount and made with Marlene Dietrich by Josef von Sternberg.[25] She worked for years on a story about the Revolution, *We the Living*, which after all the days of hard work in the writing, earned less than a hundred dollars in its original American edition. In 1959 it was brought out by a publisher in London and republished in New York; on the second time around it sold 400,000 copies in the first year.[26] But by then Ayn Rand was one of the most successful novelists in history.

In 1938, after no less than four years of research and planning, she sat down to write a novel about an architect, brilliant and obsessed with the integrity of his own artistic vision, which he refused to compromise for money or love. The writing was slow, and her money was running out. She turned once again to writing for the theater. A series of disasters, personal and professional, distracted her. But she kept on writing. In the spring of 1943 Bobbs-Merrill finally agreed to take the novel, which was published as *The Fountainhead*.[27] The reviews, except for one in the *New York Times Book Review*, were dismissive; the sales, from the start, were buoyant, but Bobbs-Merrill seemed not to believe in the book, which kept appearing in tiny editions, then going out of print again. Such was the beginning of one of the most extraordinary stories in the history of New York publishing. In 1948 alone, *The Fountainhead* sold 400,000 copies. Altogether by now it has sold over four million copies, and Rand's next book, *Atlas Shrugged*, has sold over five million. Altogether, Ayn Rand's books have sold more than twenty million copies. And that success was achieved, as she herself was fairly to claim, in spite of the publishing industry, not thanks to it. "It was rejected by twelve publishers who declared it had no commercial possibilities, it would not sell, it was 'too intellectual,' it was 'too unconventional,' it went against every popular trend. Yet the success of *The Fountainhead* was made by the public. Not by the public as an organized *collective* — but by single individual readers who discovered it of their own choice, who read in on their own initiative and recommended it on their own judgment."

Something was going on.

The Fountainhead is certainly an unusual best seller.[28] It is, for a start, a novel of ideas. It has a strong story line. It is plotted with great skill, and it certainly has all the qualities of suspense, excitement, narrative drive that have always been part of the recipe for popular success. It is, at one level, as they say, about the trials of a young man of great talent and a young woman of great beauty and great intellect on their way to what can only be called a conventional happy ending — even if it takes place on a hoist to the top of a skyscraper and after a love story that begins with rape and passes through betrayal, adultery, and as many misunderstandings as any Victorian three-volume novel, and this is by any standards a very long book. It is not only a novel of ideas; it is a novel of particular ideas that were, at least according to the prevailing intellectual fashions of the day, profoundly unpopular.

It is the story of an architect, Howard Roark, born with flaming red hair and even more inflammatory talent. He is being expelled from architecture school for the intransigence with which he rejects "second-hand" ideas. The prize that was his for the taking goes instead to his friend and antithesis, Peter Keating, portrayed as the epitome of the second rate. Rejected and unemployed, even though he has designed one impressively original building, Roark goes to work in a marble quarry belonging to a fashionable architect, whose daughter, Dominique Francon, falls in love with him. He visits her at night and rapes her. She marries Keating. Roark builds a temple to humanity around a naked statue of Dominique. He is sued by the man who has paid for the temple, and the architectural establishment lines up to denounce him. Only Dominique gives evidence for him. "Howard Roark built a temple to the human spirit. He saw man as strong, proud, clean, wise and fearless . . . as a heroic being." But, says Dominique, don't expect men to achieve self-respect. "They will hate your soul."

In the novel, Ayn Rand, through Roark, pleads on behalf of the men, among whom he counts himself, who throughout history have been the creators, the men of "unborrowed vision." They have always stood alone against the men of their time, Roark says, but they went ahead. These creators, he argues, have not been selfless. Their motive was creation itself, not the benefits others might derive from it. He draws a distinction between the creator, whose basic need is independence; and the "second-hander," who needs ties with others. The second-hander, Roark argues contemptuously, declares that man exists to serve others because he, unlike the true creator, needs others. He preaches altruism; but altruism to him is a mere weapon of exploitation. Indeed, the man who attempts to live for others is a dependent and a parasite, and makes parasites of those he claims to serve.

So far Roark's — and Ayn Rand's — philosophy is Nietzschean. He and she are preaching the dangerous doctrine of the supremacy of the Superman over the rank and file of mankind. They are also arguing the paradoxical but not altogether serious notion that the selfishness of the creator is more virtuous than the assumed altruism of the man who attempts to live for others. There is something in this of the *fin-de-siècle* cult of art for art's sake, something of the fashion set by George Bernard Shaw and other writers of the turn of the century who liked to rattle the intellectual bars of the bourgeois cage.

Then, suddenly and perhaps unconsciously, the speech makes a shift from the philosophical, or pseudo-philosophical, into another key: the more familiar key of political ideology. The contest between the creator — who is "denied, opposed, persecuted, exploited," says Roark, but who "carries all humanity forward on his energy" — and the second-rater has another name. It is also the struggle between the individual and the collective. And Ayn Rand propels her creature, Roark, into a passionate exposition of her own views.

The common good of some collective grouping — a race, a class, a state — was the justification of every tyranny in history, and every horror in history was committed in the name of an altruistic motive. "The most dreadful butchers were the most sincere," and the only good men can do to one another, the only statement of their proper relationship is to say, "Hands off!"

In the next step of her argument, Rand the immigrant introduces the dimension of American exceptionalism. Contrast the horrors committed in the name of altruism with "this, our country. The noblest country in the history of men, the country of the greatest achievement, the greatest prosperity, the greatest freedom." America was not built on selfless service or altruism, Rand says through the mouth of Roark. "It was based on a man's right to the pursuit of happiness. His own happiness. Not anyone else's. A private, personal, selfish motive."

For his peroration, Roark says that collectivism is running amuck. "It has brought men to a level of intellectual indecency never equaled on earth. It has reached a scale of horror without precedent. It has poisoned every mind. It has swallowed most of Europe. It is engulfing our country . . . The world is perishing from an orgy of self-sacrificing."

It was, to say the least of it, a peculiar interpretation of what was happening in Europe and the world in 1943. Collectivism was running amuck, all right, in Nazi Germany and in Soviet Russia. But only the most perverse observer could see the Holocaust and the *gulag* as the consequences of altruism or self-sacrifice on the part of their perpetrators. Only the most unscrupulous could argue that the mild experiments of the New Deal, in a country then flat out in victorious battle against one form of collectivist horror and soon to gird its loins for a long Cold War against the other, could be said to have "engulfed" America. Nor could the New Deal be decently compared to the absolutism of either Hitlerian fascism or Stalin's communism.

What gave *The Fountainhead* its extraordinary popular appeal was certainly not any special coherence of its ideas, but its force. Ayn Rand had crafted a best seller out of the usual ingredients: a dynamic if implausible plot; strong if unsubtle characterization; and, much less usual, ideas, expressed both in the plot itself and in set-piece speeches by the protagonists, which carry the reader along because of the sheer conviction of the writer. Crucially, however, she had also done something else. She had put her finger on a sensitive place in the consciousness of millions, especially but not only in the United States: a feeling that mass society, bureaucracy, mediocrity, were robbing the individual, as citizen, as employee, as consumer and human being, of individuality. Ayn Rand appealed from what she portrayed as the new and dangerous forces of collectivism, not to traditional conservative values, but to the will of the exceptionally gifted individual, to something recognizably related to the Nietzschean Superman. She worshiped, in short, something not so clearly distinguished from the celebration of the Leader's will that lay at the heart of the "ancient monster," which had broken loose and was terrifying the world in the 1930s and 1940s. She chose to call that monster "collectivism." But if you examined the reality of Hitler and Stalin, Mussolini and Chiang Kai-shek, and all their tinpot imitators in the 1930s and 1940s, in another light, their ideologies and –isms strangely resemble her own cult of the superior individual. This is not to say that Ayn Rand was a fascist writer. Certainly, however, it was not the New Dealers but the dictators who shared her contempt for liberal altruism and the democratic search for collectivist solutions.

From the day *The Fountainhead* was published, it evoked in a significant proportion of its readers something more than mere agreement. The book made converts. Millions read it to the last page, closed it, and said, "That's it! She's right! They're all wrong, and she and I are right!" For all its obvious faults, it was a book that altered consciousness, changed lives. It was a book of power and paradox. It could hardly have contrasted more sharply with another book published in the same year: a brief, gracefully argued treatise about political economy: *The Road to Serfdom.*

"PEOPLE WHO WERE not born then," wrote the Austrian novelist Robert Musil decades later about the mood in Vienna in 1900, "will find it difficult to believe, but the fact is that even then time was moving faster than a cavalry camel . . . But in those days no one knew what it was moving towards."[29] Austrian society, so civilized and *gemütlich*, was like a liquid whose temperature, under its smooth surface, was rising toward the boiling point. The constitutional system had to all intents broken down under the tension between Magyars, Czechs, and German-speakers. A few years earlier, Karl Lüger, an avowed anti-Semite, had overcome the emperor's fastidious opposition and become mayor of Vienna, a city whose culture in the age of Mahler and Freud was very largely Jewish. Many Viennese — Freud, the painter Gustav Klimt, and the musician Arnold Schönberg among them — had reacted to this crisis of bourgeois liberal society by abandoning its values and plunging into the introspective study of the Self. *Flectere si nequeo superos,* Freud chose as the motto of one of his papers, *Acheronta movebo:* "If I cannot bend the Gods above, I will move the Underworld." It was into this world, self-consciously poised above the abyss, questioning all and daring all, that Friedrich von Hayek was born, in 1899. His family were scientists and academics, loyal and unquestioning servants of the imperial and royal monarchy of Austria-Hungary.[30] Hayek was profoundly influenced *intellectually* by the crisis in Austrian civilization, the war, the falling apart of the Empire, near-revolution in the streets of Vienna, and the destruction of the culture of Mitteleuropa. But personally he seems to have been strangely untouched. In Vienna and then in London, in Chicago, and once again in Germany and Austria at the end of his life, he kept the even tenor of his way, living the life of the Herr Professor, quiet, polite, conscientious, and heroically hard-working, apparently unscathed by the surrounding chaos. The father was a doctor of medicine who did research in botany and lectured as a *professor extraordinarius* at the University of Vienna. The mother's father was a professor of constitutional law and a statistician who ended up as the president of the Imperial and Royal Central Statistical Commission.

Friedrich Hayek, as a student, was saved from military service in the terrible campaigns in Galicia, Serbia, and Italy that bled two empires to death. In 1921 he received his first doctorate from the University in Vienna, in law, and two years later a second doctorate, in political science. He became an economist, though for the rest of his life he continued to write learned articles on political and legal topics, on the philosophy of science, and even on psychology. By 1927 he was the director of the Austrian Institute for Economic Research, where, in February 1929, he caused something of a stir in the world of professional economists by predicting a sharp downturn in the economy of the United States. In 1931 an invitation to lecture in London led to his being made the Tooke Professor of Economic Science and Statistics at the University of London, where he remained for the next twenty years.

In the 1930s Hayek worked on a number of technical problems that preoccupied the economics profession at the time. By 1935 he was regarded as the principal theoretical rival of John Maynard Keynes.[31] He even became one of the two duelists in a famous jousting match with Keynes. Hayek's friend Lionel Robbins, the conservative economist who had brought him to London and later became head of the London School of Economics,[32] assigned Keynes's *Treatise on Money* to Hayek to review in a leading London economic journal, *Economica*; while Keynes assigned Hayek's *Prices and Production*, which covered much the same ground from a different point of view, to his brilliant Cambridge disciple Piero Sraffa. At the time, Hayek's review annoyed Keynes's friends at Cambridge and elsewhere. The episode may have laid the foundations for future polemics. For the time being, however, Hayek slogged away at the theory of capital, understandably not a very fashionable field at a time when the world was being gradually sucked into total war. Then, in 1943, he published *The Road to Serfdom:* brief, passionate, addressed in simple, even emotional language to a general audience.

Until 1943, although he had read voraciously in several fields, Hayek was thought of, and presumably thought of himself, primarily as an economist. In 1950, after the publication of *The Road to Serfdom*, he broadened his range. That year, he accepted a chair at Chicago as professor of social and moral sciences. Under Robert Hutchins the university had been in the forefront of the reaction against the antiacademic precepts of the school established by John Dewey, and by 1950 it was at the height of its vigor. The South Side of Chicago had not yet experienced the social collapse that was to follow, and the campus around the Midway had not yet become a precarious settlement in the middle of hostile territory.

Shirley Robin Letwin has given a marvelous picture of Hayek's seminar, held every Wednesday after dinner "around a massive oval oak table in a mock Gothic chamber." Participants included two atomic physicists, one an Italian holding a Nobel Prize, the other a Hungarian,

> [a] profuse inventor of projects, physical, cinematic, political and of every other sort; an Irish classicist and farmer, as completely master of Shakespeare, Gibbon, and Tolstoy as of Sophocles, Plato, and Thucydides; a French Thomist of great piety and philosophical precision who admired Pascal, Proudhon, and T. S. Eliot; an arch grassroots American, founder of the Chicago school of economists and a belligerent atheist with a passion for theological inquiry; the leading monetary theorist, fascinated by the sun-seeking motives of leaves on trees and the optimistic behaviors of economic actors; a classical archaeologist, educated in the iconographic tradition of Munich and Berlin, who conducted classes on Nietzsche and tutorials on Proust; the author of *The Gothic Cathedral;* and the author of *The Lonely Crowd;* as well as the inventor of the "folk society" and the discoverer of early industrial revolutions

— not to mention a rich mixture of students from the United States, Europe, Japan, and the Middle East. Hayek presided over this intellectual bear garden with unflustered tolerance, old-fashioned intellectual good manners, and erudition prodigious in its depth and width alike. During his Chicago years Hayek was at work on his second political masterpiece, *The Constitution of Liberty,* but he still found time, as he had done in Vienna and London, to read hugely, browsing over great prairies of literature until his eye was drawn by some flower of theory or example.

The Road to Serfdom was a small book,[33] yet it had the explosive blast and the fallout released by the splitting of a tiny but dense nucleus. Its thesis can be stated very simply. Hayek argued that political freedom is inseparable from economic freedom. He insisted that Russian communism and German national socialism were two manifestations of the

same disastrous collectivist tendencies to be found in all forms of socialism. And he warned — writing as he did primarily for British readers in
wartime — against the implications of German ideas, meaning not the
national socialist ideas of Hitler, but the nationalism and socialism of the
apparently civilized Germany in the years just before the First World
War. Britain, he said, had moved much more slowly on the same path as
Russia, Italy, and Germany. Those countries were in irreconcilable conflict with British democracy, "but it is the same path."

Britain had followed the rest of Europe, Hayek taught, in moving
away from "the basic ideas on which European civilization has been
built." Most fundamental of those ideas is that of personal and economic
liberty. "We have progressively abandoned that freedom in economic
affairs without which personal and political liberty has never existed in
the past." The gradual transformation of the rigidly hierarchical society
of feudal Europe into one "where men could at least attempt to shape
their own life," Hayek insisted, "is closely associated with the growth of
commerce." Money, he believed, was "one of the greatest instruments of
freedom."

Hayek particularly singled out for assault the idea, fundamental to
the history of socialist thought, that political liberty is worthless without
economic prosperity. This is the idea first associated, during the French
Revolution, with Babeuf and memorably expressed by Anatole France in
his famous sarcasm, that "the law in its majestic equality forbids rich and
poor alike to sleep under the bridges."[34] Hayek had no patience with the
socialist idea of a "new freedom," meaning freedom not from coercion
but from necessity.[35] This, he said, is a dangerous misuse of words, at
best intellectual confusion, at worst deliberate casuistry. Freedom from
necessity is not freedom at all. It is simply another name for power or
wealth. It is an arguable point, but to Hayek it was plain unarguable.

Historically, he insisted, socialism has always been authoritarian. It
developed out of a reaction against the liberalism of the French Revolution.[36] Only for tactical reasons, because of the need to ally themselves
with middle-class liberals at the time of the revolutions all over Europe
in 1848, did the socialists start talking about freedom. The early socialists, he pointed out, did nothing of the kind. The saintly Saint-Simon
even predicted that those who did not adopt his ideas would be "treated
as cattle." Logically, too, according to Hayek, this would always be so.
Socialism is necessarily authoritarian. "Socialism can be put into practice only by methods of which most socialists disapprove."[37] And he unleashed a string of quotations from the mouth of the most harmless-

sounding social democrats, democratic socialists, and Fabians, including Sidney and Beatrice Webb and George Bernard Shaw, not to mention his *bête noire* colleague from the London School of Economics, Harold Laski, to show that "liberal socialism" is purely theoretical, while "the practice of socialism is everywhere totalitarian."[38]

The form this totalitarian impulse of socialism takes, for Hayek, is planning, and planning, he insisted, is the "very opposite" of the Rule of Law, the foundation of liberty and one of the noblest achievements of the liberal age.[39] Planning, for Hayek, even of the ostensibly mild sort envisaged by the Webbs and the British Labour Party, involves "that glorification of power which easily leads from socialism to nationalism and which profoundly affects the ethical views of all collectivists."[40] Indeed, he insisted that planning leads, by no long or tortuous road, to a totalitarian state. "To be a useful assistant in the running of a totalitarian state," he said, "it is not enough that a man should be prepared to accept specious justification of vile deeds"; he must be ready to break every moral rule. The nationalization of industry, what is more, goes hand in hand with the nationalization of thought. Totalitarian systems must use propaganda, and totalitarian propaganda is destructive of all morals because it undermines respect for the foundation of all morals, respect for the truth.

Against collectivism in all its forms, fierce or mild, Hayek raised the old banners of liberalism, in its classic, European sense.[41] He also dared to recommend individualism. Individualism had a bad name, he conceded. It was often linked to egotism or selfishness. But there need be no such connection. The fundamental principle, for Hayek, was that we cannot plan or ordain the world we want to see, but must "make as much use as possible of the spontaneous forces of society, and resort as little as possible to coercion." Individual freedom was the supreme value. It "cannot be reconciled with the supremacy of one single purpose to which the whole of society must be entirely and permanently subordinated."[42] It was not by trying to plan and organize their world that men could progress. That, indeed, was the road to serfdom and barbarism. It was by submitting to the impersonal forces of the market that in the past men had been able to make possible the growth of civilization.

So Friedrich Hayek the economic liberal, disciple of Adam Smith, met Hayek the political liberal, admirer (and collector of the letters of) John Stuart Mill. In 1947, Hayek invited like-minded liberals to meet at Mont Pélerin, near Vevey, within sight of Lake Geneva, to exchange ideas about the nature of a free society, the dangers to its survival, and ways to strengthen it.[43] Those who attended the conference in April that year included economists, philosophers, historians, lawyers, and intellectuals from many other disciplines, from Europe and from the United States. They agreed on a statement of aims, among them the redefinition of the functions of the state "so as to distinguish more clearly between the totalitarian and the liberal order" and "re-establishing the rule of law" so that no one should encroach upon the freedom of others. To further these aims, Hayek and his friends, who included Lionel Robbins, his sponsor at the London School of Economics, the Princeton economist Fritz Machlup (a pupil of Ludwig von Mises in Vienna), and his future Chicago friend Milton Friedman, founded what became known as the Mont Pelerin Society. It is revealing that Hayek wanted to call it the John Stuart Mill Society, but was overruled because of Mill's flirtation with ethical socialism in his old age.

The society said it did not engage in propaganda. But over the next quarter of a century its influence, in Europe and in the United States, in creating a core of antisocialist, anticollectivist intellectuals and in combating the idea that classical liberalism was dead, was very great. One of the headwaters that fed the conservative flood began on that hillside above the lake associated with the names of Voltaire and Jean-Jacques Rousseau.

ANOTHER SPRANG in an even more surprising way from the sluggish ground water of the "stump country" in central Michigan. Ten years after publication of *The Road to Serfdom*, by which time Friedrich Hayek had already moved to Chicago,[44] a young scholar from Mecosta, Michigan, Russell Kirk, published a book called *The Conservative Mind*.[45] Kirk, whose father was a railroad engineer, and whose family had lost a fortune in the Depression, inherited a strong dislike for the "assembly line civilization" whose cutting edge was in Detroit. He graduated in 1940 from Michigan State,[46] where the "peanut butter and crackers" culture and intellectual conformity irked the young man, and took himself off to Duke, still home to a congenial spirit of Southern conservatism. There, Kirk read Sir Walter Scott, embraced "Jeffersonian principles," and identified with the Agrarian romanticism of Southern writers like John Crowe Ransom and Robert Penn Warren, expressed in their manifesto *I'll Take My Stand*. At Duke he wrote his master's thesis on the Southern archconservative John Randolph of Roanoke. It was a work of precocious maturity, later published as a book.

In 1941, as the United States was bucketing, largely unknowing, toward global war, Kirk worked briefly at Greenfield Village, the outdoors museum established by Henry Ford, and then at Ford's giant River Rouge plant. The experiences confirmed Kirk's distaste for big business, big labor, and big government. For a while he was even attracted by the leftish progressivism of Thurman Arnold, the New Deal lawyer who wrote *The Folklore of Capitalism*, and in 1944 he was to vote for the Socialist candidate for the presidency, Norman Thomas. But Kirk's political faith was grounded in the traditional individualist conservatism of the Middle West. In 1942, to his disgust, he was drafted into the army, which he disdained as "slavery"; he spent four years in Utah and Florida as a sergeant in a chemical warfare unit. The years of military tedium, however, qualified Kirk to benefit from the most imaginative and perhaps the most beneficent social legislation of the 1940s, the G.I. Bill. It enabled Kirk to travel, at the federal government's expense, to Scotland, to the ancient University of St. Andrews, in its gray granite town between the world's most famous golf links and the cold North Sea; and there Kirk had an intellectual experience that not only formed his personal development but was to irradiate American conservatism for the next thirty years. He fell in love with Edmund Burke.

Kirk wrote his doctoral thesis at St. Andrews on Burke and later expanded it into the fourth of the books under discussion, *The Conservative Mind*, published in 1953. It starts from the incomparably elegant writings of that deceptively complex political operative and philosopher, Edmund Burke. A Protestant Irishman who had embraced the American Revolution and then denounced its sequel in France with equal eloquence, a Whig who became the philosophical icon of Tories both in Britain and America, Burke defended against the levelers and radicals of his day that "natural aristocracy, without which there is no nation," by which he meant not only the hereditary owners of the land, but also administrators, professors, and successful businessmen.

Burke did not, like Hayek and the liberal tradition he represented, reject the state; he glorified it. He saw it as "a divinely ordained moral essence," a spiritual union of the dead, the living, and those yet unborn. Kirk's book is essentially a history, beautifully written and unashamedly reactionary, of the influence of Burke's ideas in Britain and the United States. Of continental Europe, unlike Hayek, he has little or nothing, and certainly nothing good, to say.

Kirk admired John Adams, whom he termed "the father of true conservatism in America," and who, he said, "more than anyone else . . . kept the American government one of laws, not of men." Following Burke, Kirk maintained that the American Revolution was not really a revolution, "not an innovating upheaval, but a conservative restoration of colonial prerogatives."[47] Only Burke's attachment to the English crown and his defense of the established church put him in conflict with Adams's idea.

Friedrich Hayek admired John Stuart Mill so much that only with difficulty was he persuaded not to call his society after him. Kirk, on the contrary, detested Mill as the heir of Jeremy Bentham, whom Mill himself had called "the father of English innovation, both in doctrine and institution . . . the great subversive." Kirk stood with the Romantics, led by his beloved Sir Walter Scott, against Bentham and his Utilitarian school, who held that everything must be judged according to the "calculus of pains and pleasures." Their test was whether it contributed to "the greatest good of the greatest number." "What the Romantics dreaded in a world subjected to Utilitarian domination," Kirk saw, was "an indiscriminate destruction of variety, loveliness, and ancient rights in the name of a devouring industrialism and a Philistine materialism . . . the age of the machine, the hell-hole city and the barrenness of liberal morality."[48] He might have been writing of the 1830s in England and the coming of the Industrial Revolution to London and Manchester; but who can doubt that he had the River Rouge plant and the city of Detroit in his mind's sights?

Much of the book is taken up with deft, sympathetic sketches of such various conservative writers as John Randolph and John C. Calhoun in the South, Fenimore Cooper and James Russell Lowell in the North, Samuel Taylor Coleridge and his defense of religion and order, W. H. Mallock and his assault on equality. He revived and defended such American conservatives as Irving Babbitt,[49] whose task, as he saw it, was to "remind society of its spiritual reality," and Paul Elmer More,[50] who believed that Americans needed to find a natural aristocracy without the insignia of prescriptive rights, and wrote that "to acknowledge this aristocracy, we must be frankly and nobly reactionary."

Kirk summed up the task for "intelligent conservatives" in the twentieth century under four headings. There was "the problem of spiritual and moral regeneration . . . the restoration of the ethical system and the religious sanction upon which any life worth living is founded."[51] There was the problem of leadership, including the "purgation of our system of education"; there, at least, Kirk found himself in total agreement with Albert Jay Nock. There was the problem of "the proletariat"; how could "the mass of men" find "status and hope" in American society, changed as it had been? And there was the problem of economic stability.

In his closing pages, Kirk turned to consider the contemporary world of British and American politics. Frankly reactionary he was prepared to be in his insistence on the importance of order, prescriptive rights, and the religious basis of political society. But Kirk was also, perhaps surprisingly, mildly optimistic about the world he looked at. Conservatism might have been routed, though not conquered; conservatives might have retreated, but they had not been beaten. And the radical tradition, too, was in trouble. Successive movements had disappeared: Jacobins, Benthamites, ethical socialists of the school of William Morris, had all passed away. Marxism had been made hideous by its association with Russian communism. He listed the objects of his abhorrence and summed up his hopes in a splendid paragraph:

> Respect for established usage and longing for continuity are not dead among English-speaking peoples, either. Despite the disruptive forces of mass communication, rapid transportation, industrial standardization, a cheap press, and Gresham's Law operating in affairs of the mind, despite the radical consequences of vulgarized scientific speculation and weakened private morality, despite the decay of the family economy and family affections, most men and women in the twentieth century still feel veneration for what their ancestors have believed, and express a pathetic eagerness to find stability in a time of flux . . . Conservatives may yet appeal to an unsatisfied emotion of gigantic potency.[52]

The Americans, Kirk reminded his countrymen, had "always been a conservative people." Doctrinaire radicalism had never flourished among them. Their conservatism was perhaps inarticulate, but then, as his beloved Burke had said, conservatism everywhere is like the "placidity of cattle browsing under the oaks."[53] Looking back into the past, Russell Kirk, who was pleased to call himself "the bonnet laird of the stump country," saw himself as the heir to a long and honorable tradition of thinkers who had rejected the secular, equalizing purposes of the French Revolution and its heirs. Looking to the future, he believed that Americans' inherent conservative prejudices — his word — would revive and would be applied to their present discontents.

IN THAT, he was unmistakably correct. His own book, his publisher said, had caught on "beyond all expectations."[54] With Hayek, a historian has said, "Kirk had made it respectable again to be a man of the Right." By the beginning of the Eisenhower administration, there was a vast disillusion, a chafing impatience, with the liberal orthodoxy. That was what brought Eisenhower to power, as we shall see. Along with those negative emotions toward liberalism, there went a widespread curiosity about what modern conservatism might be like. Conservatism, for the first time since 1929, was in the air. That mood explains the success of the four books I have described: the effect of Albert Jay Nock on an influential remnant, the massive sales of Ayn Rand's novels, the impact of *The Road to Serfdom* on economists and political philosophers, the sudden enthusiasm for something so unlikely as the handing down, by a young graduate student from Michigan by way of Scotland, of the philosophical tablets bequeathed by an eighteenth-century British Whig.

It has to be said, though, that these proto-conservatives were an odd bunch in themselves, and it cannot be denied that they were at odds with one another to an embarrassing degree. Ayn Rand, Russian-born, cherished the classic immigrant's romantic passion for the idea of America, the clanging, jostling America of Hollywood and New York, symbolized by that archemblem of modernity and megalopolis, the skyscraper. But that was precisely the world that horrified Nock and Kirk, both of whom fled from it, Kirk to Scotland and Nock to Belgium, for long periods. Their patriotism was directed not toward the builders of the Empire State Building, but toward the lost worlds of the nineteenth century, the world of Thomas Jefferson and John Adams, just as Richard Weaver had retreated first to the antebellum South, then even farther back, to the schools of Paris before they were tempted by the new logic of William of Occam. Nock and Kirk shared a detestation for the innovations of John Dewey and his peers, but Kirk remained until his death a mentor of the Anglican Communion and a Christian moralist in the tradition of Hooker's *Ecclesiastical Polity*, where Nock, a lapsed Episcopalian minister, abandoned his family and was in the latter years of his life a bohemian and a skeptic. Kirk shared with Hayek a passionate commitment to the ideal of personal liberty, a conviction that political and economic liberty are indivisible, and a detestation for socialism. In other respects the Austrian aristocrat and the Midwestern admirer of aristocracy could hardly have been more different thinkers. Russell Kirk embraced conservatism and traced its roots to European monarchy and law, to the yearning for order and the search for legitimacy. Hayek cared very little about such things.

Indeed, he went so far as to tack onto his second major book, *The Constitution of Liberty*, a little essay called "Why I Am Not a Conservative."[55] In it, there was even a veiled criticism of Russell Kirk. Hayek wrote that the confusion between the European and American uses of the word "liberal" "was made worse by the recent attempt to transplant to America the European type of conservatism, which, being alien to the

American tradition, has acquired a somewhat odd character."[56] The decisive objection to conservatism, Hayek wrote, is that by its very nature
it cannot offer an alternative to the drift toward collectivism, but only
slow it down. The liberal, Hayek insisted, must actively oppose some of
the basic conceptions that most conservatives share with socialists; the
main one is the conservative's "characteristic complacency" toward established authority. Conservatives, said Hayek, lack principles. They do
not lack moral conviction. But they have no political principles that will
enable them to work with people who do not share those convictions. To
the liberal, again, neither moral nor religious ideas are proper objects of
coercion. Conservatives incline to defend the established order, while
liberals feel that no established values can justify privilege, monopoly,
or any other action of the state. Conservatives blame the evils of the
time on democracy; liberals believe that the chief evil is unlimited government.

Some of these writers, in short, like some of the many who turned
toward conservative ideas in the new and dismaying circumstances of
the Cold War, were more inclined to be libertarian, some more authoritarian. Some saw big business as an engine of progress and a spring of
healthy vitality. Others saw it as a sordid conspiracy vulgarizing the
purity of American democracy. Some saw conservatism as the shield and
sword of spiritual truth; others were skeptics in religion and all else. It
would be a mistake to exaggerate their differences, but the differences in
perception, in instinct, in values and aims of the first prophets of a new
intellectual conservatism were so great as to amount virtually to contradictions, and forewarned of disagreements to come.

So books like the four I have described at some length were straws in
the wind only. Their success was a sign of a new readiness, in the minds
of many different Americans, to consider conservative ideas, not yet
evidence of an assured, let alone a successful, conservative movement.

That had to wait for two developments of the 1950s. One happened
in the arena of public politics. A series of political events on the surface
discredited the new conservatism, but also hardened in the fire of almost
hysterical controversy a new generation of conservative politicians. The
other was the work done by a new generation of conservative intellectuals — the very phrase would have sounded like a contradiction in terms
to most people in 1945 — who first fused the diverse and often contradictory ideas of the conservative pioneers into a coherent conservative
ideology, and then organized cadres of disciples to preach the new gospel across America.

⊭ 3 ⊭

Mainstream: The 1950s

And not by eastern windows only
When daylight comes, comes in the light,
In front, the sun climbs slow, how slowly,
But westward, look, the land is bright.

— *Arthur Hugh Clough,*
"Say Not the Struggle Naught Availeth"

THE FORTUNES OF American conservatism in the twenty years after World War II can be seen from two points of view. Looking outward, the performance of conservative candidates in the electoral field is a story of revival after the near-eclipse of conservatism during the New Deal years. Gradually, great slabs of the New Deal's support among the voters split off and drifted to the right. They became at least available to be won by conservative Republican candidates, both nationally and at the state and local level, and in due course, under the pressure of events, that is exactly what happened.

Looking inward at the conservatives themselves, it is the story of how a substantially new conservatism was forged in a struggle that was not only electoral but also ideological: a war on many fronts whose stake was nothing less than hegemony over American life.

The struggle was a bitter one. There were harsh accusations on either side, and they led to the merciless political destruction of those not strong enough to survive. At first the conservatives were a despised, almost insignificant minority. As they fought to reassert their legitimacy and their right to a share of the spoils of national leadership, many of them were toughened, some into insensitivity. The traditional conservatism had been all but swept away by the Great Depression, the New Deal, and the prestige with which the liberal majority and the Democratic Party emerged from the victorious struggle against Germany and Japan. The new conservatism was forged in the heat of those conflicts into something both harder and sharper.

As long as the war lasted, Roosevelt was something more than a political chieftain; indeed, something more than president of the United States. He really was what has paradoxically become an empty phrase since the collapse of communism: leader of the Free World. Ironically, his death and the triumphant conclusion of the war made some kind of conservative revival possible and ultimately inevitable. Roosevelt was a titanic figure. It is commonplace now to point out that the New Deal didn't end the Depression, and to draw attention to Roosevelt's shortcomings and contradictions as a leader in peace and war. But until the war was over, it was plain to contemporaries that he would remain invincible. In 1944 even Robert Alphonso Taft, champion of Middle Western conservatism and archenemy of the New Deal, did not think it likely that Franklin Roosevelt could be beaten.[1] All political calculations revolved around the assumption that if Roosevelt chose to run, he would win. Many therefore focused on the secondary question: who would be his choice for vice president and so the heir apparent of a man whose health was unmistakably fragile?

By 1948 that had all changed. In the 1946 midterm elections the Republicans recaptured control of both houses of Congress for the first time since 1930 and proceeded to pass a solid portfolio of anti–New Deal legislation. Harry Truman was no titan. In foreign policy, he rose magnificently to the challenge of Stalinist truculence. But there was something perhaps a little patronizing about the way men like Dean Acheson said so.[2] The mere presence of Harry Truman in the White House made the old Republican warhorses paw the ground and sniff the air with a new sense of hope.

Between 1944 and 1948, in other words, the reign of the New Deal came to an end. It is true that the Truman administration offered a parcel of policies labeled the Fair Deal, and that these represented in a general sense a continuation of the Roosevelt policies. It is also true that it was to be another two decades before the supremacy of a sort of liberal consensus faded away.[3] Nonetheless, after 1945 the New Deal's task was done. The Great Depression was over. To borrow Roosevelt's own phrase, Dr. Win-the-War had succeeded where Dr. New Deal had failed. After the war, America was inundated and irrigated by a great flood of prosperity. And the war was won. Americans, not least those who had been overseas to fight, felt they could relax and go back to normal life. "Normalcy" had been a Republican slogan.[4] The heroic years of struggle that had evoked the Roosevelt miracles were over. And now Roosevelt himself was dead. Suddenly, Republican conservatives could see that they once again had a realistic prospect of winning the White House, controlling the Congress, and climbing into the national driving seat again. But first they had to work out what pitch they would make to the voters.

In 1948 Dewey's widely unexpected defeat confirmed the need for new thinking. Republicans suddenly came to terms with the fact that they were not going to win automatically; there would be no pendulum to swing Republicans back into power, whatever they stood for. Once they grasped that, Republicans realized they would have to decide what they did stand for, and that realization, in turn, unleashed a ferocious conflict within the Republican Party, truly a battle for the party's soul.

Taft was bitterly disappointed when he lost the Republican presidential nomination to Tom Dewey. But the consolation was that he believed that Dewey and his running mate, Earl Warren, would easily defeat the incumbent, Harry Truman. So when the unthinkable happened, and Dewey was beaten by Truman, the bitter divisions within the Republican Party could no longer be hidden or healed.[5]

To understand who were the combatants in that battle and what it was about, you have to understand that American conservatism, while decisively beaten in 1932, 1936, 1940, and 1944, had not actually melted away. Many conservatives, of course, remained conservative throughout the years of the New Deal. In the South, most of them continued to vote for Democrats as they and their grandfathers before them had done, because the South was not yet ready to forget that it was the Republicans who had overthrown the Confederacy and emancipated the slaves. In the rest of the country, most of them voted Republican. As one group after another peeled off and joined the Roosevelt coalition, the Republican Party was stripped down to its hard core.

Or, rather, to its two hard cores. One was the old, predominantly Eastern upper class, heirs and in many cases descendants of the men who had built big business in America. On Wall Street and on Boston's State Street, in their homes on Long Island or on the Philadelphia Main Line, many of these bankers and brokers, and scions of great wealth earned in oil and steel, railroading, and mining, denounced the New Deal in extravagant terms over the Scotch Roosevelt had allowed them to drink legally once again. They can be called the Eastern wing of the Republican Party, so long as it is remembered that people essentially like them were also to be found in the older, richer suburbs of Western cities: in Shaker Heights, Ohio, Evanston and Winnetka, Illinois, in St. Louis, on Nob Hill in San Francisco, as well as in small clusters that James Reichley, in a perceptive article in *Fortune*, once called "Elm Street," the street of old shade trees and spacious frame houses where "the nicest families" in every town in America lived. "At the root of the rivalry," wrote Taft's biographer, "was the sectional-ideological split in the party that had pitted the Taft-Bricker-Midwestern wing against the Willkie-Dewey-Eastern wing as early as 1940."[6] The Eastern wing might not necessarily live in the East, but they sent their children east to be educated. They thought that big government and big unions were taking the country to the dogs, and called Roosevelt a "traitor to his class." At the same time these were not fanatics. Their business experience had taught them to be practical and realistic, and their political instinct was to come to terms with the New Deal as long as they had to. They found it particularly easy to go along with its foreign policy, for most of the Easterners were internationalists after their fashion; and their leaders, men like Henry L. Stimson, Wendell Willkie, Tom Dewey, were strong internationalists.

When they called FDR a traitor to his class, the Eastern internationalists acknowledged in a backhanded way what the other strand of Republican conservatism would have angrily denied: that there was an American upper class. For the other strand in Republican conservatism, essentially Middle Western but also Western, was made up of businessmen who saw themselves, not as a silk stocking aristocracy, but as the plain people who had prospered by keeping alive the flame of traditional values. Some of them, like Robert Taft himself, might seem to outsiders hard to distinguish from the Eastern aristocracy of wealth. Son of the only man to serve both as president of the United States and as chief justice of the Supreme Court, Taft was educated at the Taft School, founded by his uncle; then at Yale, where, like his grandfather, father, and four uncles, he was a member of the most famous and influential secret society in America, Skull and Bones; and finally polished at Harvard Law School. His family constituted almost in themselves the aristocracy of Cincinnati, where they owned one of the newspapers, founded the symphony and the art museum, and endowed a university. Yet to Taft himself the distinction was clear. He saw himself as a plain Midwestern American. He remained to the end of his life an isolationist at heart. Although he was proud of America's and his own "English heritage," as he put it in a 1946 speech at Kenyon College, which his biographer said came as close as anything he ever said to setting out his fundamental convictions, he contrasted "European selfishness" with "American idealism."[7] He was skeptical about the Truman Doctrine, in which the president committed Americans to helping countries fight communism, and he opposed the Marshall Plan. In a major speech in Chicago before the end of the war he attacked the very idea of a postwar military alliance, which he said would "create a profession of militarists" in America. "Political power over other nations," he said, "however benevolent its purposes, leads inevitably to imperialism."[8] It is strange to note how much common ground there was between some of the isolationist conservatives of the 1930s and 1940s and the antiwar radicals of the 1960s.

Taft also fully shared the Midwestern suspicion of those Eastern Republicans who had accommodated the New Deal. If Taft had been nominated in 1948, he believed, he could have won. The way to do it, he observed, was "to hit Truman every time he opened his mouth."[9] Even if Dewey, having got the nomination, had won the election, it might still have been possible to preserve the party's unity. It was the combination of Taft's rejection and Dewey's failure that made a bitter *post mortem* inevitable. Four years later, in 1952, Taft was passed over again in favor of the candidate the Eastern Republicans had cleverly brought in because he could win and they knew that one of their own could not. The abyss between the Midwesterners and the Easterners became unbridgeably wide, and the recriminations too bitter for reconciliation. Between 1948 and 1952, however, other things shaped the emerging conservatism even more than the repeated rejection of Robert Taft, the champion of the Midwest.

To Midwestern isolationists, it was a disaster that American boys should have been sucked into war overseas at all. That was precisely what they had feared all along: that Franklin Roosevelt and a bunch of internationalists from the environs of New York would drag the United States once again into pulling Great Britain's chestnuts, and her Empire, out of the fire. Indeed, there were not a few who believed to the end of their days that, with his fiendish manipulative skills, Roosevelt had somehow set the whole thing up, connived with the Japanese to get them to attack Pearl Harbor, perhaps, so as to provide a pretext for getting the United States into the war. When the war did finally end, and triumphantly at that, the isolationists, and many other Republicans and conservative Democrats, were appalled to see that it had brought about the very development they had most feared ever since 1917: the spread of communism.

It hardly came as a surprise to them to see Europe divided between communists in the East and socialists in the West. What was worse, in the very moment of American triumph, when the United States ought to have been able, like Cincinnatus or George Washington, to return to its own estate and mind its own business, American invulnerability, that precious breastplate, had been pierced for the first time since the War of 1812.

Every year brought worse news. In 1946 it was plain that Stalin, so far from being "Uncle Joe" and a "gallant ally," was a dedicated and dangerous enemy of the United States and all it stood for. In 1947 the United States became committed to helping governments resist communist subversion. In 1948 Whittaker Chambers, a senior editor at *Time* magazine, testified that he had served in a communist underground in Washington and that "a member of this group . . . was Alger Hiss," a former State Department official whose brother was a law partner of Secretary of State Dean Acheson, archsymbol of all that Midwestern and other conservatives detested. Everywhere, it seemed, as the House Un-American Activities Committee pursued its outwardly impressive if in reality tacky and slipshod investigations, there was foreign conspiracy and domestic subversion. Still in 1948, as the communists took over in Czechoslovakia and tightened their grip on the rest of Eastern Europe, Whittaker Chambers led HUAC investigators to a pumpkin patch in Westminster, Maryland, where they found cached papers that made it inevitable Hiss would be indicted. We now know, from the so-called Venona cables, that Soviet espionage on a systematic scale was a reality. In 1949 it became known that the Soviet Union had tested an atomic bomb, and communist revolutionaries overthrew America's allies in China. In January 1950, Alger Hiss was convicted of perjury for denying that he had been involved in a communist espionage ring. And on February 9, 1950, Senator Joseph R. McCarthy of Wisconsin made his famous speech in Wheeling, West Virginia, in which he said that he "had in his hand" the names of 205 communists at work in Acheson's State Department.[10]

As McCarthy traveled round the country and returned to Washington, the number of these "card-carrying communists," as he began to call them, fluctuated. A forty-one-year-old recently voted the worst member of the Senate in a poll of Capitol Hill reporters, he had been flailing around in search of an issue that would make his fortune. It appears that he was handed the idea, in the course of a dinner at the Colony Restaurant in Washington, by a Roman Catholic priest, Father Edmund Walsh, of Georgetown University, who urged him to take up the issue of communist subversion. Walsh meant the real threat of communism abroad. McCarthy talked about the less substantial threat posed by communists closer to home. He had found his issue and for a while was able to set the political agenda.

It is tempting to see McCarthy as nothing more than a self-interested buffoon with primitive Red-baiting ideas. And there is a rich irony in the way Dean Acheson, a deeply conservative and patriotic Christian Brahmin with passionate anticommunist beliefs, was McCarthy's principal target. McCarthy's language was almost manically violent. "When this pompous diplomat in striped pants, with the phony British accent," McCarthy said, "proclaimed to the American people that Christ in the Sermon on the Mount endorsed communism, the blasphemy was so great that it awakened the dormant indignation of the American people."[11] In part, of course, McCarthy was expressing, and at the same time whipping up, traditional isolationist attitudes. But there was more to it than that.

It is impossible to understand the ferocity of the right's charges against Acheson, the State Department, and the Truman administration, and their plausibility for many, except in the context of the apparent triumphs of communism in the five years after World War II in general, and in particular of the triumph of the communists in China. The collapse of the Nationalist regime in China was followed within six months by the news of the Russian atomic bomb, the conviction of Alger Hiss, and the news of the treason of the atomic scientist Klaus Fuchs, who confessed in London to having passed nuclear secrets to the Soviet Union. "How much more are we going to have to have to take?" asked Indiana's conservative Republican senator, Homer Capehart, and there were many who wondered along with him.

At the same time, the turmoil and tension of the period from 1945 to 1960 was due to the connection some made, and others as passionately denied, between the unmistakable challenge of communism abroad and domestic radicalism. As early as 1945 the issue of this connection was raised by the House of Representatives Un-American Activities Committee and its investigations into communist subversion in Hollywood and elsewhere. It was thrown into relief in the context of the Chinese revolution by the distinctly murky *Amerasia* case. *Amerasia* was a review of Asian affairs run by a businessman, Philip Jaffe, who was close to the

Communist Party. He was a friend of the former American Communist leader, Earl Browder, and also had contacts with the Soviet Union. In 1945 an analyst with the Office of Strategic Services (the forerunner of the CIA) saw an article in *Amerasia* that was closely based on a top-secret document he himself had written. When government agents broke into the *Amerasia* offices, they found hundreds of secret government papers. Surveillance led to espionage charges being brought against Jaffe and several other people, one of them a well-known diplomat and expert on China, John Stewart Service.

Service was one of a number of "China Hands," or China experts (not, as was later to be charged, members of a group, for they were not all in close contact with one another). They included Dr. Owen Lattimore, John Carter Vincent, and others. All to a greater or lesser degree felt that the United States had become too closely tied to Chiang Kai-shek and his Kuomintang government and that the future of China might lie with the communists.

They were thus fiercely at odds with the China Lobby, a group of more or less conservative Republicans who clung to Chiang and sought to defend him against what they saw as betrayal by the Democrats and their "China Hand" advisers. The China Lobby included former ambassador to Chiang, Patrick J. Hurley; General Albert C. Wedemeyer, who had commanded U.S. forces in China; Senator Kenneth Wherry of Nebraska; Senator Bill Knowland of California, whose family owned the *Oakland Tribune*; and a number of influential Republicans with personal connections to Protestant and Roman Catholic missions to China, including Representative Walter Judd of Minnesota, a former medical missionary in China, and no less a publicist than Henry Luce, the publisher of *Time*, *Life*, and *Fortune*, whose parents had also been missionaries in China.

Service was no communist. But he had undoubtedly been leaking secret government documents to Jaffe, who was close to being one, if he was not actually a party member. For the Truman administration, therefore, the *Amerasia* case was acutely embarrassing. The attorney general, Tom Clark, worked out a deal with the former New Deal aide Tommy Corcoran. He was the Chinese Nationalists' lobbyist in Washington, and it was not in the Nationalists' interest to draw attention to the extent to which the administration's own experts were losing faith in them.

In a very Washington way a deal was cut. The grand jury found no bill against Service. The State Department cleared him of disloyalty and let him go. Jaffe successfully bargained for a plea of guilty to a minor charge of possessing government documents. And for years some Republicans suspected that the Truman administration had deliberately covered up communist espionage at almost as sensitive a moment for foreign policy as could be imagined: at the point where the United States was deciding whether to shift its diplomatic and perhaps more practical support from the anticommunist Kuomintang to the Chinese communists.

The *Amerasia* case is interesting because it disposes of the cruder stereotypes on both sides. The Democrats' behavior was hardly impeccable. Yet the Republicans' charges did not hold water. The Democrats could hardly deny that one of their top advisers on China was leaking sensitive secret documents to a left-wing journal close to the Communist Party, or that they fixed legal proceedings to cover up what had happened. The Republicans, on the other hand, were equally wide of the mark when they charged Service and the China Hands, let alone the Truman administration, with being soft on Communism. So the *Amerasia* case set the scene for ten years of angry charges, uneasy denials, and reciprocal paranoia, which together played a not insignificant part in fertilizing the political soil in which a new conservatism was to grow.

If concern about the power of communism in Europe and the Far East grew steadily from 1945, so too did concern about domestic loyalty in the United States. The issue was exploited by politicians: first by men like Representatives John Rankin and J. Parnell Thomas in their HUAC hearings, later by altogether more formidable figures such as Joseph R. McCarthy and Richard M. Nixon. But it will not do to brush aside the loyalty issue, as Dean Acheson and many less exalted liberal Democrats did, as "the revolt of the primitives." For one thing, there really was widespread communist espionage, before, during, and after World War II. And for another, the politicians did not create public concern; they reflected it.

It is not always easy to distinguish between spontaneous popular anticommunism and the synthetic version whipped up by preachers, newspapers, and politicians. Still, it is plain from the attacks on communists indicted in the *Dennis* trial of the Communist Party leadership, under the Smith Act in 1949, that there was a strong anticommunist mood in the country. Poll data support this. Support for outlawing the party altogether declined, as might be expected, during the war, from about 70 percent to under 50 percent in 1946. But by May 1948, 77 percent thought communists should have to register with the government and by a margin of two-to-one Americans thought that communists were loyal to the Soviet Union, not to the United States.[12] The four million people who turned out in 350 cities in 1947 to board the Freedom Train and be exhorted about the Constitution and the virtues of free enterprise bear witness to the prevailing political climate of the Truman years. Several states, including California, Michigan, Mississippi, Pennsylvania, and Ohio, passed various laws to harass "subversives," and so did some cities, including Los Angeles and Detroit, then the third and fifth biggest in the nation. The hunt for subversives was particularly hot in areas with a strong radical tradition in politics and the unions.

The unveiling of communist spies, such as Judith Coplon in 1949, Klaus Fuchs in February 1950, and Julius Rosenberg in July of that same year, contributed to public conviction that communist subversion was a real danger. It also underlined to Republican politicians the Truman administration's vulnerability to the charge that it had been "soft" on domestic communist subversion.

It was in those very years that the Democrats divided precisely on the issue of communism. There was what has been called a Popular Front wing, prominently represented in 1948 by Henry Wallace, which still sought to rally "progressive forces," including the communists and their fellow travelers. Opposing the Wallaceites were the anticommunist "Cold War liberals." They included younger intellectuals like the group that met at the Willard Hotel in Washington in January 1947 to found Americans for Democratic Action, people like Arthur M. Schlesinger, Jr., whose anticommunist manifesto, *The Vital Center,* was published in 1949.[13] They were also young Democratic politicians like the mayor of Minneapolis, Hubert H. Humphrey, who had cut their teeth in fights with local communists. Yet try as they did to emphasize their own (absolutely genuine) anticommunist credentials, President Truman, Secretary of State Dean Acheson, and other top administration officials could never quite free themselves from association with the Popular Front hangers-on who had indeed been honored supporters of the Roosevelt administrations.

Senator Joseph McCarthy's Wheeling speech was made in February 1950, but it was the outbreak of the Korean War, five months later, that ushered in the acute phase of the national obsession with domestic subversion. From then until his censure, in December 1954, McCarthy terrified the Democrats, and put the wind up a good few Republicans as well. The nature of his hold on the political imagination, and the manner of his fall, both contributed to the mythology and the mood that created the new conservatism.

McCarthy inspired a sort of panic, especially among those Eastern intellectuals who had themselves been attracted to left-wing ideas of one strength or another in the 1930s. Many of them were of recent immigrant stock, and many of those were Jewish. The Jewish intellectuals, in particular, came from families that had known religious and ethnic persecution only too well before they left Europe. They had experienced milder but still disagreeable anti-Semitism in America. And they had only just been confronted with the full horror of what had happened to European Jewry in the Holocaust. Those who faced public pillorying, the loss of their jobs, even prison, could be forgiven for fearing McCarthy's demagoguery. But the fear spread far wider than that, and it has contributed to a widespread and lasting misunderstanding of what McCarthyism was and what it was not.[14]

One group of intellectuals, typified by Theodor W. Adorno, a Marxist who was himself a refugee from Nazi Germany, interpreted McCarthyism in terms of "the authoritarian personality."[15] Others saw McCarthy as the harbinger of a "native American fascism." More widely accepted was the interpretation publicized by the journalist and political analyst Samuel Lubell[16] and by the highly influential group of contributors to the collection of essays edited by Daniel Bell and called *The New American Right*.[17] It explained McCarthy's support among the general public in terms of a new politics of "status anxiety." In the impoverished past, Bell and such fellow authors as Seymour Martin Lipset argued, politics was about economics and was divided along class lines. In the brave new world of postwar American prosperity, they claimed, class politics were a thing of the past. The support for McCarthy, they said, expressed a new noneconomic politics. They proceeded to list over forty groups in American society, from "oil wildcatters," "shabby genteel Protestants," "people from South Boston," to real estate manipulators and Daughters of the American Revolution, who were unduly prone to be led by "status anxieties" to support McCarthy.

Individually brilliant as the contributors to this volume were, their interpretation looks, at an interval of forty years, like nothing so much as a topology of the pet hates of New York intellectuals at the time. (Another reflection prompted by a rereading of *The New American Right* is how many of its authors subsequently crossed no man's land and joined ideological forces with the wildcatters, South Boston, and the Daughters of the American Revolution in embracing one or another variant of "neoconservatism"! But that is a thought for a later stage in this story.) Perhaps McCarthyism was not directly about economic issues, but it was emphatically about politics, not psychology. It was the projection of traditional political divisions in a new context.

The clearest identification that can be made on the basis of quantitative evidence (from polls and surveys) is not between support for McCarthy and one or another status group or personality type. It is between support for McCarthy and Republicanism. McCarthyism was political, in the narrow, party sense of the word. McCarthy, one political scientist has concluded,[18] "was unusually dependent upon regular Republican support both in the Senate and in his home state." He was also used by Republican politicians as "the weapon of a desperate Republican party ... Senator Taft's famous advice [to McCarthy], 'if one case doesn't work, then bring up another,' is a measure of the lengths to which Republicans were willing to go in those days to embarrass a long-entrenched Democratic administration."

The context was new, in two respects. As we have seen, McCarthy, and the other politicians like Bourke Hickenlooper, Karl Mundt, and Richard Nixon, who exploited the domestic subversion issue, flourished against the background of real concern about genuine communist subversion. They were also operating in a new political context in the sense that they were learning to use the new media, and in particular television. McCarthy learned how to manipulate the "artillery of the press." And he learned how to use television, making an implication, then moving on, so that the truth could never catch him up.

Joe McCarthy, who had lived by the sword of television, died by it too. It was Edward R. Murrow's exposure on *See It Now* in April 1954, and even more the Army-McCarthy hearings, televised live between April and July, that finished him. By the fall McCarthy, who had been so much in demand to speak for Republican candidates in 1950 and 1952, was a pariah. Then and only then did the Senate establishment decide it was time to be done with him. For that is what happened. He was censured not for his "McCarthyite" assaults on the civil liberties of Americans, but for bringing the Senate into disrepute by being rude about its members.

McCarthy's fall was greeted with relief, not only by those who could imagine themselves being his victims, but also by politicians generally. In his heyday, there was a feeling, exaggerated by the eternal isolation of Washington from the rest of the country, that McCarthy knew something other politicians did not, that somehow he could tap hidden springs of Americanism, or of populism, or of Know-Nothingism, depending on your point of view. The truth was less mysterious than that. Joe McCarthy at the height of his power and reputation was a slick, dangerous, political assassin equipped with fairly conventional Midwestern Republican politics, with a glib tongue, and a convenient lack of scruple where the truth was concerned. He also had a brass neck that would have done credit to the crocodile Behemoth in the Book of Job: "Consider now the great Behemoth," might have been his epitaph: "his bones are of brass."

When he did fall, as the phrase went in those days, he had it coming. He had lived so dangerously, talked and picked fights, made enemies and drunk whiskey so recklessly, that it was not really surprising that he would disappear so swiftly. Even those respectable Republicans who had been glad to use him were in no hurry to pay tribute to his memory. Yet to a minority, the manner of his fall left a bad taste in the mouth, and the questions he had briefly raised so saliently remained suspiciously unanswered. The high tide of anticommunism in the United States has been so associated with the name of Joe McCarthy that it is easy to forget that his erasure left millions as uneasy as ever about the threat of communism and the strange unwillingness not only of liberals and Democrats, but of many Republicans too, to see the matter in as serious a light as they did.

Other events between the outbreak of the Korean War and the eclipse of Joe McCarthy contributed to the suspicions and to the isolation of his followers. The first was the nomination and election of General Eisenhower. Aware that they could not successfully nominate an "Eastern," moderate Republican, the party's (predominantly Eastern) managers turned their backs on the Midwestern conservatives and chose instead a man who was arguably not a Republican at all, and who had certainly been actively sounded out as a candidate by the Democrats only a few months previously. That in itself was a slap in the face to conservatives. But when Eisenhower reached the White House, the men he surrounded himself with, while conservative enough in all conscience, were figures from the past of the Republican Party. The secretary of state was John Foster Dulles, partner in the Sullivan and Cromwell law firm, the very epitome of Wall Street internationalism. The secretary of the treasury was George M. Humphrey, the head of the M. A. Hanna company, founded by the greatest Republican political boss of the late nineteenth century. The secretary of agriculture was Ezra Taft Benson, conservative even by the standards of his fellow Mormon bishops. These were conservatives, but in the manner of the 1920s. They were for the most part utterly innocent of the new ideas that were stirring among a younger generation of conservatives.

IN 1946, and again two years later, a candy company executive, Robert Welch, from Belmont, Massachusetts, a suburb of Boston, visited England to study the effects of socialist government there.[19] In 1949 he spent a month flying round the world, focusing his attention mostly on Asia. What he saw on his travels frightened him and determined him to devote his life to educating the world about the dangers of communism. In 1952, after an unsuccessful run for Republican lieutenant governor of Massachusetts, he worked for Senator Taft. When Taft lost, Welch believed that communists and one-worlders had stolen the nomination and given it to their hand-picked front man, Eisenhower. From that point on, Welch believed quite literally, the Republic was in danger. In 1955 he was in Asia again; as a vice president of the National Association of Manufacturers he had enough influence to arrange appointments with President Syngman Rhee of South Korea and with General Chiang Kai-shek in Taiwan. In 1956 he was in Germany, where he interviewed the chancellor of the Federal Republic, Konrad Adenauer. In that year he decided to give up business, which had made him modestly prosperous, and throw himself full time into the fight against communism.

On December 8, 1958, he met eleven potential disciples he had invited to join him in an Indianapolis hotel, and for two days he laid out his despairing analysis of the state of the world, the advance of communism, and the need for an educational and political campaign to reverse "the gradual surrender of the United States" to communism. He told his friends that he proposed to found a national right-wing organization, and that he had decided to call it after John Birch, a twenty-six-year-old fundamentalist Baptist preacher from Macon, Georgia, who, Welch said, had fought against the Japanese in China, and had then been murdered by the Chinese communists "because of the powerful resistance he would have been able to inspire against them." Welch wrote a biography of his hero, in which he said:

> We have built this sermon around John Birch, for in one blade of grass lies the key to all creation, could we only understand it; and in the forces that swirled around John Birch lay all the conflicts, of philosophy and implementation with which our world is now so imperatively concerned. Therein lay the significance of his life and death. Actually we must choose between the civilization, the form of society, and the expression of human life, as represented by John Birch, and their parallels as envisioned by Karl Marx and his spiritual successors. There is no middle ground.

Welch duly proceeded to set up the John Birch Society, whose aim was to alert the American people to the onward march of communism, in the world but especially in the United States. The society was to be a secretive, authoritarian membership organization. It would be divided into chapters of "from 10 to 20 dedicated patriots" who would work at the level of local communities to educate people about the imminence of the communist threat. Originally it seems that Welch envisaged it as primarily educational, working through local government, Parent-Teacher Associations, church groups, and voluntary associations. Welch declared that he hoped to recruit a million members. By 1962, press estimates of membership ran from fifty thousand to a hundred thousand, though financial statements filed with the attorney general of Massachusetts suggest that at the time it was no more than twenty-four thousand.[20] In 1967, when the John Birch Society was at the height of its influence, two experts estimated that it had some eighty thousand members in four thousand chapters.

The air of mystery surrounding the society did nothing to minimize concern about its influence. At least two members, John Rousselot and Edgar Hiestand, were elected to Congress as Republicans from California, and there are reports that as many as five Birchers won Republican nominations for the House of Representatives or for state legislatures in 1964. The John Birch Society was especially effective at the local level. In Amarillo, Texas, for example, a Birch member ran for mayor and won 42 percent of the vote after a bitter and divisive campaign. In a smaller Texas town, Midlothian, fire bombs were thrown through the office of the local newspaper after it reported a speech by a leading local John Birch Society member. Speaking in the public high school, he said that President Franklin D. Roosevelt was responsible for the existence of communism, and that President Truman was a cold-blooded murderer.[21]

Perhaps the society's most effective campaign was against the tiny trickle of imports into the United States from Eastern Europe. This involved organizing "card parties" to drop cards saying "Always buy your Communist Products at" such-and-such a store. At its height, the campaign affected 264 cities all over the United States, and intimidated major retailing corporations such as Sears, Roebuck into withdrawing Eastern European products. The society's greatest strength was in California, Texas, and Florida, with especially strong concentrations of chapters in Greater Los Angeles and Greater Houston. There were outlying redoubts in Phoenix, Birmingham, Atlanta, and Wichita; there were also thousands of members in New York, New Jersey, and Massachusetts. Everywhere, the society's appeal was in the suburbs, from Belmont, where headquarters was on the ground floor and basement of a red brick office building shared with an insurance company, to Orange County, south of Los Angeles.

The Birchers did not restrict themselves to saying that communism was a present danger in the United States. They said the communists were already in control. Robert Welch originally asserted that the country was "50–70% Communist-controlled"; by the middle 1960s, that rather meaningless numerical estimate had been increased to "60–80%." But what brought Welch national notoriety was widespread circulation of his charge, at first in the unpublished manuscript of a book called *The Politician*, that President Dwight Eisenhower — incumbent, Texas-bred, golf-playing, reassuring, deeply conservative Ike, the generalissimo of America's victorious armies in World War II — was "a dedicated, conscious agent of the Communist conspiracy." This view, Welch wrote in his manuscript version of the book, was "based on an accumulation of detailed evidence so extensive and so palpable that it seems to me to put this conviction beyond any reasonable doubt."

Reckless, paranoid, even deluded he may have been, but Welch was not an ignorant hick. He had been educated at the University of North Carolina and then at Harvard, and spent two years at the U.S. Naval Academy at Annapolis. Even so, his bald statement that President Eisenhower — and for good measure his brother Milton, president of Pennsylvania State University and Johns Hopkins, the brothers Foster and Allen Dulles, respectively secretary of state and director of central intelligence, and the late General George C. Marshall were all members of the Communist conspiracy — backfired with a noise heard across the continent. Liberals and moderate Republicans naturally treated such statements with hooting derision. But even conservative Republicans rushed to dissociate themselves from Welch's wilder accusations. When *The Politician* was finally published in 1962, Welch toned it down, saying, for example, that "Truman was passively *used* by the Communists, with his knowledge and acquiescence, as the price he consciously paid for their making him President." This was a grave enough charge in itself, in all conscience, but one that fell perceptibly short of the original charge that Truman was himself an active communist conspirator. As for President Eisenhower, said Welch evasively in his more measured version, "it is difficult to avoid raising the question of deliberate treason."

With hindsight, there is perhaps a temptation to laugh off Robert Welch and the John Birch Society as a seriocomic bubble of extremism, an essentially unimportant by-product of the tensest period of the Cold War, the time of fear from the Korean War to the Cuban missile crisis.

That is a mistake, however. For one thing, the society did have significant influence at the time. For another, it expressed what the historian Richard Hofstadter has called "the paranoid style in American politics," a traditional suspicion of collusion between privileged leaders and dark, subversive forces that goes back at least as far as the Anti-Masonic Party of the 1840s and lives on to this day in such corners of American life as the right-wing militias. What is more significant for our present purpose, it also prepared the ground, especially at the local level, for the next important manifestation of conservative political strength, the Goldwater campaign of 1964. The fact is, however, that the John Birch Society was only one of a large number of more or less extreme movements that proliferated in the 1950s and 1960s and, taken together, came to be known as the Radical Right.

There was the Christian Anti-Communist Crusade run out of Long Beach, California, by a former Australian physician, Dr. Fred C. Schwarz. There was the Christian Crusade, based in Tulsa, Oklahoma, headed by the Reverend Dr. Billy James Hargis, who roamed the country in a specially converted Greyhound bus bringing to the people the message that communism and treason were everywhere, and collecting their alms for his tax-exempt foundation in the process. Like Welch, who called for getting "the UN out of the U.S. and the U.S. out of the UN," Hargis denounced the United Nations, accused American liberals of being socialists, and charged that the media were doing the Kremlin's work. There was the Reverend Carl McIntire from Collingswood, New Jersey; Phyllis Schlafly from Illinois; Kent Courtney, who ran the Conservative Society of America and in 1961 charged Senator Barry Goldwater with being "tainted by socialism"; and numerous radio evangelists and conspiracy theorists like Clarence Manion. There was the billionaire oilman Harold Lafayette Hunt, and his employee Dan Smoot, who wrote in his 1962 book, *The Invisible Government*, that this sinister conspiracy aimed "to convert America into a socialist state and then make it a unit in a one-world socialist system"; "one world" was almost as serious a term of abuse in the language of the right as "communist" or "socialist."

These were only the apex of a whole structure of crusades, campaigns, radio stations, newsletters, magazines, storefronts, action groups, committees, lecture bureaus, lobbies, and assorted voluntary organizations of every kind devoted to warning the citizens, in a tone of voice that rarely fell below the decibel level of the primal scream, about the dangers of communism, foreign and domestic. The communists, if you believed these editors, broadcasters, lecturers, publicists, preachers, and politicians, were coming by land and by sea. They were poisoning the water supply with fluoride, and the minds of innocent children with propaganda. Their insidious wiles informed the schedules of mainstream broadcasters and the editorials of even Republican newspapers. Proteus-like, according to the admonitory propaganda of the Radical Right, the forces of left-wing evil transformed themselves into as many shapes as the Tempter himself. Like the witches and warlocks who lay in wait for the virtuous in the ages of faith, communists and socialists now disguised themselves as social workers, now as clergy from the more tolerant and affluent denominations, as historians, scientists, social scientists, hygienists, planners, liberals, Democrats, and even — so careful did one have to be — into Republicans! Worst of all, they had infiltrated the United Nations, the National Council of Churches, the Federal Reserve, the State Department, and even the White House.

To some extent, this astonishing outpouring of fearfulness had a rational basis. Stalin had murdered millions, perhaps tens of millions of people, and Roosevelt and his political allies had embraced him as "Uncle Joe." The United States had poured out its idealism, its blood, and treasure to make the world safe for democracy, twice in the lifetime of the mainly middle-aged people who formed the primary audience for the massed bullhorns of the Radical Right. Yet the world seemed more dangerous than ever. The United States, for the first time in well over a century, truly was potentially vulnerable to the attacks of what certainly were ruthless, dissembling, and dangerous foes. You did not have to be a paranoid fanatic to draw that conclusion from what had happened in Eastern Europe, China, Korea, Cuba.

There was, however, a domestic dimension to the excited warnings, the strident denunciations of the Radical Right. It was not just that Welch, Hargis, Schwarz, and their myriad imitators focused, as had the House Un-American Affairs Committee and Senator McCarthy, on communist subversion in the United States, as exerted directly by the minuscule Communist Party or indirectly through the labor unions and the political left. Both communists and socialists had been active in creating the great new industrial unions of the 1930s, and those like Welch who identified with the interests of manufacturers were determined to expose and eradicate their influence.[22] But there was something else. One essential element in the shrill tone of the new Radical Right in the 1950s was the oncoming locomotive, its smoke clearly visible across Middle America by the middle 1950s, of the civil rights revolution.

In 1954, in *Brown* v. *Board of Education of Topeka, Kansas*, the Supreme

Court declared racial segregation unconstitutional, and in the following year reiterated that states must act "with all deliberate speed" to enforce what was now the law. In 1955 blacks in Montgomery, Alabama, boycotted segregated buses. In the ensuing struggle a young, Northern-educated black minister, Dr. Martin Luther King, Jr., emerged as the charismatic leader of what came to be known as the civil rights movement. In December 1956 the Supreme Court gave King and his flock the victory by declaring Alabama's segregated public transit system unconstitutional, and in 1957 Congress passed the first, admittedly modest, modern Civil Rights Act. Soon blacks all across the South were in a ferment of newfound political enthusiasm, newly determined to vindicate their newly declared rights. The first sit-in demonstration, at Greensboro, North Carolina (Robert Welch's native state), in February 1960, handed the energized black masses a new and effective technique and made it plain that the South's social system, with its total social segregation of whites and blacks, was now squarely in the crosshairs. The tide of black protest rose until it peaked in the great March on Washington in August 1963 and found expression in the decisive Civil Rights Act of 1964 and the Voting Rights Act, whose consequences for American politics in general and conservatism in particular were profound.

By the late 1960s a real social revolution had been accomplished in the South. After 1964, the racial battle line moved to the North and West. In over a thousand American communities, blacks rioted, demanding not only legal equality, as in the South, but economic equality as well. At the same time, blacks, many of them impoverished and some disorganized, began to move into what had previously been tight working-class and middle-class city and suburban communities.

In the circumstances, it would have been surprising if both traditional and new right-wing and racist organizations had not attracted new members troubled and angry about the upheaval. It threatened to overturn the traditional American pattern of race relations, which had been based on avowed segregation and white supremacy in the South, and on a less overt but nonetheless rigid code in other sections, especially in the Border States and in areas, such as Southern California, to which substantial numbers of white Southerners had migrated in the 1920s, 1930s, and 1940s. In the Deep South, the Ku Klux Klan had been founded during Reconstruction as a secret society to restore white supremacy. It was reestablished in Atlanta in 1915 and flourished until the mid-1920s as a racist but also anti-Semitic and anti-Catholic organization, as strong in Midwestern states like Indiana and Kansas as in the old Confederacy. Its third coming was as rawly racist working-class gangsterism in the small towns of the Deep South, where Klansmen were responsible for a number of murders and other crimes in the late 1950s and 1960s.

By the 1950s, though, the South was changing rapidly. A new class of corporate executives, college graduates with professional qualifications, often tied to military industries, but also prospering in oil, insurance, health care, and other businesses, had moved out to the beautiful suburbs like those of northwest Atlanta or Birmingham south of the mountain. The crude politics of the courthouse ring and the crude intimidation of nightriding and cross burnings were not for such as these. Indeed, many Southern moderates accepted the inevitability of racial equality and social change. Others, however, were determined to resist federal pressure and preserve the South's traditional way of life. Some of them hastened to join more genteel racist organizations, like the White Citizens Councils, one of whose leaders, John Sattertfield, Jr., of Mississippi, was president of the American Bar Association, no less, in 1961–62.

Those who resented and resisted the coming of racial equality were certainly disproportionately available to hear the message of the Radical Right. In fact, while most of the new right-wing organizations maintained publicly that they were nonracist, the John Birch Society was by no means alone in arguing that, as the title of a pamphlet published by the Liberty Lobby put it in 1965, *Black Revolution Is Red Revolution.*

It is not too much to say that the John Birch Society seized on the civil rights upheaval of the middle 1960s as an opportunity to achieve the mass influence that had eluded it since Robert Welch's bizarre charges against President Eisenhower made it a laughingstock. In 1965 Welch distributed to the Birch Society chapters no fewer than 500,000 copies of a pamphlet called *Two Revolutions at Once,* which identified the civil rights movement as part of a worldwide communist revolution. Another Birch Society pamphlet, *It's Very Simple,* by Alan Stang, asserted that Martin Luther King, Jr., was "one of the country's most influential workers for Communism"; there is and never has been any evidence that King was a communist, though two of his friends and advisers, Stanley Levison and Jack O'Dell, were often said to have been close to the party.

When racial violence broke out in Watts, in south-central Los Angeles, in the summer of 1965, local Birch chapters quickly mobilized to exploit the situation for recruitment and other purposes. Within days, Dr. Fred Schwarz had mailed out a "Dear Friends" letter, bizarrely comparing the Watts violence, in which more than thirty people, almost all blacks, were killed, to the fashion for "panty raids" on college campuses and concluding, with comic portentousness, that "behind the mob there lurks the disciplined organization of the Communist Party ready to seize power once the destructive task is complete." Other right-wing propagandists poured out literature attributing the civil rights movement to a communist conspiracy and predicting disaster if civil rights legislation was passed and enforced. The Patrick Henry Press, in Richmond, Virginia, for example, mailed out half a million copies of *How Classroom Desegregation Will Work*, by one Dr. Henry E. Gannett. He did not think it would work well, to judge from another pamphlet from his pen, *Breeding Down*, which asserted that "the Negro race is less advanced in an evolutionary sense than is the white race, by perhaps 200,000 years."

There was a bewildering cross-membership between the general institutions of the Radical Right and those explicitly devoted to white resistance. In April 1965, for example, Kent Courtney of the Conservative Society of America, a Birch Society member, summoned a Congress of Conservatives in Chicago, where speakers included Robert Welch; William Douglass of Let Freedom Ring, Inc., an organization that referred to President Lyndon B. Johnson as "Mr Surrender"; Lester Maddox, the restaurateur from Atlanta, Georgia, who supplied his customers with ax handles to beat up black customers and became lieutenant governor of the state as a result; and Dr. Medford Evans, a conservative whose name was to be found on the letterhead both of the White Citizens Council and of Robert Welch's magazine, *American Opinion*.

In the John Birch Society's *Bulletin*, circulated to all members, Robert Welch wrote that "our task must be simply to make clear that the movement known as 'civil rights' is Communist-plotted, Communist-controlled and in fact . . . serves only Communist purposes." One interesting tactic the Birchers used was to circulate a reissue of a 1928 Communist Party pamphlet, *American Negro Problems*. The Birchers said it was written by a Hungarian Communist, a man of many aliases, but whose pen-and-ink portrait, circulated to the membership, looked like a Nazi anti-Semitic caricature.

The Radical Right in general and the John Birch Society in particular generally tried to distance themselves from the anti-Semitism of earlier right-wing followings, such as those of Father Coughlin, the Detroit "radio priest," and of Gerald L. K. Smith.[23] However, a number of veteran anti-Semites did attach themselves to the John Birch Society, among them James Oviatt, Merwin Hunt, Nesta Webster, and the Australian Eric Butler. Far more damaging, from Welch's point of view, was the career of the University of Illinois classics teacher, the palindromic Revilo P. Oliver, who was one of the original eleven disciples from Indianapolis in 1958, a member of the society's council and on the staff of *American Opinion*. In early 1966 the Anti-Defamation League of B'nai B'rith published a report, researched and written with the league's usual scrupulous care, charging the John Birch Society with contributing to anti-Semitism. One of the society's Eastern regional officers, Thomas J. Davis, then went on a tour from New York to San Antonio attacking the league, with Welch's explicit support in the *Bulletin*. Oliver, who had earlier addressed the White Citizens Councils' 1966 convention at Chattanooga, and had delivered himself of the opinion that it was a "lie" that people of different races were equal, chose to tell an audience of two thousand at an Independence Day rally in Boston that there was a "conspiracy of the Jews" dating back to the fifth century, of which the eighteenth-century society the Illuminati,[24] the French Revolution, and the communist movement were all consequences. He added his personal opinion that it would be a "beatific vision" if all Jews were "vaporized tomorrow."

Revilo P. Oliver was prevailed on to resign from the John Birch Society and his various offices within it, and Welch did his best to repair the damage Oliver had done. It is hard to escape the conclusion, however, that to some extent Oliver had let the cat out of the bag, in that anti-Semitism, once a widely avowed sentiment in the Know-Nothing, "Americanist" purlieus of politics, was alive and well in many of the covens of the Radical Right. It may well have been part of the motivation that attracted some members to the right's multiplying institutions.

In the climate of the 1960s, however, overt anti-Semitism was no longer respectable outside the remoter, more unreconstructed provincial crannies. Fear and suspicion of desegregation and black integration were something else. The business class's inveterate resentment of unions, taxation, regulation, and the power of government generally was one effective recruiting sergeant for conservative organizations. The fear of communism, foreign and domestic, aroused by events between 1945 and 1963 contributed a new and potent source of converts. But the evidence strongly suggests that racial prejudice and resentment against the civil rights revolution also powerfully reinforced the conservative ranks.

That is not, of course, to say that the new conservatism was in itself racist: some of its leaders condoned racism, others did not. But one essential element of the new political environment that led to the capture of the Republican nomination by Barry Goldwater in 1964 was conservative revulsion at the policies, aimed at securing at least minimal legal equality for minorities, carried out by the Supreme Court under Chief Justice Earl Warren, by the Democrat-controlled Congress, and by the Kennedy and Johnson administrations.

Before we look at the Goldwater campaign, however, we must understand the crucial developments that had taken place in the world of ideas in the late 1950s and early 1960s. For in order for conservatives to make headway in national politics, they had to answer two great questions. In the domain of ideas, they had to resolve the apparently sharp contradiction between an older, authoritarian conservative tradition and the new, libertarian interpretation of conservatism. And in the domain of political action they had to find ways of accommodating the differences between orthodox conservatism and the wilder energies of the rising Radical Right.

Watersmeet

> ... that these two streams of thought, although they are sometimes presented as mutually incompatible, can in reality be united in a single broad conservative political theory, since they have their roots in a common tradition and are arrayed against a common enemy.
> — *Frank S. Meyer*

THERE IS A POINT in the course of the Amazon where the white sand waters of the Rio Branco and the black earth waters of the Rio Negro run alongside each another for many miles before they eventually merge into the uniform soupy flood of the great river. Two streams of conservative thought had descended from American (and European) history to contribute their very different waters to the swelling flood of the new conservatism. There was the libertarian tributary, and there was the stream of religious and authoritarian tradition. Before conservatism could run down to the sea like a mighty river, those two streams would have to merge or be reconciled in one way or another. The story of how their merger, or fusion, was effected is a curious illustration of the fact (unwelcome to many impatient and practical men of affairs) that what happens in the world of ideas, in the conversation of intellectuals, and even in the columns of little magazines can powerfully influence the course of political history.

In the middle 1950s *Time* magazine, founded by Henry Luce and Briton Hadden in 1923, was certainly no little magazine.[1] With a circulation of 1.664 million in 1952,[2] it was at the height of its influence. In the internecine wars of the American right, *Time* and Henry Luce occupied a somewhat ambiguous position. *Time* was firmly committed to internationalism and had deeply angered conservatives by its support for Eisenhower in 1952. Several key members of the Eisenhower administration were Time Inc. graduates. They included C. D. Jackson, a senior White House aide, and the president's favorite speechwriter, Emmett John Hughes.[3] At the same time, Henry Luce was one of the leaders of the China Lobby and as such tolerant of at least the less rococo manifestations of McCarthyism. Above all, Henry Luce was staunchly anticommunist. Also, unlike many publishers, he appreciated the journalistic value that could be added to a publication by provocative intellectuals among its writers and editors.

So Time Inc., which owned *Life* and *Fortune* magazines as well as *Time*, became a haven for anticommunists and in particular for converts from the left, of both the American and the European varieties. Alger Hiss's denouncer, Whittaker Chambers, worked his way up from third-string drama critic to become one of the seven senior editors at *Time*. James Burnham, Trotskyist turned Jeremiah of the Cold War, thundered his prophecies in *Fortune*, as did Daniel Bell, anticommunist socialist-liberal, and that nemesis of corporate complacency, John Kenneth Galbraith. Willmoore Kendall and John Chamberlain, both former leftists who had moved to the right, worked for Henry Luce. A key position, as Luce's own editorial assistant, was held by one of Chamberlain's friends, a Jewish refugee, born in Austrian Poland in 1904, Willi Schlamm.

A small dark man who wore his hair brushed straight back, Schlamm was almost the last man you would expect to play a decisive part in the resurgence of conservatism as a potent intellectual force.[4] Once described, accurately, as the "incarnation of the Viennese coffeehouse literati," Schlamm joined the Austrian Communist Party at the age of sixteen. His disillusionment with communism is said to have begun when a party member in Moscow procured a prostitute for him. That didn't stop his becoming the editor of a communist newspaper, but he quit the Communist Party in 1929 and became the editor of a left-wing paper opposed to both fascism and communism, *Die Weltbühne*, which moved to Prague. In 1937 he published *Diktatur der Lüge* (*Dictatorship of the Lie*), but in 1938, when Hitler threatened Czechoslovakia, Schlamm fled to the United States. After working for the (left-wing but anticommunist) *New Leader*, he landed his job at *Time*. But nothing would do but he must start a magazine to carry on the fight against Stalinism. At first he hoped Henry Luce would make him the editor of a periodical called *Measure*, but Luce sold the title to the University of Chicago, which sold it to the conservative Chicago publisher Henry Regnery, and he wanted nothing to do with Schlamm's idea for a magazine.

At the time, *The Freeman*, once Albert Jay Nock's warhorse, was going through one of its recurrent crises. In Nock's day, in the 1920s, it had been a freethinking libertarian magazine. It revived again in the 1930s with the isolationist, pacifist libertarian Frank Chodorov as editor, and again collapsed. After World War II it was revived by a group of more orthodox conservatives, including Henry Hazlitt and Schlamm's friend and patron, John Chamberlain. The editors fell out with one another and with Forrest Davis, a former aide to Senator Taft, over the proper line to take on McCarthyism, and Hazlitt, Chamberlain, Suzanne La Follette, and Schlamm all resigned. *The Freeman* was bought by Leonard Read and the Foundation for Economic Education, who converted it into a monthly and made Frank Chodorov editor once again. The historian of the conservative intellectuals has written, however, that "it is difficult to convey a sense of the crucial role of *The Freeman*" between 1950 and 1954. At a time when journals of the left were numerous and well funded, it fell to *The Freeman* alone "to focus dissent, to marshal its forces, to articulate practical alternatives to the chimeras and schemes of its foes."

Still, with *The Freeman* now reduced to a monthly, it was time for the conservative banner to be picked up by a younger champion, and a younger champion was on hand. It was Willi Schlamm who made the connection. He was now on the beach, but still utterly determined to create a new magazine to represent what he called "the outs," by which he meant something very similar to what Albert Jay Nock had meant by "the Remnant." He approached a new potential backer, a young man who had just appeared on the New York conservative scene, William Frank Buckley, Jr.

Bill Buckley is probably the most important single figure in the whole history of the revival of conservatism in late twentieth-century America. John Chamberlain was to say of him that "he, more than any single figure, made conservatism a respectable force in American life." No less a luminary than Ronald Reagan called him "perhaps the most influential journalist and intellectual in our era," and added that "he changed our country, indeed our century." No one has done more to elaborate the conservative doctrine that made political victories possible; no one has done more to take the conservative intellectuals out of their Remnant ghetto and show them the possibility of moving from the contemplative to the strenuous life. He is not a politician; yet no one has done more to make it possible for conservatives to build political structures. Fanatical and easygoing, equipped with a sharp wit and a sense of humor that sometimes allowed self-deprecation, he has never seriously, in Oliver Cromwell's phrase, bethought himself in the bowels of Christ that he might be mistaken, at least on the principal lines of his religious and political faith. Yet his absolute certainty about what he considers nonnegotiable principle nevertheless permits him flexibility, even tolerance, on matters not considered essential for conservative salvation. Perhaps his greatest gift, after his absolute self-certainty, is his uncanny sense of what is essential and what is not, what tactically permissible, and what strategically fatal.

Buckley has come to occupy such an almost mythical position in the history of American conservatism that it is exceptionally important to avoid anachronism, and not to write back into the youthful entrepreneur of the 1950s the several Buckleys who appeared in subsequent decades: Buckley, for example, the politician, Buckley the Manhattan café society celeb, Buckley the talk-show gadfly, the novelist, harpsichordist, yachtsman, businessman, and philosopher.[5] In 1954 Bill Buckley was a very rich young man, or at least the son of a very rich father, newly married, who, after a career of great prominence and achievement at Yale University, had profoundly angered and scandalized Yale and its large following in the American upper class, "power elite," or Establishment, call it what you will, by publishing *God and Man at Yale*,[6] It was an arrogant and intemperate but an awkwardly persuasive book which taxed Yale with having abandoned Christianity in its public philosophy and adopted a soft kind of liberalism as its prevailing ethos. After its publication he had disappeared to work for none other than the future Watergate bugger-in-chief and author of penny dreadfuls, E. Howard Hunt, as a CIA agent in Mexico. He returned to teach an elementary course in Spanish at, of all places, godless Yale.

With boyish charm, unruly hair, and a most attractive combination of social good humor and intellectual fanaticism, like a preppy Inquisitor, Buckley was, far more than most people found it easy to credit, in deadly earnest. "I have God and my father," Buckley once told a Yale teacher; "that's all I need." To an extent that has often been concealed by his worldliness and his wit, at once sardonic and aggressive, the core of Buckley's political philosophy is his militant Roman Catholic faith. He is essentially not a conservative, but a counterrevolutionary,[7] and he acquired his counterrevolutionary commitment from his father. William Frank Buckley, Sr., known as Will Buckley, was of (originally Protestant) Irish descent. His family had converted to Catholicism. He was raised in Texas, trained as a lawyer, and won and then lost a fortune in Mexican oil during the Mexican Revolution of 1911–1921. He later made a second fortune, from oil investments first in Venezuela, later in Canada and elsewhere. But his experience of revolutionary Mexico convinced the elder Buckley that godless Marxist revolution literally threatened religion, private property, and the freedom and well-being of the United States. It was, Bill Buckley himself has suggested, because his father was an outsider and a rebel that his children did not rebel against him as the children of so many rich fathers have done. The Kennedys were superficially a similar clan. They were raised by an Irish Catholic father in a world of rich Protestants, and in a generation when the American upper class had by no means abjured anti-Irish and anti-Catholic prejudices. They displayed the same truculent solidarity toward a world that was perhaps more willing to open up to them than they were prepared to acknowledge.[8]

Like Joseph P. Kennedy, Will Buckley encouraged and challenged his children, writing them long, perceptive letters when he was away in South America or elsewhere and stimulating sharply competitive debates over the family dinner table. The family grew up on two estates, Great Elm, near Sharon, in the idyllic countryside of western Connecticut, a colonial mansion in forty-seven acres to which the Buckleys had added the exotic adornment of a Mexican patio; and Kamchatka, near Camden, in the South Carolina Piedmont.[9] In both places, the Buckleys were conscious of being outsiders: as wealthy, Catholic newcomers among the swamp Yankees of rustic Connecticut and as Yankees in South Carolina, though Bill Buckley's parents were both Southern born and bred. (His father had grown up in central Texas, and his mother came from New Orleans.) Although Will Buckley's father emigrated from Ireland by way of Canada, the Buckleys did not think of themselves as Irish Americans, but as American Catholics. Will Buckley's ten children did not take the hostility of their Connecticut neighbors lying down. On one occasion, Bill's older brothers and sisters burned a cross — symbol of the Ku Klux Klan — on the lawn of a Jewish resort.[10] They got into even more serious trouble when they sneaked into an Episcopal church, smeared the clergyman's chair, and stuck rude cartoons into his Bible.[11]

Will Buckley arrived in Tampico, then at the height of a great oil boom, in 1908, to practice law. The Mexican president, Porfirio Díaz, was pushing the country's development with the help of his friends, known as the *científicos*, and of foreign oilmen like Edward L. Doheny of Pan American, later implicated in the Teapot Dome scandal, and the Englishman Wheetman Pearson, later Lord Cowdray, of Mexican Eagle. By 1921, Mexico had become the second biggest oil producer in the world, but it had also been thrown into turmoil, and Will Buckley, having observed revolutionary violence at close quarters, committed himself irrevocably to the struggle against revolution wherever and in whatever form it might raise its head, a touchstone that was to magnetize his son for life. After the Díaz regime was overthrown, Buckley took the side of Díaz's successor, General Victoriano Huerta, against both the liberal generals Venustiano Carranza and Álvaro Obregón, and the peasant armies of Pancho Villa and Emiliano Zapata. Buckley began by organizing an underground to save priests and religious objects, then went on to organize two abortive military coups. In 1921 he was expelled from Mexico, and his oil and real estate properties there were confiscated. He transmitted to his son not just a hatred of revolution, but a deeply pessimistic sense that revolution was a real and present threat to everything a good Catholic and a good American should hold dear.[12]

Will Buckley's politics were those of the conservative Southern Democrats of his youth and the conservative Republicans among his business colleagues, sharpened by the detestation of communism he brought with him from Mexico. His son's conservatism inherited the feeling that the hour was late and the time short to fight the coming revolution. Grafted on to it, however, was a real radicalism born of his contempt for what he saw as the reckless and cowardly refusal of upper-class America to face the realities of the threat. Bill Buckley received an excellent education, including a competent grounding in the piano, more than a smattering of Latin and Greek, and fluent Spanish. At the age of thirteen he was packed off to England, and came back with an English accent, traces of which still linger incongruously more than half a century later; his sisters called him "the young Mahster." He was sent to Millbrook, a nearby prep school; while there, he read, and later met, his father's friend Albert Jay Nock, and came under the spell of his seductive theory of the beleaguered Remnant of the just.[13] Buckley never succumbed to the anti-Semitism his father expressed in private and Nock, toward the end of his life, gave vent to with embarrassing crudity in increasingly marginal journals.[14]

After Millbrook, he was drafted into the army, which he hated and which didn't like him much either. As a young man, he was regarded as almost unbearably arrogant, but his obnoxiousness was leavened by enough charm and kindness so that by the time he got to Yale he was accepted as a leader even by many of the ambitious and talented young men on campus who were his rivals. At Yale he really came into his own, making the debating team and becoming chairman of the *Yale Daily News;* it is said that he was the first choice for Skull and Bones, the prestigious (and overwhelmingly Protestant) secret senior society. If Yale, by and large, took to Buckley, Buckley, for his part, took an intense dislike to Yale.

The university administration was even sufficiently impressed by this talented and confident undergraduate that he was invited to give the student speech at the Alumni Day ceremonies. Normally this was a bland occasion, dedicated to persuading former students to unbutton their checkbooks and give generously to the dear old alma mater. The student selected for the honor of making the speech was supposed to contribute his share to the outpouring of self-congratulation. Buckley did nothing of the kind. He composed a fiery denunciation of Yale's *laissez-faire* view of education, which acted on the assumption that ideas should compete in the academic marketplace. Instead, Buckley called on Yale to declare "active Christianity the first basis of enlightened thought and action" and to proclaim "communism, socialism, collectivism, government paternalism inimical to the dignity of the individual." And he summoned the university to dismiss named faculty members if they did not adhere to these principles. The university tried to cajole him into toning down this diatribe. Its president, Charles Seymour, succeeded in maneuvering the young orator into withdrawing. Buckley never forgave Yale, and he determined to put his denunciation into hard covers. In 1951 *God and Man at Yale* became both an instant scandal and an instant success.[15]

Buckley began by raising the embarrassing question of "whether Yale fortifies or shatters the average student's faith in Christianity." And he proceeded to award grades, few of them passing grades, to a number of Yale professors in the robustest manner. Of Professor Schroeder, for example, the chairman of the religion department and an ordained minister, Buckley wrote, "Mr. Schroeder does not seek to persuade his students to believe in Christ because he has not, as I understand it, been completely able to persuade himself."[16] And so on. For Professor Ralph Linton, for example, Buckley wrote that "religion is, at best, a useful superstition";[17] and of Professor Raymond Kennedy, known as Jungle Jim, Buckley wrote that he "never left room for doubt as to the contempt in which he held religion."[18]

Irreligion was not the only charge he brought against his alma mater. The Yale economics department was greatly admired at the time, but not by the former chairman of the *Yale Daily News.* "I believe," he

announced, "the net influence of Yale economics to be thoroughly collectivist."[19] In politics, too, he said that "individualism is dying at Yale,
and without a fight."[20] But what rankled most deeply, and drew down on
the young author the heaviest guns the university could hire in its defense, was what Buckley had to say about academic freedom. That was
then an intensely sensitive subject, as great universities like Yale and
Harvard writhed under the whips of McCarthyite investigations of radical faculty members.[21] In a chapter devoted to "the superstitions of
academic freedom," Buckley concluded:

> One thing is clear: it is time that honest and discerning scholars
> cease to manipulate the term academic freedom for their own ends
> . . . For in the last analysis academic freedom must mean the freedom
> of men and women to supervise the educational activities and aims of
> the schools they oversee and support.[22]

Nor did he leave it at that. Buckley attacked what, for liberal-minded
academics and college administrators, was the most vulnerable quarter
of all: the conservative instincts of the wealthy trustees and fund raisers
and of the predominantly conservative alumni on whom Yale depended
for financial support. He reminded the university authorities that the
people on whom they depended for money were far more conservative
than they were themselves, and he raised the question of how much
influence conservative alumni ought to have over liberal educators. He
went so far as to quote the "stern warning" given at the very Alumni Day
at which he had not been allowed to make his own speech by no less a
person than George Herbert Walker, the grandfather and eponym of
President Bush, who spoke of the need for "a constant reaffirmation
of fundamental and eternal values." And he ended with two silky but
shrewdly chosen threats. They were fairly breathtaking in their audac-
ity, coming, as they did, from a young man of twenty-four with no
credentials but his own brains and self-confidence.

> I shall not say, then, what specific professors should be discharged,
> but I will say some ought to be discharged. I will not say in what
> manner the alumni ought to be consulted and polled on this issue,
> but I will say that they ought to be, and soon.[23]

With his father's help, and some of his own and his father's money,
Buckley had arranged publication, not by one of the well-known New
York publishers, but by Regnery, the small, ideologically motivated con-
servative publisher in Chicago whom Willi Schlamm had been trying to

talk into starting an anticommunist magazine. The result was startling. Publication date was in late October. By Christmas, Regnery had sold twelve thousand copies, and by the spring, thirty-five thousand. This slim book, on a recondite subject, published by an obscure press and written by an unknown, reached the *New York Times* best-seller list. The Yale Establishment did not take this assault, from one of its own who could not be dismissed as an envious outsider, lying down. A champion was armed and sent into the lists. McGeorge Bundy, himself a Skull and Bones man, then a registered Republican and as big a man on campus in his day as Buckley ever was in 1950,[24] was commissioned by the *The Atlantic Monthly* to review *God and Man*, and was primed by no less a researcher than A. Whitney Griswold, the new president of Yale. He took, he told Griswold, a "kind of savage pleasure in the composition" of his review, in which he called Buckley an "ignorant and twisted young man."[25] Other reviews were equally fierce, and even Henry Luce called *God and Man* a "brilliant but not quite honest polemic"[26] and labeled Buckley a "brat." Buckley was hurt, and even threatened libel actions against some of his critics. But none of them did him a pennyworth of harm.

It may seem lacking in proportion to elaborate at such length the argument of Bill Buckley's first youthful book. I have done so because in it all the main themes that were to animate his work as a writer and publicist for forty years were already unmistakable. His work, in turn, foreshadowed most of the main traveled roads of American conservatism for the next thirty years. There is the aggressive contempt for communism, for collectivism, and especially for liberalism. There is the indignant insistence that religious truth should not be discussed, but proclaimed, and the impatience with those who offered, in the name of academic freedom, moral relativism. There is the faith in the morality of individualism and of the free enterprise system. The content of Buckley's conservatism was all there in the egg of his first book. But so too was the style: the brash willingness to shock; the absolute seriousness concealed by a manner so outrageous that opponents were not sure how seriously to take him; and the deadly instinct for the polemical and political jugular.

It was not long before he did it again. For a while Buckley tried to settle down to working under the Alabama novelist William Bradford Huie,[27] who was taking H. L. Mencken's old magazine, the *American Mercury*, to the right. He found the job disappointing, and he rejected an offer to go to work for *The Freeman*. But with a Yale friend, L. Brent

Bozell, who had married his sister Patricia, Buckley did compose a long article on McCarthy for *The Freeman*, and Regnery offered to publish it as a short book. Instead, the two authors produced an enormous manuscript.[28] Willi Schlamm was the professional called in to cut seventy-five thousand words from it and write an introduction.[29] The book, published as *McCarthy and His Enemies*,[30] was even more provocative than *God and Man*. Instead of attacking the liberals, it tweaked their tenderest emotions by vindicating their most hated enemy. Buckley and Bozell defined McCarthyism as "a steady flow of criticism" to make the administration "get on with the elimination of security risks in government,"[31] and they did not hesitate to call for the firing not only of communists, but of officials whose advice tended to help communism. Nor did they hesitate to make themselves the arbiters of who should go and who should be allowed to stay. "We are talking not about 'who is loyal,' but about who favors those policies that are not in the national interest as we see it."[32] And they added that "the merely incompetent must go out along with the traitors."[33]

McCarthy and His Enemies came out in the spring of 1954, and in the early summer Bill Buckley and his wife, Pat, visited Willi Schlamm at his home in Vermont. About a year and a half later, on Friday, November 18, 1955, to be exact, two wooden crates, delivered to 112 East Thirty-seventh Street in New York City, were carried to a large room surrounded by cubicles.[34] The larger of the two boxes contained twelve bottles of champagne; the smaller, dispatched from the Wilson H. Lee Company of Orange, Connecticut, was eagerly prised open. For the first time the editorial staff saw the blue-and-white cover of the latest, indeed at the time virtually the *only*, conservative journal of opinion in the United States: *National Review*.

That first issue contained articles by John Chamberlain, James Burnham, Russell Kirk, Frank S. Meyer, and Willmoore Kendall. It also contained an article by the publisher, signed by William F. Buckley, Jr. *National Review*, he said, stood "athwart history, yelling 'Stop,' at a time when no one is inclined to do so." Liberal ideologues, he went on, and energetic social innovators had "simply walked in and started to run things." Conservatives, therefore, "at least those who have not made their peace with the New Deal, and there is serious question whether there are others," were "non-licensed non-conformists; and this is a dangerous business," for when they were not being suppressed or mutilated by the liberals, they were ignored or humiliated by the "well-fed Right." The new magazine added a list of what it called — a very Buckley word — *credenda*, that is, "things meet to be believed."[35]

The growth of government must be fought. The profound crisis of the day was the conflict between the Social Engineers, in capital letters, and the disciples of Truth. The most blatant force of satanic utopianism was communism, and "we find ourselves irrevocably at war with communism and shall oppose any substitute for war." But the largest cultural menace was the conformity of the intellectual cliques in education and the arts, and the most alarming danger lay in the fact that "Fabian" operators were bent on controlling both major parties "under the sanction of such fatuous . . . slogans as . . . 'middle of the road,' 'progressivism,' and 'bipartisanship.'" Finally, *National Review* promised to "tell the violated businessman's side of the story" and to expose such "superstitions" as "fashionable concepts of world government" and the United Nations. No one called this statement of principles equivocal or mealy-mouthed, though it did sound remarkably negative. No alternative vision of the good life was proposed; perhaps, as the British Conservative leader Harold Macmillan said at much the same time, if the people wanted moral leadership, they should go to their archbishops.

The magazine's finances were boosted by some rather crude ads. One, for example, from the Gray Manufacturing Company of Hartford, Connecticut, depicted a foreign-looking man, with pamphlets in his pockets labeled Lenin, Stalin, and Marx, in the act of hurling a large bomb called HATE at Mount Rushmore. To obviate all misunderstanding, a caption explained that "peaceful coexistence is bunk."[36] There was a long article by Senator William F. Knowland, attacking disarmament, and — to inaugurate a long-term tradition of family participation — an article by one of the Buckley sisters, Aloise Heath, describing how when she raised the "documented Communist-front affiliation" of the faculty at Smith College, the school was conveniently inundated with money from conservative alumni.

Willi Schlamm, mindful of the infighting at *The Freeman*, convinced Bill Buckley that he must be not only editor but also the only stockholder. Fund raising was a problem. Buckley found it hard to raise money from the rich Texans who usually supported right-wing causes, though he did get some money from Los Angeles and some from wealthy and conservative Yale alumni who had been impressed with his guts in pitching into President Seymour. But the bulk of the funding came from Will Buckley, and the magazine would have been launched even sooner if the editor's father had not suffered a stroke, from which he only partially recovered, in April 1955.[37]

From childhood, the Buckley brothers and sisters had run a family

newspaper, called, after their two homes, the *Grelmchatka*, and especially at the start there was a dash of family fun in the cocktail of *National
Review*. Besides Bill, his sisters Priscilla, who had worked for the UPI
wire service as well as for the CIA, and Maureen were hired as staff
writers. Aloise also wrote for the magazine, and Patricia and her husband, Brent Bozell, who had been working for Joe McCarthy, were also
part of the team. So large a representation of the editor's family might
have seemed elitist, even nepotistical; little Bill Buckley cared about
that. But the family did give *National Review* its peculiar tone, sarcas-
tic and sardonic, as if puncturing the pretensions of liberal intellectuals
and Eisenhower Republicans was just an extension of the family's inso-
lent yet curiously good-tempered attitude to lesser breeds outside the
charmed world of Buckleys. The other editors and contributors were
drawn from a variety of backgrounds: old hands from *The Freeman* like
John Chamberlain and the feminist Suzanne La Follette; the libertarian Frank Chodorov, who had founded first a tiny circulation magazine,
analysis, and then the right-wing student organization, the Intercollegiate Society of Individualists.[38] But most of the editors and writers
were drawn from the ranks of left-wing intellectuals who had moved to
the right: the former Communists Frank S. Meyer, Freda Utley, and
Schlamm; the former Trotskyite turned CIA official James Burnham;
the Yale philosopher Willmoore Kendall, who had been so shocked by
what he saw when working for the Republic in the Spanish Civil War
that he moved to a conservative Catholic position; and, after some difficulty caused by his suspicion that Buckley was not sufficiently admiring
of Richard M. Nixon, of the arch-convert from communism to anticommunism, Whittaker Chambers himself.

As we shall see, this stable of passionate controversialists was to
divide bitterly on a number of issues, mirroring the perplexity of conservative intellectuals generally in the Eisenhower years. From the start,
however, one or two attitudes (rather than fully developed ideological
lines) united the Babel on East Thirty-seventh Street. These, for a start,
were no isolationists: the editors of *National Review*, both those who had
worked for the CIA, like Buckley, Burnham, and Kendall, and those who
had not, were utterly committed to the need for America to take the lead
in the battle, the Last Battle, against godless communism. They were,
moreover, in the literal as well as the political sense, internationalists:
cosmopolitans, several of them Jews (Schlamm, Meyer, Frank Chodorov, Morrie Ryskind, and Ralph de Toledano, among others), several
Anglophiles (Meyer, Burnham, Kendall had all been educated partly at

Oxford, and Buckley combined generalized Anglophilia with occasional outbreaks of limey-bashing). Second, on the most burning of the domestic issues that divided American conservatives in the middle 1950s, McCarthyism, *National Review* was equally emphatic where it stood: founded less than two years after the Army-McCarthy hearings, and by an editor who had written an outspoken defense of the senator, it was an unashamedly McCarthyite journal. Indeed, on December 28, 1955, Buckley invited Joe McCarthy to review Dean Acheson's book, *A Democrat Looks at His Party.* It might have been an inspired choice by a young editor. As it turned out, the senator wrote a snide and undistinguished notice,[39] referring to the former secretary of state as "Brains" throughout, and ending, "Many people will think this book is outrageous, but I think its foolishness saves it from being that. A pathetic gesture by a discredited statesman." The same might have been said of McCarthy and his article. He who strikes at a king, they say, must strike to kill; and McCarthy had already lost the killer touch.

Finally, though on the whole it steered clear of the anti-Semitism that had been all too common on the American right,[40] *National Review* took an only very slightly reconstructed Southern position on race. In 1957, for example, Buckley, who had after all been brought up by Southern parents and in part in South Carolina, asked whether Southern whites would be justified in "taking such measures as are necessary to prevail, politically and culturally," where they did not predominate numerically. "The sober answer," he concluded, "is *Yes* — the white community is so entitled because, for the time being, it is the advanced race." It is true that, under pressure from his brother-in-law Brent Bozell, Buckley subsequently published a "clarification," in which he accepted that white Southerners ought to disenfranchise not only uneducated blacks but also uneducated whites. Yet the thrust of his earlier position was to justify denying the vote to blacks. It also defended policies aimed at preventing blacks in black majority areas in South Carolina from predominating "culturally" by means of segregation in education and public facilities. *National Review* kept its distance from crude racism, and tried to cast its conservative position in the togaed constitutionalism of a Calhoun or a Richard Brevard Russell. But it was unmistakably opposed to the civil rights revolution. Over the years it was to do its bit to make skepticism about black claims for equality seem respectable.

In an atmosphere of such intellectual fervor, given the editors' belief in the gravity and the immediacy of the communist threat, it is hardly surprising that there were divisions, feuds, ideological splits like those of the left-wing *groupuscules* from which so many of the *National Review* crowd had emerged. After repeated tantrums, threats of resignation, and strained attempts at reconciliation, all intensely painful for Buckley, his mentor Willi Schlamm finally departed.[41] The issue was his violent disagreement with James Burnham over the implications of the Soviet invasion of Hungary in 1956. *National Review*, as might have been expected, reacted with rage and anguish at Soviet repression of the uprising. The magazine invited its readers to make "the Hungary pledge," a total (though as it turned out unrealistic and ineffectual) "cultural boycott" of the Soviet Union. And it published powerful statements by Professor William Williamsen of Santa Clara College ("the Cross reels today in Hungary, but reeling stands") and by the Reverend Stanley Parry, a Notre Dame professor, who prayed that the Hungarian crisis would "stimulate us to a manliness we have of late forgotten."

James Burnham, however, drew a conclusion that shocked many of his colleagues and many of the readers as well. In *Liberation or Containment*, Burnham had argued that if the peoples of Eastern Europe were to revolt, the United States could not refuse to go to their aid. But now, faced with the reality of the revolt in Hungary, which was being put down with the utmost ruthlessness by Soviet troops in circumstances where the United States could not effectively intervene without risking a nuclear war, Burnham drew back. The "next great steps," he wrote — anticipating what was to happen in very different circumstances more than thirty years later — must be the reunification of Germany, the renegotiation of Germany's eastern border, and the withdrawal of Soviet troops from Eastern Europe. How was this to be achieved? "By neutralization." That was too much for Burnham's fellow Cold Warriors. Schlamm and Frank S. Meyer trained their heaviest ideological artillery on Burnham in the magazine, and at meetings openly impugned his loyalty to its fundamental ideals.[42] Buckley, perhaps surprisingly, defended Burnham, and Schlamm, after scenes of almost unbearable tension, left for Europe, for *American Opinion*, the organ of the John Birch Society, and for oblivion.[43]

Buckley had been immensely impressed by Whittaker Chambers's memoir, *Witness*, one of the touchstone books of the right in the 1950s.[44] To his disappointment, Chambers at first refused to join, then joined, and then resigned in 1959 in protest against the magazine's hysterical opposition to the Khrushchev visit to the United States. (Buckley threatened to dye the East River red so that Khrushchev would arrive in a river of blood!) Chambers pointed out that "Khrushchev is no monster in the sense that Stalin *was* a monster, and it does much disservice to say so."

The departure of Schlamm and Chambers was personally painful for Buckley, but it was partly compensated by two new arrivals. One was the twenty-three-year-old Jesuit seminarist at Xavier University in Ohio, Garry Wills, who replaced Schlamm as drama critic. (He caused a major upset when he came out against the Vietnam War and went on to write brilliant biographies of Richard Nixon and Ronald Reagan from a liberal point of view.)[45] Even more important for the future of the magazine, and indeed of conservatism, was Buckley's decision to hire as publisher a Princeton graduate who had flirted with Republican politics, William Rusher, to cope with the magazine's financial problems. Rusher was to play an important part in persuading Buckley and *National Review* to emerge from an elitist, purely intellectual role and play an active part in advancing the cause of conservatism in the field of practical politics and in particular in the Republican Party.

That was in the future, however, in the late 1950s, when *National Review* performed perhaps the most important of all its services to conservatism, in what Goethe called the gray realm of theory.[46] American conservative intellectuals in the 1950s were deeply divided. There were at least three main schools of thought, each subdivided into factions, and they were in danger of turning into warring tribes.

There were, first of all, the "traditionalists," sometimes known (confusingly) as the New Conservatives; men like Peter Viereck and Russell Kirk, who were shocked by what they saw as a rootless mass society around them. Kirk stated baldly that "true conservatism . . . rises at the antipodes from individualism. Individualism is social atomism; conservatism is community of spirit." The political consequence of individualism, he said, would be anarchy. Many followed Kirk in all but deifying Edmund Burke. They played down his liberal, Whig, free-trade beliefs and emphasized the side of Burke's subtle, evolving, and complex philosophy that stressed the organic character of society and the partnership between the dead, the living, and the unborn.

Other traditionalists were disciples of the great scholar Leo Strauss and the historian Eric Vögelin, both refugees from Germany. Strauss argued in his best-known book, *Natural Right and History*, that Burke was right to prefer the "authors of sound antiquity" to the "Parisian philosophers" who had perverted the ancient idea of natural right, recognized by all, into hedonism and relativism.

Richard M. Weaver's work had immense influence. He was appalled by what he saw as "rampant philistinism, abetted by technology, large-scale organization, and a complacent acceptance of success as the goal of life." Weaver's doctoral dissertation at Louisiana State University argued that the values of the antebellum South were in many ways preferable to those of the North.[47] His denunciations of materialism, mass society, and relativism had an immense influence on conservatives of many stripes in the 1950s: intellectuals and plain Christians, Northerners and Southerners. But he was only one of many teachers and writers who rejected mass society. A book that had immense popularity on campuses in the 1950s was José Ortega y Gasset's *Revolt of the Masses*, first published in 1932. Many agreed with the Episcopal clergyman Bernard Iddings Bell, a close friend of Albert Jay Nock and a professor at his alma mater, Bard College, when he assaulted the "crowd culture" of midcentury America and said the chief threat came from the "complacent, vulgar, mindless, homogenized, comfort-seeking, nouveau riche culture of the common man."[48] If the traditionalists disagreed among themselves, they had immense appeal for a society in which many people, recently released from pressing concerns about material prosperity, were beginning to raise again fundamental questions about the goals of politics, the quality of life, and its meaning. The essential link between traditionalist conservatives was their insistence on seeking, at the very base of their politics, the anchor of a transcendent moral order.

Such traditionalist conservatives stood in the corner opposite to a second tribe of conservatives. The "libertarians," who emphasized not order but freedom as their supreme value, were also divided among themselves. Some of them interpreted freedom in almost anarchist terms, like Frank Chodorov, Murray Rothbard,[49] who wanted to privatize lighthouses, and Ronald Hanovy, who thought the law should not punish libel, or even blackmail, on the grounds that it was a legitimate commercial transaction. Buckley mocked him for these ideas, and Rothbard returned the compliment by accusing Buckley and the *National Review* group of wanting to destroy the Soviet Union in a nuclear war. "The right wing," Rothbard charged, "has been captured by elitists and devotees of the European conservative ideals of order and militarism, by witch hunters and global crusaders, by statists who wish to coerce 'morality' and suppress 'sedition.'"[50] Close to this extreme strand of the libertarian tradition were Ayn Rand and her followers, both those who adopted her Objectivist philosophy and those, the "anarchocapitalists," who stressed economic over personal freedom. In its pure form the libertarian tradition was obsessed not only by personal freedom but by destroying the power of the state. There was a great gulf between the disciples of the Founding Fathers, who saw the United States Constitution as all but divinely ordained, and the extreme libertarians.

Far more important was the gathering momentum of liberal economics. By the 1950s the influence of the "Austrian School," including Friedrich Hayek, Ludwig von Mises, and Karl Popper, was growing; Hayek's *The Constitution of Liberty*[51] was published in 1960, and since 1950 he had been teaching at the University of Chicago, where a vigorous free-market school of economics had flourished since the 1930s, founded by Frank Knight, Jacob Viner, and Henry Simons, with future Nobel laureates Milton Friedman and George Stigler and the Englishman, Harry Johnston, prominent in the next generation. Friedman's magisterial *Capitalism and Freedom* appeared in 1962. It counterattacked the popular hostility to free enterprise, refuting the then widely held idea that the Great Depression had been caused by capitalism, and powerfully reasserting the nineteenth-century liberal belief, also fundamental to Hayek's thought, that economic and political freedom could not be separated. Friedman was also developing his theories of monetarism in the course of his work on *The Monetary History of the United States*. Monetarism directly challenged the guru of liberal economics, John Maynard Keynes, by insisting that inflation was solely caused by changes in the supply of money. Indirectly, by fingering inflation as the most dangerous of economic maladies, the Chicago school discredited Keynes's policy of keeping a depression at bay by using public expenditure to stimulate aggregate demand. The whole thrust of Chicago economics was to question the value and even the morality of government intervention in the economy. In the late 1950s and even more so in the early 1960s, Keynesian economics approached apotheosis as the economic doctrine of the liberal consensus. Paul Samuelson's textbook became the standard work on hundreds of college campuses,[52] Keynesians like Walter Heller, James Tobin, and Gardiner Ackley dominated the Council of Economic Advisers to President Kennedy. Yet at this very moment the counterattack was being made ready.

Finally, together with anarcholibertarians and the Chicago school, the libertarian tradition of conservatism merged gradually into the conventional wisdom of business conservatism. Not small businessmen nor self-made tycoons nor corporate executives nor for that matter the financial sector on Wall Street and elsewhere had ever taken warmly to Progressive regulation, let alone to New Deal intervention and the high taxation implied by Cold War military spending. As long as the liberal consensus held, it was only a minority of self-conscious conservatives in the various business communities who dared to challenge the liberal orthodoxy. But a huge reserve army of potential recruits to conservative economics stood ready in their uniform of business suits for the moment when the bugle would call for a libertarian, antigovernment offensive to be launched on the battlefield of ideas.

Traditionalist New Conservatives and libertarians held flatly contradictory positions on many important issues. The third conservative faction of the late 1950s, the anticommunists, did not disagree with the others on ideas so much as on priorities. The anticommunists were no more homogeneous than the libertarians or the traditionalists. There could be little in common between a Princeton- and Oxford-educated ex-leftist like James Burnham, for example, and the isolationist businessman or preacher from the heartland and the Bible Belt. European-born anticommunists like Stefan Possony and Robert Strausz-Hupé, Willi Schlamm and Ayn Rand, tended to see communism as *the* issue, as a clear and present danger, in a way that was difficult for most native conservatives, libertarian or authoritarian. Indeed, one of the defining characteristics of the *National Review* crowd was precisely the fervor of their anticommunism. It was this that underlay much of what seemed to many conservatives, and especially the majority of Eisenhower Republicans, to be frankly eccentric positions, such as their unapologetic defense of McCarthyism. But in the Eisenhower years, there were many who despaired that the communists were spreading the revolution to the Third World while the United States stood by and did nothing; and in the Kennedy years, while the president spouted a rhetoric of anticommunist militancy, he seemed even less effective at resisting the advance of communism than his benign predecessor.

National Review took the view that the United States was in a foxhole, fighting for its life. Buckley once wrote to the editor of the Jesuit magazine *America*, which had been very critical of his own stance, "When we stand together, as well we may, in that final foxhole, you will discover, as we pass the ammunition, that all along we had the same enemy."[53] Such martial language may seem shrill. But it had undoubted appeal for many who could not be reached by an economic libertarianism that looked all too much like the self-interest of the business class or by a New Conservatism that seemed to be trying to import into the United States a European elitism and an excessive interest in the eighteenth or even the thirteenth century. More than thirty years later Bill Buckley had no doubts.

Communism posed a challenge so total in its dimensions that it was required in order to respond to that challenge that you draw on the whole of your philosophical resources. Pius XII was correct when he said that there are some challenges to what we cherish so great, he might have said so convulsive, as to justify resistance on any scale.[54]

The Harvard political scientist Samuel P. Huntington put a kindred point in an interesting way in a 1957 article. Conservatism, he argued, was not truly an ideology, nor did it have any single vision of the future. He was particularly scornful of attempts by Russell Kirk and others to equip American conservatism with an intellectual past: "few enterprises could be more futile or irrelevant." (About the same time, Huntington's Harvard colleague Louis Hartz argued that there could be no true conservatism in America because it had always been a liberal society.) Rather, Huntington went on, "the impulse to conservatism comes from the social challenge before the theorist, not the intellectual tradition behind him." People became conservatives when they experienced the "horrible feeling" that a society they took for granted might suddenly cease to exist. And he added, presciently, that "the only threat extensive enough and deep enough to elicit a conservative response today is the challenge of communism and the Soviet Union to American society as a whole."[55]

By the early 1960s, at any rate, two ideas were gaining ground rapidly. The first, which attracted attention far beyond the narrow circle of members of the various conservative cults, was that there did seem to be a growing interest in something, or a whole set of ideas, called conservatism.[56] The second, fervently held within the conservative camp itself, was that it was high time for conservatives to see whether they could resolve the contradictions that divided them. By 1959 Buckley himself was calling for such a debate in his book *Up from Liberalism*. He cited a recent book by President Eisenhower's adviser Arthur Larson, *A Republican Looks at His Party*, which, he added caustically, had the "singular" distinction of having been read by Eisenhower. That was the conservatism of expediency, and it was dead. "The conservative movement in America," he concluded, "has got to put its theoretical house in order."[57] That was a task that *National Review*, its shabby office crowded with men who had cut their teeth on the lethal distinguos and contradictions of the left, was born to fulfill.

There were two or three preliminary skirmishes. First, the old leftist Max Eastman departed from the masthead when he realized that religious belief was a required component of *NR* conservatism.[58] Then, Peter Viereck's brand of New Conservatism was read out of the movement. Frank S. Meyer, the ex-communist who was now writing a column called "Principles and Heresies," and was emerging as the ideological commissar or Grand Inquisitor of the magazine, accused Viereck of the ultimate treason: he called him a liberal passing off his views as conservative.[59] Next, Whittaker Chambers declared war on Ayn Rand in a review of her second best seller, *Atlas Shrugged,* whose message, relentlessly plugged, was the ultimate in individualism. Chambers had read no other book, he said, "in which a tone of overriding arrogance was so implacably sustained. Its shrillness is without reprieve. Its dogmatism is without appeal . . . a voice can be heard, from painful necessity, commanding, 'To a gas chamber — go!'" The youthful Garry Wills agreed. He called Ayn Rand a "fanatic" and not a conservative at all. Her hero John Galt, he said, "denies history . . . the first principle of conservatism."

These preliminaries having been conducted in a satisfactorily sanguinary manner, the main bout was joined. Frank Meyer had already attacked Russell Kirk in *The Freeman;* in early 1956 he crossed swords with him over John Stuart Mill in *National Review.*[60] But when one M. Morton Auerbach attacked Kirk from a libertarian standpoint, Meyer came to his defense, writing that "the Christian understanding of the nature of man, which is the foundation of Western civilization, is always and everywhere what conservatives strive to preserve."[61] In fact, Meyer now emerged as the man of the hour, the conservative intellectual who could span the great divide. He ceased acting like an ideological prosecutor and polemicist, and became the skilled negotiator, seeking out common ground and leading the embattled partisans toward it.

An intense, slim man with deep dark rings under his eyes, Meyer chain-smoked and worked at night, constantly telephoning friends and colleagues to hammer out political and journalistic questions with them. He embodied the conservative contradictions in his own life. An ex-communist who became an implacable enemy of communism, socialism, and liberalism, Meyer was born a Jew but converted to Catholicism at the end of his life. He lived in a remote house near Woodstock, New York, and was sufficiently libertarian to educate his two sons at home rather than entrust them to the public school system. Indeed, in a 1962 book he argued that the supreme test of a political system was simply how much it allowed individual freedom.[62] Society, he said (herein anticipating Margaret Thatcher, who told a conference of Scottish conservatives there was no such thing as society) was a "myth." The state had only three legitimate functions: national defense, the preservation of order, and the administration of justice. At the same time, even before his conversion, Meyer's conservatism, like that of Whittaker Chambers or for that matter Bill Buckley's, was grounded in his belief in transcendent values, chief among them the very "constitution of being." Conservatives must therefore acknowledge both freedom and authority; the authority, not of the State, but of God.

In 1962 Meyer made a supreme effort to reconcile the two apparently contradictory traditions. The article "Freedom, Tradition, Conservatism,"[63] originally published in Frank Chodorov's magazine *Modern Age*, was subsequently issued as a pamphlet by the Intercollegiate Society of Individualists and was finally published by Holt, Rinehart and Winston in 1964 as a book called *What Is Conservatism?*[64] It was topped and tailed by Meyer essays, but with papers by a dozen protagonists expounding various strands of conservatism, including Russell Kirk, M. Stanton Evans, and Hayek, represented by his infuriatingly self-consistent essay, "Why I Am Not a Conservative,"[65] as the sandwich filling.

Meyer began, in a sense, by begging the question. He used the word "conservative," he explained, "to include two strands of thought that in practice unite to oppose the reigning ideology of collectivist Liberalism." But did they so unite? "I believe," Meyer went on,

> that these two streams of thought, although they are sometimes presented as mutually incompatible, can in reality be united in a single broad conservative political theory, since they have their roots in a common tradition and are arrayed against a common enemy.[66]

With great subtlety Meyer then began to plait together the strands of libertarian and authoritarian conservatism. "The belief in virtue as the end of man's being," for a start, "implicitly recognizes the necessity of freedom to choose that end." Truth withered when freedom died, and individualism uninformed by moral values rots at the core. Why, the whole history of the West had been "the history of reason operating within a tradition." There was an inherent dilemma for conservatives in a revolutionary era, "when the fibers of society have been rudely torn apart"; for what the conservative is committed to conserve is not whatever happens to obtain at a given moment, but "the consensus of the civilization of his country." Freedom may be the goal in the political realm; but in the moral realm, freedom is only a means to man's proper end, "which is virtue."

In his summing up, Meyer contended, a little in the manner of a skillful chairman finding a formula for the highest common degree of agreement, that consensus *was* there, hidden under apparent contradictions. It was demonstrated by the contrast between the basic assumptions of all conservatives and those of liberals. Conservatives, the chairman put it to the board, all accept "an immutable moral order" and the human individual as the center of their politics. (Many liberals could accept both of those propositions, and might well resent the conservatives claiming them as their exclusive property.) Conservatives, Meyer went on, all share a distaste for the power of the state, and planning is also anathema to them. Above all, though, they share "a devotion to Western civilization and an awareness of the necessity of defending it against the messianic world-conquering intentions of Communism." In that way were the contradictions of conservatism to be resolved, in a process that came to be known as "fusionism," and by an appeal not only to the common values that were supposed to underlie even what might look like sharply contradictory principles, but to the common fight against the twin enemies, communism abroad and liberalism within.

In time the wounds so expertly stitched up by Frank Meyer and Bill Buckley were to be torn open over such issues as abortion. With the passing of communism the appeal to form ranks and march against the enemy came to lose much of its force, even if conservatives could still rally against the menace of liberalism within. Yet fusionism was a real intellectual achievement. It did bring into existence a new American conservative consensus. It made possible the building of new conservative political institutions, in particular ones that could attract a new generation of educated young conservatives who by no means felt themselves thrust out of the mainstream of American life. What was more, it released the energies of the conservatives from intellectual dissension and debate for action in the political world. In the process, it made possible a less obvious fusion, between the extreme right of the Republican Party and all but the wildest and least presentable elements of the new Radical Right that had previously stood outside the pale of political discourse.

In short, the debate over fusionism was a necessary preliminary to the next phase of the conservative revival, that much-misunderstood tragicomedy, the Goldwater campaign of 1964. In a broader sense, it was also necessary to enable conservatives to emerge as the beneficiaries of the whole complex crisis of the liberal order, which lasted from the culmination of the civil rights rebellion and the assassination of President Kennedy in 1963 to the discrediting of Jimmy Carter in the late 1970s.

⚑ 5 ⚑

Broken Levees and
Horseshoe Lakes: 1963–1973

Extremism in the defense of liberty is no vice . . . Moderation in the pursuit of justice is no virtue.
— *Barry Goldwater, 1964*

THE CANDIDATE LOOKED every inch as if central casting had come up with exactly what the director asked for: the good-looking, Western outdoorsman who rode tall in the saddle and hewed true to his core of old American principle. Those who knew him personally saw other sides of him: the laid-back legislator, the gentle person whose pleasure it was to explore the Arizona desert with his camera, taking photographs of uncommon sensitivity, the loner who hesitated more than the square jaw line would have suggested, the unpredictable individualist who could be disarmingly kind or inexcusably rude. Still, in his supreme moment on the podium at the Cow Palace, in San Francisco, he was ramrod straight, commanding. If the line was written for him, he delivered it as if it was his innermost conviction, and perhaps it was: "I would remind you that extremism in the defense of liberty is no vice. And let me remind you also that moderation in the pursuit of justice is no virtue."

The galleries roared their rage or their approval. Veteran reporters and cynical politicians could not remember such shouts of triumph and outrage, such an intensity of partisan fervor for and against a candidate in the ranks of the well-fed and neatly brushed Republicans. The supporters of the Eastern liberal tradition, delegates pledged to Nelson Rockefeller of New York, Bill Scranton of Pennsylvania, or George Romney of Michigan, were outraged by the candidate's intransigence. But the answering howl of conservative joy also expressed a kind of rage:

the pent-up frustration and resentment that conservative Republicans had swallowed like bile for a generation.[1]

That was Barry Goldwater's hour of victory, and it was short-lived. Less than four months later, Lyndon Johnson had rolled over the Goldwater forces with the ruthless impersonality of a tank regiment. In his campaign rhetoric, and even more in his deadly campaign advertising, Johnson — a few months before he took the nation into war — portrayed his opponent as a warmonger, unstable, uncaring. Goldwater was politically annihilated. But a new conservatism was closer to being born.

For the conservative faithful, the Goldwater campaign felt like the worst of times. They, the true believers, had watched and waited. They had been disenfranchised from 1936 to 1944, then disappointed in 1948, bilked, as they saw it, in 1952, twice cheated in 1960, once because (as they devoutly believed, and not without all reason) Kennedy did not really win in Illinois or Texas, and consequently Nixon should have been elected president, and again because Nixon, originally one of their own, had compromised with the hated Eastern moderates. And now when at long last they had a candidate after their own hearts, he had been thrashed, and by Lyndon Johnson.

Yet this was truly the dark hour before the dawn for conservatism. For one thing, the Goldwater campaign proved to conservatives that they could play the game of politics and, if they learned the technical skills, even hope to win. They had learned to raise money, to organize, to compete. In the process, and this was the second lasting gain from the disaster of 1964, they had formed cadres who would fight again and win. And in the very hour of disillusion they had found the leader that Goldwater, at least in the circumstances of 1964, had proved not to be. The conservatives had passed unscathed through the waves of the Red Sea. They were to wander for some years more in the wilderness. The conservative river, having broken its banks, was to waste its strength in horseshoe lakes that led nowhere. But the discovery of 1964 was the leader who would eventually take the conservatives into the Promised Land: Ronald Reagan.

AT THE SAME time as the conservative intelligentsia were fighting the important battles in the realm of theory, the new conservatism was beginning to take its first timid steps into the world of organizational and eventually electoral politics. Of course there were plenty of robust conservatives, some wearing Republican colors, some Democrats, in Congress and in state legislatures, even during the long eclipse of conservative ideas by the dominant ideology of the New Deal. But in the 1950s, just as a new, essentially anticommunist conservatism appeared in the New York intellectual world and on college campuses, so the pioneers of these new ideas began to get involved in practical politics. One of the first places where this showed up was in the Young Republicans' national federation, which was the youth arm of the Republican National Committee. In 1952, the bitter fight between the Taft and Dewey supporters at the national convention was replicated at the Young Republicans' convention in Boston. The next year, far from media eyes, in Rapid City, South Dakota, a talented young political manager (and former political science professor) F. Clifton White led a successful operation by which the Dewey supporters took over the Young Republican federation, and at Detroit in 1955 and in Washington, D.C., in 1957, the Dewey-Eisenhower forces dominated the party's youth wing and elected their men to office in the federation.

Under the surface, however, a strange thing was happening. White and his friends were changing their own political views. By 1957 they had become consciously conservative enough to elect, without opposition, John Ashbrook of Ohio, later an outstandingly conservative Republican member of Congress, to the national chairmanship of the Young Republicans. In 1959, realizing what was happening under his own nose, Nelson Rockefeller purged the conservatives from the New York Young Republican delegation. It made no difference. At the federation's convention, in Denver that year, the inheritors of the coalition put together by White were still able to elect "what was now more or less frankly an anti-Rockefeller, anti-Eastern, and anti-liberal alliance."[2] William Rusher, himself a New York conservative Republican before he became the publisher of *National Review,* commented, "For the first time in modern Republican history, a basically conservative coalition of Southern, Midwestern, and Western Republicans had defeated the long-dominant and relatively liberal East in a convention broadly representative of the distribution of forces in the party."[3]

As early as 1953 the libertarian Frank Chodorov founded the first student conservative movement, called the Intercollegiate Society of Individualists; the name was later changed to the Intercollegiate Studies Institute. As befitted its libertarian principles, it was the most loose knit of movements, with "virtually no organization, no salesmanship, and no fanfare."[4] The first president was none other than William F. Buckley, Jr. Chodorov consciously intended the ISI as an antidote to the various socialist and leftist organizations that flourished on campuses. One of its principal activities was to circulate conservative literature, including Hayek's *The Road to Serfdom*, Buckley's *God and Man at Yale*, and Chodorov's own *One Is a Crowd*. Part of the ISI's purpose was precisely to counter the isolation that conservatives and those who challenged liberal orthodoxy felt on college campuses in the 1950s. There must have been a demand for conservative ideas nevertheless; by 1956 as many as ten thousand had joined the ISI.

The 1960 Republican convention was a traumatic event for a generation of young conservatives. Enthusiasm was beginning to stir for the senator from Arizona, Barry Goldwater. But his chances were recognized to be slim. The big question for conservatives was whether Richard Nixon would stand up for conservative principles. Instead, on the Saturday before the convention opened, the delegates assembled in Chicago read in their newspapers that Nixon had flown secretly to meet Nelson Rockefeller, his principal rival for the nomination and for conservatives the diabolical symbol of all they hated in the Eastern wing of the party. In sober realism, Nixon was virtually certain of the nomination. What he wanted was to eliminate any danger that Rockefeller, a powerful and unpredictable figure, might become a spoiler. The discussion with the New York governor focused on whether the Republican platform should embrace the achievements of the Eisenhower administration, which Nixon, as one of that administration's top members, naturally hoped it would do, or whether — as Rockefeller thought would be electorally more effective — the party should emphasize future perspectives. The conservatives were deeply suspicious. They denounced the "Compact of Fifth Avenue" as "the American Munich."

It was that September, and in that context, that Bill Buckley invited about eighty young conservatives out to his family home in Sharon. M. Stanton Evans, then a Yale student from near Corpus Christi, Texas (with a father from Mississippi), wrote a statement of principles that Buckley edited. Later known as the Sharon Statement, it followed the *National Review* line by fusing traditionalism, libertarianism, and anticommunism. At the Chicago convention, Buckley had spent some time with Martin Liebman, yet another communist turned conservative,[5] who had been one of the organizers of Buckley's Carnegie Hall rally against the Khrushchev visit the previous year. In Chicago, Liebman was organizing a boom for Walter Judd, the right-wing Minnesota representative and luminary of the China Lobby, for vice president. At the convention, Liebman and Buckley also met two students who were running something called Youth for Goldwater, Doug Caddy and David

Francke. Brought together by their anger at the American Munich, they decided to start Young Americans for Freedom. In an interview, Buckley disclaimed credit for starting YAF. "My midwifery of that was purely ceremonial," he said.[6]

The fact remains that Buckley did play an important part in this vital move from campus protest to national activism. His friend and colleague William Rusher was also involved. Doug Caddy became the first executive director of YAF. When he left to go into the army in the summer of 1961, his successor was a young Texan named Richard Viguerie. The son of a middle-management petrochemical industry executive from Houston, raised as a Roman Catholic, Viguerie attended law school in Houston but left to work full time for YAF. He hated the fund raising involved.[7] Or, rather, he hated face-to-face solicitation. Instead, he found that he had a talent for using the new computer technology to raise money by direct mail. That talent was to have no small effect on the spread of the conservative movement.

If the Compact of Fifth Avenue seemed to conservatives an argument for action, Nixon's defeat by Kennedy, and the early foreign policy blunders of the Kennedy administration, especially the Cuban adventure ending in disaster at the Bay of Pigs, made an infinitely stronger case. Nixon no longer looked like a plausible standard bearer for conservatives, and by 1962 he seemed to have committed political *hari-kiri* by his outburst to reporters after his defeat by Edmund G. Brown, Sr., in the California governorship election. All conservative eyes now turned to the man of the moment, Barry Goldwater.

On the face of it, Barry M. Goldwater might have sounded like a Western version of the country club Republicans whose conservatism was essentially an instinct for protecting their own economic interests and those of their class. An Episcopalian with a Jewish father, Goldwater had inherited the controlling interest in a department store in furiously growing Phoenix. He first got involved in politics when he was elected to the school board there, and in 1952 he was elected to the Senate, defeating no less an opponent than the Democratic majority leader, Ernest W. McFarland. For his first term Goldwater made an unexciting record as a labor expert. A fighter pilot, Goldwater also took an active part in the Air Force Reserve, in which, like other senators, he was soon promoted to general. As a Westerner, he was deeply suspicious of the federal government. One of his close friends from Arizona, a Phoenix lawyer, explained to me in 1964 just how people in Arizona felt about Washington. If land in Arizona is not a national park or a national forest, he said, then it is part of an Indian reserve or a military base. From Phoenix, he said with such unfeigned indignation that I have remembered his expression thirty years later, "Washington looks like a colonial power." But what was not common or conventional about the young Senator Goldwater, even in the context of the Southwest in the 1950s, was the vehemence of his anticommunism. He became a close friend of Senator Joe McCarthy's. (Goldwater has a great capacity for friendship; another of his Senate friends was the junior senator from Massachusetts, John F. Kennedy.) When in November 1954 the Senate was debating McCarthy's condemnation, Goldwater went out of his way to defend him, and to attack not only Democrats who were for the censure motion, but even more his fellow Republicans.[8] To vote to censure McCarthy would be "the culminating act in the merciless fight to destroy a United States senator and the fight against communism," he said. He used language almost as strong as McCarthy's own about the "masterminds," the "unknown engineers" of censure.

> All the discredited and embittered figures of the Hiss-Yalta period of American dishonor have crawled out from under their logs . . . The news columns and the airways have been filled with their talk about "civil liberties" . . . while these people have dipped in the smut pot to discredit Senator McCarthy and his work against communism.

Even so, in his first term Goldwater attracted no special attention. The turning point that made him something more than just another attractive young Western anticommunist, with tough views on labor and defense, was his reelection in 1958. Washington politicians, and not only politicians in Washington, looked up when, for the second time, he thrashed McFarland, who had in the meantime been elected governor of Arizona. In 1959 he became the ranking Republican member of the Senate Labor Committee. Its Republican counsel, Mike Bernstein, became his mentor there, and suggested that Goldwater focus on being a spokesman for "the forgotten American."[9]

What really attracted attention was his principled resistance to what he saw as a weak and bad labor bill, sponsored by Senators John F. Kennedy and Sam Ervin. Goldwater was the only senator to vote against it. But then the Senate voted 95 to 2 for the tougher House bill, Landrum-Griffin. The bill, which responded to public fears of union racketeering aroused by the McClellan committee disclosures on union corruption, was regarded by unions as a disaster, because it made it much harder for them to recruit members. Business groups welcomed it for incorporating changes from the Taft-Hartley bill recommended by President Eisenhower. Goldwater was widely credited with a stunning legislative turnaround. That fall he was introduced to a Republican dinner in South Carolina by the state chairman, Gregory D. Shorey, as his choice for the 1960 Republican presidential nomination. It is worth noting the importance of South Carolina, perhaps the most conservative state in the South, then confronting the inevitability of conflict with the federal government over desegregation, in the story of Barry Goldwater's emergence as the national conservative standard bearer. In many ways the South was to count for as much in the new conservatism as in the old.

In January 1960 Goldwater had become sufficiently well known to be invited to write a column three times a week in the *Los Angeles Times*, and shortly afterward Clarence Manion, the retired dean of the Notre Dame Law School (and former member of the John Birch Society), arranged for publication of a book signed by Goldwater but written by Bill Buckley's brother-in-law L. Brent Bozell. *The Conscience of a Conservative* was a forthright statement of strongly anticommunist conservative views, and it was a runaway success. By 1964 it had sold 3.5 million copies.[10] Even discounting the propensity of right-wing organizations to buy huge quantities of conservative books and distribute them at a loss, that in itself suggests how strong were the currents of conservative yearning and curiosity by the end of the Eisenhower years. At the same time, Barry Goldwater was chairman of the Senate Republican campaign committee. That gave him the opportunity to travel around the country incessantly, raising money for Republican candidates, getting to know Republicans in every corner of the Union, and charming them with his open manner and uncomplicated conservative commitment.

By 1960 Goldwater was nationally known. That spring a Republican state convention in South Carolina, led by the Goldwater boosters Greg Shorey and Roger Milliken (heir to a textile fortune in South Carolina and neighbor of the Buckleys at Sharon, who, with his brother Jeremiah, was one of the angels of *National Review*,) pledged their delegation to support a Goldwater presidential nomination at the Chicago convention that year. The senator was able to convince his Republican friends in Arizona, led by the governor, Paul Fannin, and the state party chairman, Richard Kleindienst, that he would "look a fool" if Arizona, too, did not support his nomination.[11] Goldwater's attitude toward being a presidential candidate was ambivalent, to say the least. He discouraged attempts to promote him as a serious candidate in 1960, and when, after

Nixon's defeat by Kennedy in November 1960, there was talk of Goldwater emerging as the candidate for 1964, Goldwater discouraged it.

For example, a few weeks after Kennedy was elected, six men met with Senator Goldwater in a room at the Jefferson Hotel in Washington. They included Goldwater's campaign manager and ghostwriter from Arizona, Stephen Shadegg; Roger Milliken; Charles Barr, an oil company executive from Chicago; William R. Spear of Nebraska; Dick Herman, president of an Omaha trucking firm; and G. R. Herberger, a Minnesota department store owner who spent his winters in Arizona.[12] All were committed Goldwater supporters. But as soon as discussion turned to the senator's prospects in 1964, Goldwater cut it short.

Even so, after Nixon's defeat, conservatives had to look for a candidate to carry their standard against the Eastern candidates who were bound to come forward, led by the governor of New York, Nelson Rockefeller, the very epitome of the Eastern financial Establishment that Southern and Western conservatives wanted to overthrow. A couple of weeks after the election Goldwater made a speech (once again written by Bozell) that helped to establish him still more clearly as the natural candidate of the right of the party. The rhetoric foreshadowed the language of his more famous 1964 acceptance speech. "Peace is a worthy objective," he told his audience at the Air War College in Montgomery, Alabama, "but if it means letting Communists into Berlin, then we must fight . . . Justice is a worthy objective, but if justice for the Bantus entails driving the government of the Union of South Africa away from the West, then the Bantus must be prepared to carry their identification cards yet a while longer." And he ended by placing anticommunism at the very heart of his system of political belief: "The indispensable condition for a tolerable world — the absence of Soviet Communist power — must take precedence over other 'worthy objectives.'"[13]

In the South especially, spurred by unease about the rising civil rights movement, but also by deep suspicion of the Kennedy administration's policy toward Nikita Khrushchev and the Soviet Union, conservative sentiment was spreading with amazing speed. More and more it was being diverted from classic conservative Democrats to a new breed of educated, suburban, conservative Republicans. In May 1961 John Tower, a college professor and a perfect example of the new breed, was elected to the Senate from Texas. Goldwater was called by *Time* magazine "the hottest political figure this side of Jack Kennedy." But still Goldwater would not move. "I have no plans for it," he said when asked whether he would run. "I have no staff for it, no program for it, and no ambition for it."[14]

Others, however, had the ambition and the program for him, and were prepared to act voluntarily as his staff. Three men in particular took the initiative. One was Representative John Ashbrook of Ohio. The second was William Rusher of *National Review*.[15] And the third was F. Clifton White, the former Cornell political science instructor and organizer of the conservative caucus in the Young Republican movement. At a series of meetings in New York and Washington, they drew up a list of twenty-six people and invited them to meet in a Chicago motel to save the Republic. There was no mention of Senator Goldwater. "We said that the three of us felt it was important enough for them to be there," White remembered later, "and they came."[16]

On October 18, 1961, in fact, twenty-two men met at a motel in the Chicago Loop. (In the time-pressed style of American politics, borrowed from the executive culture, history is made in interchangeable motel and hotel rooms.) Besides White, Rusher, and Ashbrook, and Roger and Jeremiah Milliken, they included one congressman, Donald Bruce from Indianapolis, and a sprinkling of Republican state chairmen and national committeemen. The purpose of the meeting was to see whether it was desirable and practicable to launch a Draft Goldwater movement, and after the meeting Clif White was deputed to tell the senator in a general way what was afoot.

After a second meeting in Chicago that December, the Texas and Mississippi Republican chairmen came on board, and Clif White was set up in New York with a full-time office in Suite 3505 of the art deco Chanin Building, at the corner of Forty-second Street and Lexington Avenue, and a budget of $65,000, only two thirds of which was ever raised.[17] Rita Bree, chair of the Young Women's Republican Club of New York, gave up her job as an insurance manager with an investment trust to be what was called in those days White's Girl Friday and women's coordinator.[18] Together, they set to work to organize the national Draft Goldwater campaign. White alone traveled over a million miles between 1961 and 1964, setting up state organizations to choose Goldwater delegates through primaries or at state conventions. By the end of 1962, there were organizations in place in forty-two states.

In the middle of 1962, there was a Valley Forge period, when money ran very low. But the fortunes of conservative Republicans continued to rise. The signs were everywhere. A congressional Senate and House joint committee on Republican principles, chaired by the highly intelligent Republican representative from Wisconsin, Melvin Laird, took the conservative line on foreign policy: "an active strategy aimed at victory does not increase the risk of nuclear war." That was what Goldwater was trying to say. At the National Federation of Republican Women's convention, coincidentally in Phoenix, conservatives were voted into all offices and liberals rejected. As the 1962 midterm elections drew near, many Republicans agreed with a column by the AP political commentator Lyle Wilson, who wrote that what the Republicans needed was "a set of courageous political principles that clearly distinguish it from the Democratic Party." That too was what Goldwater and his conservative backers were trying to get across.[19]

After the elections Clif White held another meeting in yet another Chicago motel, but this time the press got wind of it, and the cat was out of the bag.[20] There were headlines like GOLDWATER '64 BOOM: MOVE TO BLOCK ROCKY in the *New York Herald Tribune*.[21] "Somehow," William Rusher commented in *National Review*, "Mr. Rockefeller's nomination never seemed quite so 'inevitable' again." That was all very well. But would the candidate back his backers? On January 14, Clif White flew to Washington and had a nasty shock.

"I'm not a candidate," said Goldwater. "And I'm not going to be. I have no intention of running for the presidency."

With a bleak smile, White tried to laugh it off. "Well, we thought we might have to draft you."

Goldwater lost his temper. "Draft nothing. I've told you I'm not going to run. And I'm telling you, don't paint me into a corner."

White left the room, and the door shut behind him, as he graphically put it later, with all the finality of a coffin being lowered into a grave.[22]

The next meeting of White's group, at the O'Hare Inn near the Chicago airport in February, was gloomy. There was only one thing to do, they decided, and that was to draft their man. At a meeting of the Downtown Association just off Wall Street (in the camp of the enemy, so to speak), Peter O'Donnell of Texas agreed to be the chairman of the Draft Goldwater Committee, White was named national director, and Bill Middendorf, a New York investment banker, became treasurer.[23] Ione Harrington was named women's director and co-chair. On April 8 the committee went public with a press conference at the Mayflower Hotel in Washington. The great worry was what Goldwater himself would say. He took no position. But at least he stopped short of taking the "Sherman position" his friend had been afraid of.[24] And indeed within weeks he was beginning to say things like "a man would be a damned fool to predict with finality what he would do," which was something definitely less definite than a Sherman declaration.

In May 1963 the political scene was transformed by several dramatic developments. Michigan Governor George Romney's incipient campaign was deflated by a *Detroit News* editorial which reminded him of all the problems that needed to be tackled in Michigan, saying: "Come home, George, and let's get on with the chores." Richard Nixon took himself out of the race by announcing that he was moving to New York to practice law. Far the most important, and unexpected, Nelson Rockefeller announced that he had married a neighbor, Happy Murphy. Both the governor and his wife were divorced, she only a month earlier. In the context of Republican politics at the time, that was just not done. Within a month, Rockefeller's standing in the Gallup Poll had slumped by fourteen points, to 29 percent; Goldwater's had risen by the same margin, to 40 percent. Suddenly Goldwater's situation was transformed. By June, *Time* magazine was reporting that if the Republican convention were to be held then, rather than in a year's time, Goldwater would win. Robert Novak, who had recently left the *Wall Street Journal* to become, with Rowland Evans, Jr., one of the best informed journalists on Republican politics, wrote on June 24 that "the fact that Senator Barry Goldwater is so far in front for the Republican presidential nomination is proof of a little-understood transformation in the party's power structure . . . nothing less than a quiet revolt. The aggressive postwar club of conservative young Republicans from the small states of the West and South are seizing power." On Independence Day — only weeks before Martin Luther King's triumphal March on Washington — White's organization was able to fill the District of Columbia Armory with thousands of cheering Goldwater supporters.[25] By August, White was beginning to worry about complacency in the ranks, because so many Republicans, both in Washington and in state organizations, believed that Goldwater had the Republican nomination sewn up.

At the same time as Clif White was mounting this informal Draft Goldwater campaign, with the double ambition of making Barry Goldwater the Republican candidate for president and himself the chairman of the Republican National Committee, Goldwater loyalists from Arizona and elsewhere were doing their best by private intercession to persuade a reluctant Goldwater to run. The leader of this operation was Denison Kitchel, an Arizonan lawyer whose roots were deep in the Eastern Establishment and in one of its strongest outposts in the West. Kitchel was a graduate of Yale and Harvard Law and was married to Naomi Douglas, whose uncle, "Rawhide Jimmy" Douglas, had built up what became the giant Phelps Dodge copper empire; Lewis Douglas, the ambassador to the Court of St. James's, was a cousin. Kitchel, an early member of the John Birch Society, had resigned when Robert Welch insisted that President Eisenhower was a communist. Other members of this faction were William Baroody, Sr., a former New Dealer and founder of the American Enterprise Institute in Washington; Ed McCabe, a Washington lawyer; and Arizona associates like Dean Burch and Richard G. Kleindienst. Goldwater's supporters were riven with jealousy, and this group in particular did everything it could to keep the White-Rusher-Ashbrook Draft Goldwater Committee at arm's length. They also drove off Bill Buckley and Brent Bozell by leaking to the *New York Times* word of a private meeting. At the beginning of 1963 a Goldwater for President Committee had been started in Phoenix, and by midsummer Kitchel, who had been commuting to Washington for months, rented an apartment there and opened a campaign office at the Carroll Arms on Capitol Hill.

By the fall of 1963 there was real political excitement in the conservative camp. One issue that helped the conservatives was Cuba. It was becoming plain that, so far from standing firm against Khrushchev, President Kennedy had done a secret deal, negotiating away NATO missiles in Europe and Turkey in return for the removal of Soviet missiles from Cuba. Moreover, the civil rights movement was producing a white backlash in the very sections of the population that were turning to Goldwater and conservatism: in the South, among older blue-collar workers, especially those from "ethnic" groups, and in working-class neighborhoods in the cities.

In September, Goldwater voted against the test ban treaty, to the delight of his supporters, saying, "I do not vote against the hope of peace, but against the illusion of it. I do not vote for war, but for the strength to prevent it." By now Goldwater had broken openly with Rockefeller, and Rockefeller and conservative operatives clashed nastily at the Young Republicans' convention in the summer of 1963. In September, President Kennedy turned his fire on Goldwater in a speech at the Mormon Tabernacle in Salt Lake City.[26] It was obvious that Kennedy and his advisers now saw Goldwater as the man they had to beat.

The putative candidate, however, still would not commit himself to either of his potential teams of boosters. By the fall he had privately decided to run. But he had still not made his intentions publicly known when the assassination of President Kennedy, on November 22, changed everything. At first, Goldwater ordered his would-be drafters to stand down their operations. It was not just that he responded to the shock, as others did, with a sense of futility; he also calculated, as he admitted later,[27] that "I didn't feel Johnson could be beaten, because Johnson was a Southerner and he would or should carry the South." But that mood did not last long. He was convinced that to take himself out of the race would be to betray the conservative cause. And on January 3, on the steps of Yavapai County Courthouse in Prescott, Arizona, his foot in a cast from a skiing accident, he duly announced that he was indeed a candidate for president.

The preconvention campaign was not impressive. The Arizona mafia around Denison Kitchel froze out the Draft Goldwater people, who had, after all, built a national organization. Reporters found it easy to confront the senator with extreme or eccentric-sounding statements he had made in *The Conscience of a Conservative* or in earlier speeches. He either said, or allowed himself to appear to have said, that he would cut Social Security and that U.S. long-range missiles were not reliable. There was, inevitably, dissension between the Kitchel and White factions in the campaign, and the first advertising agency retained was caught ripping off the campaign. As a result, in New Hampshire, Goldwater, who was thought to be far ahead, came in second by a wide margin to Henry Cabot Lodge, exemplar of the Eastern Republican Establishment. Worse, in Oregon he ran third behind Nelson Rockefeller and Lodge. Only a last-minute blitz, backed by the enthusiasm of his Southern California supporters, could give him a victory in the California primary.

Yet in spite of everything, Goldwater arrived at the Cow Palace with a sure 770 votes against the 655 needed for victory. On the first trial vote on the platform he easily won nearly 900. His first choice for running mate was probably the Eastern but attractive and moderately conservative Bill Scranton, former governor of Pennsylvania. But on the eve of the convention Scranton circulated a letter to all delegates so violent in its attacks on the front runner that a Goldwater-Scranton ticket was unthinkable. "Goldwaterism," the Pennsylvanian wrote, "has come to stand for a whole crazy quilt of absurd and dangerous positions that would be soundly repudiated by the American people in November." Instead of Scranton, Goldwater chose as his vice presidential running mate the obscure congressman Bill Miller, from Buffalo, New York, whose only recommendations were that he was a Roman Catholic and that his style of below-the-belt infighting was so egregious that it was hoped — vainly hoped — it would throw Lyndon Johnson off his stride. The logic was much the same as that behind the "extremism is no vice" rhetoric in the acceptance speech. It was almost as if the conservatives at this stage cared more about sticking it to their liberals, especially those in Republican ranks, than about winning the general election.

The Goldwater campaign was if anything even more ineptly managed after the nominating convention than before. The candidate made 162 appearances in forty-five states, but much good it did him. Recklessly, he chose to attack Social Security in Florida, cotton subsidies in Memphis, and the Tennessee Valley Authority in Knoxville. In Wisconsin, in October, state Republican leaders were corralled for a live rally, only to find that they had been upstaged by some clips of earlier speeches by the candidate; they were not strongly motivated to pull out the last stop on his behalf. It is fair to say that even if Goldwater had spoken with the tongues of men and of angels, yea, and given his body to be burnt, he would have had a hard time making himself heard over the uproar of perhaps the most one-sided and unfair press coverage ever deployed in a presidential campaign.

The columnist Joseph Alsop, a lifelong Republican, wrote of Goldwater's "itchy finger on the nuclear trigger," while in the *New York Times* Charles Mohr quoted former President Eisenhower as musing that Goldwater "might take this country into war." Walter Lippmann called him a "war hawk," and Cyrus L. Sulzberger wrote in his family's newspaper, the *Times*, that if Goldwater were elected, "there might not be a day-after-tomorrow." Not content with outrageously negative comment, newspapers and television vied with one another to misreport what Goldwater actually said, though in all conscience it was scary enough — because he spoke so insouciantly off the top of his head — even when he was reported straight. When he replied to a question by Howard K. Smith on ABC's *Issues and Answers*, for example, that "defoliation of the forests by low-yield atomic weapons" was a possible solution to the infiltration of men and arms into South Vietnam along the so-called Ho Chi Minh Trail, the *San Francisco Examiner* headlined GOLDWATER'S PLAN TO USE VIET A-BOMB, and rubbed it in with a second-deck headline saying, in quotes, "I'd Risk a War." *Good Housekeeping* magazine weighed in with a — completely untrue and unsourced — report that Goldwater had had two nervous breakdowns in the 1930s. And CBS's Daniel Schorr, followed up by Arthur J. Olsen in the *New York Times*, asserted, without a shred of justification, that Goldwater was "in touch with the Right Wing in Germany."

With the candidate caroming to and fro across the country with his foot in his mouth, and with newspapers, both Republican- and Democrat-owned, and television roughing him up in this cheerfully ruthless fashion, the campaign was listing heavily and taking on water even before the Johnson-Humphrey artillery got its range. When the Democrats did open up, they blasted away at two themes above all. One was that Goldwater was going to cut and eventually end Social Security. Barry Goldwater despises poor people, said David McDonald of the Steelworkers' Union, and wants to destroy unions. "If you want to be unemployed and live in filth and degradation," he went on, then you should vote for Goldwater. It is true that twenty years later, under Goldwater's ideological ally Ronald Reagan, unions did take a notable pasting. Still, the political rhetoric of 1964 went beyond measured prediction. The Johnson campaign TV ads focused on fear. One, which has become perhaps the classic political ad of all time, showed a dear little girl plucking the petals from a daisy. Vote for Goldwater, was the message, and innocent young lives would be whisked away on a nuclear wind. More generally, Johnson occupied the middle ground so firmly that Goldwater could make few inroads beyond the most solidly partisan Republicans and the deepest-dyed conservatives.

The result of the presidential election came as no surprise. Johnson carried forty-four states and the District of Columbia (voting for the first time).[28] He carried New York by more than two million votes and Pennsylvania, Massachusetts, and Michigan by more than a million each; in Illinois his margin fell just short of a million. What was even more significant, he won California, which had delivered the nomination to Goldwater, by another clear million votes. In all the Pacific and Mountain states, Goldwater's presumed heartland, Goldwater carried only his home state, Arizona. The only section where he ran strongly was the South, and there it was Johnson who carried the growing, modernizing states like Texas, Florida, and North Carolina, while Goldwater carried Alabama, Georgia, Louisiana, and South Carolina, the most traditional states, where his opposition to the civil rights movement matched unreconstructed values. Concealed in the results in the South, however, was that it was the African American vote that delivered the Johnson majority in Texas, Florida, and North Carolina. In the Electoral College, Johnson won 486 and Goldwater 52. In the popular vote, Johnson won more than forty-three million votes, or 61 percent, a slightly higher percentage than Roosevelt in 1936 (though not as high as Harding and Coolidge in the Republican years of the 1920s). Goldwater and Miller won just over twenty-seven million votes. Johnson's coattails elected an additional thirty-eight Democratic representatives and two new Democratic senators.

For Goldwater, it was an absolutely shattering defeat, and it was understandable that at first it was also taken as a resounding national repudiation of his entire philosophy. It was not that. The conventional wisdom was that what one writer called "the Goldwater caper" was an aberration from which the Republican Party would recover once it came to its senses and rejected the Goldwater philosophy. The historian George H. Mayer, for example, rushed out a second edition of his authoritative history of the Republican Party so as to include an account of, and his analysis of, the 1964 campaign, which he referred to as "the Amateur Hour."[29] The party, he consoled himself, "seemed certain to regain some of its lost supporters in the North once the controversial Goldwater had vacated the center of the stage." As for the South, he judged that while the Republicans there "did elect a few more congressmen and state legislators by running candidates who professed to be more conservative on the race question than their Democratic opponents," the gains from this policy were more than counterbalanced by the adverse effect on blacks in the North. In short, he concluded regretfully, the Republicans in national politics must reconcile themselves to another long stint as the minority party, hoping that "the burgeoning problems of the city" would produce a split in the Democratic ranks, and consoling themselves with the reflection that "long periods of one-party supremacy have been the rule rather than the exception."[30]

The Republican Party, concurred the authoritative *Congress and the Nation* study published by Congressional Quarterly, "reduced to a nadir in modern-day strength by Goldwater's candidacy and right-wing philosophy," was engaged in a deep internal debate about its own future. Goldwater supporters might reject moderates like Governors Rockefeller, Romney, and Scranton and Senators Tommy Kuchel of California, Clifford Case of New Jersey, and Hugh Scott of Pennsylvania as "so-called Republicans," and want to read them out of the party. But there were many others who agreed with Governor Robert Smyllie of Idaho, the chairman of the Republican Governors' Association, when he argued that what the party needed was "to get back into the middle of the road that was satisfactory to the American people, and that this is the middle road of the Eisenhower years." The Ripon Society, founded in 1962 to promote mainstream Republicanism among the younger professionals and academics, charged that "the architects of this right-wing crusade [had] in their zeal to promote an ideological cause" willfully sacrificed the interests of the party.[31]

Such analyses of the consequences of the Goldwater campaign were understandable at the time. From Washington and from the offices of national news organizations in New York they may even have looked compelling. In fact, they completely missed the campaign's significance for the future. Looked at in retrospect, however, it is clear that the Goldwater campaign of 1964 was a watershed in the history of American conservatism. For one thing, Goldwater's campaign was fatally handicapped by three circumstances: the ferocious attacks on him by fellow Republicans; the quite exceptionally uniform hostility of the news media; and, perhaps most fatal of all, the Kennedy assassination. It has been pointed out that previous political assassinations, those of Lincoln in 1865 and McKinley in 1900, had the effect of keeping the victim's party in power for a generation. Then, decisive as Johnson's defeat of Goldwater was, it was not wholly inevitable. Before Kennedy's assassination, before Goldwater had even officially thrown his hat into the ring, and in September 1964, before the sheer ruthless weight of the Johnson campaign had begun to have its effect, there were strong signs that Goldwater was voicing concerns that were on the minds of many Americans. New groups, disturbed by the civil rights movement, by urban conflict, and perhaps by a diffuse sense that values and traditional *mores*, as well as neighborhoods, were under attack, were responding to various strands of the conservative message. Such people — the 1964 equivalent of the Reagan Democrats of 1980 — were peeling off from the liberal consensus and from traditional Democratic loyalties.

One extraordinary indication of this popular receptivity to conservative ideas was to be seen in the sales of conservative books. Three books in particular racked up sales figures in 1964 that were nothing short of prodigious, even if one takes due account of mass purchases by conservative organizations. J. Evetts Haley's *A Texan Looks at Lyndon: A Study in Illegitimate Power*, John A. Stormer's *None Dare Call It Treason*, and Phyllis Schlafly's *A Choice, Not an Echo*, are said to have sold between them sixteen million copies. Add to those Goldwater's own book, and you have a total sale of twenty million copies of four nonfiction books, all taking the same strongly conservative ideological tack. From Washington, that might seem evidence of no more than a further "rebellion of the primitives," a weird stirring in the hinterland. From close up, it was more rational to assume that a very large number of people were very unhappy about what was happening, and in particular about the government's involvement in the cause of black civil rights. They were not likely to be reassured by those in either party who had signed off on the liberal consensus. Instead, they were prepared to listen to what the conservatives had to say.

This was one of the lessons of the Goldwater campaign. There were indeed people who wanted "a choice, not an echo." Another was that a new generation of conservative activists had emerged on the right, in no way less fervent in their beliefs or less dedicated in their loyalty than the new generation of pro–civil rights, antiwar militants on the left. The Goldwater campaign blooded new conservative cadres. There were those, like Goldwater's speechwriter Karl Hess, who were so shaken by the defeat that they moved across to the New Left. They were hugely outnumbered by those who decided to sign on for the long march and to work for an eventual conservative victory, however distant it might seem.

The cadres of the Nixon and Reagan campaigns, not to mention dozens of congressional and state campaigns, were recruited in the Goldwater effort. So was a new generation of Southern Republicans. W. Henson Moore II, for example, a Republican representative from Baton Rouge, Louisiana, got his first taste of politics working for Democrats for Goldwater.[32] In Mississippi, Trent Lott, who was to become first Republican whip in the House of Representatives, then a senator, and eventually Republican majority leader, admits that the Goldwater campaign was "the first time that we really started thinking, 'Gee, maybe we are Republicans.'"[33] Mayor E. Clay Shaw of Fort Lauderdale, Florida, switched from Democrat to Republican because of the 1964 Goldwater campaign. David Keene, who had grown up in a union, gut-Democrat family in Illinois and Wisconsin, switched to work for Goldwater, Spiro Agnew, James Buckley, Ronald Reagan, and George Bush. He pointed out that the 1964 Goldwater campaign did for a generation of conservatives what the McCarthy and McGovern campaigns later did for the Democrats. "You almost need those things once in a while," he mused to the *Washington Post*'s political editor, David Broder. "It's only a campaign like Goldwater's that is emotionally exciting and ideological and non-Establishment that allows new people to come in."[34]

There was another enduring and very practical consequence of the Goldwater campaign. Suddenly conservatives could raise very large sums of money. These were the years when political advertising, especially on television, and the cost of producing it and buying time for it, made campaign finance, on an undreamed-of scale, critical to political success. The Goldwater campaign demonstrated that a lot of money could be raised in the old-fashioned way, from well-known wealthy individual contributors, for convincing and outspoken conservative candidates. It also led directly to the arrival of a new technique, direct mail solicitation. Direct mail revolutionized campaign finance for all parties, but specifically it gave great influence to a small group of people on the New Right led by the former YAF executive director, Richard Viguerie, and those who shared his beliefs.

Goldwater's official finance committee eventually represented a compromise between the true believers of the Draft Goldwater effort (the Milliken brothers and Bill Middendorf, the New York investment banker); Arizonans, some of them with Midwestern connections, like Herberger, the department store magnate with real estate in Arizona; and traditional Republican fund raisers like George M. Humphrey in Cleveland, secretary of the treasury in the Eisenhower administration who chaired the Goldwater finance committee in the Midwest. The overall chairman, Dan Rainey, claimed, perhaps only half in jest, that he got the job because he spent his winters on a farm in Arizona, so he "was not regarded as an alien by Denison Kitchel and his crew." Altogether these men of means raised $3.5 million to get the campaign going. Henry Salvatori, an oil geologist from Los Angeles, chairman of the board of the Western Geophysical company, garnered another million dollars, independently of the main campaign, for the California primary. Much of it was raised at receptions and dinners in the Hollywood community, where such figures as John Wayne, Efrem Zimbalist, Jr., of TV's FBI show, and Hedda Hopper were strong Goldwater supporters. By way of comparison, the Rockefeller campaign, helped by such powerful business and political leaders as Leonard K. Firestone, Justin Dart, and Jack Warner of Warner Brothers, is said to have spent between $3.5 million and $5 million in the California primary alone.

Still, what was striking about the fund raising for Goldwater was not the admittedly huge sums raised from wealthy businessmen and show business moguls, but the substantial amounts contributed by small donors. "Unlike so many other campaigns," commented Clif White, "the money for this one was raised without promises of political patronage. And the money came not from a small group of wealthy contributors seeking a measure of control over the national government, or a Cabinet post or some ambassadorship. It came from thousands of people in all walks of life who saw in Goldwater's candidacy a more lasting promise for their country."[35]

There was a paradox or at least an apparent contradiction here. While the Goldwater campaign was supported by thousands of wealthy businessmen, there was nevertheless a strange role reversal. In 1964, it was the Democrats, traditionally the party of underdogs — industrial workers, minorities, and the South, always the poorest part of the country — who had become the Establishment. The Republicans, historically seen as the party of the haves, the respectables, and the white Protestant ascendancy, who had always dominated America, suddenly looked like radicals and outsiders. That was what Goldwater and his insurgents achieved; and in part that reversal became permanent. The Republican triumph in 1980 was nothing if not a victory for conservatives who saw themselves as radicals.

Henry Salvatori was one of a group of wealthy businessmen from Southern California ready to raise and to spend enormous sums of their own and their friends' money if it would help to elect candidates who met their exacting standards of conservatism. Most of them lived in or around Los Angeles, though some of them had Midwestern connections too. Leland Kaiser, of the shipbuilding and steel family, and A. C. (Cy) Rubel, of the Union Oil company, later raised large sums to elect a governor of California. But their man made his first appearance on the national scene on October 27, 1964, when the Goldwater campaign seemed to be slipping hopelessly beyond rescue. He gave a speech called "A Time for Choosing," and although it was written by others, it was delivered, with memorable aplomb, by a former Hollywood actor named Ronald Reagan.

Reagan had always been a strong anticommunist. Even before he discovered that he was not a Democrat, as his father had been, but a Republican, he was a conservative. From 1954 until 1962, he worked for General Electric. Part of the duties for which he was handsomely paid involved presenting and occasionally acting in the carefully uncontroversial TV plays in *The General Electric Theater.* But even more important was his role as a presenter of the company image to the outside world and of its philosophy within the company.[36] Reagan claims to have visited more than 130 GE plants in every corner of the United States, giving what came to be known as "the Speech." He also gave the Speech to political audiences. He had become caught up in the excitement of the Radical Right in Southern California, and had given a version of the Speech in 1961 to Dr. Fred Schwarz's Christian Anti-Communist Crusade, and even in 1962 at a fund raiser for John Rousselot, the Republican congressman who was an officer of the John Birch Society.

One night in the summer of 1964 he gave "basically the same talk I'd been giving for years, altering it slightly so that it became a campaign speech for Barry," to an audience of eight hundred Republicans at the Coconut Grove in the Ambassador Hotel in Los Angeles. After dinner, five or six of the audience came up and asked whether he would join them at their table. While the waiters were noisily clearing away the glasses, the group, which included some of the biggest Republican contributors in California, led by Salvatori, asked him to repeat the speech on television. "Sure," he said, "if you think it would do any good!"[37] They bought half an hour of time on NBC, and Reagan taped the speech in front of an invited group of Republicans, to simulate the kind of audience he was used to.

The basic theme of this last effort to shore up the failing fortunes of the Goldwater campaign was anticommunist, of course. In it, Reagan warned his listeners of the danger from the Soviet Union and world communism. But what he emphasized even more was the danger from the inroads of domestic "communism" in the insidious shape of high taxes, unions, government regulation, and every other kind of interference sanctioned since the New Deal into the God-given freedom of the American businessman to make and spend his dough. Reagan was utterly sincere about this. He "criticized liberal Democrats for taking the country down the road to socialism," as he put it. At the same time, what the Speech did, and what made it catnip to millionaires, self-made or otherwise, was the identification it suggested — all the more effective for never being a formal argument — between the New Deal and communism. When he called his telecast *A Time for Choosing*, he was picking up another of the themes of the new conservatives. Phyllis Schlafly's book was *A Choice, Not an Echo*. People were being told, he said as he moved into his peroration, to choose between left and right. "There is only an up or down: up to man's age-old dream — the ultimate in individual freedom consistent with law and order — or down to the ant heap of totalitarianism." And he ended, strangely enough, with a phrase from his old hero, the creator of the New Deal, Franklin D. Roosevelt:

> You and I have a rendezvous with destiny. We will preserve for our children this, the last best hope of man on earth, or we will sentence them to take the last step into a thousand years of darkness.

That theme of *choice* was, of course, a slogan calculated not so much to recruit Democrats to the Republican Party as to call upon Republicans to turn from the moderate leadership and embrace full-blooded conservatism. Not the least of the consequences of the 1964 Goldwater adventure was that it defined the distinction so that the choice was not between Republicans and Democrats, parties characterized by the quarrels of the distant past, but between conservatism and liberalism. From 1964 on, the contest was between two ideologies whose differences related to the recent past, the present, and the future.

Since 1962, when he handed over the general running of Young Americans for Freedom to David Jones, Richard Viguerie had been using first card files and then computers to send letters to prospects who, because of their previous contributions to conservative candidates or organizations, were likely contributors to the conservative cause. ("I'm not sure we would have called it a conservative movement at that point," he recalls.) Even before Goldwater's defeat, Viguerie had a brain wave. He went to the office of the clerk of the House of Representatives on Capitol Hill, where by law the name of anyone who had contributed more than $50 to a political campaign was filed, and started copying down names by hand. In January he decided to do the job properly. He formed a company, hired half a dozen women to copy the names, gave the names to a computer firm, and said, "Put 'em on a computer for me." At the time he knew so little about the technology that when, a few weeks later, the first batch of names came back, he didn't know what to expect. "I remember very clearly unrolling the first twenty or thirty feet of tape, and I looked at the fellow, and said, 'Where are my names?' That just shows the level of my sophistication at that time. Commercial organizations had started doing direct mail, but there was really no one doing ideological direct mail, left or right. I just started doing computer letters. I learned by doing it. There was nobody to teach me."[38]

He learned well. In the early 1960s, Marvin Liebman kept the names of contributors to Young Americans for Freedom on three-by-five cards. No less an authority than William Rusher believes that "the mailing lists accumulated during the Goldwater campaign were the foundation of all subsequent organized political activity on the part of American conservatives."

Altogether, Goldwater's campaign staff mailed more than fifteen million fund-raising appeals and raised $5.8 million at an estimated cost of just over $1 million. Goldwater received 380,000 responses with contributions under $100 each. In 1968, Richard Viguerie raised $6 million through direct mail for George Wallace's presidential campaign; that amounted to 76 percent of the Wallace campaign's budget. In 1972, Viguerie's company, RAVCO, declined to work for the liberal Democratic candidate, George McGovern. McGovern went to another direct mail company, which raised $15 million for him at a cost of $4.5 million. Direct mail fund raising is extremely profitable, and Viguerie has made a fortune by using the technique for commercial advertising as well as for religious and other ideological purposes.[39] In 1975, for example, Viguerie's company raised $5.8 million for the National Rifle Association at a cost of $3.2 million, and an NRA spokesman said the organization was quite content. On the other hand, in 1974 Viguerie raised money for Americans for Effective Law Enforcement, a law-and-order lobby based in Evanston, Illinois. Viguerie warned the group's executive director, Frank Carrington, that he would "barely break even," and in the end RAVCO raised $202,000 at a cost of $198,000. Carrington, disillusioned, concluded he was just "trading dollars." In 1976 RAVCO began direct mail fund raising for another group, Bibles for the World, which distributes Bibles in Asia. A year later, the solicitation had raised just over $802,000 at a cost of $889,000, or 112 percent of the sum raised.

A quiet, thoughtful man, deeply involved in his family, Viguerie finds his favorite relaxation in playing golf (he plans meticulously a golfing vacation in Scotland most summers.) He makes a great deal of money out of direct mail fund raising. But his chief motivation is ideological. In 1972 existing conservative organizations raised about $250,000 for congressional campaigns. By 1976 New Right political action committees, most of them using Viguerie as their direct mail fund raiser, collected $5.6 million. By 1979 Viguerie had moved to Georgetown, home of the Washington political elite, while the Richard A. Viguerie Company's head offices moved to an elegant modern office building on the edge of a lake in the Virginia suburbs, where two big mainframe computers held the names and addresses of more than 10 percent of the U.S. population on more than three thousand reels of magnetic tape. High-speed printers bombard carefully selected targets with highly emotional appeals, many of them relying heavily on fear and deliberately calculated to arouse the anger of potential donors. It was not long before Viguerie had competitors, including two former employees, one of them Bruce W. Eberle, whose firm is said to have raised more money for Ronald Reagan in 1976 than had ever been raised for any candidate, though the $6 million Viguerie raised for Jesse Helms to be elected senator from North Carolina would also take some beating for a state race.

Not only was, and is, Richard Viguerie intensely ideological, a man who really cares about the dangers of abortion, pornography, and other scourges that he attributes to liberal philosophy; he worked closely with a tight group of conservative organizers, including Paul Weyrich of the Committee for the Survival of a Free Congress, Howard Phillips of the Conservative Caucus, and the late John Terry Dolan of the National Political Action Committee. The ability of these groups, coordinating efforts with Viguerie and other direct mail fund raisers, to collect large sums of money for conservative causes resulted from the application of a new technology to the new legal framework for campaign finance. (This was set up by the Federal Electoral Campaign legislation of 1971 and 1974.[40]) They called themselves the New Right. Their rise was a direct consequence of Viguerie's perception that the Goldwater campaign showed there was money out there if you could scare or cajole it out of troubled conservatives.

So great was the response Goldwater aroused, so fervent the spontaneous support, that the question arises why the conservative triumph, which finally arrived with Ronald Reagan at its head sixteen long years later, did not come sooner. There were in fact three moments of opportunity for the conservatives in national electoral politics, not one. Goldwater failed to take full advantage of the first. Richard Nixon threw away a second. "He either fears his fate too much, or his deserts are small, Who will not put it to the touch, to win or lose it all."[41] Goldwater's political deserts were perhaps after all too limited. Richard Nixon feared his fate too much, and in the desperate intensity of his wish to make assurance doubly sure, he was caught cheating in so abjectly corrupt a way that the triumph of conservatism was delayed again by the philosophy's association with this unworthy prophet. In the immediate aftermath of the Goldwater debacle in November 1964, it was Ayn Rand who got it right. "It was earlier than you think," she said, "not later."[42]

IN 1964, to revisit the appropriate Old Testament metaphor, the conservatives did pass through the Red Sea out of Egypt. Before reaching the Promised Land, however, they still had to endure sixteen years in the wilderness. First came the years of national trauma, almost, it seemed at times, like a collective national breakdown, between 1965 and 1968. In retrospect, those years helped to convert tens of millions of Americans to the conservative creed. But at the time it looked as if everything conservatives held dear was being torn to shreds. Abroad, the nation experienced frustration, humiliation, and eventually defeat in Southeast Asia, and as a consequence the prestige America had earned by a generation of economic and military success wavered. At home, the cities were full of rioters, and raucous voices challenged every cherished relationship and hallowed belief. Many conservatives in those years must have asked themselves, as Goldwater's own friend and campaign manager, Stephen Shadegg, did in a 1965 book, "Was his nomination the mistake which subsequent events seem to indicate? Is conservatism dead, outmoded, no longer useful?"[43] Another of Goldwater's aides, sharp in his criticism of Shadegg in other respects, expressed an almost identical thought: conservatism, he wrote, "that weary and not terribly meaningful word."

The midterm elections of 1966 were heartening. By and large Republicans had supported the Vietnam War. Certainly they had opposed those on the left of the Democratic Party who had denounced it. But by 1966 the war was unpopular. Lyndon Johnson was unpopular. The Great Society programs no longer seemed to offer something for almost every section of the electorate, as they had when Johnson first announced them. Rather, the administration's inability to deliver on its grandiloquent promises began to call into question the very welfare liberal policies that had elected it. The Democrats were visibly divided; they were becoming discredited.

On the surface, the tide still seemed to be flowing strongly in the liberal direction in the Kennedy and Johnson years. In reality, the currents were eddying and swirling as they do when the ebb is about to begin. The very years that saw the culmination of the liberal consensus, working itself out in its most characteristic actions — legislative monuments like the Civil Rights and Voting Rights Acts, the introduction of Medicare and Medicaid, and the participatory political action of the Great Society social programs — also saw the beginnings of the reaction. To a remarkable extent, the historical processes that created a new conservative consensus, or at least made it possible, were *reactive*.

The most fundamental turning point of all came in the field of civil rights, between Martin Luther King's great speech at the March on Washington in 1963 and his murder in 1968. As long as the civil rights movement demanded constitutional and legal equality for blacks in the South, it was working with the American grain. Even the majority of white Southerners found it hard to maintain that equality before the law could be denied forever to black citizens. Overt defenders of segregation, whether erudite, like John C. Satterfield, the Georgia segregationist who was president of the American Bar Association from 1961 to 1962, or crudely racist, like the Klansmen and night riding thugs in small Southern towns, became marginal in the face of this massive national consensus that the time to end legal segregation had come.

As soon, however, as black leaders — at this point the term "civil rights leaders" becomes a euphemism — began to demand not juridical equality, but substantial equality of economic condition for blacks outside the South, as they did from 1965 onward, they were asking for something for which there was in fact no national consensus. Go so far, said tens of millions of Americans, and especially tens of millions of working-class Americans, and we are on your side. Go further, use the power we have given the government with our votes to give others an unfair advantage over us, and you will have us to reckon with.

To achieve equality of condition for blacks would have been difficult with the best will in the world. It would inevitably imply competition — for jobs, for homes, for status — with other groups, almost equally disadvantaged and at least as sure that they were deserving. Members of these other groups would not give up their jobs or their schools without resentment and resistance. Moreover, in practice the chance of achieving *de facto* equality within a period measured in decades rather than centuries could be contemplated only through compensatory action, and by the government, and probably the federal government, at that. President Johnson in his speech at Howard University, on June 4, 1965, committed his administration to the effort to achieve equality for black people; by implication, he committed it to special help for black people to compensate for the damage done to them and to the structure of black families and the black community by slavery and oppression. From 1964 on, there were riots in hundreds of cities all over the country. While most of the rioters were black, and the great majority of the victims were black too, this wave of violence created a "white backlash" of indignation and anger not only against black rioters, but also against Democrats and liberals who seemed to tolerate if not to encourage lawlessness.

If the efforts of the Executive Branch of the federal government produced an angry reaction from many ordinary white people, in Northern cities as much as in the South, the efforts of the federal courts to give effect to the 1954 *Brown* decision, outlawing segregation in education, was even more vehement. By 1974, when mildly violent resistance to school busing erupted even in supposedly liberal Boston, home of the abolitionists, the Kennedys, and the Harvard liberal community, something vital had changed. Something similar was happening in Canarsie, a working-class section of New York City; in South Philadelphia; on the near West Side in Chicago and in Cicero, Illinois; in Detroit. It was not just that blacks seemed more aggressive, that black crime was increasing and seemed to be protected by liberal legislation and court decisions. There was a physical pressure, too, as blacks and other minorities blockbusted one stable working-class neighborhood after another. A new majority was forming. It opposed compensatory social action. It suspected that government social programs for blacks and other disadvantaged groups made things worse, not better. And it resented the arrogance of those who wanted to "engineer" a better society, sometimes at the expense of others, and so often seemed to make bad worse.

Although efforts have been made to portray the Vietcong's Tet offensive in the spring of 1968 as a military defeat for the Vietnamese communists, it was in strategic reality a decisive blow to American policy in Southeast Asia, and for a simple reason. However many casualties the Viet Cong sustained, after Tet large numbers of Americans turned against the war. It was in acknowledgment of that reality that Lyndon Johnson abdicated the presidency a few weeks later. From that point on, polls showed a growing majority of Americans "against the war." This negative majority, however, concealed a vital asymmetry. Some Americans, a small minority, had come to believe that the war, perhaps any war, certainly one against a Third World nation, was wrong in itself. A far larger group, swelling the size of the overall "against the war" number in the polls, had merely decided pragmatically that this particular war could not be won.

Consequently, to send American young men to kill and be killed in it was wasteful and foolish. These two schools, the moralist and the pragmatic, came together and made common cause tactically on the narrow issue of whether the war should be fought on to victory at any cost. But on every other issue, and in particular in their attitude to American motives for getting into the war and the justification for it, they were fundamentally in disagreement. What was more, many of those who believed pragmatically that the war could not be won deeply disliked and resented those who contended that it was morally wrong. A new majority was forming. Its patriotism was affronted by those who questioned American motives and morality. It yearned for new fields, where American idealism could be vindicated by victorious military action. And it seethed with anger against moralists, pacifists, and defeatists, all the more so because many of the new majority had — for pragmatic reasons — joined the informal coalition against the war, but bitterly resented the company they found themselves in.

In those same years of the mid-1960s, heady for some and terrifying for others, the Oedipal conflict between generations boiled over into the counterculture. It was not just the images, soon to become clichés, the film clips and soundbites, the draft cards burned, the bras thrown away, upper-middle-class students playing at revolution, and adolescents claiming to be the people their parents warned them against. There was an authentic and widespread reaction against the complacent conformism, rigid authoritarianism, and narrow rationalism of the organizations — corporations, military services, universities — that controlled Americans' lives as the 1950s ended. Some honest thought, some talent, went into the resulting rebellion of the young. But there was also much self-advertisement, much frivolity, much guttersnipery, and not a little bullying. The threat to society was not in truth great, nor was it prolonged. By the middle 1970s, the campuses were quiet and the students, intent on qualifying themselves for jobs, as good as gold.[44]

The great upheaval had achieved little of its own deeply confused and contradictory agenda. But it had provoked a reaction that was, from the point of view of the adherents of the counterculture, catastrophic. In the citizenry as a whole it provoked a mixture of fear, anger, and contempt, even if many citizens were secretly not a little attracted by the thought of more sex, less puritanism, and an occasional toke of marijuana. The campus revolt had a special effect on the unfortunate group that had borne the brunt of the campus rebels' scorn, their pranks and their occasional violence: the professors. The academic world divided. Some floated off into a world of ineffectual theoretical Marxism or post-Marxism. A crucial group, numbering many who had thought of themselves as the staunchest of liberals, turned to a new search, this time not for social reform but for stability and a new defense of nationalism. These were the intellectuals who came to be called the "neoconservatives." They were to have a disproportionate influence on the evolution of American conservatism.

Another cause that achieved startling and far more lasting momentum by the end of the 1960s was the women's movement. It too evoked an equal and opposite reaction. Modeled at first to some extent in its rhetoric on civil rights and antiwar activities, the women's movement proved far more durable. In the end, it has transformed American life even more than the civil rights revolution. But in the short term the women's movement added to the turmoil that made many turn to conservative ideas. On one crucial issue for feminists, abortion, the pro-choice movement ran head-on into a pro-life movement, just as passionate, just as sure of its rightness, and at least as willing to shock and disturb people to make its point. The full story of the abortion conflict and its effect on the spreading acceptance of conservative ideas belongs to the 1970s, and will be treated later. It was, however, one of the main areas where reaction against the perceived excesses of "the Sixties," and the liberal consensus associated with that decade, prepared the ground for the conservative advance in the 1970s. Together with the challenge to racial patterns of subordination, the perceived threat to the traditional American family, whether it took the form of abortion, of advocacy of lesbian and gay rights, new theories of childrearing, or simply a new permissiveness, a new assertiveness on the part of women in relation to men, was *the* major cause of the shift of values toward conservatism.

The structure of what had once been one-party politics in the South was being redesigned from top to bottom by the consequences of the civil rights revolution, the Black Power movement (which surfaced in 1966), and the Voting Rights Act of the previous year.

The result was that in 1966 a Republican Party that had looked close to inanition, if not extinction, suddenly sprang up, Lazarus-like, from its bier. Republicans gained forty-seven seats in the House and three in the Senate; they won eight new governorships, tipping the balance from thirty-three to seventeen, or virtually two-to-one in favor of Democrats before the election, to parity. It is true that this was not, on the surface, specifically a *conservative* victory. Ronald Reagan was elected governor of California by almost a million votes, and Governor John Rhodes of Ohio and Senator John Tower of Texas, both strong conservatives, were both easily reelected. But moderate Republicans like Charles H. Percy, elected to the Senate from Illinois, and George Romney, reelected governor of Michigan, did just as well. In Massachusetts, Edward Brooke was the first black man to be elected to the United States Senate since Reconstruction, and he was a Republican. The party doubled the tally of its House seats in the South, from fourteen to twenty-eight. Republican governors were elected in Arkansas (Winthrop Rockefeller), Florida (Claude R. Kirk), and Maryland (Spiro Agnew). In Georgia, deepest of Democratic territory, Howard (Bo) Callaway won a plurality of the votes, but because under Georgia law he failed to win a majority, the election was thrown into the legislature, which chose the segregationist Democratic restaurant owner Lester Maddox.[45] In most of these states, a Republican governor would have been, even half a dozen years earlier, a chimera. Yet it was noticeable that overtly racist or "backlash" candidates, such as Mahoney in Maryland, whose campaign slogan was "Your home is your castle — protect it!" did not flourish. The meaning of 1966 was not that the Republican Party had been captured by conservatism, still less by extremism; it was that the Republican Party was now turning away from the "me-too" policies it had followed since the New Deal. It might still be groping for a coherent philosophy. But it was establishing itself firmly as a serious competitor to the Democrats, and that on a fully national basis, in the South and East almost as much as in the Middle West and the West.

One of the big winners of 1966 was Richard Nixon, even though he was elected to no office that year. Campaigning tirelessly for Republican candidates of all ideological stripes and all over the country, he quieted the questions raised about his character and his political appeal by the unhappy 1962 California governorship race. When, four years after the worst slough of despond, he entered the White House at last, it was admittedly as a Republican centrist, rather than as a full-blooded conservative. But his administration already gave out a more rousing tone than the subdued harmonies of the Eisenhower administration, in which he had served, almost on sufferance, as vice president. From a conservative point of view, of course, the foreign policy mapped out by Nixon and his national security adviser, Henry Kissinger, was very far from perfect; while as long as Kissinger's fellow Harvard professor, Daniel Patrick Moynihan, was bemusing the president with the sorcery of his talk about "Tory men and Whig measures" in imitation of Benjamin Disraeli, domestic policy was even further from the all-American conservative ideal.

Yet in important ways Nixon's victory in 1968, and Nixon's strategy in the White House, marked a sharp and, for conservatives, a heartily welcome break with the "me-too," "yes-but" school of Republicanism of the years of frustration and apology. Conservatives might dislike the element of retreat in the Nixon Doctrine, which meant getting America's allies to fight a bigger share of her wars, and so represented a retreat of American power.[46] On the other hand, there were welcome echoes of an isolationist determination not to be at the beck and call of every last foreigner about the doctrine. Conservatives certainly did dislike the Nixon-Kissinger emphasis on *détente*. But at least the odd couple in the White House did seem to want to assert American determination to defend American interests. Even in the impenetrable discussions of strategic weapons limitation, there was a welcome undertone of confrontation beneath the surface of diplomacy.

It was good for conservatives to see a Republican president speak with homespun frankness to the Soviet Union. It was better still to see an American president in China, always dear to conservative hearts as the place where there would one day be the most souls to save and the most business to be done. On balance, the Nixon-Kissinger foreign policy was worrying for conservatives. The years of agony and frustration in Southeast Asia saw an ominous advance for the forces of communism and socialism in places as far apart as Chile, Italy, the Middle East, and various parts of Africa. The time had not yet come for the collectivist tide to turn; but at least with Nixon in the White House there need be no doubt about the essential commitment of the United States to resistance.

Domestically, again, the Nixon administration, from a conservative point of view, was equally imperfect. Yet there were encouraging developments. After the abandonment of the Moynihan Family Income Plan in 1971, Nixon broke decisively with the essence of the liberal domestic policies of the Democratic years, indeed with the "liberal consensus," which had ruled almost as much under Eisenhower as under Truman, Kennedy, and Johnson. The search for the Great Society was abandoned. No longer was the power of the federal government to be exerted without stint to seek equality for black Americans and other minorities. The pulse of enforcement of the courts' decisions on school segregation, to take a salient example, slowed almost to coma level. The touted New Federalism was not very effective in braking the relentless growth of federal expenditure on welfare and entitlement programs. Still, it was plainly meant to put an end to more than thirty years of steady accretion of revenue and power by the federal government. Moreover, it clearly ushered in a shift in the beneficiaries of government largesse, from the poor to the middle class. At least there was an end to what conservatives saw as the wanton outrage of federal subsidies for radical "community action" programs.

Even more important, Nixon's victory in 1968 was achieved by a conscious "Southern strategy." Already, by the beginning of that tumultuous year, the hard-line conservatives, the remnant of those who had gone down to defeat with Barry Goldwater in 1964, were for Reagan, and nowhere was that more true than among the growing ranks of the Republicans in the Deep South. A small clutch of Southern Republican state chairmen, led by Harry Dent, the party chairman in South Carolina, Clark Reed of Mississippi, and Bill Murfin of Florida (they called themselves the Greenville group, after Reed's home town), while attracted by Reagan, tried to deliver the Southern delegations to the Miami Beach convention to Nixon.[47] To some extent, they consciously played off Reagan and Nixon against each another. Only by making the South vital for whoever wanted to win the Republican nomination, they believed, could they help the South gain the influence it needed and they sought.

This is not the place to follow the byzantine twists of their political maneuvers, but the first decisive meeting had been at the Marriott motel in Atlanta on May 31 and June 1. In Atlanta Nixon realized that Harry Dent's friend Senator Strom Thurmond could help him cope with both dangers. In Miami, as enthusiasm for Ronald Reagan spread round the Southern delegations along the beach like summer lightning, Thurmond was the man who kept the Southerners in line. A tape recording of Nixon's meeting with the delegates from seven Southern states and the District of Columbia gives the flavor of the understanding that was reached there. At this level in politics agreements are not written down, not even necessarily expressed in words. Nixon left Miami Beach with the nomination because he was able to convince the Southern Republicans that he understood their fears (and the subtle, euphemistic language about "guidelines" and the like in which they expressed them). He convinced the Southerners that if he had slipped from the path of conservative righteousness by supporting a federal open-housing bill, for example, it was from purely, or impurely, tactical motives, not out of any lurking liberal conviction.

In order to win the presidency, Nixon had to satisfy the Southern Republicans that he was not seriously committed to civil rights; there was a serious risk that they would have gone for Reagan at the convention and that some of them might even have gone for Wallace in the fall if he had not done so. And as a consequence the Nixon administration did in fact show a good deal of sensitivity toward Southern pride and prejudice. Two of Nixon's more uncharacteristically inept political missteps in his first term, his unsuccessful nomination of two conservative Southern judges, Clement F. Haynsworth of South Carolina and G. Harrold Carswell of Georgia for the Supreme Court, can be explained only by his wish to reassure the Southern Republicans (and potential Southern Republican voters) that he was on their side. Their nomination had been "in tune with his overall Southern Strategy," commented a sympathetic biographer.[48] When the Senate rejected Carswell, Nixon lashed out at the "vicious assaults" and "hypocrisy" of the two judges' opponents and issued a press release, saying, "I understand the bitter feelings of millions of Americans who live in the South about the act of regional discrimination that took place in the Senate yesterday."

Of course, it can be argued that Nixon's understanding of the South was like General de Gaulle's understanding of the white Algerians: he told them he understood them — and then he betrayed them.[49] For it was during Nixon's first term that the desegregation of the Southern school systems took place.[50] But Nixon *did* understand the South. He had gone to law school at Duke, and Whittier, where he grew up, was largely peopled by migrants from the South. He did sympathize with Southern conservatives, and he did take great pains to avoid using the power of the federal government to bring unnecessary upheaval to their society or to hurt their sensibilities. Under Nixon, the Southernization of national politics took a giant step forward.

MOST EXCITING OF ALL, from a conservative standpoint, about the Nixon years was the possibility, itself a logical outgrowth and a goal of the Southern strategy, of a historic realignment of the party system. If conservative Southern Democrats in sufficient numbers could be persuaded to abandon their loyalty to the Democratic Party — a loyalty, after all, that harked back to the distant events of the War between the States and the Reconstruction era — the whole political scene would be transformed, and not just in the South, but nationally. The prospect opened up of achieving what conservatives had dreamed of for a generation and more: to split conservative Democrats away from their ill-assorted liberal bedfellows in the North and bring them home rejoicing into the bosom of a new, conservative-dominated Republican Party. That would achieve three grand strategic goals at one blow. It would pit conservatives against liberals, not Republicans against Democrats; and conservative strategists like William Rusher were forever pointing out that poll data proved that "conservative" was a far more popular label in America than "Republican."[51] More immediately alluring, it would rob the Democrats of the near-automatic majority they had enjoyed since the New Deal. In particular, it would strip away the conservative Democrats (former Dixiecrats, future Boll Weevils) who had delivered countless majorities on Capitol Hill for liberal Democratic policies. And lastly, it would shift the center of gravity within the Republican Party itself, endowing it with a permanent conservative majority for as far ahead as anyone could see. That would drive a stake at last through the heart of the hated moderate Eastern Republicans, whose domination of the party the conservatives had so bitterly resented for a generation.

For decades, political scientists like Walter Dean Burnham of the Massachusetts Institute of Technology have elaborated a theory of political realignment. They use the term to refer to those rare occasions in the history of American politics when whole blocks of voters have shifted their allegiance, not just to bring one party in and kick another out in Congress or the White House, but to change the very nature of the parties themselves. In this sense, the Civil War was a major realignment. So too was the 1912 presidential election, when the Republican Party split between its Progressive, or Bull Moose wing, and the regular wing. Franklin Roosevelt's victory in 1932, while arguably not strictly a realignment, because both the Democratic and Republican Parties remained intact, was so one-sided that it amounted to a realignment; whole groups of voters who had voted Republican for decades transferred their support to the Democrats.

The 1968 election was a dramatic, violent conflict. It revealed deep divisions in the Democratic Party, especially, but not only, over the war. Yet when the dust had settled, and Richard Nixon had moved into the White House, realignment had not taken place. What was needed for a true realignment, completing the effect of the Southern strategy successfully worked by Nixon and his operatives in the course of the 1968 campaign (and brilliantly rationalized in Kevin P. Phillips's best-selling political analysis, published in 1968, *The Emerging Republican Majority*), was for the conservative Southern Democrats to stampede out of the party whose liberal policies had troubled and often disgusted them for years, and switch their allegiance to the Republicans.

That realignment nearly happened, not as a construct puffed out of their pipes by professors of political science, but as the hardest actuality of practical politics. The realignment that nearly happened over the Christmas holidays in 1972–1973 is one of the great untold tales of American politics. It is astonishing, indeed it is a serious reflection on the competence with which the Congress is, or was then, covered by mainstream newspapers and by television, that although pieces of this enormously significant nonevent have been reported here and there, the story as a whole has never been told. There is no mystery about why this occurred. The realignment-that-nearly-happened was not reported for the same reason that it didn't happen. It was killed by the explosion of the Watergate affair. And it was knocked off front pages and nightly news bulletins by the unprecedented media and public interest in the unfolding of the Watergate investigation, especially from the time the Ervin committee opened hearings, on May 17, 1973. Within days, the whole country had become mesmerized by the story of "the President's men." Even sooner, shrewd Southern congressmen could see that the game would have to wait. There was no mileage in jumping the Democratic ship. And that was exactly what a substantial proportion of them were planning to do.

Nixon and Spiro Agnew won the 1972 election in a landslide. They got 60.7 percent of the popular vote, against 37.5 percent for George McGovern and Sargent Shriver; in the Electoral College, they won by 520 votes to 17. Normally, with such a one-sided vote in the presidential elections, the presidential candidate's coattails are long enough to elect a majority in the House of Representatives. But that did not happen. Republicans picked up only thirteen House seats, far below the thirty-nine they needed for control. In the Senate, they fared even worse. They won seventeen out of the thirty-three seats contested, but overall the number of Republicans in the House fell by two.

Conservative Democrats, however, and not only in the South, had been troubled by what was happening to their party. North and South they were bitterly angry about the Democratic Party's internal reforms, pushed through by the Mikulski and McGovern committees.[52] The reforms produced the Miami convention. Large numbers of "citizen politicians," many of them women, some of them black, and a high proportion of them young, displaced many party warriors who had fought the party's battles for decades and who expected as a matter of course to travel to the party's nominating convention. Labor union organizers, who had provided the men and the money for so many Democratic victories in the past, now found themselves rejected, sometimes abused. Men like the Steelworkers' Union president, I. W. Abel, to take a single example, who failed to be selected as a member of the Pennsylvania delegation, were deeply unhappy. The fall campaign did not heal the wounds of the preconvention campaign. Democratic professionals, especially those of conservative temperament or with conservative constituencies, detested what they saw as the amateurism of the campaign as much as they disliked its tone. The Vietnam War was the ostensible division between the conservative Democrats and the McGovernites; in truth that issue only served as a shibboleth distinguishing two wholly inimical political cultures.

The South was a special case. Many Southern Democrats deeply disliked the Civil Rights and Voting Rights Acts of 1964 and 1965. They disliked even more the way the renascent Southern Republicans were cashing in on their constituents' distaste for the policies of the national Democrats. When Congress met in December and began its organizing meetings, the Louisiana Democrat Joe D. Waggoner opened discussions with Republican leaders.[53] Many of his Democratic colleagues, he pointed out, had accumulated long years of seniority. That provided an additional motive for ranking Democrats to switch parties, or would have done if the necessary deals could be made. For the Democrats, under pressure from the Democratic Study Group, a reform caucus within the congressional Democratic Party, were proposing to abolish the automatic award of committee chairmanships by seniority, and the seniority system was duly abolished. Waggoner took the lead in asking the Republicans on what terms ranking Democrats would be welcomed into Republican ranks.

This was not a wholly new idea. As early as 1969 President Nixon told a Republican senator that he was involved in top-secret negotiations with some of the Southern Democrats. Harry Dent was the White House official who explored with several Southern Democrats whether they would either become Republicans (as Dent's political mentor Senator Strom Thurmond had already done) or at least commit themselves to vote with the Republicans to create a new conservative majority. Nevertheless, it was too unfamiliar an idea, and it involved deals that were too delicate, to be resolved during the official organizing process in December. The real negotiations took place after Christmas, in January, February, and March 1973. Altogether, a total of some forty Democrats entered into negotiations about becoming Republicans. There were several Western congressmen and several Democratic House members from the big cities, including Frank Annunzio from Chicago. Several of the Democrats who contemplated changing party were far from conservative in ideological terms; they were simply disgusted with what was happening in their party, and, in some cases, resentful that the Kennedy and Johnson administrations had done nothing, or less than nothing, for them politically. If forty of them had switched, that would have reduced the Democratic ranks from 243 to 203 and increased the Republican strength from 192 to 232, handing clear control to the Republicans. Even if in the end the number of defectors had been only twenty-six, that would have been enough to hand control of the House by a bare margin to the Republicans.[54]

Younger Republicans, especially the new members elected in November, were all in favor of the ranking Republicans standing down to hand their committee chairmanships or desirable assignments to converts from the Democratic ranks. They made the argument that it would be far better to have a part in a controlling majority than to have what crumbs might fall from a Democrat-controlled Congress. Older Republicans who had acquired substantial seniority were understandably not so keen to throw away what they had worked and waited for thirty years in some cases. The negotiations were complicated by the fact that half a dozen of these, including Silvio Conte of Massachusetts, threatened to cross the floor and become Democrats if the scheme went through. Nevertheless, there were detailed discussions between Waggoner and his friends and the Republican leadership. It went committee by committee; the ranking member in each case was asked whether he would be willing to stand aside and let a Democratic convert take over the chairmanship. In the end, half of those who were asked said they were willing to do just that. It was only the opening of the Ervin committee hearings, and the cumulative evidence of wrongdoing and hubris in the Nixon White House, that killed the truly dramatic possibility that control of the House of Representatives might have slipped to the minority party, not as a result of an election, but because of a split within the majority party.

Of course deals and crossing of the party line on Capitol Hill are one thing; shifts in voting loyalty patterns in the country are quite another. Still, the Southern strategy on Capitol Hill represented not just the split in the Democratic Party and the personal disillusion and even bitterness of individual Democratic politicians, but also profound shifts in the tectonic plates of American politics. Economic, industrial, and demographic change were working together to transform the country. They were tilting it toward the South and West. Economic vitality, population, and political influence were flowing away from the traditional power centers of the East and the Middle West toward what Kevin Phillips dubbed "the Sunbelt": Florida, Texas, the Southwest, above all Southern California. Great new forces had been unleashed, and most of them favored the conservatives, who were far better placed to surf on the demographic and geopolitical rollers.

That was the next and final stage of the conservative march to power. But the triumph that eventually happened under Reagan in 1980 might very well have happened in the second Nixon term if it had not been for the revelation, in the course of the Watergate affair, of the folly and arrogance of the Nixon White House. Eight years later, when the political issues, the mood of the country, and the temper of the conservatives themselves had all moved on, the realignment that did take place was in several respects different from what might have happened in 1973–1974. But the fact that Watergate seemed to conservatives to have bilked them of the fruits of victory was reason enough in their eyes for the fury they directed at the liberals whom they blamed for their disappointment.

6

Out of the Alcove

That isn't neoconservatism; that's just Irving.
— *Daniel Bell on Irving Kristol*

IN OCTOBER 1971 the mild-mannered social scientist Nathan Glazer, then a professor at Harvard, and previously best known for writing, with Daniel Patrick Moynihan, a groundbreaking study of the ethnic politics of New York City called *Beyond the Melting Pot*,[1] published an article in *Commentary* magazine called "On Being Deradicalized."[2] How, Glazer began by asking,

> does a radical — a mild radical, it is true, but still someone who felt closer to radical than to liberal writers and politicians in the late 1950s — end up by early 1970 a conservative, a mild conservative, but still closer to those who now call themselves conservatives than to those who call themselves liberals?

Not that he had ever been very far to the left, Glazer hastened to explain. He had never been an apologist for Soviet or Chinese communism. Still, he had demonstrated against nuclear deterrence. He had opposed NATO, disliked the big bureaucracies of federal, state, and city government, universities, and corporations. That, in the 1950s, was radicalism. Looking back on his earlier feelings from the beginning of the 1970s, Glazer conceded that his radicalism had always seemed a bit like conservatism in certain respects: the bias against government intervention; the suspicion that the massive structures created by New Deal and Cold War liberals to make the world over according to their theories would not work; the "allergy toward Communist oppression."

Still, Glazer recognized, he had changed too. He listed half a dozen reasons for the change. For a start, he had spent a year in Washington, early in the Kennedy administration, working on housing policy. It had taught him that reform was not as easy, nor perhaps as necessary, as he had supposed. In 1963 he had moved to Berkeley, in time to witness the student revolt there, which began in 1964. He found himself out of sympathy with the peace movement; "it was impossible for those of us who were alive and conscious during World War II and Korea to take the same easy path." He was dismayed by the racial turmoil of the late 1960s, by the "increasing radicalization, increasing vituperation, increasing disaffection with the country and its institutions." As he watched the agitators for racial change, it seemed to him he was being asked, "Do you hate [President] Johnson enough?. . . Do you hate the Southerners enough, or the Northern white middle classes, or the Northern white workers, or the Jewish schoolteachers of New York?" To his own surprise, he found himself detesting what the radical movements were doing to the university and to the country. Now, he felt, the main task for people like himself, who had always thought of themselves as intellectuals, liberals, radicals, must be to combat the new radicalism.

Glazer was not alone in this reaction. A little more than five years earlier, he had been one of a group of like-minded intellectuals, all former liberals if not former radicals, almost all of them originally from New York, and — not entirely coincidentally — most of them Jewish, who founded a journal called *The Public Interest*.[3] The first issue, in April 1965, contained an editorial jointly signed by Irving Kristol and Daniel Bell, as well as articles by Bell, Martin Diamond, Nathan Glazer, Daniel Patrick Moynihan, and Robert Nisbet. Ten years later, when the magazine published a special issue to celebrate simultaneously (with what might be called a characteristic lack of modesty) its own tenth and the Republic's two-hundredth birthday, the same six men were still contributors, and most of them were members of the publication committee, though they were joined as contributors by four other eminent social scientists, all long associated with the magazine: Samuel P. Huntington, Seymour Martin Lipset, James Q. Wilson, and Aaron Wildavsky.[4]

"When we began," wrote Moynihan almost plaintively in the Bicentennial issue, "almost all the editors and contributors would have described themselves as liberals. But before long we began to find ourselves depicted as conservatives." In time, he went on, a new label, "neoconservatives," was invented, in the first place to describe Moynihan himself, Nathan Glazer, and Daniel Bell, and later to describe a whole group of writers and thinkers. Their importance in the development of American conservatism can hardly be exaggerated.

It is true that not all of the friends who founded *The Public Interest* together, many of whom also contributed over the years to the New York monthly *Commentary*, published by the American Jewish Committee, can be called conservatives, neo- or otherwise. Senator Moynihan, after a decade of belaboring the crimes and follies of liberalism, and even taking his dissent to the point of serving Richard Nixon in the White House, subsequently proved, in three terms as senator from New York, to be the doughtiest of warriors for the Democratic legacy. Daniel Bell still maintains that he is a socialist, at least in his economic thinking. He resigned from *The Public Interest* in 1972 and supported McGovern that year. "When I read about neoconservatism," says Bell, "I think, 'That isn't neoconservatism; that's just Irving.'"[5] Irving, it goes without saying, is his friend Irving Kristol.

The original neoconservatives were never anything like a political party. They were a cross between a generation of New York intellectuals, a coterie, and a tendency. Their failings were not hard to see. They reflected comparatively small and sheltered corners of American life: essentially, the great elite graduate schools and a corner of the New York literary world. Although many of them claimed to be "scholars" or "social scientists," their real gifts, in most cases, were for a particular style of what used to be called "the higher journalism," more French in many ways than American, in which they slashed away at the errors of those who disagreed with them in great and sometimes cloudy realms of high policy and national destiny. They were frequently unjustifiably rude to their opponents. Often they contradicted each other and themselves. Still, they made the decisive breach in the defenses of the liberal orthodoxy, because they succeeded in stripping liberalism in the public mind of its monopoly of expertise.

Since 1933, indeed to some extent since 1913, however bitterly many conservative Americans may have resented the fact, it was generally assumed that the overwhelming consensus of experts in political science, economics, and the social sciences were of one mind: that the improvement of society could best be achieved by the intervention of government, which would carry out policies supplied by experts and intellectuals, in the main liberal. Now here were some of the most highly qualified and highly praised social scientists in America saying that it was not so. Government did not necessarily know what it was doing. Liberal experts often caused more harm than good. The lesson to be drawn from the turmoil of the 1960s was to rely less, not more, on government intervention. In short, the brightest suns of the liberal intelligentsia were suddenly preaching a conservative gospel.

In certain respects the neoconservatives had never been as "liberal" as they were painted or as they painted themselves. As Nathan Glazer saw, their radicalism had always been surprisingly close in many of its tenets to conservatism. Even when they had been "on the left," they had mostly been on the right-hand side of the left. The members of the core group had been, for a start, without exception strong anticommunists, even in their teens, which is to say in the late 1930s, when communist influence was stronger in America than at any time before or since. The heart of what later became the neoconservative crowd attended City College of New York.[6] Kristol, Bell, Lipset, and Glazer were all there together (as was Moynihan a couple of years later). The critic Alfred Kazin, who was also there, and whose sister is married to Bell, recalls that there were "two Nobel Prize-winners, or three" in his class, "not to mention personalities of some fame in later life, like Zero Mostel, Bernard Malamud, and Albert Wohlstetter." Another classmate was Irving Howe, the historian of Jewish immigration to New York, who recalled the influence of the brilliant philosophy teacher Morris Raphael Cohen, whose gentle manner did not prevent him from being constantly challenging. Howe considered that Cohen contributed to "a sense of intellectual life as a form of combat," which marked many of the City College products of the 1930s. This also had its origins, he added, "in the . . . talmudic disputatiousness" and in "the Russian political-intellectual world, which was ferocious."

Outside the classroom, the arena for displays of this disputatious spirit was in the alcoves, "kind of booths . . . adjoining the cafeteria," where students spent their lunch hours and time between classes. One alcove became by prescription the home of Orthodox Jews, another of Zionists; others were the turf respectively of the Catholic Newman Club, of the few blacks, and of the even fewer jocks. But the two alcoves that counted were Alcove Number 1, occupied by the anti-Stalinist socialists of every variety and sub-variety, and Alcove No. 2, the turf of the orthodox Stalinist communists.[7] (In those years, recollected a very different graduate, Bernard Cornfeld, the founder of the mushroom investment empire Investors Overseas Services, "all you needed was a telephone and a mimeograph machine, and you were in business as a party of the American Left!"[8]) The point is that, from their tenderest youth, the future neoconservatives — unlike many other ambitious and idealistic people of their generation, in New York and elsewhere — were always staunchly and even bitterly anticommunist. Moreover, however far to the left they may have been by the standards of other worlds — by those of Midwestern farmers, for example, or Harvard professors — by their own standards, and in their own world, they were not on the leftward end, and so were always, subjectively, if not on the right, at least in the center.

Irving Kristol has described his own trajectory by saying he had been edging away from liberalism for twenty years. Starting out as a Trotskyist in Alcove Number 1, he graduated in 1940 as a member of the Young People's Socialist League. Soon after graduation, however, he left YPSL and joined the Socialist Party. Then he went into the army, "which cured me of socialism. I decided that the proletariat was not my cup of tea, that one couldn't really build socialism with them."[9] Under the influence of the (liberal) Christian writer Reinhold Niebuhr and the critic Lionel Trilling, and somewhat later of the philosopher Leo Strauss, he started "to move slowly to the right." He joined the staff of *Commentary* and then became the editor of a London periodical, *Encounter*.

That phase of his life has been the subject of some controversy. Much later it became known that *Encounter*, and the organization that sponsored it, the American Congress for Cultural Freedom, were funded by the Central Intelligence Agency.[10] From a very early stage after the war Kristol became a conscious conservative. The two master themes of his conservatism were, on the one hand, a hatred of communism and, on the other, a passionate Americanism, or more specifically a fierce anti-anti-Americanism.[11] This denounced, as either inspired by communism or tending to give comfort to communism, any serious radical or liberal criticism of the *status quo* in that best of all possible countries, the United States.

Kristol even supported Senator Joseph McCarthy, regarded by almost all of his future comrades in neoconservative arms as a dangerous demagogue and a serious threat to civil liberties. "There is one thing that the American people know about Senator McCarthy," Kristol wrote in *Commentary* in March 1952; "he, like them, is unequivocally anti-Communist. About the spokesmen for American liberalism, they feel they know no such thing." The statement is not wholly unambiguous; a faint whiff of the weasel hangs over the qualifier "they *feel*." But the general import was plain enough. Most of the future neoconservatives, including Nathan Glazer and Norman Podhoretz, while criticizing McCarthy more or less strongly, were even at the time more concerned to attack his enemies than to condemn his excesses.

So, when other intellectuals of his acquaintance were shocked to discover that their cherished view of themselves as liberals was giving way before the indignation with which they observed the excesses of the peace movement, the civil rights movement, and the counterculture, Kristol had long gone before to the other shore. The group who founded *The Public Interest* represented the core of what later became the neoconservative movement. But there was no orthodoxy. Some, like Moynihan, ceased to be neoconservatives. Others, like Bell, had always stopped well short of identifying themselves as conservatives in the first place.

Nonetheless, beginning in the late 1960s, this group did develop a cluster of ideas and attitudes that were characteristic of what evolved into an identifiable neoconservative movement. It was to have an immense effect on the form American conservatism took in the 1970s and 1980s. Perhaps the absolutely fundamental neoconservative idea was the need to reassert American nationalism or patriotism or "Americanism" or "American exceptionalism": the idea that American society, however flawed, is not only essentially good but somehow morally superior to other societies.[12] This belief has been deeply ingrained in the United States since the Revolution. It was strong in the American colonies before the Revolution. It has origins in the puritanism of the English Revolution in the seventeenth century, and it has religious overtones, in the idea that it is the destiny of the United States to "redeem" a sinful world, as well as nationalist ones. Indeed, it has sometimes been called a "secular religion." It is found in every corner of the country geographically and in Americans of every ethnic origin and social class, even among many black Americans.

At the same time it is especially associated with immigration. The future neoconservatives mostly came from relatively recent immigrant stock. It is arguable, though certainly unproven, that such people in America feel a stronger need than those of longer American lineage to display their credentials as Americans; or rather, that those whose families came over on the Mayflower feel that there is nothing incompatible between deep patriotism and a propensity to shout about what needs to be changed.[13] "One of the longest journeys in the world," wrote Norman Podhoretz, "is the journey from Brooklyn to Manhattan."[14] The bright, ambitious young men who sharpened their wits on one another in Alcove Number 1 at CCNY came from Brownsville, where they grew up in "a half-English, half-Yiddish environment." Most of them, "including myself," Daniel Bell has written, "were ashamed of our parents."[15] Yet their parents, however unadjusted to American society, knew clearly who they were. They were Jews. *"Os mir seinem, seinem mir,"* says the old Yiddish song; *"Ober Jüden seinem mir"*[16] (What we are, we don't know / But Jews we are.) The agonizing dilemma of those of the younger generation growing up in the 1920s and 1930s — Kristol and Bell's generation — was that they knew no such thing. "Clearly perceived as Jews in the Gentile world," wrote Alexander Bloom, "they were less clear as to what that meant to them personally."[17]

A whole department of twentieth-century American literature has chronicled the fierce determination of these young men, whose families had fled across the ocean from the insults and hardships of Eastern Europe and then been dropped at the foot of the cliffs of American life, to scale the heights and "make it."[18] What has been less fully recorded is the deep gratitude they felt toward a society that had allowed at least the strongest and the most talented of them to make the climb. At first, in the 1930s, they were radicals. They burned to bring the ideas of the European left to bear on American life. They wanted to give a fairer share of its bounty to people like themselves, but also to others: Southern blacks, Mexican *braceros*, Slav factory workers. By the end of the war, with prosperity transforming many areas of American life, including theirs, their radicalism was already dropping away. In 1952, long before the shocks and frights brought by the excesses of the counterculture, *Partisan Review*, the voice of the more radical section of the New York Jewish intelligentsia, was already asserting, in a symposium called "Our Country and Our Culture," that "more and more writers" — read, in the main, "more and more New York Jewish writers" — "have ceased to think of themselves as rebels and exiles. They now believe that their values, if they are to be realized at all, must be realized in America and in relation to the actuality of American life."[19] At the same time, in the postwar years, these ex-rebels, these exiles-come-home, found, in the original sense, an alma mater, a nourishing mother: the ample breasts of the expanding university of the G.I. Bill, Cold War era.[20]

These were men who knew that they had climbed to higher places than they could have dreamed of in American society, partly by their own brains and energies, but partly too because American society, in the end, had not excluded them. No wonder they were affronted by the apparently heedless assaults on the icons of a fiercely held patriotism. Jewish Americans, contemplating the probability that if their families had remained in Europe instead of emigrating, they would have perished miserably in the Holocaust, might well have felt especially outraged by the apparent disloyalty of the young, as evidenced by such adolescent gestures as spelling the word "Amerika" and burning the American flag. "But for an accident of geography," exclaimed Irving Howe, "we might also be bars of soap." The fact that many of the most ungrateful young were, so to speak, their own children only made their behavior more unbearable.

At any rate, from this need to reassert not just conventional patriotism, but a philosophical quasi-religion of Americanism, it is easy to trace connections to most of the other characteristic ideas of the evolving neoconservative creed. The central doctrine of Americanism, Daniel Bell wrote, "was the idea of individual achievement free of class origins; of individual mobility, geographical and social; of equality of opportunity, and the acceptance of the risks of failure. The central image was the idea of individual enterprise." It is questionable whether Thomas Jefferson or George Washington, or even Henry Adams or Theodore Roosevelt, let alone Commodore Vanderbilt or John C. Calhoun, would have subscribed to that definition of the American creed; but that only goes to show how profoundly the United States was transformed by mass immigration.

Americanism was directly opposed, of course, to communism, in the works of New York intellectuals like the neoconservatives just as much as in the business lunch rhetoric of corporate conservatives. Long before they became neoconservatives, writers like the sociologist Seymour Martin Lipset placed a heavy emphasis on the pluralism of American society. All the contributors to the *New American Right*, the book edited by Bell that sought (unconvincingly) to explain McCarthyism in terms of "status politics," shared this emphasis. The argument was that in exceptional America, unlike in effete Europe or benighted Asia, the "people of plenty"[21] did not need to concern themselves with economic issues or with social class, but could afford to let their political preferences be determined by "status anxieties." "Status politics" is a concept that does not hold up well under close examination. In particular, it is not entirely easy to distinguish from class politics. But it was a key idea in the writings of the historian Richard Hofstadter[22] as well as of Seymour Martin Lipset.[23] Whatever its other defects, it had the merit of making even McCarthyism evidence of the advanced character of American society.

Another key idea was "the end of ideology."[24] Lipset himself subsequently admitted that "the end of ideology" was not far from being an ideology in itself, and it is not clear that it ever meant much more than the decline of socialism. It was a kind of recantation by intellectuals who had grown up in the socialist faith. If it did have any specific content, it was perhaps related to what Moynihan called "the professionalization of reform." In the bad old days of ideology, the argument ran, calls for reform came from the victims of the economic system or from their middle-class allies; now the agenda was being set by a "new class" of professional reformers: administrators, welfare workers, and the like. The implication was that such vicarious protest was somehow less authentic, even less honest, than the spontaneous eruption of the sons of toil.

The "new class" was another neoconservative concept. Like "status politics" or "the end of ideology," it tends to melt in the heat from the candle of analysis into an amorphous, self-contradictory rhetoric that says more about the neoconservatives' irritation with those who disagreed with them than about any specific idea. For what precisely was the sociological distinction between the "new class," defined by Irving Kristol in 1983 as consisting of "scientists, lawyers, city planners, social workers, educators, criminologists, sociologists, public health doctors, and so forth" and the neoconservatives themselves? What was Seymour Martin Lipset if not a sociologist, James Q. Wilson if not a criminologist? What were Samuel Huntington, a Harvard professor, or Kristol himself, the Henry Luce Professor of Urban Values at NYU, if not "educators"? Just as "status politics" were unheedingly invoked out of a desperate need to prove that the "class politics" of their socialist youth did not exist in exceptional America, and "the end of ideology" meant little more than "down with the socialist ideology I no longer subscribe to," so the "new class" seems to have consisted, for the neoconservatives, of "those intellectuals who do not agree with us."

Amorphous and ambiguous as so many of their favorite ideas turn out to be, the neoconservatives were nevertheless immensely influential. They achieved something that neither the motley journalists of the Buckley circle nor the formidable economists of the Chicago school could have done: they enabled conservatives to say that liberal ideas were no longer endorsed *even* by the very people — New York intellectuals, professors, and contributors to the upscale monthlies and quarterlies — who had been assumed, since the New Deal and indeed since the founding of *The New Republic* in 1910, to legitimate liberal orthodoxy.

Moreover, this defection of one key segment of the liberal intelligentsia was of its nature self-multiplying. Because of the authority and weight of the writing as well as the freshness of its ideas, the prestige of

The Public Interest increased. *Commentary*, under the editorship of Norman Podhoretz, picked up and promoted the *Public Interest* editors and their causes: Irving Kristol, after all, had worked for *Commentary* as an editor before leaving for London. It has been pointed out[25] that *Commentary* came out in neoconservative colors surprisingly long after the wave of political and cultural radicalism had subsided. Nevertheless over the winter of 1970–1971 Podhoretz published in *Commentary* a whole series of articles lambasting the New Left, the counterculture, the women's movement, the environmental movement, and many aspects of liberalism, especially upper-middle-class liberalism. By March 1971, in an editorial headlined, "Come On In, the Water's Fine," even *National Review* welcomed *Commentary* as a surprising but useful recruit to the propagation of the conservative cause.

In 1968 Kristol began to write a column called "Books & Ideas" for *Fortune* magazine.[26] And in 1972 he joined the Board of Contributors of the *Wall Street Journal*. He soon began to use the wonderfully influential platform of its editorial page, read by almost every serious banker and corporate executive in America, to reach powerful people, not in the main much given to theoretical speculation, with his ideas. Finally, Kristol moved to the American Enterprise Institute in Washington. There he was able to place his protégés in many strategic corners of American intellectual, journalistic, and business life. In 1968 he had supported Humphrey for the nomination (the old pattern, since this placed him on the right of the left). But by March 1970 he was dining with President Nixon in the White House. The *New York Times* reported that discussion at the dinner, which took place on the day bombs set by New Left extremists exploded in three Manhattan office buildings, focused on the parallel between young middle-class Americans and nineteenth-century Russian revolutionaries and "between militant black nationalists here and Algerian revolutionaries." In 1972 Kristol endorsed Nixon and was invited to a white-tie party at the White House, along with John Connally, Bob Hope, Norman Vincent Peale, and Billy Graham. By the 1970s, in short, Kristol was a fully fledged conservative. His formidable energies and polemical skills were concentrated on counterattacking liberals, radicals, students, black activists, and other groups who had the temerity to call in question the exceptional moral superiority of American society.

Daniel Patrick Moynihan's conversion, if less lasting, was even more spectacular. He had worked for Governor Harriman in Albany in the 1950s and came to Washington as a dedicated supporter of the Kennedy

New Frontier, for which he worked as deputy assistant secretary of labor. In 1965 he became known overnight for the "Moynihan report," a paper he had written for circulation inside government. It drew upon social science (much of it by black academics like Dr. Kenneth Clark and E. Franklin Frazier) to suggest that the problems of the urban black poor stemmed from the collapse of the black family.[27] The paper also advocated a strategy for the civil rights movement, and for the government, then still seen as committed to some degree of alliance with that movement, which would target public expenditure to the family as opposed to the individual. The strategy was perhaps influenced by Moynihan's own experience of poverty as a child, itself the result of the breakup of his parents' marriage, and perhaps also by the Catholic Church's traditional emphasis on the family. Certainly it was written in the context of a moment of hesitation and perplexity for the civil rights movement, the liberal community generally, and the Johnson administration, the moment (signaled by the urban riots of the summer of 1964) when it became plain that economic equality for blacks in the North would be far harder to achieve than legal equality in the South.

Even more controversial, in the long run, was the policy of which Moynihan became a principal advocate within the Johnson administration, of compensatory assistance to minorities. This approach, Moynihan and others argued, was justified by the historic wrongs done to blacks in slavery and since. It was needed because without positive discrimination they could not hope to achieve equality in any reasonable period of time. Moreover, the Moynihan report specifically argued that the very term "equality" had come to mean something different for blacks than for whites. Where whites could ask for mere equality of opportunity, the experience of blacks had taught them that they must address the equality not just of individuals, but of groups. They must therefore demand, beyond equality of opportunity, the equality of results. Indeed, he quoted Nathan Glazer to this very effect.[28] These same ideas found their way into the speech, drafted at least in part by Moynihan,[29] that President Johnson gave at Howard University on Independence Day in 1965. "We seek," the president said in that solemn, incantatory tone, which led wits to say he was dictating to a stonemason, "not just equality as a right and a theory, but equality as a fact and a result."

That was the high point of the drive for compensatory policies and for positive discrimination, the twin excesses of 1960s liberalism that were to attract the neoconservatives' fiercest indignation. It is curious, but it is a demonstrated fact, that the clearest and most influential statements of those twin policies came from two of the future members of the publication committee of *The Public Interest*, two of the founding fathers of neoconservatism. Moreover, the Moynihan report ended in just the tone that neoconservatism was most to reproach the liberals for, by threatening that if the government did not act soon enough and effectively enough to produce equality of condition for blacks as a group, then "there will be no social peace in the United States for a generation."

WHETHER OR NOT "government action" could justifiably be singled out as the main cause, in most of the cities and some of the suburbs across the United States in the late 1960s resentment certainly boiled. Turf was fiercely disputed. Anger had surely arisen. Black rage boiled over in rioting in hundreds of cities. It began in Newark, New Jersey, in 1964. It reached a new peak of violence in Watts (south-central Los Angeles) in 1965. It culminated in the Detroit riot of 1967, when the president had to order in an airborne division, and it reached to within a dozen blocks of the White House and ripped through every major city in America after the murder of Dr. Martin Luther King in April of 1968.

White anger was less explosive, but at least as lethal. (Most of the casualties in, for example, Watts and Detroit were caused by white policemen shooting black citizens. Whatever justification can be advanced for police gunfire in these circumstances is silenced by the question: would police have fired as randomly as they did if they had been in white neighborhoods?) Civilian white anger boiled away, half-silent and sullen, through the second half of the 1960s. It could be seen in the support for Alabama governor George Wallace when he ran for the presidency in 1968. Wallace had started life as a Southern populist, pitching his appeal to deep-seated racial fears and hostilities. But in 1968 he realized that the whole country had been so shaken by black militancy that

> if the politicians get in the way in 1968, a lot of them are going to get run over by this average man in the street, this man in the textile mill, this man in the steel mill, this barber, the beautician, the policemen on the beat . . . and the little businessman.[30]

In early 1968 an anonymous Georgian, straightening up from under a truck he was fixing, gave vent to sentiments that were soon to be staples of a new conservatism, even if he expressed them in language that was then unusually frank.

> I don't intend to vote for anyone up in Washington again, and I'll tell ya why. When I get to thinking about how hard I work, and how damn greasy I get, and I start thinking about how much you-all take out of my paycheck for taxes and all, and I see those people setting on their porches spending my money, why, I get so damn mad I just say to myself, "I ain't never going to vote for them sons-of-bitches again!"[31]

Before 1964, most people in the North and West of the country would have typecast that as a typical Southern attitude. But in 1964, capitalizing on sympathy with his stand against desegregation in Alabama and on the publicity he won by his "stand in the schoolhouse door" to prevent black students from enrolling at the university the previous year, Wallace entered Democratic primary elections in states outside the South. In Wisconsin, he won 33.8 percent of the vote. In Indiana, 29.8 percent. In Maryland, no less than 42.8 percent.[32] Hundreds of thousands of voters of precisely the kind that Franklin D. Roosevelt and Harry Truman had counted on with little question, including blue-collar workers, many of them union members, in typical industrial cities like Milwaukee, Gary, South Bend, and Baltimore, had voted for a self-proclaimed Southern segregationist.[33]

In electoral terms, the significance of the Wallace vote in the spring of 1964 was concealed by the overwhelming margin of Lyndon Johnson's victory over Goldwater in the fall of that year. But Johnson was the incumbent president. He was a Southerner, strongly nationalist and anticommunist, and widely (though wrongly) perceived in the Senate as a conservative. Over the next four years, as riots flared in hundreds of cities, as students (seen in working-class circles as spoiled and privileged) seemed to trample on all the traditional values, insulting the flag, proudly proclaiming their unwillingness to fight for their country, and flaunting their contempt for the sexual decencies, tens of millions of ordinary working Americans all over the country — "the barber, the beautician" — shared at least some of that bitter disillusion with politicians in general and liberal politicians in particular which had inspired the 1964 primary vote for Wallace.

In February 1968 a slightly retooled Wallace, stripping his pitch of raw redneck rhetoric, declared for president. That year a reporter for *The Saturday Evening Post* reported on a visit to an idyllic small town in central Pennsylvania. In particular he talked to five Millersburg ladies and found they were all in fear of the "communist plot to destroy us." On pressing them to explain whether they believed in this threat as a clear and present danger, he was told, "Well, it is all part of the same thing. Crime, the streets being unsafe, strikes, the trouble with the colored, all this dope-taking, people leaving the churches. It is sort of a breakdown of our standards, the American way of life."

Now, there is nothing particularly surprising about finding this primal conservatism in a small town world. But two things were so surprising that they stood on their head the assumptions most journalists and politicians had made for thirty-five years. The first was that such feelings of bewildered anger at what was happening in their world were being expressed just as much in big cities as in small towns and suburbs. And the other was that they were expressed just as much, if not more, by people who had voted Democratic all their lives as by registered Republicans. The most dramatic way such people could express their anger and disillusion with the established politicians of both major parties was by voting for George Wallace, the antithesis of the Washington represented by both Eisenhower and Kennedy. Again and again in American history waves of populist rage had surged out of the hinterland, like fierce nomads on the march. George Wallace was one of the first leaders of a new populist insurgency, but unlike most of its predecessors, the new populism, though radical enough, was also recognizably conservative.

At first Wallace bumped along at about 13 percent in the polls. In July his poll standing began to climb. Senators, congressmen, Washington insiders, pollsters, and reporters all began to predict that Wallace would get fifty, even seventy votes in the Electoral College, and even perhaps force the election to be decided, for the first time in American history, by the House of Representatives.[34] By October Wallace had raised between $10 and 12 million, much of it from modest contributors. He claimed that he would win 170 votes in the Electoral College, and even the Nixon campaign was prepared to concede that he might win half as many as that. The *New York Times* thought he might be running ahead of Hubert Humphrey, the official Democratic candidate. George Wallace, in fact, riding on a whirlwind of rumors about the alienation of the voters in the South and in the great northern cities, had thoroughly spooked the political class in America. And he had done so with an appeal that was only in part racial, but wholly conservative.

In the event, it is true, Wallace faded. He shrank back into the position from which he had emerged in 1963, as an extremist Southern politician. He carried no state outside the Deep South, won only 13.5 percent of the popular vote, and only 10 percent of the vote outside the South. There were many reasons for that. His choice of General Curtis E. LeMay, who had offered to bomb North Vietnam "back to the Stone Age," was too strong political meat even for some of his potential supporters. His campaign was inept, and it was handicapped by the candidate's concern with his wife's poor health. Most significant of all, many of Wallace's populist and cryptically racist themes were appropriated by Nixon (and by his running mate, Spiro Agnew). It has been calculated[35] that two Wallace voters out of every three would have voted for Nixon if Wallace had not been running. The Wallace candidacy may therefore have served to conceal how much of the old Roosevelt coalition had already swung to a conservative position.

George Wallace was not quite finished by his poor showing in 1968. He ran again in 1972 and accumulated the third highest number of delegates to the Democratic convention, even though he was incapacitated and almost killed in an assassination attempt in mid-May. His disappearance from the field contributed to the decisive margin of President Nixon's reelection that fall. The ground was now clear for conservative Democrats and the new blue-collar conservatives in the Northern industrial regions to move to the Republican Party. As we have seen, had it not been for the Watergate scandal, which swept away President Nixon's credibility for all but his staunchest supporters by the summer of 1973, there might have been a decisive party realignment in that year.

It was plain that the Roosevelt coalition in electoral politics and the liberal consensus in the wider polity were over. What is still not plain is the exact nature of the shift that had occurred. It became the conventional wisdom to refer to the Wallace phenomenon as a "white backlash." Wallace and his supporters indignantly denied that his appeal was essentially to racism or racial fears. They attributed it to the general frustration and disgust of working-class and "Middle American" voters at the overweening claims of imperial liberalism, the arrogance of intellectuals (Wallace called them "pointy heads"), and the indiscipline of students. Some conservative commentators agreed with him. Wallace's surprisingly strong support in his presidential forays, however, was by no means the only evidence of a new mood among working-class voters, strongest in the very places where liberalism previously had counted on the most automatic and the most class-conscious support. In Cicero, Illinois, and Gary, Indiana, in Detroit and South Philadelphia, Democratic politicians detected a boiling anger under the political waters. Strangest of all, nowhere was this new working-class rebellion against the liberal orthodoxy angrier than in those twin heartlands of liberalism and the intelligentsia, Boston and New York.

One lunchtime, early in 1968, I ran into an acquaintance, Jason Epstein, who had founded *The New York Review of Books* five years earlier.[36] If I wanted to understand what was going on in American politics, he told me meaningfully, the key was to be found in a place called Ocean Hill–Brownsville. He explained that, among other things, the conflict over Ocean Hill–Brownsville's schools was important because it was driving a wedge between the blacks and the Jews. Nor was he entirely wrong.[37] Two years later, in a ninety-page introduction to the second edition of their classic *Beyond the Melting Pot*, Nathan Glazer and Daniel Patrick Moynihan, who were by then clearly on the other side of the bitter rift that had developed between the intellectuals gathered around *Commentary* magazine and the older-style liberals who wrote for Epstein's *New York Review*, came to exactly the same conclusion. They described how in New York City the blacks and some — not all — Puerto Ricans stood in liberal alliance with Manhattan, "and that means whites of high social and economic position, largely Jewish and white Anglo-Saxon, with a mixture of better-off Catholics." They were generally opposed, from a conservative position, by working-class and lower-middle-class Catholics, Irish, and Italian, in the other boroughs. In the middle, Jews were the "swing group."

> Perhaps the most important development in the current crisis is the shifting of middle- and working-class Jews, in large numbers, from one side to another, a move hastened by the referendum on the police Civilian Review Board in 1966, the school strike over decentralization in 1968, and rising black — and occasionally anti-Semitic — militancy . . . For the first time in New York City's history . . . racial conflict, which can also be viewed as ethnic conflict, became determinative for the city's politics.[38]

In the 1880s and 1890s and the early years of the twentieth century, as Jewish immigrants from Eastern and Central Europe poured into the United States, they gathered, largely voluntarily, in neighborhoods not wholly different from the imposed ghettoes they had left behind. There were Jewish ghettoes in Chicago and Philadelphia, in Boston and Newark and the East Bronx. But the biggest by far, and the site of the most fertile incubation of energy and talent, was Brooklyn, and particularly the central Brooklyn neighborhood known as Brownsville. The critic Alfred Kazin has described "Brownsville's ancestral stress on food, the Yiddish theater, the left-wing, right-wing arguments around the tables in Hoffman's cafeteria [and] the sidewalks jammed with political discussions on Pitkin Avenue."[39] Irving Howe, the socialist polymath who wrote the richest historical portrait of this vanished *World of Our Fathers*, locates the heart of Brownsville on Southern Boulevard.[40] Irving Kristol came from Brownsville. So did Daniel Bell. So did Nathan Glazer. From Brooklyn, "making it" might mean moving to a modest Long Island suburb, to New Jersey, to the Upper West Side, to Miami Beach or Cambridge or Beverly Hills, according to the degree and the nature of personal success. But the modest apartment houses, the synagogues, and yeshivas of Brownsville were the heartland, and it was precisely this homeland of the New York Jews, the "swing group" in the city's increasingly ethnic politics and dynamo of its media culture — with an influence over the nation, through newspapers, magazines, universities, television, and Hollywood that can hardly be exaggerated — which was to be the scene of a tragic ethnic confrontation in the critical year: 1968.

By the late 1960s, many of the apartment blocks in which devoted parents had brought up young men and women, sharpening their wits in the knowledge that they would fly away from them and from much in their way of life, were peeling and unsanitary. They were now largely inhabited by black newcomers, from Harlem or from the South. (Though many of these were as hard-working and affectionate as their predecessors, I have graphic memories of a night in 1967 patrolling there in a police cruiser. There was an emergency call to a shooting or a stabbing every hour or so, and most of both victims and perpetrators were black.) Between 1950 and 1965 the proportion of blacks and Puerto Ricans in Brooklyn rose from 9 percent to 29 percent. In the Ocean Hill–Brownsville neighborhoods, in the center of the borough, the concentration was far heavier. The success of the civil rights movement in the South had focused attention on the economic deprivation of black people; and in truth, as the sociologist Herman P. Miller demonstrated, black income had scarcely risen since the 1950s. An air of freedom, of excitement, and of faith in the efficacy of direct action was blowing in the outside world. Change could be watched on television even in the most crumbling rat-infested tenement in Brooklyn; yet, so it seemed to those who lived there, nothing was changing for them.

At the heart of black frustration in New York (and other great

Northern cities) was the differential in opportunities for employment. Middle-class black parents in particular clung to the traditional method by which newly arrived or disadvantaged groups in American society had always moved up and out into the wider society: education. Frustration focused on the inadequacies, and as it seemed to many angry black parents and teachers, the deliberately differential inadequacy, of public schools in black neighborhoods. In Harlem, fifty years after the Harlem Renaissance drew attention to the talents of black American men and women, only one young person graduated from the only high school, which was all black, and 85 percent of students in the intermediate school were more than two years behind the national average in reading. Black parents, in effect, refused to accept the view of teachers and administrators that their children were ineducable. They determined to try to do the job themselves.[41]

On the opening day of the school year in the fall of 1966 angry parents had boycotted one Harlem school, Intermediate School 201. The catchword of the day was community control, and the parents at I.S. 201 demanded that the school be either racially integrated (which meant busing) or handed over to them. The demand for community control of schools spread across the city. In Ocean Hill–Brownsville, black parents declared themselves the school board in District 17. At first the teachers' union (with a significant proportion of Jewish members) welcomed their initiative. But when the New York City Board of Education set up an experiment by which schools would be run by (largely black) local boards in three districts, including Ocean Hill–Brownsville, the teachers were worried. In the fall of 1967 they went on strike for a new contract.[42] Things went from bad to worse. In May 1968 the Ocean Hill–Brownsville board, black-controlled, ordered the involuntary transfer of thirteen teachers and six administrators. The union struck again. The Ford Foundation, led by McGeorge Bundy (Boston Brahmin and former national security adviser to Presidents Kennedy and Johnson), New York Governor Nelson Rockefeller, and New York Mayor John V. Lindsay, patrician liberal Republicans, favored "community control" in one form or another.[43] After three citywide strikes, marred by anger and racial bitterness, the courts stepped in and ended the community-control experiment.

The Ocean Hill–Brownsville affair inflicted permanent damage on the New York public school system, once the envy of the nation and indeed the world. (It did not escape notice that the upper and upper-middle classes, who supported experiments in community control, were in the habit of sending their own children to private schools.) It embittered race relations and political debate in New York City, once seen as a model of tolerance. It accelerated the alienation of many middle-class Jews from their traditional liberal loyalty.[44] More generally, it discredited activist liberalism, positive discrimination, community control, and all the other nostrums of the liberal consensus. In the process, it transformed many New Yorkers, once citizens of the most reliable liberal bastion in the country, into conservatives.

Ocean Hill–Brownsville was not the only community in New York City to be torn apart by the new mood of racial competition and confrontation. As recently as the 1930s, Canarsie had been a "sparsely settled community laid out in dispiriting flatlands, smoked over by the perpetual reek of fires in the vast refuse dump at its western end." To this unpromising promised land came Italian truck farmers and masons and Jewish tailors and teachers, cultivating neighborliness and the family values they respectively described as *amicizia* and *fraindlichkeit*. By the 1950s Canarsie was "Brooklyn's last frontier." The developers Harry and Sidney Waxman covered two hundred acres with forty blocks of Cape Cod, ranch-style, split-level, and row houses, selling for $13,000 each. By 1970 the population, still mostly Jewish and Italian, had more than doubled, to eighty thousand. Most of the Italians were working-class machinery operators; half of the Jewish families had a white-collar breadwinner, but their income, too, was modest.

Blacks began to move into Brooklyn in the 1940s, pushing out from neighborhood to neighborhood. The blockbusting of East Flatbush in the late 1960s created a stampede to Canarsie. And after the Jews and Italians began moving out of neighborhoods that blacks were moving into, there came the scouts of what Canarsie perceived as an invading army: the first black families looking for a Cape Cod or a split-level to raise their children in. Traditionally, the peoples of Europe saw the invaders from the East — Goths, Vandals, Huns, and the rest — as savage predators. Research has shown that, however ferocious they may have seemed when they appeared on the farmlands of earlier settlers, they too were victims, driven from farther east by hunger or by earlier waves of migrants, themselves driven by famine deep in Asia. So it was in Canarsie — and in countless other working-class neighborhoods in Chicago and Cleveland, Detroit and Philadelphia. People who were poor themselves, or at best were clinging insecurely to modest security, found themselves threatened by a wave of minority migrants worse off than themselves. "From where they stood," a social scientist commented, "the people of Canarsie thought *they* were the victims. The issue of race frightened them too immediately to permit the grace of compassion. They viewed the shifts in Brooklyn's racial complexion as an invasion by a hostile army. A Jewish community leader offered the image of menaced Israel and vowed, 'We ran once, but we've nowhere else to go. We're surrounded. The water is at our backs.'"[45]

It was not just blockbusting and the pressure of minorities on Italian or Jewish neighborhoods. They saw themselves as caught in a general squeeze, at home, at work. An Italian analyzed his own situation bitterly. "The average guy who makes $20,000 a year is basically coming out with the same amount as the guy on welfare . . . Middle income is a federal term to make people good before they pick their pockets." Jonathan Rieder's study is an anthology of desperation. White people in Canarsie used the most violent language to express how they felt "stretched to the limits of their endurance": they were "raped," "fucked up the ass," by rising utility rates, taxes, and busing. "It's all in danger," said one resident. "The house you always wanted is in danger, the kids are in danger, the neighborhood is in danger. It's all slipping away." "The middle classes," said another, "are the lost people." A Jewish carpenter who had voted for George McGovern in 1972 said, "I want to keep mine and fuck everyone else. Those niggers are the marauders of Brownsville. They ruined Brownsville, but I won't let them ruin Canarsie. I'll join a terror squad to keep them out." Another Democrat said, "This is a Warsaw ghetto mentality in Canarsie. It's an uprising like at Masada. When you can't do anything, when you're pushed to the wall, you fight back."[46]

Leader of the Canarsie resistance was Alan Erlichman, who had grown up in integrated Bensonhurst, playing ball and rhythm-and-blues with black friends. He considered that "Italians were the vanguard, Jews the laggards, in the movement toward backlash." He did not blame black people themselves. His fiercest anger was directed at the "injustice [that] holds us responsible for the inequities within the minority cultures." He laid the blame for that squarely on "the sanctimonious liberals, social planners, and suburbanites."[47]

In the early 1970s much emphasis was laid on the "ethnic" character of the new antiliberal mood. What was happening in Canarsie, for example, was largely described locally and reported elsewhere as the anger of the Jewish and Italian "communities" in that section of Brooklyn. In 1972 magazines and newspapers devoted many hundreds of thousands of column inches to analyses of the "ethnic vote." A voluble Catholic sociologist at the Catholic University in Washington, Monsignor Geno Baroni, seized on the use of the word "pigs," borrowed by student radicals from black street speech as slang for the police, to invent a new term: PIGS, meaning "Poles, Italians, Greeks, and Slavs."

The idea was carried forward by one of those slapdash, specious phenomena of the New York book-publishing world, a sort of neo-conservative answer to Charles Reich's *The Greening of America*, called *The Rise of the Unmeltable Ethnics*. Written by a Catholic academic of Slovakian ancestry named Michael Novak, it reported with considerable acuity and a mass of anecdote the new mood of anger of what he called "ethnics." The term itself was imprecise. Sometimes it seemed to include Irish Americans, at other times to exclude them. (It was strong on ethnic generalizations like "The Italians and the Slavs are no admirers of either the Irish or the Irish church."[48]) Novak started from the premise that "there is no such thing as *homo Americanus*. There is no single culture *here*." It is a dubious, even a meaningless proposition, if only because Novak made no attempt to define what he meant by a culture. Still more dubious was what Novak stuck together as the major premise for his argument: "three sets of figures." Seventy million Americans lived in families with incomes between $5,000 and $10,000 a year; there were seventy million descendants of immigrants from Ireland, Italy, Spain, Greece, Armenia, and the Slavic nations; and there were nearly fifty million Catholics in the country. From those three "facts," he argued, without ever actually saying so, that some fifty to seventy million "ethnics" were in revolt or, alternatively, on the "rise."

The truth was that many working-class Americans of every religious and ethnic background, Catholic, Jewish, and Protestant, of immigrant and of the oldest American stock, were by the late 1960s deeply worried by the social and political change of the past decade. They were turning away from "liberalism," and they were displaying a new hostility to black people and to those who seemed to take their part. But they were not doing so because they were "ethnics" or because they were Catholics. Still less were they doing so because they lived in ethnic neighborhoods in Northern cities. Something alike was happening in the South, in cities where Poles and Greeks, Slavs and Armenians, were rare, and in small towns and rural areas where Americans of such exotic ancestry were all but unknown.

Anxious (like so many of his neoconservative allies) to deny the existence of class differentiation in America, Novak, and many like him, saw a classic class phenomenon as an "ethnic" one. The phenomenon itself, unfortunately, was undeniable. It was painful. And it was of the greatest significance for the future of American politics. Tens of millions of working-class (or, if the C word offends you, "less well off," "lower middle," "ordinary," or "Middle") Americans, North and South, no longer saw the Roosevelt coalition as the natural political defender of their interests. Nor did this growing segment of the population accept the "liberal" philosophy of governmental activism on behalf of the disadvantaged as the proper rationale of political action. Many of them decided, sometimes disguising their shame at the decision by more or less ingenious rationalizations, that they no longer shared a basic community of interests with blacks and other members of minorities.

This titanic shift in the political mood of a decisive proportion of the population did not in itself constitute a conservative revolution. It made one inevitable. All that remained to be decided was who would organize the revolution, who would lead it, and how lasting it would be.

BROOKLYN'S ONCE tolerant middle classes seethed with rage. Jewish accountants remembered Masada. Italian truck drivers went to Madison Garden to hear Tony Imperiale cry out, "The blood of Roman gladiators runs in your veins."[49] And the city that perhaps in all America had the proudest attachment to the ideals of liberty was being torn apart by the same demons of resentment and rage as New York.

Boston was the home of abolitionism. It was in Boston churches and in Harvard's Memorial Hall that abolitionist orators worked up proper Bostonians to passionate commitment to an ethical politics that transcended their economic interests. In the 1950s Greater Boston was the intellectual metropolis of America. The Massachusetts Institute of Technology was in the forefront of the new computer science and of such key new intellectual techniques as econometrics and systems analysis. The Harvard Medical School and Massachusetts General Hospital were on the frontier of the new medicine. It was at Harvard and MIT that the new ideas about government, about national security and nuclear war, were generated and then brought down to Washington by Cambridge and Boston's favorite son, John F. Kennedy, and his escort of professors. As late as 1962 the youngest Kennedy brother, Edward M. Kennedy, polled 94 percent of the vote in Charlestown, the working-class, overwhelmingly Irish neighborhood where the Kennedys had first flourished under the granite monument to the defeat of the British at Bunker Hill in 1775.

Between 1940 and 1960, though, Boston's black population nearly tripled, from 24,000 to 63,000. By the middle of the sixties many working-class and middle-class white Bostonians were beginning to ask whether the Kennedys and their brand of liberalism had their interests sincerely at heart.[50] As early as November 1967, the mayor of Boston, Kevin White, the very model of a modern, Kennedy-style Boston Irish politician, came within twelve thousand votes of being beaten by the former school board member Louise Day Hicks. She had made herself immensely popular in the city by insisting that if schools in Boston were *de facto* segregated, this resulted solely from residential segregation, and that no one could do anything about that. The rising tensions were bottled up for some years by legal struggles over plans for integrating Boston schools by busing. But on May 10, 1975, Judge W. Arthur Garrity handed down a judgment that increased the number of students who would have to be bused from 14,900 to 25,000.[51] This number Louise Day Hicks and her organization, ROAR, which stood for Restore Our Alienated Rights, already regarded as intolerably too many.

When school opened in September, and the second phase of the busing plan was due to be implemented, there were scenes in Charlestown reminiscent of those which had shocked television audiences when Central High School in Little Rock, Arkansas, was desegregated in 1957. A sophomore hung outside the school a dummy with a cardboard sign saying, "Nigger, burn!" The crowd burned it, shouting, "Burn, nigger, burn," as if they were playing a lynch mob in a movie about Southern bigotry. When Senator Kennedy attempted to speak at a ROAR meeting outside City Hall, one of Mrs. Hicks's lieutenants introduced two supporters in chicken masks as "the white chicken, Senator Kennedy, and the black chicken, Senator Brooke." (Edward W. Brooke, Massachusetts' other senator, was an African American Republican.) Kennedy was pelted with tomatoes and eggs, then hit and kicked as he ran for safety inside City Hall. The senator's own staff warned him it would be unwise for him to attend the Bicentennial celebrations of the Battle of Bunker Hill. When the day of the ceremony came, the black students at Charlestown High School remained seated rather than say the words "one nation, under God, indivisible." A group of white students marched downtown, where they chanted "Niggers suck!" and "Bushboogies back to Africa." Six of them were arrested.

A few days later the students who had been arrested (and released) set out to lobby, or intimidate, Judge Garrity. As they crossed the plaza in front of City Hall, they fell into a confrontation that encapsulated the bizarre and tragic ironies implicit in the collapse of liberal attempts to abolish black inequality. Theodore Landsmark, a black lawyer wearing a three-piece suit, happened to be crossing the plaza to chair an equal-opportunities hearing. Born in Harlem, Landsmark (who had changed his name to that of a Jamaican slave in order to emphasize his solidarity with black people) had been educated, on scholarship, at St. Paul's School, Harvard, and Yale Law School. He had been a partner in one of the most prestigious Boston law firms, Hill and Barlow. As they saw Landsmark, the six white boys from Charlestown shouted, "There's a nigger! Get him!" Landsmark was not seriously hurt. But there was a painful symbolism in the fact that, in the mêlée, one of the white boys' kids tried to spear him with the staff of an American flag.

ONE OF THE neoconservatives' favorite concepts was the "law of unintended, or unanticipated, consequences."[52] They used it to warn against attempts on the part of government to transform society, arguing that such social engineering always produced unintended and unwelcome effects. But as the civil rights legislation and litigation of the 1960s began to work through the system, it produced a consequence, unheeded if not unintended, that was far from unwelcome to new converts to conservatism as well as to old conservatives: the discrediting of affirmative action.

In the middle 1960s, about the time of the passage of the Civil Rights Act in 1964 and the Johnson administration's initiation of its Great Society programs, black and other minority Americans were still greatly underrepresented in the professions.[53] In 1965, for example, 11 percent of the U.S. population was black, but only 2 percent of the lawyers were. Nor were professional schools making serious inroads into that imbalance. Only 1.3 percent of law school students in that year were black. Altogether, the law schools accredited by the American Bar Association had admitted a total of 434 black students, or only three each. (That came close to the tokenism indicated by a 1960s joke. "Certainly our school has an equal opportunities policy," the private school headmaster says to the gushing liberal mother. "Why, there he goes right now!") It was much the same with medicine. In 1961–1962, 78 percent of black medical students were in two all-black medical schools, Howard in Washington and Meharry in Nashville. As late as 1970 the proportion of physicians in the United States who were black was the same as in 1950: 2 percent.

School administrators and faculty, backed by trustees, felt this to be an inadequate response to black demands for equality. They were also afraid of litigation under civil rights legislation and of enforcement action by federal and state authorities. So professional schools began to adopt a variety of "special" admissions programs intended in one way or another to increase recruitment of blacks and other minority students. These programs generally favored Native American, Hispanic, and Asian students as well as African Americans. In practice, most of those admitted under them were black.

At the same time, for a number of reasons — among them rising prosperity, the G.I. Bill, the differential inflation of professional incomes — there was a sharp rise in the number of qualified white students applying to professional schools. In 1971, for example, seventy thousand students applied for the thirty-five thousand places available in all U.S. law schools. By the same period it was not unknown for Americans to seek medical qualifications in Western Europe, in Mexico, and even in Romania. The pressure on the better schools was correspondingly more intense.

In 1967, for example, there were 618 applicants for 150 places at the University of Washington Law School, in Seattle. Four years later there were 1,601 applicants for the same number of places. By 1973–1974 there were 2,464 applicants for a hundred places at the medical school at the University of California at Davis; the very next year that number had risen to 3,737. In 1970 and again in the following year a resident of the State of Washington, named Marco DeFunis, Jr., applied for admission to the University of Washington Law School.[54] On the second occasion he did well enough on his Law School Aptitude Test to put him in the top 7 percent nationally, though on the average of all his scores he did less well. He could have gone to the law school at the University of Oregon for the same fees as at Washington. But then he would have lost his part-time job with the Seattle Park Service, and his wife, a dental technician, might not have been able to find as good a job. DeFunis sued.[55] His case was a marginal one. If the University of Washington Law School had not operated a special admissions program, some white students who had been rejected might have been admitted; DeFunis might or might not have been one of them. Pending resolution of his suit, and on the order of the state court, the university admitted him. In 1974 — by which time DeFunis was within a few months of finishing law school — the United States Supreme Court declared his case "moot"; that is, because it no longer affected a real issue, the Court declined to adjudicate it.

By then a far more dangerous and difficult case, brought by a formidably determined litigant, was making its own way through the courts.

Since 1945 perhaps only the *Brown* case of 1954 and *Roe* v. *Wade* in 1973 had raised so many, so difficult, and such painful issues. Over twenty years later, they have not wholly been laid to rest. The Supreme Court itself has been unable to produce an entirely clear and coherent resolution of them. And powerful critics have dealt weighty blows of the ax to the roots of the decisions it did reach.[56] Nevertheless, the *Bakke* case is a watershed in the decline of liberal and the rise of conservative consensus in the United States.

When Allan Paul Bakke filed his suit, the consensus in the United States was probably that the positive discrimination of which he had been a victim, while perhaps unjust to him as an individual, was required in the interests of a larger justice, that of achieving "equality as a result" for minority groups. By the time the Supreme Court decided *Bakke*, that view was in eclipse.

Bakke was born in Minneapolis in 1940 to a family of Norwegian ancestry and modest means. His father was a mailman, his mother a teacher.[57] They moved to Florida, where Allan went to school. In 1962 he got his bachelor of science degree in engineering, with B+ to A- grades, at the University of Minnesota. Having helped to pay his way through school by joining the naval reserve, he served his four-year obligation as an officer in the marine corps and spent seven months in Vietnam as commander of an antiaircraft unit, rising to the rank of captain. On discharge he took a job with NASA as an engineer at the Ames Research Center, near the Stanford campus in Palo Alto, California. Because he had now decided he wanted to work in medical engineering, he also took premed courses at Stanford and San Jose State. By this stage he had developed what some witnesses called "an almost religious conviction" and others an "obsession." He concluded his application to one medical school with the emphatic words "I want to study medicine."

It was not easy to fulfill that honorable ambition. In 1972 he applied to the University of Southern California and Northwestern medical schools; both rejected him. In the next year he applied to eleven medical schools, again without success. He did, however, score high marks (468 out of 500) and created a very favorable impression at the University of California Medical School at Davis; the professor who interviewed him called him "a well-qualified candidate," though a little old, and "a very desirable applicant"; he formally recommended acceptance. Unfortunately, at this point Bakke's mother was dying of cancer, and his application was delayed. By the time his application was received, the scales had tilted against him. On July 1, 1973, having received no reply to an earlier letter from the chairman of the admissions committee, he wrote a second letter referring to the "quotas, open or covert, for racial minorities" at UC. "I realize," he explained, "that the rationale for these quotas is that they attempt to atone for past racial discrimination. But instituting a new racial bias, in favor of minorities, is not a just solution."

It seems, too, that he was encouraged — inadvertently or otherwise — to consider litigation by one of the admissions dean's own assistants. Bakke certainly became aware that the university not only practiced a discriminatory admissions system to favor minority applicants, but also kept five places a year for relatives of faculty, politicians, and influential local businessmen. It turned out that the medical school, in order to choose among the thousands of applicants for its hundred places, operated two separate admission processes. Eighty-four of the places were reserved for regular admission of nonminority students: in 1974 there were 3,104 applicants for these 84 places. The remaining 16 places were reserved for minorities, known euphemistically as "disadvantaged" students. In reality, these students were far from disadvantaged by the admissions procedure of this medical school: over the four years from 1971 through 1974, 11 percent of the applicants were from minorities, and they received 27 percent of the places in the school.[58]

In November 1973 Bakke complained formally to the federal Office of Civil Rights in San Francisco that he had been "the victim of racial discrimination," and on June 20, 1974, he filed suit against the university. *Bakke v. the Regents of the University of California* was not a class action but a private suit, which sought to compel the medical school to admit an individual. Bakke had written in early 1973 that "my first concern is to be allowed to study medicine . . . Challenging the concept of racial quotas is secondary." Nevertheless, he and his lawyer, Reynold Colvin, brought suit on the grounds that he had been discriminated against for reasons of race. They cited the fact that he had higher qualifications than those of the sixteen students admitted under the special minority admissions process. Colvin, though he liked to portray himself as a "little old country lawyer," was a former U.S. assistant district attorney. He had already won one case in federal court opposing racial quotas, to which, as a prominent member of the San Francisco Jewish community, he had a strong antipathy.[59]

In September 1976 the California Supreme Court (by reputation one of the most liberal in the country) upheld Bakke's claim by a six-to-one decision. It ruled that race could not be used as a criterion for admission and held that the "equal protection" clause of the Fourteenth Amendment applies equally to "any person," white or black.[60] It also ordered Bakke's admission, but that part of the order was stayed when the university, through its board of regents, appealed to the Supreme Court of the United States. The university was in an awkward position. It could not easily yield to the California court's decision without the risk of having its whole admissions procedure declared unconstitutional. It had argued in the California Supreme Court that "it is far more important for the university to obtain the most authoritative decision possible on the legality of its admissions procedure than to argue over whether Bakke would or would not have been admitted in the absence of its special admissions procedure."

The United States Supreme Court accepted the case in February 1977. It heard oral argument on October 12, 1977, when Reynold Colvin wasted much of the forty minutes he was given by the Court in reciting the facts, which were well-known to the justices. He was opposed, on behalf of the university, by no less a pillar of the liberal Establishment than Archibald Cox of the Harvard Law School, who had served as solicitor general (and therefore argued frequently in the Supreme Court) in the Kennedy administration. (It was his dismissal on President Nixon's orders as special Watergate prosecutor in what the press called the "Saturday night massacre" that touched off the wildest crisis of the whole Watergate affair.) Naturally he had the best of the oral argument. Yet the justices (a majority of them Nixon appointees) did not find *Bakke* easy to decide.

When, on June 28, after weeks of feverish speculation in Washington and in the legal community across the nation, Justice Lewis Powell rose to announce the Court's decisions, he began by saying truly that "we speak today with a notable lack of unanimity." The case, "intrinsically difficult," had received the justices' "most thoughtful attention over many months." And ... the Court had not been able to agree.

There were three questions before it. Should Allan Bakke be admitted to the medical school of the University of California at Davis? Was the medical school's special admissions procedure constitutional? And could race legally be a factor in a university's admissions procedure? The arguments, intrinsically difficult in any case, were complicated by the fact that Bakke had argued that the Davis quota procedure under which he had been rejected was illegal, first, under the Civil Rights Act of 1964, which says that no one should be discriminated against on grounds of race under any program receiving federal aid, and, second, that it denied Bakke the equal protection guaranteed by the Fourteenth Amendment.

Five out of the nine justices held that Bakke had no case under the Civil Rights Act, because that act made illegal only practices that would be prohibited by the Fourteenth Amendment's equal protection clause anyway. The remaining four justices found that Bakke *was* justified by the Civil Rights Act, and that they did not therefore have to consider the constitutional argument. One justice, Lewis Powell, took the position that the Constitution, through its equal protection clause, *does* prohibit quotas, *unless* a school can show that they were needed for reasons of compelling importance. Powell found that the university had not met that test. But he also found that race *may* be taken into account as one of several factors aimed at achieving a desirable diversity in a student body, and he cited the Harvard College admissions program as an example of how that could be done legally. So the Court had in effect divided into two groups of four justices each, with Powell in the middle. The Court affirmed the California court's order that Bakke must be admitted. But it reversed that court's prohibition against taking race into account. Both sides in the larger quarrel, therefore, could claim victory. Those — let us call them Great Society liberals — who believed in affirmative action to discriminate positively in favor of minorities could now claim that such policies were constitutional. Indeed, the opinion of the four justices — Brennan, White, Marshall, and Blackmun — who found that racial preference could be justified marked the first time that position had come so close to being affirmed by a majority of the Supreme Court. Those, on the other hand — let us call them conservatives plus neoconservatives — who thought that positive action had gone too far could cite Bakke's personal victory in support of their view, and that they emphatically proceeded to do.[61]

The classic liberal position had been restated by the *New York Times* in June 1977 in an unusual half-page editorial headed "Reparation, American Style," which concluded that "it is in the national interest that Mr. Bakke should lose his case." A dozen years earlier, that might have been the prevailing opinion, at least among the accredited authorities of Northeastern liberalism. Indeed, eight months before the Court's judgment the *New York Times* headlined a conscientious trawl of opinion in education schools, "Educators Fear a Ruling for Bakke Would Undo Minorities' Vast Gains." Some may have feared that, but others feared positive discrimination more. At Yale, for example, Professor Alexander M. Bickel of the law school thundered his disapproval of all forms of quota:

. . . invidious in principle as well as in practice . . . The history of the racial quota is a history of subjugation, not of benevolence . . . a divider of society, a creator of castes.[62]

At Harvard, Nathan Glazer was no less emphatic.

Thus the nation is by government action increasingly divided into racial and ethnic categories with differential origins. The Orwellian nightmare, "All animals are equal, but some animals are more equal than others," comes closer . . . New lines of conflict are created by government action. New resentments are created; new turfs are to be protected; new angers arise; and one sees them on both sides of the line.[63]

The California pollster Mervyn Field defined the change in the national mood rather differently. "It has become much more acceptable," he said, "to be less generous."[64] He was not speaking only of the case of *Bakke* v. *the Regents of the University of California.*

7

Tributaries:
The River of Jordan

Jordan's river is deep and wide —
Alleluia!
— *Traditional spiritual*

IN THE 1950s, American conservatism was a stream so narrow you could step across it. Its transformation into a broad river, sweeping through wide stretches of the nation's political and social life, came about because powerful tributaries poured in from different directions. Three, in particular, brought water from distant watersheds, deep in half-forgotten hinterlands of American history.

One flowed in from the hills inhabited by all those who were troubled by the apparent decline of the country's influence and reputation in the world and by their desire for a more assertive foreign policy. These were the Americans whose emotions were aroused by the fall of Saigon in 1975, with its implication that the whole agony of Vietnam had been wasted, and by increasingly aggressive Soviet behavior in Africa, the Middle East, and even in the Pacific. Many were shocked, as well as inconvenienced, by the revelation of American vulnerability to the Middle East oil embargo. They saw on the nightly television news that the United States was no longer treated with the same respect in the world as in the past. These were the issues of the flag.

A second tributary, fast-flowing and turbulent, was the stream of economic concerns: the dollar-and-cents issues. Americans were perplexed, as well as inconvenienced, by the impact of the twin energy crises, the first after the Arab oil embargo of 1973 and the second after the fall of the Shah of Iran, in 1979. There was widespread concern about inflation, combined in an unfamiliar way with economic stagnation to produce what was known as "stagflation." The dollar had already been effectively devalued twice, once by the Smithsonian Agreement of December 1971 and again formally by 10 percent on February 12, 1973. In the late 1970s there was growing awareness of rising unemployment and falling productivity and even more with the rise of Japanese and European competition. Those were the dollar issues. They were important enough in themselves. But what made them contribute so powerfully to the conservative tide was the accompanying perception that liberal pundits did not know what to do about them, so that attention turned to new gurus. Some of these, like the monetarists, had been around, heard but little listened to, for years. Others offered the unfamiliar but tempting new panaceas of the "supply side."

The contributions of both flag issues and dollar issues to the growing appeal of conservatism will be looked at in Chapters 8 and 9 respectively. Arguably even more decisive was the contribution of the New Right. The name was claimed by activists who were outraged over what they called the "social issues," but can be more accurately called ethical and religious issues. One of these was abortion. But a whole cluster of other issues was raised by changing mores and changing morals: school busing, school prayer, homosexuality, the protection of the traditional family, and all the questions attendant on the new assertiveness of women. As they appeared to conservative Christians, these were the issues of God. The conservative religious uprising of the 1970s needs to be understood, however, against the background both of the long history of evangelical Protestantism in America, and of the changes in society that made evangelicals and fundamentalists decide to abandon their long tradition of standing apart from politics and commit themselves instead to political, as well as social, conservatism.

IN MANY FIELDS and many ways the spread of conservatism was driven by reaction against the perceived threat of new ideas, new fashions, new lifestyles. In no department of American life was this more true than in religion. From the late 1960s on, among some Catholics and Jews as well as Protestants, ideas that were often called fundamentalist, but were more truly traditional, reasserted themselves in the face of what was seen as a widespread assault by "radicals" or members of the counterculture on the God-fearing and their way of life. Finally, in 1980, evangelical Protestants, especially from the South, the Border States, and the West, who had traditionally sat on their hands on Election Day, turned out in large numbers to vote for Ronald Reagan. That strengthened the impression, widespread in the media at the time, that Reagan's victory was largely won by these Christian soldiers.

There was of course nothing new about the evangelical tradition in America or in the South. What was new was the way it became harnessed to conservative politics. The terms "fundamentalist" and "evangelical" are loosely used, and they also overlap. Sometimes adherents of either tradition will lay stress on the distinctions between them. At other times they will emphasize the unity of all "Christians." But for the present purpose one can say that *evangelical* Christians are those whose religion is anchored by the acceptance of Jesus Christ as "personal Savior and Lord." This acceptance springs from the believer's decision to deliver himself to redemption through an experience often called being "born again." Evangelicals, finally, usually feel obliged to "witness" to their faith to those not yet "saved." *Fundamentalist* Christians accept these elements of the evangelical creed, but they also accept the literal truth of the Scriptures. They believe the Old Testament's account of the origins of the universe. They believe in miracles, in the Devil, in eternal damnation, in hell, and in the Second Coming of Christ in majesty.[1] They also take literally the injunction in 2 Corinthians 6:17, to "come out from among them, and be ye separate."[2] At the core of the evangelical belief is the double injunction: the Christian must seek individual salvation and must actively proselytize nonbelievers to seek their salvation, too.[3]

Theologians distinguish between four strands of evangelicalism: the Baptist tradition, the pentecostal tradition, the anabaptist tradition, and the reformational traditional.[4] Pentecostal Christians, among whom the largest denomination is the Assemblies of God, accept, in addition, as a sign of baptism the ancient custom of "speaking in tongues."[5] At one time the evangelical and fundamentalist denominations refused to accept the Pentecostals, but by the 1940s successful attempts were being made to heal this breach. The Anabaptist tradition, drawn from continental Europe, maintains a sharp suspicion of government and opposes war and violence of all kinds. The reformational-confessional tradition has had little influence on the politicized conservative Christianity of the last quarter of the twentieth century.[6]

Evangelical Christianity has a long history in North America, stretching back to the First Great Awakening, which began in New England about 1734. It fits the democratic and egalitarian temper of American life, because it offers salvation not to all those who obey a set of rules imposed by authority, but to all who choose to repent their sins.

Since colonial times, it has also been closely related to American nationalism. It saw the United States as God's chosen nation with a special destiny to renew the world. "America," one scholar wrote, "was seen as the 'new' Israel; Americans, having a covenant with God, were the chosen people entrusted with the responsibility of establishing a 'righteous empire' or a Christian commonwealth within this new land."[7]

In the late twentieth century evangelicalism in America has become associated with social and political conservatism. But this was not always so. Indeed, it was largely evangelicals who denounced slavery and demanded its abolition. Between the hammer of the abolitionist conviction that slavery was sinful, and the anvil of the South's conviction that its "peculiar institution" was divinely ordained, the American evangelical tradition split into two. In the middle of the nineteenth century Presbyterians, Methodists, and Baptists all split into Northern and Southern denominations; Baptists and Methodists each split into three, with separate communities for African Americans.[8] The modern evangelical tradition descends from the Southern churches that justified slavery, not from the abolitionist Northern branches.

Toward the end of the nineteenth century, the Protestant evangelical tradition began to weaken. In its place there emerged a more secular consensus. By the 1950s this had evolved into what the church historian Martin E. Marty has called a "four-faith pluralism": mainstream liberal Protestantism, Catholicism, Judaism, and a tolerant, liberal, secular morality. Squeezed out of the consensus was the conservative evangelical religious culture of the South and the Midwestern small towns. In 1925, at the time of the Scopes trial in Dayton, Tennessee, which drew national attention to the fact that a teacher could lose his job in Appalachia for teaching the theory of evolution, fundamentalism looked in danger of becoming confined to backward corners of the rural South. In the trial fundamentalist beliefs were derided by Scopes's attorney, Clarence Darrow, to the glee of the North. It confirmed many fundamentalists in their view that American society was damned and doomed. Most of them concluded that their best course was to withdraw from what they regarded as a corrupt and hostile secular society, pursue their own salvation, and bring their children up in righteousness. In the 1930s, for example, Carl McIntire left the Presbyterian mainstream and founded a breakaway communion of fundamentalist Presbyterian churches linked together in the American Council of Christian Churches to oppose the World Council of Churches, already detested by conservative Christians for its ecumenical and "social gospel" orientation.

The shift to the political right in the fundamentalist churches accelerated during and after World War II as the new generation of evangelists launched their various crusades against communism. With the coming of the Cold War, a significant minority of fundamentalist evangelists began to mobilize under the banner of anticommunism. They included Billy James Hargis and the Christian Crusade, Edgar C. Bundy and the Church League of America, and the Australian Dr. Fred C. Schwarz. All of them taught conservative social doctrines and unyielding anticommunism at home and abroad. They were given additional impetus in the South and the West, the homelands of conservative Christianity, by resentment of the government's growing willingness to stretch out into hitherto private domains. Not that the fundamentalists had any objection to the growth of the federal government's power when it was a matter of fighting communism. In 1967, for example, the general council of the Assemblies of God formally struck out that denomination's fifty-year-old bylaw objecting to participation in war, replacing it with a clause that left it up to the individual whether or not to fight.

It was when the federal government, or state governments, for that matter, presumed to intervene in what conservative Christians saw as private matters, such as the family or schooling, that the fundamentalists were first worried, then appalled. Finally they determined to stand and fight for cherished beliefs they saw as being under threat. One of those beliefs, for many fundamentalist Protestants, was the assumption of white supremacy. In 1954 came the Supreme Court's decision in the *Brown* case that segregation was unconstitutional. That deeply shook the South, and the South was after all the bastion and heartland of fundamentalism, even if its sons and daughters had carried their old-time religion with them to the Southwest and especially to Southern California.

IN HIS 1936 novel *The Grapes of Wrath* John Steinbeck unforgettably traced the story of an imaginary family, the Joads, from a small town in eastern Oklahoma to the Central Valley of California. In his 1992 book, *Rising in the West*, a *Washington Post* reporter, Dan Morgan, followed the fortunes of a real family, the Tathams, who made a journey that was so similar to the Joads', it was almost uncanny.[9] The Tathams left Drake's Prairie, near Sallisaw, Oklahoma, in August 1934. Sixteen of them crammed into a Chevy truck for the journey. Oca Tatham, aged twenty-three, was at the wheel. Not counting the $24 Oca needed to buy title to the truck so that it could cross state lines, they had less than $50 between them.

The Tathams' experience illustrates how the plain people of the South and Border preserved their old-time religion, in their case conservative Protestantism modified by the comparatively recent pentecostal tradition, as a lodestone to guide them through swirling economic and social change. By the 1980s, both the Tathams and their dollars had increased and multiplied exceedingly. Oca started life as a trader who bought and sold used truck parts and anything else he could see a profit in. He bought a state-owned hospital at auction and built up a chain of nursing homes in time to prosper when Medicare and its California equivalent, Cal-aid, came along in the 1960s. Some Tathams did better than others. One of Oca's sons, Bill Tatham, became very rich, progressing from nursing homes to real estate developments to savings and loans to pro football. Along with the likes of Donald Trump, Bill Tatham was involved first in trying to float the United States Football League and later with NFL franchises in Tulsa and then in Phoenix. The Tathams, in fact, were a part of that social and economic revolution in the Sunbelt which brought new men to the top in business, in politics, and in religion.

Some Tathams were more religious than others. Some enjoyed, at least for periods of their lives, the hedonism of California life. But few of them forgot the religion they had brought with them in that battered truck, a tradition handed down from Isaac Tatham, the first of the family to settle in Missouri in the 1800s. As one of the younger generation, an affluent lawyer in Fresno, put it: "If you're a Tatham, the religion you inherit is almost too much to bear."

The same, after all, can be said of Americans as a whole. In the 1960s there was a widespread assumption that religion in America was in decline. But over the next twenty years that assumption was refuted by a religious resurgence that was unmistakable, whether you looked at the impact on political life or at the statistical evidence and the surveys. In 1989 the sociologist and priest, Father Andrew Greeley, wrote that in every Gallup Poll from 1944 to 1989 more than 90 percent of Americans said they believed in the existence of God; three-quarters also believed in the divinity of Jesus Christ and in life after death.[10] Nine Americans out of ten say they have prayed to God. Two out of every three claim to be members of a church (or synagogue). And two Americans out of every five attend a religious service at least once a week, a proportion that has hardly changed since the 1960s and is, incidentally, far higher than in most countries. Indeed, there is some evidence that Americans are becoming, at least in outward respects, even more religious than they were in the recent past. When in 1979 researchers revisited Muncie, Indiana, the site of Robert and Helen Lynd's pioneering sociological study, *Middletown*, in the late 1920s, they found that in respect of two thirds of a list of specific questions, the residents of Muncie had become more religious than their grandparents were.[11]

True, that deeply embedded religious life flourishes in the midst of a society that is in its public, political, business, and cultural life firmly secular. "The nation is as pluralist as ever," wrote Martin Marty, "and in the operative aspects of its national life — in the university, the marketplace, or the legislature — America remains secular, with no single transcendent symbol to live by."[12] He went on to say that unless theologians understood *both* the pervasive religion *and* the persistent secularity, they would not understand the place of religion in America. True, too, that religious faith may be for many Americans an affirmation of belonging, a search for meaning, consolation, or life guidance, rather than a matter of deep knowledge or full acceptance of the church's tradition. The problem with Americans, it has been said, "is not that they refuse to believe in anything, but that they believe in far too many things, and would believe in everything if they could."[13] "Although 94 percent of Americans believe in God, and 84 percent think Jesus was the son of God," Stephen Bates pointed out, "only four in ten know who delivered the Sermon on the Mount, or can name the four Gospels or five of the Ten Commandments."[14]

Americans a hundred years ago were probably more thoroughly instructed in the doctrine of whatever denomination they followed and in the Bible as a whole. There are other changes. One is surely a welcome one. Americans, when they think of religion, think of it primarily in terms of three great religious communities: Protestants, Catholics, and Jews.[15] (There are of course increasing numbers of Americans whose religious roots lie in Asian religions. And there are significant sects or religious groups that, though "sociologically" Protestant, are not strictly Protestant or in some cases arguably not strictly Christian at all, including Mormons, Quakers, and Unitarians.) There is a good deal of evidence that conflict among denominations, and also among the three great religious communities, is on the whole much less sharp than it was.

The social position of these three communities and of the denominations that go to make up the Protestant community, still by far the largest, has changed significantly. American Judaism has been to a certain extent a victim of its success. Though their intellectual and spiritual life is immensely rich and intense, strengthened by the twin tasks of remembering the Holocaust and nurturing Israel, American Jews have been leaving their Jewish roots and to some extent their Jewish community in large numbers through the simple experience of assimilation, often symbolized by marriage to non-Jews.

The Catholic Church in America, likewise, has passed through difficult times, though for a very different reason. Two events, in particular, came as rude shocks to American Catholics. The first was the reforming action of the Second Vatican Council, which sat from 1962 to 1965. The second and on the whole more damaging was the papal encyclical *Humanae Vitae* (1968), which, at the very height of the questioning of traditional sexual morality and the position of women in the secular society, flatly reaffirmed the church's traditional teaching on contraception and the family. The consequences can be tracked unmistakably in the statistics for church attendance.[16] The proportion of Catholics who actually go to Mass fell sharply, from 72 percent in the early 1960s to around half, where it has stuck for the last quarter of a century. Father Greeley, for one, attributes this directly to the church's teaching on sexual morality. "The decline in church attendance," he says, "began immediately after the birth control encyclical and ended when Catholic readiness to accept the Church's teaching on birth control and premarital sex reached rock bottom." The Catholic Church has also experienced significant difficulty in recruiting priests. No more than 12 percent of the Catholic laity, it has been calculated, accept the church's teaching on contraception. The Roman communion in America, numerous, rich, and powerful though it remains, is troubled.

A minority of Jews and Catholics, therefore, have turned to conservative religious beliefs in a spirit strikingly similar to that with which broad swathes of conservative Protestants, feeling their traditional beliefs to be under attack, have defied modernism and all its works. The pressures experienced by the Jewish and Catholic communities, predominantly found in urban and industrial areas and in the great metropolitan areas, were felt even more painfully by what were until quite recently the most powerful Protestant denominations in America. Episcopalians, Presbyterians, Lutherans, Methodists, and the United Church of Christ, the very denominations that had led the way toward liberal theology, all experienced steep drops in membership. The United Methodist Church had over 11 million members in 1965; by 1980 that was down to 9.5 million. Membership in the United Presbyterian Church fell by almost a third over the same period, from 3.3 million to 2.4 million, while the Episcopal Church has fallen from over 3.4

million to under 2.7 million. This fall in membership was accompanied in the 1960s, in the case of all the traditional mainstream Northern Protestant denominations, by even sharper falls in enrollment in church schools and by lower contributions, leading to budget and staff cutbacks.

Contrast that with the explosive growth in membership in those Protestant denominations which once catered predominantly to people who were marginal to the mainstream of American life: the evangelical, fundamentalist, charismatic, and Pentecostal churches. The most powerful grouping, the Southern Baptist Convention, had 10.8 million members in 1965, but 13.6 million by 1980. The Assemblies of God, a Pentecostal denomination, almost doubled its membership over the same period, from 570,000 to 1.1 million. Striking gains were also achieved by such small conservative groups as the Churches of God, the Church of the Nazarene, the Jehovah's Witnesses, and the Seventh-Day Adventists.[17] "While most of the mainline Protestant denominations are trying to survive what they hope will be but a temporary adversity," wrote Dean M. Kelley in 1977, "other denominations are overflowing with vitality."[18]

Between the 1960s and 1980, in fact, the traditional mainstream Protestant churches were losing influence and self-confidence. In most of these Establishment denominations, there was a split between the silent, traditionalist rank-and-file and a minority in the ordained ministry, and especially in the national leadership, that espoused liberal and even radical politics and doctrinal innovation. At the same time, the churches that can loosely be described as fundamentalist were growing in numbers. The regions where they were concentrated, in a great crescent from Virginia south and west through the old Confederacy across Texas to Southern California, were getting richer, both absolutely and in relation to the Northeast and the Middle West. Many committed Christians in those fundamentalist churches had become individually rich enough to fund church and political activities. The fundamentalist churches themselves, in response to what they perceived as threats from the outside, were girding on the temporal sword to fight the good political fight. They were creating institutions, and forming alliances, that gave them far more political power at just the moment when they were prepared to use it.

TO WHAT EXTENT was the wave of conservatism in the Protestant churches of the South and the Southwest ultimately inspired by racial fear or hostility? Indeed, to what extent was the new conservatism as a whole a rationalization for what were at bottom racist emotions? Those questions cannot be definitively answered. Clearly, many conservative Christians held what can charitably be called conservative positions on racial issues. Equally, not all conservatives are racists, any more than all political liberals are models of racial brotherhood in their private behavior. It can fairly be said that fear of change in the deep racial structures of American society was the ground bass to the growing chorus of conservatism from the 1950s to the 1970s. Other matters also troubled conservative Christians, who were in the process of being turned into Christian conservatives.

Ever since the New Deal, the federal government had intervened in the lives of families, businesses, and communities in ways that fundamentalist Christians found objectionable. As prosperity returned in the 1950s, that trend did not abate. The government seemed to be moving away from its traditional stance as the protector of Christianity and the family. Once again, as with racial desegregation, the Supreme Court was out in front. In 1957 it issued the first of a series of more than thirty rulings setting ever stricter standards for prosecutions for obscenity. In 1960 the Federal Drug Administration approved Enovid, the first effective oral contraceptive for women.

More immediately threatening were the Court's school prayer decisions, *Engel* v. *Vitale* in 1962 and *School District of Abington Township* v. *Schempp* in 1963. In 1951 the New York State Board of Regents, under pressure from agnostic, Jewish, and other parents and organizations who objected to public prayer and Bible readings in public schools, composed a nondenominational prayer it hoped would quiet these objections. "Almighty God," it said, "we acknowledge our dependence on Thee, and we beg Thy blessings upon us, our parents, our teachers, and our country." In the context of New York, that might have seemed a harmless text to finesse the differences of a pluralist, largely secular society. In the context of most of the Southern half of the nation, it was, for a politically formidable and respected segment of the population, an outrageous attack on God's word. In 1959, presumably unaware of the hornet's nest they were poking, five parents in a Long Island suburb of New York City, New Hyde Park, filed suit against the prayer, not on the grounds that would have made it objectionable across the South, that there was too little religion in it, but, on the contrary, that it breached the constitutional prohibition on the establishment of religion.

Two of the plaintiffs in *Engel* v. *Vitale* were Jews, one was a Unitarian, one a member of the Society for Ethical Culture, and one an agnostic.

They lost at all three levels of the state judicial system. But the United States Supreme Court found, through the mouth of Justice Hugo Black (a native Alabamian), that it was "no part of the business of government to compose official prayers." Francis Cardinal Spellman of New York said he was "shocked and frightened." Richard Cardinal Cushing of Boston said the communists must be enjoying the decision. And another Alabamian, Representative George Andrews, said, "They put the Negroes in the schools and now they're driving God out."

The Court's ruling in the second case, which came from Pennsylvania, was more diplomatically expressed, but thrust even deeper into the customs and beliefs of the South. It simply struck down, as unconstitutional, all oral prayers and Bible readings in school. This was a good example of the principle that the declaration of substantive law will not receive acceptance, even from deeply law-abiding citizens, and however logical its interpretation of the Constitution, if the ruling departs too far from the citizens' actual practice. In this case, as in many others, the Court ran up against the very substantial differences between practice in different sections of the country. In Texas, for example, even four years after the Court's ruling in *Schempp*, 90 percent of Texas school districts still *required* daily prayers. Twenty years later, 20 percent of all schools in the South had Bible readings and no less than 43 percent, in open breach of the declared law of the land, held spoken prayers.[19]

Oca Tatham was one of millions of Bible Christians who watched these developments and, as the Good Book says, pondered them in his heart. Remembering the bitter years of the Depression, he asked, years later, "Did we need the church in the Depression? You bet we did. What else did we have? We had no one else to turn to. And you know something? We didn't have everything, but we had peace and joy." By 1951, a relatively rich man now, Oca went to a meeting in the traditional Pentecostal "upper room" in Fresno at which the celebrated healing preacher Oral Roberts spoke. At the meeting Oca and other members of the Tatham family joined what they called the Full Gospel Businessmen's Fellowship, a group where men like Oca, who had started life as farm-workers, traders, or truck drivers but were now successful businessmen, could feel comfortable, as they might not have done in the churches of the business elite in the San Joaquin Valley. In 1964 Oca was attracted to Barry Goldwater as "a fellow free man of the Western republic." When Goldwater spoke of freedom, he wasn't speaking of civil rights, but of throwing off the constraints of government.[20] Oca practiced what he preached. He went down to Mexico to help little storefront Protestant churches, and he loved the simplicity of the religion he found there. But he settled as a member of a little church that had become a big church: People's Church, a Pentecostal church which was now the biggest in Fresno. By the time Jimmy Carter ran successfully for the presidency in 1976, Oca Tatham "detested Carter." Dan Morgan commented: "Carter's presidency appears to have been the point at which millions of conservative Christians like Oca became terminally fed up and began to think about what they wanted in political terms. Suddenly the joining of populist religion and populist politics seemed feasible."

Oca Tatham's slow evolution from an apolitical businessman, wholly wrapped up in making his way in business, in bringing up his family, and in caring for his own soul, into a conscious member of a conservative political movement was repeated in the lives of many millions of Americans. A figure that has often been used is that the Reagan campaign of 1980 brought twenty million evangelical Christians to the polls who had never voted before. Suddenly in the middle 1970s a new conservatism arose. It was forged from an alliance between evangelical and fundamentalist Protestants, Pentecostal Christians, Mormons, Roman Catholic traditionalists, and Orthodox Jews. For the first time in the twentieth century, it looked as if this conservative block was in the strategic center of public life in America.

In June 1978 the ribbon was cut on a new People's church on Herndon Avenue in Fresno. It was a $4.5 million facility, a far cry from the simple places of worship Pentecostals had been used to in Oklahoma and Texas when Oca was growing up. One of Oca Tatham's sons had given $300,000 to start the building. A local rancher, Sherman Thomas, had risen in his place one Sunday service and presented the pastor with a check for one million dollars, the fruits of some complex real estate transactions. The new church was impressive, both as a structure and as a center for the Christian life. There was a robed choir with excellent music, and no speaking in tongues, at least not at the main Sunday service. The church ran its own high school for the Fresno Christian Education System, and its nonprofit foundation produced the Sunday services for the local TV channel, KJEO, the ABC affiliate, so that a large audience heard Pastor G. L. Johnson's sermons.

There was nothing remotely exceptional, however, about People's Church in Fresno. All over the South, from Pat Robertson's church in Norfolk, Virginia, by way of Charles Stanley's First Baptist Church in Atlanta and D. James Kennedy's Coral Ridge Presbyterian in Fort Lauderdale, Florida, across the Sunbelt to Tim LaHaye's Scott Memorial

Baptist Church in San Diego, energetic leaders were building super-churches. They were creating church communities with financial and human resources compared to which the best-run suburban brick church of the 1950s, with its colonial architecture and neat spire, stood in comparison as a Liberty ship to a supertanker. There was Northside Baptist in Charlotte, North Carolina, with six thousand members. Its Christian academy accepted pupils from kindergarten through twelfth grade, and the sermons of its pastor, Jack Hudson, could be heard over twenty-six radio stations. Jerry Falwell in 1956 began his ministry in an unused soda bottling plant in Lynchburg, Virginia, with only a handful in his congregation. By 1964 he had built a church with seats for a thousand, and three years later that was too small. In 1988 his Thomas Road Baptist Church had eighteen thousand members, guided by sixty associate pastors. Falwell's Liberty Baptist College had fifteen hundred students by 1976 and in 1985 it was accredited as Liberty University by the Southern Association of Colleges and Schools.[21] Mightiest of all, with its twenty-three thousand members, the largest Southern Baptist congregation in America, was W. A. Criswell's giant First Baptist Church in Dallas. First Baptist ministered to the body as well as to the soul. It had its own twin gymnasiums (one for men, one for women), with its own Nautilus machines, sauna, skating rink, bowling alleys, and racquetball courts. Its academy by the late 1970s had an enrollment in kindergarten through twelfth grade of over six hundred, and that led on to the Criswell Center for Biblical Studies,[22] with over 275 students, an FM radio station, not to mention a fellowship of Christian truckers.

By the 1970s evangelical America was building institutions of all kinds: Christian summer camps, retirement homes, hospitals, universities like Bob Jones University in South Carolina, Oral Roberts University, Criswell Center, Jerry Falwell's Liberty Baptist College in Lynchburg, Virginia, and Pat Robertson's Regent University in Norfolk. To dubious outsiders, especially among those writing for mainstream newspapers and magazines, this institution-building often seemed evidence of muscle-flexing. Certainly it reflected a new economic power and social confidence. But the spirit was more defensive than offensive. The evangelical and fundamentalist Christians continued to be suspicious of the "mainstream." Their first instinct was still to separate themselves from a secular culture that, after all, they believed to be not only wicked but also doomed to destruction, at no late date, by the Second Coming foretold in the Scriptures.

It was the search for shelter by Christian people from the turbulent waters of what they saw as an increasingly secular and immoral society that motivated the most remarkable and conceivably the most lasting institution-building by the conservative Protestants in the 1970s. Between 1970 and 1980 overall public school enrollment in the United States actually declined by 13.6 percent. The main reason was that over that same period enrollment in independent Christian schools virtually doubled. By the mid-1980s, 2.5 million students were reported to be enrolled in more than seventeen thousand Christian academies.[23] It was widely assumed in the North that the prime motive for the independent Christian school movement was revulsion against the desegregation of Southern public schools. There was more to the movement than racism, however. In February 1979 the sociologist Peter Skerry visited a number of Christian schools in North Carolina, nearly all of them started within the previous ten years. Most of them were small in size; the average was two hundred students. Most were in modest buildings. A lot of the furnishing and carpentry had been done by parent volunteers, which gave most of the schools a "homey and noninstitutional" feel. Teachers had to settle for extremely modest pay, around $6,000 a year. Fundamentalist religious and social values pervaded the schools. Each day began with a salute to both the American flag and a Christian flag. Discipline was old-fashioned. Students had to stand when addressing a teacher and use "sir" or "ma'am." The disciplinary code was enforced with the threat of corporal punishment or expulsion.

Yet Skerry found the relationship between teachers and students marked by mutual respect and friendliness, and behavior was good. He concluded that concern over desegregation was part of the reason for the shift into Christian schools, but not the main reason. Pastors readily admitted that some parents sent their children to Christian schools because they didn't like blacks. But he believed that those who saw Christian schools as nothing more than segregation academies had to confront the fact that there was no evidence of racist ideas being taught in them. And he cited the case of Riverdale Baptist High School in Prince George's County, Maryland, in the middle-income Washington suburban belt. The school was founded in 1971. The next year, after court-ordered busing was introduced in the county, the enrollment jumped from fifty to five hundred. By 1977 the school had thirteen hundred students, 20 percent of them black. Skerry's judgment was confirmed by the sociologist Steve Bruce: "The vast majority of conservative school founders deny racist intent and declare that it was the generally liberal socio-moral climate of the public schools which they found offensive."

Even if skepticism is in order about the protestations of those who ran or used the schools, it is probably the case that, as Skerry put it, desegregation symbolized the social turmoil and alien values parents saw in the public schools. One mother said the last straw that made her take her nine-year-old out of public school was discovering that he and his peers were allowed to play records for an hour every day and that he had become infatuated with a rock group specializing in demonic lyrics and pretending to vomit blood over its fans. For such Christian parents in a small North Carolina town, desegregation was "more like the last in a long series of affronts." Of course, seeing desegregation as an affront may in itself be taken as evidence of racist attitudes. That is not quite the same as seeing the independent Christian schools as simply so many attempts to evade court-ordered desegregation.

The separatist impulse among conservative Christians, however, existed in tandem with missionary zeal. The new wealth of some evangelicals made it possible for their churches to gain access to technology that had previously been the preserve of the secular culture. Christian book and periodical publishing flourished, and here I am using the word "Christian" in the way American evangelicals and fundamentalists use it, to refer to themselves, not to those formerly mainstream denominations which were scarcely seen as deserving the name of Christians. Far more important for the evangelicals were the new opportunities for preaching and conversion offered by what began to be called "the electric church."

That phrase was invented by Ben Armstrong, the executive director of National Religious Broadcasters. He claimed in 1979 that "every Sunday nearly 130 million Americans tune their radio and television sets to the 'electric church.'" Armstrong explained that he used the word "electric" in a double sense: the message of television and radio preachers was transmitted thanks to electricity, but it was also electrifying. Citing five religious broadcast networks, more than sixty syndicated television programs, and an expanding number of TV and radio stations owned by churches and religious groups, Armstrong called religious broadcasting "a major sociopolitical movement of our time." One of its purposes, he said, was to "revitalize" the churches because of the "rapidly diminishing time span before the return of Jesus Christ," and he argued that worshiping at home was "a revolution as dramatic" as the sixteenth-century Reformation.

Most others who have studied the rise of religious broadcasting would not go as far as Armstrong, either in his sense of the immediacy of the Second Coming or in his estimate of the size of the audience. The Gallup Poll recorded in 1980 that 32 percent, almost a third, of viewers watch religious broadcasts. But this is suspiciously high. Perhaps people claim to watch more religious TV than they really do. The researchers Jeffrey Hadden and C. E. Swann, using Arbitron ratings in February 1980, found that there were no more than twenty million viewers for all the syndicated religious TV programs (a figure no higher than that of five years earlier).[24] The highest ratings, moreover, went to nonpolitical preachers like Oral Roberts of Tulsa (2.7 million viewers) and Rex Humbard of Akron, Ohio (2.4 million), with Jerry Falwell, the highest-rating of the political preachers, coming in sixth, with only 1.5 million viewers. The media, caught between the self-serving claims of religious broadcasters and the nervousness of secular metropolitan viewers and readers, have systematically exaggerated the strength and also the politicization of the religious broadcasters and their audience. A survey of white middle-class neighborhoods in Dallas, in the heart of the Bible Belt and the home of the Southern Baptist Convention, found that only 16 percent of those who had heard of the Moral Majority approved of it! Claims made about the audience and the influence of religious broadcasting should be treated with skepticism. Still, no one should underestimate the importance or the sheer passion of "televangelists" like Jerry Falwell, Marion G. (Pat) Robertson, or James Robison of Dallas, all of whom specialized in interweaving patriotism, political conservatism, and cultural fundamentalism with their specifically religious message.

In the early days of radio, there were several dozen radio stations owned by churches or institutions under church influence. By the 1930s, however, radio licenses had become so valuable that these church-owned stations disappeared. Religious broadcasting was available either in "sustained time," provided by the stations under the Federal Communications Commission's rules, or in commercial time, paid for by the churches. By and large the mainline churches used sustained time, and the independent and evangelical preachers raised money and paid for their time. This pattern began to change in the 1960s, however, as the loss of tobacco and liquor ads obliged stations to seek other sources of revenue. Changes in FCC regulations and network policy allowed stations to sell air time to religious organizations, thus generating revenue on time dedicated to fulfilling regulatory obligations. Since the mainstream denominations traditionally relied on sustained time, and could not afford to compete with preachers who often used a third of their air time to solicit for contributions, the vast majority of religious broadcasting in the United States came to be controlled by evangelicals.

The first evangelist to switch from radio was Billy Graham. Rex Humbard, Oral Roberts, and others soon followed. Later, Pat Robertson started the Christian Broadcast Network in Virginia Beach, Virginia, which helped to parlay him toward a presidential candidacy. The flagship of the Christian Broadcast Network is a ninety-minute show, the *700 Club*, compered by Robertson. By 1979 it was said to be shown on 150 TV stations and eighteen hundred cable TV systems, and it claimed $54 million income. Some of the claims made for the influence of televangelism were greatly exaggerated. Underneath all the hype, however, a shift of enormous significance for the future of American politics had taken place. It was not a change in the underlying beliefs of American evangelicals. Still less was it a mass conversion of unbelievers to the evangelical persuasion. Rather, it was a decision on the part of many of the most powerful leaders of evangelical Protestantism to become active in politics. This had certain immediate political consequences. More important, it marked a historic departure for those conservative Christians in America who for several generations had turned their backs on the mainstream culture of the "four faith consensus," with its strongly secular belief in liberal reform. The decision was to abandon separatism and get in there and fight.

The civil rights revolution of the 1960s caused profound unease in the South and far beyond. It was not just the desegregation of Southern schools in response to *Brown*, which began to reach even the most conservative corners of the South in the early 1970s. The social desegregation mandated by the Civil Rights Act of 1964 was accepted with remarkably little resentment in the South. All but the most conservative Southerners had already come to accept the inevitability and the reasonableness of desegregating restaurants, hotels, swimming pools, and the like. In any case, middle-class whites were in practice sheltered by economic protections from abrupt change. (Those few black families, for example, who could afford to move into previously all-white suburbs were not likely to be very threatening.) More disturbing, for many conservative white Southerners, were the complex consequences of the Voting Rights Act of 1965 and the subsequent voter registration drives.

Although by the 1970s there was no Southern state in which African Americans were still in a majority, they were numerous enough in most Southern states to affect the whole context of politics. In response to prevalent African American block voting for Democrats, substantial numbers of conservative whites who had previously voted for Democratic candidates began to vote for Republicans, and a new style of conservatism was seen in southern politics. It was suburban and educated where the old conservatives had been raw and rustic; this was the style of the corporate boardroom and the country club rather than that of the courthouse ring and the Klavern. Social and political conservatism was rescued from the ungodly and passed into the hands of people who might well be members and deacons of conservative churches.

These broad transformations of Southern society in the decade of 1965 to 1975 would not have developed had it not been for what Southern conservative Christians, and their coreligionists in the West, perceived as a series of gratuitous assaults on their most cherished values, some of them carried out by the federal government. We have seen how the Supreme Court, in the early 1960s, handed down a series of judgments on school prayer and Bible reading that were deeply offensive to Southern Christian opinion. The late 1960s and early 1970s were the highwater mark of what was called "permissiveness." The women's movement loudly proclaimed a whole series of positions and objectives, summed up in the Equal Rights Amendment, which ran flat counter to fundamentalist teaching and the traditional view of the family. The veteran Catholic conservative activist Phyllis Schlafly set up an organization with two names, Eagle Forum and Stop-ERA, which by the late 1970s claimed fifty thousand members.[25]

Even more objectionable to many religious conservatives was the increasingly outspoken gay rights' movement. In 1977 Anita Bryant became a national symbol of conservative resistance to homosexual emancipation when she campaigned successfully against a "gay rights" ordinance in Dade County, Florida; half a dozen other successful campaigns were mounted elsewhere in imitation of what she had achieved.[26] She followed through by setting up a national organization called Save Our Children, Inc. Paul Weyrich's Committee for a Free Congress backed Enrique Rueda's *Homosexual Network* with a carefully written argument that the government was supporting the homosexual movement, which he portrayed as a conspiracy against conventional morality; that was just another sign of the growing rally of conservatives around what were coming to be called the social issues.[27]

By far the most potent issue in arousing public disquiet over what conservatives saw as a government-sponsored attack on traditional morality was abortion. As early as the late 1960s, opinion was polarizing between pro-life groups, largely Catholic, and pro-choice activists, most of them associated with the women's movement. Then in 1973 the Supreme Court decided, in *Roe* v. *Wade*, that the abortion law of Texas, which made abortion a crime except to save a mother's life, was unconstitutional. The Court went further. It said that any state law that forbade abortion before the seventh month of pregnancy in order to protect a fetus was unconstitutional. It thus held, by a majority of seven justices to two, that the law of almost all the fifty states must be changed.

For some, especially for many women, the decision was a cause for rejoicing. But it is hard to exaggerate how grievous a blow the Court's decision was for religious conservatives. They believed that fetuses were living human beings and that terminating their existence was nothing less than hideous murder, and murder that was being practiced, for remuneration, on an almost genocidal scale. That this decision should be handed down by a distant federal court of justices who had been appointed, not elected, was bad enough; that supposed conservatives had joined with avowed liberals and secularists was an added cause of indignation. There was nothing for it, legions of conservative Christians decided after the *Roe* judgment, but to organize and fight the political fight. Pro-life groups got into politics. Catholics and fundamentalist Protestants, once at best mutually suspicious, at worst viciously antagonistic, formed common cause, and many conservative Jews joined with them.

School prayer, the Equal Rights Amendment, gay rights, abortion — all of these issues aroused evangelical and other conservatives and helped to forge a new political coalition on the right. But the evidence suggests that it was another issue, far less noticed at the time, that was decisive in turning evangelical and fundamentalist Christians from isolation to political involvement. In August 1978 the Internal Revenue Service began to challenge the charitable status and therefore the tax exemptions of independent Christian schools.[28] Prompted by civil rights and public interest law groups, the IRS issued guidelines that stated:

> A prima facie case of racial discrimination arises from evidence that the school (1) was formed or substantially expanded at or about the time of desegregation of the public schools, and (2) has an insignificant number of minority students. In such a case, the school has the burden of clearly and convincingly rebutting this prima facie case of racial discrimination by showing that it has undertaken affirmative steps to secure minority students. Mere denial of a discriminatory purpose is insufficient.

The IRS went on to define an "insignificant" number of minority students as "less than twenty percent of the minority school age population in the community served by the school." Any school against which such a *prima facie* case was established, by summary administrative process, would not only lose its exemption from paying federal taxes (including Social Security and unemployment contributions for staff); private donors, on whom the Christian schools heavily depended, would lose the right to deduct their contributions from taxable income.

From the point of view of traditional liberals and even more of minorities, this was reasonable enough. As Clarence Mitchell, Washington representative of the National Association for the Advancement of Colored People, put it, "Every school that's been started to evade desegregation has called itself Christian. That's not my idea of being Christian." But for evangelical Christians across the nation it was an outrage, the final evidence that the federal government was vindictively hostile to conservative Christianity. The IRS received more than 120,000 letters of protest, more than it had ever received on any other proposed change. By late 1979 Congress had held hearings and passed legislation blocking application of the new guidelines. But by then the harm, both from the conservative and the liberal points of view, had been done.

For the liberals, the IRS's guidelines were a political disaster. As if from dragons' teeth, soldiers of the fundamentalist church militant sprang up in their thousands. The fact that this had happened under a president, Jimmy Carter, who was the first born-again evangelical to sit in the White House in the twentieth century, was merely an ironic accident. The evangelical movement had long ago cast off Carter as a false brother; to them, to be a genuine evangelical meant to be a conservative. The IRS school guidelines were the last nail in the coffin of any idea that evangelical Christianity was politically neutral. For conservatives, the message was now clear. Paul Weyrich, perhaps the most sagacious political strategist of the New Right, explained to a conference in Washington why the schools guidelines were so important.

> Most people who comment on the evangelical movement picture it as an offensive movement politically. It is not. It is a *defensive* movement. The people who are involved . . . had accepted the notion (which may have taken root historically at the Scopes trial) that a good Christian would raise his family in the proper manner and would not participate very much in public life. If you did that, you could avoid all the corruption that was manifest in politics. What changed all that was not the school-prayer issue, and it was not the abortion issue. I had discussions with all the leading lights of the movement in the late 1970s and early 1980s, post *Roe* v. *Wade*, and they were all arguing that the decision was one more reason why

Christians had to isolate themselves from the rest of the world. Certainly no Christian was going to have an abortion, and they could teach that to their children.

What caused the movement to surface was the federal government's moves against the Christian schools. This absolutely shattered the Christian community's notion that Christians could isolate themselves inside their own institutions and teach what they pleased. The realization that they could not do so linked up with the long-held conservative view that government is too powerful and intrusive, and this linkage was what made evangelicals active. It wasn't the abortion issue; that wasn't sufficient. It was the recognition that isolation simply would no longer work in this society.

Weyrich expanded the point in an interview with the author. When the Supreme Court decided *Roe* v. *Wade*, he explained, "the Baptists said, 'This just proves we should have nothing to do with politics, and keep ourselves to ourselves'." After all, they said, if you raise girls right, they don't need abortions.

A less well-known figure, Edward G. Dobson, pastor of Calvary Church, Grand Rapids, Michigan, agreed. "The Religious New Right did not start because of a concern about abortion," he said.

> I sat in the non-smoke-filled back room with the Moral Majority, and I frankly do not remember abortion ever being mentioned as a reason why we ought to do something. I think there was a perceived threat, but not the singular threat, of what the government was going to do to Christian schools that prompted the activism. I think a series of threats, broadly described as "secular humanism," caused a community that had been separatist for fifty years to act. It acted because, all of a sudden, the larger secular world was having an impact on their members "separated" lives, through gay-rights issues, moral erosion in the public schools, banning prayer in the schools, and government interference in Christian schools.

How a group of prominent evangelical preachers got together with conservative political operatives to throw the weight of millions of evangelical and other religious Americans into the political scales is a twice-told tale. Conservative Christians had been edging into the political arena for some years. Even before the Goldwater campaign of 1964, evangelical Christians were active in conservative causes, and this increased noticeably after the fall of Richard Nixon in 1974. Paul Weyrich claimed that he saw the potential of the evangelical vote as early as 1962, when he was still working as a radio journalist in Wisconsin. "The Supreme Court came down with its decision on school prayer," he recalled. "I saw the possibilities of that, and I called Claude Jasper, who was the Republican state chairman for Wisconsin. I said, 'Look, I shouldn't be doing this, but this decision is a means to ignite people who do not normally support Republicans.' He thought I was crazy."[29]

Richard Viguerie remembers President Ford's decision to appoint Nelson Rockefeller, a divorced man, as vice president as a watermark in evangelical indignation.[30] In 1975, Representative John B. Conlan (Republican of Arizona) got together with Bill Bright, the leader of the Campus Crusade for Christ, and other influential and wealthy evangelicals to campaign for conservative Christians running for public office. Working quietly through Bright's Christian Embassy, the Christian Freedom Association, and Third Century Publishers, they aimed to create an evangelical vanguard for a presidential bid by Ronald Reagan.[31]

The Reagan connection was odd in certain respects. After all, Reagan had been a movie star, and Hollywood and all its works had long been anathema to strict evangelicals. Worse than that, he was divorced and remarried, and known as a ladies' man in his bachelor periods. A "light drinker" and fond of telling off-color stories, Reagan had a family life that was in several respects by no means a model of evangelical purity. In spite of these shortcomings, evangelicals in California embraced Reagan from the time of his first campaign for governor in 1966; their commitment to conservative politics was so strong that they were prepared to overlook personal backslidings in a politician who, like Reagan, would talk about the evangelical beliefs he had inherited from his mother, a keen member of the Disciples of Christ.[32] At his inauguration as governor in January 1967, for example, Reagan promised to try "very hard" to follow the teachings of Jesus Christ as his guide in public office. The Conlan-Bright effort petered out after it was exposed in an investigative article in *Sojourners* magazine, a liberal Christian publication. The following year Conlan was defeated in a bid for the United States Senate in a campaign marked on his side by anti-Semitism and bigotry.[33]

In 1978 the New Right had already demonstrated its political muscle by targeting and defeating several prominent liberals, especially those who could be portrayed as supporting abortion. There were a number of personal links between the political operatives of the New Right —

men like Paul Weyrich of the Committee for a Free Congress and the Heritage Foundation, Howard Phillips of the Conservative Caucus, and Richard Viguerie, the direct mail fund raiser — and the religious right.[34] One was Ed McAteer, a former salesman for Colgate-Palmolive who had worked for the Tennessee Baptist Foundation and then for the Christian Freedom Foundation, which propagated free market economic ideas among conservative Christians. When Howard Phillips started the Conservative Caucus in 1977, Ed McAteer went to work for him. Another was the Reverend Robert Billings, a graduate of Bob Jones University and an enthusiast of the Christian schools movement.[35] One of the first organizations to express the political instincts of conservative Christians was Christian Voice, founded in 1978 by two Baptists, the Reverend Robert Grant and Richard Zone; it was also strongly supported by the very conservative Senator Orrin Hatch of Utah, himself a Mormon.[36]

In early 1979, as he told it in his book *Listen America*, the Reverend Jerry Falwell was flying back to Lynchburg when suddenly in the darkness he felt that God was calling him to bring "the good people of America" together to fight permissiveness and moral decay.[37] In April 1979 Falwell announced at a rally on Capitol Hill that the time had come to "fight the pornography, obscenity, vulgarity, profanity that under the guise of sex education and 'values clarification'" pervaded public school education. Falwell had not always felt this way. In 1965 he preached against Martin Luther King's civil rights ministry. "We are not told," he said then, "to wage war against bootleggers, liquor stores, gamblers, murderers, prostitutes, racketeers, prejudiced persons, or institutions or against any existing evil as such . . . Preachers are not called to be politicians, but soul-winners."[38] Now the boot was on the other foot, and Jerry Falwell felt that he had been called to be, if not a politician, at least politically committed.

The organization he set up was called, cleverly, the Moral Majority. Paul Weyrich has claimed that the phrase was his. Jerry Falwell sent his plane to fly Weyrich down from Washington to Lynchburg. Howard Phillips was also invited, but he was driving, and as it happened he was late. So Eddie McAteer turned to Weyrich and said:

> While we are waiting for Howard, why don't you give Jerry a briefing on the political situation. So I said, "Out there is what you might call a Moral Majority. They are politically and socially conservative. If we could get these people active in politics there is no limit

to what we could do." Falwell interrupted me and said, "What did you say?" So I started repeating what I had said, and he said, "No, no, you used a phrase back there, there was a something out there," and I couldn't remember at first what phrase I had used, so then I said, "Yeah, there is a moral majority out there," and he said, "That's it! That's the phrase I've been looking for!"

Now he had a name as well as a strategy for his organization. Among those he invited to join its board were such preeminent superchurch pastors and exponents of the electronic ministry as Charles Stanley of First Baptist in Indiana, a former head of the Southern Baptist Convention; James Kennedy of Coral Ridge Presbyterian in Fort Lauderdale, Florida; and Tim LaHaye of Scott Memorial Baptist Church in San Diego and husband of the outspoken conservative publicist Beverly LaHaye.[39] In January 1979 she founded Concerned Women for America, based in San Diego, which by 1993 claimed 600,000 members. CWA offers women a way of being politically active "from the kitchen table," that is, while remaining in a traditional role. It opposes abortion, pornography, violence on TV, gay rights, and a nuclear freeze. It supports teaching creationism in biology classes and full funding for the Strategic Defense Initiative. Ms. LaHaye believes that "feminism and the sexual revolution are tentacles of the octopus humanism."[40]

Tim LaHaye's career has faltered somewhat. In 1980 there were reports that his church's literature spoke of the Catholic Church as "the old harlot church still sitting on the seven hills of Rome, drunk with the blood of martyrs and fornicating with the political leaders of the world." In 1985 it was alleged that he had received help from Sun Myung Moon's Unification Church, and in 1987 he resigned as co-chair of the Jack Kemp presidential campaign after reports that he had written offensively about Catholics and Jews.[41]

There was one major hurdle to overcome, the fact that many leading evangelicals, especially Pat Robertson, whose father had sat as a Democratic U.S. senator from Virginia for many years, had a residual loyalty to the Democratic Party. They did not feel happy about getting involved in a purely Republican operation. Their conservative politics had become so important to many of them that they preferred a conservative Republican like Ronald Reagan, who was visibly uneasy when questioned about whether he had had a rebirth experience, to an unmistakably pietist Southern Baptist who happened also to be a moderately liberal Democrat. Weyrich contended to the author that the decisive event which overcame this reluctance to abandon Carter was the White House Conference on Families. Weyrich said that when the evangelical ministers went to those conferences and saw who was there, "all the radical feminists and the lesbians," and saw what the White House was pushing, all of a sudden they said, "You were right!"

There were in fact three conferences, in Baltimore, Minneapolis, and Los Angeles, in May, June, and August 1980. Even before the last of them, on June 24, there was a meeting of the Moral Majority in Atlanta, convened by Charles Stanley. Two hundred ministers from half a dozen Southern states were there, troubled and puzzled as to what action they could take during what they regarded as a crisis for Christian America. There were only three speakers. One was Weyrich, who had absolutely no doubt about what they should do. They should mobilize their flocks to vote for Republican candidates in general and for Ronald Reagan in particular. And that, by and large, when November came, is what they proceeded to do.

It remained only for Ronald Reagan to ask the evangelicals for their help. He did that brilliantly at a National Affairs Briefing in Dallas on August 22. For good measure Reagan distanced himself from the theory of evolution. "It is a scientific theory only," he said, "and it has in recent years been challenged in the world of science, and it is not now believed in the scientific community to be infallible as was once believed." Thus, by a speechwriter's deft touch, conservatism was made to sound like the philosophy of the future, and what had been generally accepted by science since 1859 was relegated to the status of one theory competing among others for acceptance. If there was a whirring noise in the air, it must have been the sound of John T. Scopes revolving in his grave. And then, with a characteristically sure instinct for the politics of a situation, Reagan told the assembled evangelicals, "I know you can't endorse me, but I want you to know that I endorse you and what you are doing."

There was only one false note in the acclamation. "With all due respect to those dear people," said the Reverend Bailey Smith, president of the Southern Baptist Convention, in his invocation, "God does not hear the prayer of a Jew."[42] No doubt in his own mind the Reverend Smith was doing no more than preaching sound and settled evangelical doctrine. Still, at that moment it could be said that the four faith consensus was truly dead. Conservative Christians had indeed become Christian conservatives.

There was an immediate demonstration of the new muscle evangelical voters, led by conservative preachers and conservative politicians, could bring to electoral politics. In 1978 conservative organizations targeted liberal senators and representatives of whom they disapproved and, in a number of highly publicized instances, were able to pick off their targets. One notable victory was the defeat of Senator Dick Clark, chairman of the Senate's Africa Subcommittee, by Roger Jepsen, whose intriguing motto, "I'm a conservative because I'm for change," provides Chapter 1 with its epigraph. By 1979 the New Right held some forty seats in the House of Representatives and ten seats in the United States Senate, besides countless seats in state legislatures and places on city councils and school boards and other local offices.

After the 1980 elections commentators sat up and noticed the dramatic successes that the New Right, in alliance with the evangelicals, had been able to achieve. The National Conservative Political Action Committee (NCPAC) announced with a flourish that it was targeting six liberal senators in the November 1980 elections: Birch Bayh of Indiana; John Culver of Iowa; George McGovern of South Dakota (the Democratic presidential standard bearer in 1972); Thomas F. Eagleton (McGovern's running mate in the same year, until his earlier psychiatric problems were revealed); Frank Church of Idaho, chairman of the Foreign Relations Committee and of the Church Commission, which investigated the CIA; and Alan Cranston of California. Four of the six were defeated.

The demonstration of the conservatives' power to punish outspoken liberals was not lost on Democratic office holders in the years that followed. Quite apart from these highly publicized instances where the Moral Majority openly attacked liberal candidates, a number of senior Democrats lost their seats, including Warren Magnuson of Washington, chairman of the Appropriations Committee; Herman Talmadge of Georgia, chairman of the Agriculture Committee; and Gaylord Nelson of Wisconsin, chairman of the Small Business Committee, all incumbents whose committee positions would normally have made them proof against attack.

In other congressional races the Moral Majority was highly active in trying to elect as many conservative candidates as possible to reverse what its members openly denounced as moral decay sapping the country's strength. One of the most impressive illustrations of the Moral Majority's new strength came in Oklahoma, where a freshman state senator, Don Nickles, upset the Republican leadership to win the party's nomination, outvoting a well-known businessman in the runoff primary by two to one, and then winning the election to replace Henry Bellmon in the Senate. In Alabama, retired Admiral Jeremiah Denton, a former Vietnam prisoner of war and strong fundamentalist, won a surprisingly easy victory in the Senate election. In the House, too, the Republicans, while still far short of winning control, managed a net gain of thirty-three seats, the largest since 1966. Helped by a $9 million media campaign that urged voters to "Vote Republican, For a Change," the party succeeded in defeating eight senior Democrats who had served for more than eighteen years each, including the Democratic whip, John Brademas of Indiana, and the chairman of Ways and Means, Al Ullman of Oregon.[43]

Even more dramatic, of course, was the overwhelming defeat of the sitting president, Jimmy Carter, by Ronald Reagan, clearly identified both as a conservative Republican and as one who had sought evangelical endorsement and support. Neither polls nor pundits had predicted the scale of Reagan's sweep. Carter had tried to portray Reagan as outside the mainstream of American politics, as Johnson had done with Goldwater. It didn't work. Polls showed an exceptionally large number of voters undecided up until the last minute. Millions dropped off the fence on the Reagan side in the last few hours.

After the election, press comment focused strongly on the role played by the new evangelical commitment to conservative politics in the Republican victories. New Right spokesmen have understandably exaggerated the evangelicals' part in the election. What is more, evangelical leaders, including the leaders of the Moral Majority and the New Christian Right, also exaggerate their influence over the larger body of evangelical voters. Still, a number of conclusions can be tentatively drawn from such sources as the Gallup, *Los Angeles Times*, and National Opinion Research Center surveys, the National Election Studies of the Center for Political Studies at the University of Michigan, and exit polls conducted by CBS News and the *New York Times*.[44] Such data are copious for the 1976, 1980, and 1984 presidential elections.

The first fact that can be established from such data is that evangelicals, however precisely defined, are a sizable and apparently growing proportion of the electorate. The Gallup-type surveys track the evangelicals in the electorate as having risen from 21 percent in 1976 to 23 percent in August 1980, thereafter rising, with fluctuations, to a peak of 32 percent in 1987, from which they declined to 26 percent in 1988. The Center for Political Studies numbers show them rising more gently, from 15 percent in 1980 to 17 percent in November 1984. White evangelicals are heavily concentrated in the South. Elsewhere in the nation they amount to slightly over a tenth of the white electorate, whereas in the South they are close to a third of the same group. Before 1980, evangelicals were less likely than nonevangelicals to be politically active. In the late 1970s and early 1980s great efforts were made to politicize evangelicals, including voter registration drives and efforts to get them to the polls. Evangelicals had already become considerably more politicized shortly before 1976 than over the previous, say, fifty years. It is also likely that the combination of political and social turmoil and the appearance of a Southern born-again Baptist as the presidential candidate in 1976 helped to bring evangelicals back into politics. If so, the tragic irony is that Jimmy Carter's historical legacy may have been a new evangelical constituency that, disillusioned with Carter's politics, helped to install Ronald Reagan in the White House.

White evangelicals in the South largely opted out of politics in the South from the 1920s (perhaps earlier) until the 1970s, then returned to the political fight from 1976 on. Several reasons could be advanced for that: they didn't need to get involved, because the "Solid South" had a political system that protected the *status quo*, including the religious interests of evangelicals (and perhaps also their racial attitudes); only after the impact of "liberalism" or "secular humanism" was felt in various ways (through Supreme Court decisions, federal enforcement programs, the civil rights movement) did evangelicals feel called upon to get down into the political arena. It certainly appears[45] that *since* 1980, while evangelical participation in politics outside the South has grown steadily but slightly from a low base, in the South it has fluctuated wildly. North and South, there has been a shift toward the Republican Party, and that shift has been even more pronounced in the South than elsewhere in the nation. In religious and perhaps in other ways, the shift toward conservatism in politics is intimately connected with the continuing consequences of the energies released, as in a nuclear fission, by the splitting apart of the one-party Democratic regime in the South.

Important as was the part evangelical Protestantism played in these political transformations, other factors were at work. The issues of God would not have been enough to redraw the political map of the United States had it not been that, in the second half of the 1970s, tens of millions of Americans were so shaken by international and economic issues that they were ready to turn toward conservative leadership, which, only a few years before, would have seemed strange and frightening.

¤ 8 ¤

The Strange Death of
John Maynard Keynes

There has been an intellectual revolution moving with the power
and speed of a glacier. Glaciers move very slowly, but they move
with irresistible force. As the glacier gets closer and closer to fifty
percent, everyone says there has been a sudden change. But in fact,
underneath, the intellectual change is smooth and unstoppable.
Ideas do move the world.
— *Martin Anderson, interview with the author, 1995*

IN THE 1930s, the American economy was subjected to a crisis so
severe that it came close to destroying the political system of the United
States. As a consequence of that cataclysm, which halved the gross national product (GNP) and made a quarter of the workforce unemployed, American economic thought was turned upside down. By the
end of the 1930s, in the worlds of politics and business, all but the
deepest-dyed conservatives had come to accept a leading role for the
government in guiding and stimulating the economy. In the academic
economics profession, all but the crustiest had accepted what was known
as the Keynesian revolution.

The real John Maynard Keynes, a Cambridge economics professor,
intermittently successful market speculator, and adviser to British governments and to the Bank of England, was both complex and to some extent self-contradictory. His views were diverse. They were certainly very
different from the simplistic picture that has been handed down of him
as a socialist arch-priest of the all-powerful state. He was, if anything, a
liberal in the older, European sense of the word. He was a believer in
capitalism who was trying to rescue as much as possible of the capitalist

system at a time when it was being battered by terrifying storms of war and inflation, unemployment, and deflation. Still, the gospel according to Keynes, as welcomed to the United States by the likes of Harvard's Alvin Hansen and his disciples, such as John Kenneth Galbraith and a whole generation of young academic economists, did emphasize the right and the responsibility of the government to intervene in order to maintain the aggregate demand for goods and services. It did see the government as the people's protector against the wild winds of unregulated economic forces. And it did usher in a third of a century during which public economic policy was dominated by a loose, uneasy consensus between labor and management, liberals and conservatives.

In their hearts, no doubt, most bankers and corporate managers never liked the American welfare state and the high level of taxation needed to pay for it. They were profoundly ambivalent about the extent to which they found themselves obliged to share power on the factory floor with the new giant industrial unions. But from the late 1930s until the 1970s, most conservatives grudgingly accepted the need for a more or less comprehensive welfare state as the lesser of two evils when contrasted with the specter of class war and class politics raised by the industrial conflicts of the Depression years. The boom years of the 1950s, based on full employment, high wages, and collective bargaining between big business and big unions, seemed to many to show that this was a better way than the old era of raw industrial conflict. So, until the fall of Lyndon Johnson in 1968, the American version of Keynesianism reigned in the White House, where one Keynes disciple succeeded another on the President's Council of Economic Advisers. The election of Richard Nixon put an end to that succession, but for a few years longer Keynesian doctrine predominated in most great American graduate schools — the University of Chicago always excepted.

The economic stresses of the 1970s and the early 1980s were less dramatic than those of the 1930s, though the recession of 1981–1982 was deeper than any since the Great Depression of the 1930s. But they too saw the overthrow of the prevailing economic orthodoxy. Tom Sargent, of the University of Minnesota economics department, later a champion of the new conservative doctrines, remembered his own reluctant conversion. "When I started teaching I gave my students the standard Keynesian stuff. It was the most careful presentation I could give as a true believer." For Sargent the moment of truth came while he was working with Neil Wallace on a project at the Federal Reserve Bank in Minneapolis. "This study was the apotheosis of Keynesianism. We were thrilled to be working on it. But about eighteen months into the project, Neil and I realized that it was flawed. It was a tragic realization — and painful. We scrapped the project, and that hurt."[1] If there had been statues of John Maynard Keynes on the leading Ivy League campuses — and in retrospect it seems an unaccountable oversight that there were none — then by the late 1970s eager teams of monetarist graduate students would have been yoking up tractors and cranes to topple them like the statue of Feliks Dzerzhinsky outside the Lubyanka in 1991.

The age of Keynes ended. Once again, there were complex, subtle interactions between the world of ideas and the swirl of world events. From the late 1960s on, the silent plague of inflation began to corrupt the economies of the industrialized world. (Some thought it was caused by the Johnson administration's decision to increase military expenditure for the Vietnam War without increasing taxes; nonsense, said others.) Even if inflation was already present in the system by the late 1960s, however, the biggest single cause of the economic transformation that ended the years of almost continuous economic growth, and the corresponding optimism of the years of the liberal consensus, was the doubling of the crude oil price as a result of the Arab oil boycott in 1973. There was then a further quadrupling in the oil price as a result of the Iranian revolution of 1979. Together, the two sharp price rises ended the biggest single advantage the developed countries in general and the United States especially had enjoyed: cheap energy.

The crisis had crept up stealthily. Between 1957 and 1963, surplus capacity in the United States totaled about four million barrels of oil a day.[2] By early 1971, for the first time, the Texas Railroad Commission, and the similar regulatory bodies in Oklahoma, Louisiana, and the other oil-producing states, allowed production at 100 percent of capacity. By 1973, even before the Arab oil embargo, imports of oil were supplying 36 percent of U.S. demand. That spring, James Akins, then President Nixon's adviser on energy policy, wrote an article in the influential journal *Foreign Affairs* called "The Oil Crisis: This Time the Wolf Is Here." The wolf came down on the fold that fall in the shape of the Arab oil boycott and the OPEC price rise. But the gate had already been opened by the exhaustion of domestic oilfields.

At the same time, the world economy was hit by other causes of inflation. There was a comparable jump in the price of other commodities, notably wheat, the price of which rose sharply as a result of the disastrous crop failures in the late 1960s in the "virgin lands" of Kazakhstan and other parts of the Soviet Union. The Soviet government, instead of relying on the vast wheatfields of southern Russia, was driven into the world market to buy from Midwestern, Canadian, and other western suppliers. These inflationary pressures caused real economic damage. This was graphically presented[3] by comparing the average performance of the U.S. economy in three vital respects over the period from 1962 to 1973 with its performance in those same three respects over the next dozen years, from 1973 to 1986. Before the oil price rise, the unemployment rate averaged 4.7 percent. Over the later period, it averaged 7.4 percent. Inflation averaged 4.1 percent over the first period and 6.7 percent over the second. And the gross national product, which rose on the average by just under 4 percent in the Kennedy-Johnson-Nixon period, crept up after the oil shock by an average of only 2.3 percent. What was more, the lowest annual unemployment of the years 1974 to 1986 was roughly the same as the highest unemployment rate of the 1959–1973 period, and the lowest annual inflation rate of the 1973–1986 period was roughly the same as the highest inflation rate of the previous quarter century.

By 1974 inflation had reached the highest level seen in the United States since 1919. Output at the same time was soggy, and unemployment rose inexorably. President Nixon and his economic advisers worried constantly about the dilemma of rising inflation and rising unemployment. It bothered them especially in the runup to the 1972 election. But it was not until after the 1973 oil shock that there was a general perception that the United States and the developed world as a whole faced a new situation, which was soon given a new name: stagflation.

The energy crisis, inflation, and the combination of inflation with stagnant production and high unemployment, now called stagflation, were all in greater or less degree world problems. But in the later 1970s, first American corporate management and then Washington became aware that certain problems were afflicting the United States selectively. The economies of Western Europe and Japan were not only competing successfully with American exporters in other markets; they were beginning to penetrate the American domestic market itself. For the first time in its history, the United States had to worry about relative economic decline. And this was not a distant, long-term worry. It showed in the place where corporate managers feel pain first: on the bottom line.[4]

For one thing, after twenty years of uproarious growth, the domestic market for some industries was approaching saturation. By 1979, for example, there was one car for every two residents in the United States, against one for every four in the 1950s.[5] By 1970, 99 percent of American homes had refrigerators, electric irons, and radios. Not only that: American manufacturers, for the first time ever, found themselves faced with serious foreign competition in the domestic market, not just for a few lines of luxury goods, but on their strongest ground: in domestic appliances, electronics, automobiles, aircraft engines. In 1969 imported merchandise accounted for less than 14 percent of GNP in the U.S. manufacturing sector. Ten years later, that proportion had grown to 37.8 percent, and by 1986 it was almost 45 percent.[6]

Caught in a classic squeeze between rising costs and prices held down by foreign competition, profits collapsed. The average net profit after tax of U.S. nonfinancial corporations fell from almost 10 percent in 1965 to an average of about 6 percent in the second half of the 1970s and to under 5 percent by 1980.[7]

At this point both corporate management and government decided that something must be done. Suddenly, workers found themselves in a new, harsher climate. "It's freeze time, boys!" cried the new hero of corporate business, Chrysler's Lee Iacocca.[8] Corporate business adopted a number of strategies whose underlying strategic aim was to restore profitability and also to restore management's sense of being master in its own house.

One strategy was dubbed by no less an expert on manufacturing than Akio Morita, the founder of Sony, as the "hollowing" of American industry. Indeed, Morita went so far as to say that the United States "is abandoning its status as an industrial power." He exaggerated. But in the late 1970s, American corporate management launched into a systematic effort to "outsource" production in the cheapest labor market. Production was shifted to *maquiladora* plants built in a favorable tax regime on the Mexican side of the Rio Grande, or subcontracted to producers in the newly industrializing countries of Southeast Asia, where wage levels, though rising fast, were still fractions of American rates.

Foreign competition for American labor facilitated the second major strategy, indiscreetly named by an assistant secretary of labor in the Nixon administration as "zapping labor."[9] "Beginning in 1978," wrote Bennett Harrison and Barry Bluestone,

and increasingly after the election of President Ronald Reagan, the administration and the Congress intervened in a very different way. Washington began to adopt policies that effectively forced workers to accept wage concessions, discredited the trade union movement, and reduced the cost to business of complying with government regulations.[10]

The consequence was a historic reversal in the long-term trend of American wages. After 1973, real after-tax wages for American workers stagnated. The economy created more than thirty million new jobs. The official number of the unemployed, which had risen to almost 11 percent during the midterm election campaign of 1982, fell to below 6 percent. But the jobs were not as good as those the workers had left. Although efforts have been made to deny this,[11] there is no getting away from the fact that millions of American workers left well-paid, unionized jobs and, often after being softened up by a prolonged period of unemployment, were driven to accept nonunion jobs at substantially lower rates of pay. According to the government's own figures, 11.5 million workers lost their jobs because of plant closures or employment cutbacks between 1979 and 1993 alone. The power of the labor unions was broken. In his magisterial biography of Walter Reuther, of the United Auto Workers, the archetypal leader of an industrial union during the unions' heyday, Nelson Lichtenstein summed up. Since the 1970s, he judged,

> the fortunes of the American trade union movement have fallen more sharply and more continuously than at any time since late in the nineteenth century. [Union members] declined from 30 percent to less than 17 percent, and in the Rust Belt industries, where the CIO once claimed supremacy, a wave of layoffs, plant closures, and outright deunionizations has stripped millions of workers from labor's roll. The UAW lost six hundred thousand [more than a third of its peak membership] in the years after 1970, and like many other trade unions it negotiated a series of concessionary labor contracts that actually reduced wages and benefits . . . For the vast majority of Americans, real wages have been flat and good jobs hard to find during the last two decades.[12]

There was a third strategy that many businessmen adopted. If it was so hard to make a dollar in intensely competitive global manufacturing markets, they reasoned, why not get into service industries, especially into financial services and finance itself? In this they were unconsciously following the advice of the 1960s offshore investment wizard Bernie Cornfeld, whose Investors Overseas Services crashed in 1970. "If you want to make money," that tarnished sage used to say, "don't horse around with steel or light bulbs. Work directly with money!"[13] This is not the place to retell the oft-told story of the great Wall Street boom of 1982–1987. Between 1980 and 1985 the number of shares of stock traded on the New York Stock Exchange doubled. Turnover in government securities quadrupled. And business in futures and more exotic derivative instruments increased even more astronomically.

If you took into consideration the new global character of markets, the convertibility of currencies, the securitization of many kinds of debt, and the psychological climate of the time, it was as if all the money in the world had become available for speculation, and much of it was actually being used for that purpose.

The furious investment in financial markets, and in speculative plays in the shares even of companies that did have a real manufacturing base under the stock-price bubble, was in large part a consequence of the previous squeeze on manufacturing profits. Despairing of making the return their stockholders demanded in manufacturing, many corporate managers turned to mergers, acquisitions, and various forms of corporate restructuring. Corporations were bought, their assets "redeployed," often sold off, unprofitable divisions closed down, investment programs cut back, union agreements repudiated, workers — and this was the real bottom line — forced to make concessions or be fired. What prevailed was an attitude, even an ideology, that emphasized maximum freedom from controls and regulation.

The consequence of this activity, and of corporate management's new strategies to restore profitability generally, was not only to stop the long rise in real wages. It was also, sharply and in reversal of the trend of many previous decades, to increase inequality in America. "After about 1973," wrote Harrison and Bluestone, "the direction changed. Wages, adjusted for inflation, began a long downward trend. Median annual family income stopped growing, even though more family members were working than ever before."

It was not only labor economists or Democrats who thought that. By the end of the Reagan years, the *Wall Street Journal* itself, the bible of business conservatism, conceded that "statistical evidence suggests that the American dream is fading."[14] The role of the Reagan revolution in causing this greater inequality, not just between successful and less successful individuals, but between groups of workers, including men and women and whites and minorities, will be examined in Chapter 10. In the meantime it is worth underlining once again that it was not Ronald

Reagan, nor his administration, who brought in a new economic environment that was starkly less favorable for most Americans while bountiful for a fortunate few. That had already begun to happen when Reagan was inaugurated president.

The tide had begun to turn in the middle 1970s, especially after the oil price rise of 1973. Government policy — responding to crisis levels of inflation — began to shift under President Jimmy Carter. It was Carter's chairman of the Federal Reserve Board, Paul Volcker, who ratcheted the prime rate (the interest rate banks charge their best customers) up to 20 percent in 1978. It worked. The rate of inflation in the price of consumer goods fell to 6.1 percent in 1982 and 3.2 percent in 1983. Both the Carter administration, in 1980, and even more so the Reagan administration, in 1981–1982, deliberately brought about recessions through their use of policy tools. Their reasons, in each case, were well intentioned according to their lights. They decided they must choke back inflation and expand the productivity and therefore the competitiveness and profitability of American industry. They both achieved their goals. But the price, in the loss of income, jobs, and hopes of the good life, was bitterly high. And it was unequally distributed.

THIS REVOLUTION had severe economic consequences. It had bewildering *intellectual* consequences as well. The best known of them is the shift of emphasis from what is called the "demand side" of economic analysis to the "supply side," and the rise, in place of the vanquished Keynesians, of a new school of conservative economists known as supply-siders. You might suppose that the dismal science of economics does not lend itself to mythology, but you would be wrong. History is peppered by examples of economic myth and legend, and none is more appealing, or more misleading, than the myth of Arthur Laffer, the curve, and the napkin.

The myth is that one day in 1974 economic orthodoxy in the United States changed when an economist named Arthur Laffer, while having lunch in a restaurant called the Two Continents, near the Treasury Department in Washington, took a pencil and drew a curve on a paper napkin. It showed how, as the rate of taxation increases from zero to 100 percent, the revenue raised by the tax responds. The hump-backed curve illustrates how as the tax rate rises from zero, revenue will increase, but as it approaches 100 percent, with potential taxpayers avoiding and evading the tax, revenue will fall back toward zero.

Laffer and his friends, so the myth goes, drew the conclusion that government's economic policy should focus on doing things for businessmen on the supply side of the primal supply-demand equation, as opposed to doing things for consumers on the demand side. In particular, the argument focused on taxation. In its calmer, more rational version, it argued that when government cut taxes, it would not lose as much revenue in the short term as you might think, because the stimulating effect on the economy would increase the tax base. But it came to be caricatured — by incautious conservative enthusiasts as well as by those who did not buy the supply-side case — as a claim that if you cut taxes, you would stimulate the economy so much that you would almost immediately receive more revenue from lower taxes.

The fundamental proposition of the supply-side argument is not new.[15] In 1776 Adam Smith saw that "high taxes, sometimes by diminishing the consumption of taxed commodities" — Smith was writing at a time when taxes on income did not exist and was therefore thinking of excise taxes — "and sometimes by encouraging smuggling, frequently afford a smaller revenue to government than what might be drawn from more moderate taxes." In the 1920s Andrew Mellon understood that "more revenue may often be obtained by lower taxes." Even John Maynard Keynes, later demonized by conservatives as the very antithesis of their supply-side dogma, wrote in 1933 that "given sufficient time to gather the fruits, a reduction of taxation will run a better chance than an increase of balancing the budget."

The curve-napkin myth is a charming piece of journalistic license. For one thing, the Two Continents is a posh place with expensive damask napkins; you would have to be a boor to try to draw on them. For another, Arthur Laffer has said he has no recollection of doing anything of the kind.[16] The story was the invention of a journalist and talented publicist named Jude Wanniski, who became in effect chief public relations officer for the thoughts of Arthur Laffer.

Laffer graduated from Yale in 1963 and, after earning his doctorate at Stanford, joined the faculty of the University of Chicago, an institution that has played a vital role in the development of conservative ideas about economics. (It is ironic that for a long time conservatives detested Chicago because of what they saw as the liberal influence of president Robert M. Hutchins.) At Chicago Laffer came under the influence of Robert Mundell, a Canadian economist who later moved to Columbia University in New York. It was Mundell who drew Laffer's attention to the relationship between tax *rates* and tax *revenues*.

Jude Wanniski came to his fateful partnership with Laffer by a very different route. A liberal Democrat who had campaigned for Adlai Stevenson and even flirted with the Young People's Socialist League, Wanniski graduated from the University of California at Los Angeles in 1959. By 1968 he had so far moved from his youthful loyalties as to vote for Nixon. In 1971, when he met Laffer, he was working for a mildly conservative paper, the *National Observer.* In 1972 he moved to the *Wall Street Journal,* where he persuaded the editorial page editor, Robert Bartley, who had recently replaced the more traditional conservative Vermont Royster, to give his and Laffer's ideas the credibility conveyed by the *Journal.* It was in its pages, on December 11, 1974, that Wanniski wrote what was to be the supply-side manifesto. "The level of U.S. taxes," he wrote, "has become a drag on economic growth in the United States. The national economy is being choked by taxes — asphyxiated . . . A tax cut not only increases demand, but increases the incentive to produce . . . With lower taxes, it is more attractive to invest and more attractive to work; demand is increased, but so is supply."

Soon Wanniski's theorizing was receiving powerful support from Irving Kristol, who had hitched his wagon to the star of the *Journal.* It was Herb Stein, Nixon's former economic adviser, who found the name for this newborn school. He called them the "supply-side fiscalists," meaning those who would use fiscal policy to strengthen the supply-side of the national economy. Wanniski embraced the supply-side label, but dropped "fiscalist," perhaps because it sounded too technical. In any case, the machinery of the new conservative institutions was about to scoop up Wanniski and roll him along. In 1976 Leslie Lenkovsky, director of the Richardson Foundation, which applied the accumulated profits of Vicks VapoRub as aroma therapy for the new ideas of the right, gave Wanniski $40,000 to write a book on economic policy.

Thus subsidized, and published in 1978 as *The Way the World Works,* the book exemplified a new arrogance among intellectuals on the right. Wanniski's theories were not tentatively offered; they were stated as "the way the world works." His book was much more than an exposition of the supply-side theory about taxation. It was a full-throated defense of capitalism. He dismissed the "limits to growth" argument, made fashionable by the Club of Rome in the early 1970s, with a confident half-truth: yes, there are physical limits, but they can be relentlessly overpowered by "intellectual growth." The trouble with intellectual growth is that it cannot be measured in a coinage that is universally accepted. One man's intellectual growth is another man's error. Wanniski, however, laid about him in energetic fashion, asserting now that the "relative peacefulness of Europe between 1815 and 1914 was in part due to the open frontier in America," now that "it is by no means clear that the [Soviet Union's] political economy is inferior to that of the United States," or again that "the driving force of civilization is a quest for a system that will maximize capital." But the core of his thesis, decorated with suchlike hyperbole, was an argument against socialism that depended on another idea of Arthur Laffer's.

In 1974 Laffer had sent a memo to William Simon, then secretary of the treasury, arguing that "marginal taxes of all sorts [were] a wedge between what an employer pays his factors of production and what they ultimately received in after-tax income." The socialist system, Wanniski argued, was grossly inefficient, because the task of distributing resources of labor and other resources was too difficult for a bureaucracy; it could be better performed by the market. Yet the market system, too, became "grossly inefficient, perhaps even more than the socialist system, when the expanding government wedge crushes out incentives and underemploys a whole economy."

Whatever the merits of Arthur Laffer's arguments, as served up by such master publicists as Irving Kristol and Jude Wanniski, the real origins of the conservative revolution in economic thinking did not lie in the inspired theorizing of a small coterie of supply-side economists, with or without napkins. It was, as we have seen, a response to the totally new economic situation faced by the developed world as a result of a number of events in the outside world in the late 1960s and 1970s. To a substantial extent, these problems originated outside the United States. The revolution also represented the maturing of an intellectual reaction to the prevailing ideas, usually, if somewhat inaccurately, labeled "Keynesian," which had been going on for decades in such quiet places as the economics department of the University of Chicago.

AT THE HEART of the prevailing Keynesian orthodoxy was the idea that there was a trade-off between inflation and unemployment. Let unemployment rise, the Keynesians assumed, and government had only to stimulate aggregate demand, either by public investment or by cutting taxes, and all would be well. This orthodoxy was enshrined in the Phillips curve, a graph representing the relation between employment and inflation.[17] Now, suddenly, instead of inflation rising as unemployment declined, and unemployment rising if inflation was forced down, both unemployment *and* inflation were running at historically high levels. For policymakers, the question was, as always, "What is to be done?" But for some economists, with varying degrees of excitement and even glee, it was, "Is the reign of Keynesian orthodoxy at long last coming to an end?"

The conservative revolution in economics in the 1970s was certainly not just a matter of Arthur Laffer and his evangelist, Jude Wanniski, discovering the virtues of the fiscal supply side. Nor was it merely a matter of rejecting the Keynesian trade-off between inflation and unemployment, though the arrival of stagflation certainly focused minds on the limitations of Keynesian orthodoxy as it had been taught and understood in the United States for three decades. Rather, the new circumstances seemed to baffle the analytical thinking of the prevailing Keynesian orthodoxy, so that many economists thought it might be worth trying some of the alternative ideas.

One of these was the theory known as monetarism. Younger economists also lengthened the time horizon of their analysis, looking at lifetime earnings and long-term decisions rather than at short-term cash flows. They looked at expectations. And they thought about incentives: what makes people decide to work, to invest, to buy, or to sell.[18]

Monetarism was the oldest of these new economic theories, and the soonest to be abandoned, at least in its stricter definition. The vogue for monetarism and the overthrow of Keynesian orthodoxy can be traced to two seminal papers written as early as 1967. (The term "monetarism" itself was apparently coined in 1968 by Professor Karl Brunner of the University of Rochester.) One was by Edward Phelps. The other was a presidential address to the American Economic Association by Professor Milton Friedman of the University of Chicago. More revered on the right than any of the gurus of American Keynesianism ever was on the left, more influential than Paul Samuelson or Robert Solow, James Tobin or John Kenneth Galbraith, Milton Friedman came in time to occupy a position on the right comparable with the eminence of Keynes himself for liberals.

Professor Friedman confirmed in an interview[19] his belief that "the watershed in the abandonment of Keynesian doctrine was the conflict between Keynesian orthodoxy and the Phillips curve." That was the terminal point, as he saw it, of a debate that had been going on for many years. The conflict of ideas was decisively resolved, he maintained, by an external event: "the experience of the stagflation of the 1970s." Or as he put it more formally in his 1976 Nobel lecture:

> The hypothesis that there is a stable relation between the level of unemployment and the rate of inflation was adopted by the economics profession with alacrity. It filled a gap in Keynes's theoretical

structure . . . But as the 1950s turned into the 1960s, and the 1960s into the 1970s, it became increasingly difficult to accept the hypothesis in its simple form. It seemed to take larger and larger doses of inflation to keep down the level of unemployment. Stagflation reared its ugly head.[20]

To Friedman and other conservatives, that phenomenon — of unemployment and inflation rising hand in hand when there was supposed to be a trade-off between them — could not be explained in Keynesian terms; but it was something "which we had predicted."

Throughout his career, Milton Friedman pursued with rare intellectual clarity and equal determination two connected but distinguishable ideas. One lies in the field of political economy, the other in technical economics. Or, as he put it to me, "My work has been in two categories: strictly scientific work on monetarism and so on. And political work on freedom. Fundamentally the emphasis has been on freedom." The inescapable logical inference is that, for all the brilliance of Friedman's work on economic theory, and particularly in the fields of economic theory, monetary analysis, and monetary policy, it has been fundamentally political. The driving engine of his formidable achievement has been a lifelong conviction that political and economic freedom are inextricably connected.[21]

An amiable man whose manners are most gentle and generous when he is most determinedly upsetting the apple cart of conventional wisdom, Friedman was born in 1912 in Brooklyn, the only son of a family of Jewish immigrants from Carpatho-Ruthenia, one of the poorest provinces of Europe, then part of Austro-Hungary, subsequently part of Czechoslovakia, and now part of Ukraine. His parents moved from New York to Rahway, New Jersey, when he was one year old, and when he was still in high school his father died. In 1928, financed by odd jobs and a scholarship, he entered Rutgers University, where he majored in mathematics and economics. At Rutgers he was a pupil of two remarkable men, the white-haired, pipe-smoking Arthur F. Burns, later President Nixon's White House counselor and chairman of the Federal Reserve Board, himself an immigrant from Austria; and the economist Homer Jones. Thanks to Jones, he was offered a scholarship to do graduate work in economics at the University of Chicago. There, he was a pupil of Jacob Viner and other powerful, and conservative, economists. In the 1930s, he was exposed to a variety of economic ideas at Columbia University, where he did his doctoral work, and elsewhere, and acquired experience at various government institutes, among them the National Bureau of Economic Research, where he worked on medical incomes with Simon Kuznets, the inventor of modern study of national income. During the war, he worked for the U.S. Treasury.

In 1946 he succeeded Jacob Viner in his chair at Chicago, and he stayed there, in a faculty of brilliant economists that included Hayek, George Stigler, and many others. He traveled to the first meeting of the Mont Pélerin Society in 1947, worked for a year for the Marshall Plan in Paris, and in 1953–1954 spent some time at John Maynard Keynes's alma mater, Cambridge. In the early 1960s the two themes of his life work both came to fruition within a year of each other. The theoretical work culminated in his publication (with the economic historian Anna Schwartz) of *A Monetary History of the United States*. The eight-hundred-page magnum opus drew both on the theory being developed at the University of Chicago and on empirical studies he had been asked (by his old patron Arthur Burns) to do for the National Bureau of Economic Research on the role of money in the trade cycle.

In 1938 Friedman married a Chicago colleague, Rose Director, who shared her husband's concern about the threat to personal freedom from collectivism. In 1962, they published *Capitalism and Freedom*, which argued the case for competitive capitalism and attacked government intervention. Little noticed when it was first published, the book has subsequently sold more than half a million copies. Friedman was becoming a political economist. He was an informal adviser to the Goldwater campaign in 1964. More formally, he advised Richard Nixon both in his election campaign in 1968 and in office. He was also an adviser to Ronald Reagan in his 1980 campaign, and in the spring of that year he and his wife published *Free to Choose*, a popular version of their argument for personal freedom and against government intervention. It was the nonfiction best seller of the year in the United States and, something that does not happen to many books about economics, was turned into a highly successful ten-part television series. When Reagan became president, Friedman served him in a number of capacities, among them as a member of several White House commissions. In 1977, on his retirement from Chicago, Friedman moved to the Hoover Institution at Stanford.

This brief biographic sketch makes the point that Friedman was always *both* an economic analyst *and* a conservative political philosopher or, if you prefer, a libertarian ideologue. Out of his technical work on

money there emerged a doctrine, monetarism, that was at once technical and, in its implications, as Friedman of course clearly understood,
highly political. The heart of his work was an analysis of the relation
between changes in money and changes in nominal income (the sum of
output and prices) in the modern history of the United States, from
1865 to 1960. From this he derived four propositions.[22]

1. That if there is to be price stability, the money stock must grow
without inflation.

2. That economic growth can be achieved with either rising or falling prices, provided price changes are moderate and predictable.

3. That the relations between changes in money and changes in the
variables money affects are unchanging.

4. That changes in money cause changes in income, and not the
other way around.

The finding that was at first received by orthodox economists with
something close to incredulity was drawn from Friedman's account of
the Great Depression of 1929 to 1933. This was the key to the history of
economic thought since the 1930s, and the very catastrophe that had
handed to Keynes the crown of his influence, because Keynes had argued that in the right circumstances unemployment could have been
brought down by appropriate inflationary spending. No, said Friedman,
the Great Depression was essentially the result of mistakes in monetary
policy. "The Great Contraction," Friedman wrote in his famous presidential lecture to the American Economic Association, "is tragic testi-
mony to the power of monetary policy, not — as Keynes and so many of
his contemporaries believed — evidence of its impotence."[23]

That 1967 lecture was a turning point in economic fashion; indeed,
in the history of modern conservatism. Friedman has always generously shared credit for the intellectual revolution with the economist Ed
Phelps.[24] Both Phelps and Friedman argued that, so far from inflation
being a condition that could be ameliorated by government spending,
there was a "natural" rate of inflation, and that trying to push unemployment below its natural rate for a long period would only lead to high and
accelerating inflation.[25] Friedman believed that interest rates were less
useful as evidence of what was happening in the economy than changes
in the quantity of money. He also suggested that, just as economists had
argued for decades that there was a "natural" interest rate, so there was a
natural rate of unemployment.[26]

This conclusion led him through a rather abstruse argument about
the difference between the real quantities in the economy — of money,
prices, wages, employment — and the nominal quantities, the only ones

the authorities can control. That brought him to another front in his assault on the Keynesians, in Friedman's mind so logically connected to the flaws in Keynes's assumptions about the trade-off between inflation and unemployment as to be the second wing of the same proposition. This was Friedman's belief in the determining importance of monetary policy.

Just as Friedman's ideas about inflation were based on a massive study of the monetary history of the United States,[27] so his monetary theory was rooted in an exhaustive statistical study.[28] In it, he showed that, at least at certain periods, growth in the money supply and in the gross national product seemed to rise and fall together. Courageously, Friedman disinterred the "quantity theory of money," which had been largely discredited since the 1929 crash. Only at the University of Chicago had a flickering flame of interest in this theory been kept alight.

This is not the place to unpick the complex arguments that led Friedman to his conclusions. It is the conclusions that matter. Friedman put forward as a theory that growth in the velocity with which money circulates is a highly reliable predictor of growth in the GNP. Gradually he and his disciples elaborated a whole theory of monetarism that opposed Keynesianism. Again, the role of the University of Chicago can hardly be exaggerated; while not all of the influential monetarists were to be found there at any one time, few of them had not passed through that seminary of the new classical economics at some stage in their careers.

The monetarists put their emphasis on the money supply, and specifically on the velocity of the circulation of money, as the most important determinant of total spending and therefore of the growth of the economy. They advocated slower, smoother growth of the money supply. In layman's language, the monetarists, more convinced that the economy could right itself, were less keen on the government's intervening to manage the economy than their Keynesian opponents. Their ideas fit with the general conservative bias against government activism and undercut the liberal faith in governmental intervention.

The supply of money, in Friedman's new universe, was the master key. The most audacious, and the most influential, of his claims in the field of theoretical economics, as a guide for policy, was his insistence that the sole cause of inflation, the scourge that had reappeared to ravage the economies and threaten the social peace of the last quarter of the twentieth century, was the money supply. He went so far as to say that "inflation is always and everywhere a monetary phenomenon."[29]

Monetarism caught on swiftly in the economics profession. It was soon flanked by two refinements: supply-side economics and the "rational expectations" school of economic analysis. We have already outlined the supply-side argument. Analysis of rational expectations in relation to price movements originated in an idea floated by the economist John F. Muth in a 1961 article.[30] This was picked up and developed by two disciples of Friedman's, Robert Lucas and Thomas Sargent. They applied the rational expectations hypothesis to econometric models. The details of the argument are highly complex (and also disputed). The point in the context of the history of conservative ideas is that this hypothesis, too, also tended to undermine the case for systematic monetary policy on the part of government.

Monetarism, supply-side economics, and rational expectations analysis are highly technical fields of economic study. Together, they formed what came to be known as New Classical Economics. It was not a development that made much impact on the nightly television news; the principles were not those with which you could start a mob or even sell an evening newspaper. But lurking behind the learned statistical studies, the sophisticated analysis, and the persuasive argumentation, as a shark lurks in the water, was a harsh, ultimately political preference. The monetarists and their allies argued that it was not as easy as the Keynesians had supposed for government to bring down the unemployment rate by allowing inflation to grow. What they did not say openly was that, for them, it was also not so important. If you had to choose, they believed, unemployment was a lesser evil than inflation.[31]

Friedman has admitted that his political work is more important to him than his technical economic analysis. It is therefore fair to examine the political impact even of his "scientific" work. Given his powerful intellect, it is reasonable to infer that he was perfectly aware of its political implications. He has acknowledged a preference for private over public action, and has devoted huge energy to demolishing the Keynesian proposition that by allowing some inflation we may reduce unemployment.

The choice between inflation and unemployment is no arid academic exercise. Still less is it politically neutral. Inflation damages certain groups in society — in any society — more than others. So does unemployment. Among the groups which have an interest in holding down inflation, even if that means a rise in unemployment, are businessmen, investors, those whose savings supply a major part of their income — in short, those whose position depends on the possession of capital. Among those who fear unemployment more than inflation are those whose only source of income is the wages and salaries they can hope to earn in work. The choice between unemployment and inflation, in a word, is a political choice between capital and labor.

This may sound like simple stuff, even crude, but it is true nonetheless. Moreover, while Milton Friedman himself has always expressed his economic arguments with restraint, some of the New Classical school were not so sober in their language. When the inflation rate passed 6 percent, for example, James Buchanan and his co-author, Richard Wagner, openly associated inflation with the end of civilization as they knew it. They detected "a generalized erosion in public and private manners, increasingly liberalized attitudes toward sexual activities, a declining vitality of the Puritan work ethic . . . explosion of the welfare rolls, widespread corruption," and they asked, "Who can deny that inflation plays some role?"[32] This is not the language of serious academic inquiry.

Such jeremiads were common in the 1970s, and it was becoming equally commonplace to associate all that seemed distasteful and menacing in society with inflation and the liberal economic doctrines that — justly or unjustly — were blamed for it. It is also true that the rise of monetarism coincided historically with the period when the almost unbroken prosperity of the postwar expansion had come to an end. The terms of trade were moving against the men and women who depended mainly on selling their labor. The age of monetarism was also, not coincidentally, an age when money was becoming once again a commodity in short supply. Whatever their intentions may have been, those who put forward the supply of money as the principal, perhaps the only, determinant of economic activity were establishing a case that was bound to be attractive to those who had money to supply.

SO FAR WE have been talking about the great subterranean shift in economic thinking which took place in the 1970s inside the walls of the academy and in its fragile outposts, in such places as the President's Council of Economic Advisers and the Federal Reserve system. That profound change was expressed in seminars and learned papers, in abstruse equations and econometric models. In those same years, however, a far more boisterous change was taking place in economic politics in the grittiest and most basic way. It took the shape of a tax rebellion, a familiar feature of American populism since the days of Shays' Rebellion and the Whiskey Rebellion. While the professors were excited by the idea that it was the monetary side of public policy that ought to be emphasized, the citizens' rebellion was strictly fiscal. And if in academic halls arguments were polite and abstract, the ringleaders of tax rebellion were loud and to the point.

Why do people rebel? Not necessarily because life is intolerable. More often it is a perceived inequity, a change for the worse, fear for the future, that calls out the rebels. In California in the 1970s, all those circumstances were present, and so were some special factors. For one thing, where in the 1970s federal income taxes were progressive — meaning that the higher your income, the more tax you paid — state property taxes were sharply regressive. One economist showed, for example, that in the mid-1970s a family of four with an income of $10,000 a year paid more state and local tax than a similar family with an income of $25,000 a year.[33]

In California, this inequity was made harder to bear because of a specific local shift in the burden of property tax from business property to private homes. In June 1965 a corrupt tax assessor in San Francisco was caught and sent to prison. In 1966 the California State assembly responded by passing an "assessment reform act." It was expected to reduce property taxes for homeowners. In fact, it had the opposite effect. By causing all property to be assessed at 25 percent of its actual value, the act shifted half a million dollars of assessed valuation from commercial to residential property.[34]

The surge in tax assessments came in two waves. The first, caused by the 1966 act, was largely nullified by two "homestead exceptions," which the Assembly hastily passed in 1968 and again in 1972. But the second wave followed. Because the oil price rise made people wary of moving too far out of town into new subdivisions, it drove up the price of existing homes. There was also an astonishing increase of more than 50 percent in personal income in California between 1973 and 1978. House prices exploded. Between April 1974 and April 1978 the average price of a single-family home in Los Angeles jumped from $37,000 to $83,000. At the same time, personal income taxes rose by more than 150 percent. State aid for schools, welfare, and other community spending went down, because the relevant formulae were inversely related to a community's property values! Middle- and lower-income Californians caught it all ways. Income tax went up, property taxes went up, and state contributions to local spending on services went down. A political revolt was inevitable, and in 1977 it duly happened.

The official Democratic leadership failed to take its opportunity. Governor Jerry Brown, loftily absorbed by his unearthly New Age preoccupations and his entirely down-to-earth political ambitions, was unsympathetic to the angry suburbanites. So was Willie Brown, the powerful chair of the Revenue and Taxation Committee in the Assembly's lower house, and now mayor of San Francisco. A number of local politicians picked up the issue. By May 1977 one of them had gathered 400,000 signatures in Southern California for an initiative on the ballot, and another had gathered 300,000 in the North. Once they joined forces, they mustered well over the half million votes needed, and by Election Day they had in fact collected 1.2 million signatures.

The driving force behind this extraordinarily effective grass-roots movement for tax reform was Howard Jarvis, a maverick conservative who had been around California politics since Franklin D. Roosevelt was president. Brought up in Utah, where he had played semipro baseball and fought twenty-one professional bouts as a boxer, Jarvis moved to California in 1931 and became a successful home appliance manufacturer and an activist in a long series of conservative causes. At different times he founded a right-to-work committee and lobbied for repeal of the federal income tax. He was criticized for retaining most of the money he raised for Businessmen for Goldwater in 1964.[35]

Jarvis's Proposition 13 promised that all property would be taxed at a flat 1 percent of actual value, and that there would be no new taxes. It meant that taxes would be rolled back almost to 1975–1976 levels. But while it saved homeowners $2 billion, it saved $3.5 billion for the owners of commercial property. And it cut the revenue of local governments by 23 percent.

The pros and the antis were equally balanced until Jarvis and his PR agency adopted the direct mail technique that had already made Richard Viguerie such an important figure in the conservative movement in the East. A taxpayer would receive a computer-written letter in which Jarvis said he was shocked to learn that the taxpayer's 1977 property tax was such-and-such, and then predicted that this high figure would treble within three years. The prediction was untrue, but it looked plausible because of current rumors that the 1978 reassessment of property in sought-after West Los Angeles would triple.

Proposition 13 duly passed, sending shock waves to many other parts of the country. "That was a bullet from a loaded gun that went off in California," said an Oregon state legislator. "But it's still on its way to its ultimate target — the high level of federal spending." Even before Proposition 13 passed, the tax revolt had reached the national stage.

One important underlying reason for the tax revolt at local, state, and federal levels was that dread consequence of inflation known as "bracket creep." Levels of taxation will rise, even if tax rates do not, as long as the nominal value of either income or property is being swollen by inflation. In 1961, marginal rates of income tax in the federal code varied from 20 percent to 91 percent. But 88 percent of all tax returns paid between 20 and 22 percent, while only 2 percent paid over 32 percent. Almost nine taxpayers out of ten paid, in effect, a flat tax of 22 percent. By the end of the 1970s that had changed dramatically: 45 percent of all taxpayers paid marginal tax rates of more than 23 percent. "Millions of American taxpayers," commented Robert E. Hall and Alvin Rabushka, taxation experts from the Hoover Institution and the originators of the "flat tax" idea promoted by Malcolm (Steve) Forbes in the 1996 Republican presidential primaries, "paid marginal rates that had been intended only for the very rich just two decades earlier."[36] No wonder there was hunger and thirsting after cuts in income tax among the citizens; and no wonder that politicians were drawn to income tax cuts as a policy. By the middle 1970s, many politicians had developed an acute interest in finding ways to meet the voters' wishes at least in this respect.

It is not only individual voters who pay taxes, however. Corporations do too. By the mid-1970s, a formidable new lobby for lower business taxes had emerged in Washington. Traditional business lobby groups, such as the National Association of Manufacturers and the United States Chambers of Commerce, had for decades lobbied for lower taxes with every argument and pressure they could think of. But now, faced with the new and frightening phenomena of stagflation and bracket creep, a new generation of lobbyists went to work with a new concept. They talked about "capital formation," arguing that high taxes were eroding industry's ability to invest and therefore to compete in productivity and ultimately in sales with foreign rivals.

First, in the early 1970s, came the Business Roundtable. Its membership was made up of the chief executives of the very biggest Fortune 500 corporations. The executive culture of these giant businesses had long been not particularly friendly to what was seen as the radical new conservatism. Company executives might be keen enough on corporate profit and personal prosperity, but they were also concerned about their corporate reputation as "good citizens." They had lived long enough with Democratic office holders and the liberal climate to be inhibited in their attacks on high taxes. Under the pressure of economic recession and social turmoil in the 1970s, two new brands of conservative business leaders appeared. Some of them cherished fierce conservative doctrine in their bosoms, but dared to growl their real thoughts only at the country club or to their wives. Others had internalized the liberal climate so much that they supported liberal or professedly apolitical citizens' groups, like Common Cause.

In the 1970s a new generation within the ranks of big business broke with this corporate me-tooism. John Harper, a former chairman of the board of Alcoa, was one of the first to see the need for a new style of business leadership. "What we were doing wasn't working," he said. "All the polls showed business in disfavor. We didn't think people understood how the economic system works. We were getting short shrift from Congress. I thought we were powerless in spite of the stories about how we could manipulate everything." In 1971, with Nixon in the White House, Harper was in Washington. Among the friends he talked with were Arthur Burns, then chairman of the Federal Reserve Board, and John Connally, secretary of the treasury. (No one could say that top business leaders had no access to the higher levels of the Nixon administration!) They advised him that it was no good business trying to operate through lawyers, lobbyists, and corporate vice presidents for public affairs; the chief executives themselves must get involved. So in 1972 Harper founded the Business Roundtable. For the first time for many decades, here was an organization that brought together the CEOs, to lobby not for the narrow interests of their own corporations, but for the interests of corporate business itself, as a whole and on broad, long-term themes. The Business Roundtable was nonpartisan and pragmatic. But the issues its members rallied around were conservative issues: lower business taxes, less regulation, less hobbling of business with environmental regulations in particular.

After Nixon was replaced in the White House by Gerald Ford, former governor John Connally, who had headed up Democrats for Nixon in 1972 and was a corporate lawyer from Texas close to the Richardsons, Basses, and other big Texas oil interests, was succeeded by an even more explicit and ideological conservative, William Simon, a former partner in Salomon Brothers. Throughout the 1970s, Simon was propagating the ideas he published in a 1978 best seller, *A Time for Truth*,[37] in which he lambasted liberalism as "the New Despotism"[38] and called in more restrained terms for a conservative crusade "to avert the threatening collapse of our political and economic order."

Simon understood the importance of winning the intellectual battle, and he used his influence with half a dozen middle-sized foundations — the John M. Olin Foundation, the Heritage Foundation, the Hoover Institution, the Manhattan Institute, and the Institute for Educational

Affairs among them — to reward writers and scholars whose views coincided with his own preferences: for free markets, small government, low taxes, and cuts in welfare expenditure. One issue he tried to project into the limelight was that of "capital formation," which, being interpreted, meant tax breaks for corporations to encourage them to make investments. The IEA, on the other hand, fought the good conservative fight on the cultural and patriotic level, offering "major support" to reinterpretation of the Vietnam War and attacking liberalism as "an established cultural system that condemns the society that sustains it."

With men like Connally and Simon, Burns, and other conservative intellectuals now office holders in Republican administrations, a new and highly effective form of lobbying, more aggressive in style and more in tune with the developing new conservatism, took over the running in Washington. A long-established outfit, unpromisingly called the American Council on Capital Gains and Estate Taxation — a title suggesting that its focus was limited to defending the interests of the stuffiest coupon clippers — changed its name to the American Council for Capital Formation.[39] Great in Washington is the power of euphemism. In 1975 it acquired as its new director an experienced Washington conservative operator, Charls E. Walker, known for his formidable connections in both politics and business as "the insider's insider." A softspoken Texan with a Ph.D. in economics, Walker had worked for Robert Anderson at the Treasury Department in the Eisenhower administration, spent eight years as executive head of the American Bankers Association, in which capacity he was its chief lobbyist, and then served as deputy secretary of the treasury in the Nixon administration. In 1973 he founded his own lobbying firm, Charls Walker Associates, with offices a block from the White House on Pennsylvania Avenue. Among his clients were Alcoa, Ford, GE, Procter and Gamble — and the Business Roundtable.

In 1978 Walker took up the capital formation issue as chairman of the American Council on Capital Formation. Initial funding came from the Weyerhaeuser Company, the Northwestern lumber and wood products company, long associated with conservative politics and the National Forest Products Association.[40] Walker soon put together a powerful cross-party coalition for business tax cutting. Democratic powerhouses in the world of Washington lobbying like the lawyers Clark Clifford and Edward Bennett Williams rubbed shoulders there with chief executives and Republican politicos. In 1978 the council successfully lobbied Congress for a reduction in capital gains tax. The measure was advocated as a spur to investment and productivity. In practice it operated essentially as a set of tax breaks for middle-income and well-to-do Americans, coupled with a modest cut in corporate tax rates and substantial investment tax credits.[41]

This was only the beginning of the consequences for national politics of the victory of Proposition 13 in California. Right-wing groups, including the John Birch Society, seized on the tax-cut issue. The Birchers set up TRIM (Tax Reform Immediately) committees in more than three hundred congressional districts.[42] In Congress, the tax-cut issue launched the career of a major Republican politician. One of the earliest and most enthusiastic converts was Representative Jack Kemp of Buffalo, a former quarterback for the Buffalo Bills, whose district, the archetypal Rust Belt area, was economically ravaged by the recession of the 1970s. Kemp had been captured by the supply-side crowd. His two economic advisers were both conservatives. One, the Texan Paul Craig Roberts, had been hired by Robert Bartley to replace Wanniski on the editorial board of the *Wall Street Journal* when Wanniski went off to write his book and was later to be an assistant secretary of the treasury in the Reagan administration. The other was a conservative economist named Norman Ture: together, they had been working on a Jobs Creation Act.

Again, Jude Wanniski had a colorful story of how that came to change.[43] In 1976 he was working on a story about the scandal of the day, the involvement of Democratic Representative Wayne Hays of Ohio with a secretary named Elizabeth Ray, whose duties were strictly non-stenographic. Wanniski was on his way to interview a stern conservative moralist, Robert Baumann — who later came out and admitted that he was both a homosexual and an alcoholic — when he found himself outside Kemp's office with fifteen minutes to kill. It turned out that Kemp was already a convert to Wanniski's views. "I had finally found an elected representative of the people who was as fanatical as I was," Wanniski commented. In no time at all, the Jobs Creation Act had been scrapped, and Wanniski had plugged the representative into the supply-side network. The result was Kemp-Roth.

Together with Senator William V. Roth of Delaware, once virtually the fief of the Du Pont Company, but now almost as badly hit by the recession in manufacturing as Buffalo, Kemp launched a bold initiative to slash federal income tax. The Kemp-Roth bill proposed a 10 percent cut in federal income taxes every year for three years. Defeated in 1978, it was reintroduced in modified form by the Republican leadership in 1980, with the support of presidential candidate Ronald Reagan. In fact, Kemp-Roth was the subject of one of those intriguing deals, never publicly acknowledged, but nonetheless real as historical events, which divert the course of political history into new channels. In the fall of 1979 Ronald Reagan's top political advisers, especially the much admired John Sears, were beginning to worry about the rising star of Jack Kemp as a conservative Republican presidential candidate, and therefore as a potential rival to their man. So a deal was done.[44] Kemp would drop his presidential campaign, as he was a much younger man, only for the time being. In return Reagan would endorse Kemp-Roth. That, Sears successfully convinced Kemp, would give Kemp national gratitude and prominence. It would also remove a dangerous competitor for the working-class voters Reagan hoped to win, and indeed did win, in 1980, while leaving Kemp in good shape for 1988.

Later, Reagan was to gain support from an astonishing variety of Americans, including those Reagan Democrats who might have gone for Kemp. But much can usually be learned about a politician from his earliest band of supporters, the political equivalent of the Old Bolsheviks or of the Gaullists of the First Hour or of the unconditional loyalists who have followed so many great leaders home from exile. So it should not be forgotten that the initial core of Reagan's support was a group of businessmen, many of them personal friends, and most of them based in California, who made up his "kitchen cabinet." They included the automobile dealer Holmes Tuttle, the oilman A. C. (Cy) Rubel, the oil geologist Henry Salvatori, the brewer Joseph Coors, the publisher Walter Annenberg, the nursing home investor Charles Z. Wick, and the chain-drugstore owner Justin Dart. All were wealthy men, though some were much wealthier than others. Collectively, they represented the mobilization behind conservative politics of a new kind of business lobby. It might be called Little Big Business, though some of the companies owned by kitchen cabinet members — Annenberg's or Coors's, for example — were little only in a relative sense. Unarguably, though, the core of Reagan backers — most of whom had actively supported Barry Goldwater before Reagan — represented an anti-Establishment Establishment. Mostly Californians, though in many cases with family or business connections in the Midwest, these men instinctively rejected the policy of the old Eastern Establishment in the Republican Party, symbolized by David Rockefeller and those other New York business princes who had subscribed to the "liberal consensus."

The Eastern Establishment, on the defensive against charges of economic royalism and of betraying the country into the Great Depression, had been willing to go along, grudgingly but without effective protest, with the policies of Democratic administrations from FDR to Johnson. The new entrepreneurs, from California, Texas, and the rest of the Sunbelt, neither shared any sense of guilt for the failures of business in the 1930s nor saw any merit in compromising with liberal policies. Like William Simon and the new breed of corporate chief executives, like the conservative intelligentsia, these entrepreneurs were aggressive apologists for capitalism, for free markets, and for the capacity of business, freed from the shackles of government regulation and taxation, to lift the economy out of its post–oil-shock doldrums. As much as the ethical and social conservatism of the New Right or the new nationalism of the neoconservatives, the new free market evangelists prepared the ground for the coming of Ronald Reagan.

THE SHOCK TROOPS of supply-side dogma played their part in the tax-cut rebellion. Arthur Laffer sat on the board of Charls Walker's council, and Jude Wanniski supported the campaign in the *Wall Street Journal.* Irving Kristol advised William Simon on which of the bumper crop of new conservative intellectuals should be rewarded with foundation grants and publishing contracts. From the point of view of the great transformation of American political attitudes that swept away the liberal consensus and shifted the center of gravity of political debate so many points to the right in the course of the 1970s, however, the evangelists of supply-side doctrine were only one among many influences at work, and perhaps not the most important. The cautious but effective Republican mandarins were now alert to new, more conservative ideas and to their political promise.

On December 16, 1975, Ronald Reagan, as a former governor of California seriously contemplating a run for the presidential nomination in 1976, held his first meeting with a group of economic advisers assembled by Martin Anderson, then a scholar at the Hoover Institution. Those invited included Arthur Laffer and Milton Friedman, neither of whom was present in the event, as well as Professors C. Lowell Harriss from Columbia, Hendrik Houthakker from Harvard, and Murray L. Weidenbaum of Washington. In an interview, Anderson expanded on one of the themes of his book, the continuity of Republican economic thinking from eras long before Reagan, a continuity supplied by men like Arthur Burns, a sufficiently venerable figure to have been Milton Friedman's teacher, the guru's guru.

"The economic policy Burns suggested to Nixon in 1969," Anderson maintained, and he did work closely with Burns and Nixon at the time, "contained the essence of the economic program President Reagan proposed twelve years later: (1) control spending and seek a balanced budget; and (2) reduce tax rates systematically and simultaneously." "One thing people got completely wrong," he told me in an interview. "People talk about the religious right, the New Right, the neoconservatives. But they ignore the importance of a powerful hard core of mainstream Republican intellectuals." He was referring to men like Burns, George Shultz, and Alan Greenspan. He listed the members of Reagan's economic policy task forces in the 1980 presidential campaign.[45] By the closing phase of the campaign he had six of them. They were controlled and coordinated by an economic policy coordinating committee chaired by George Shultz. Originally a labor economist from the University of Chicago, Shultz had served as secretary of labor under Nixon and secretary of the treasury under Ford. His credentials, in other words, were good with both the Friedmanite conservative economists and mainstream political Republicans. The other members, besides Milton Friedman and Jack Kemp, were Paul McCracken, who had been chairman of President Nixon's Council of Economic Advisers; Alan Greenspan, who had held the same office under Ford; Caspar Weinberger and James T. Lynn, former directors of the Office of Management and Budget under Nixon and Ford respectively; three former high treasury officials in Republican administrations, William Simon, Charls Walker, and Murray Weidenbaum; and from Wall Street none other than the legendary Walter B. Wriston, chairman of Citibank and Citicorp.

Greenspan headed the task force on the budget. The inflation policy task force was chaired by Paul McCracken, the international monetary policy group by Arthur Burns, and the regulatory reform task force by Murray Weidenbaum. Weinberger, Greenspan, and William Howard Taft IV, the inheritor of the grandest of all Republican names since Lincoln, were on the spending control panel, and the tax policy task force, including Arthur Laffer, Paul Craig Roberts, and Norman Ture, was chaired by none other than Charls Walker. Of course, it could be argued that by late 1980 these former heavyweights of earlier Republican administrations had simply jumped on the bandwagon of what would soon be called Reaganomics. But that doesn't hold water. As early as 1974 Reagan, then governor of California, had called in George Shultz for advice, and by July 1978 Shultz was on board: in that month he hosted a working dinner at his home on the Stanford campus for Reagan at which Alan Greenspan, William Simon, and Milton Friedman were among the guests.[46]

The great shift in economic policy, in fact, did owe much to the evangelical activities of a number of missionaries for the new conservative economics. The clique of true believers in the magic powers of supply-side economics certainly played an important part in that crusade. But in a sense they were pushing at an open door on behalf of an idea whose time had come. There could be no clearer example of the interweaving of developments in the world of academia and the intellectuals, on the one hand, and the turning tide of national politics. Far back in the different world of the 1950s, a handful of men like Friedman, whose teachers (including Burns) had never accepted the new orthodoxy of the New Deal, the welfare state, and Keynesianism, worked away at a number of lines of criticism of that system of economic ideas.

By the 1970s, the economists' world was changing very fast. The Bretton Woods system, predicated on the assumption that the United States would remain the guarantor of the world economic system, collapsed after President Nixon "closed the gold window" in 1971. The U.S. balance of payments was knocked sideways by trade deficits, by the cost of maintaining Pax Americana with military deployments and aid, and by the cost of the Vietnam War. Inflation took hold. Then, as described above, came the sharp rises in the price of several basic commodities, and especially the doubling of the price of oil in 1973–1974, later quadrupled in 1979–1980.

Inflation worked its way through from commodity prices into every cranny of the economy. When it reached the price of real estate in Southern California, and therefore the level of property taxes for middle-income Californians, it touched off a tax rebellion, first in California, then in the whole of the West, and finally nationwide. Politicians were itching to cut taxes, and here was a school of economic thought, certified by the most respectable authorities, which said that it was all right to cut them. Businessmen were feeling sore. They felt overtaxed, overregulated, unappreciated, unloved. Their profits were squeezed, their financial interests threatened in unforeseen ways.

The new environmental regulations were a good example. To the general public they seemed a protection against half-understood dangers; to businessmen, they were a monstrous imposition, creating needless bureaucracy, interfering with the managers' right to manage, and adding to costs. Regulation was all the harder to bear because American businessmen believed that they labored under a heavier load of environmental and other strictures than their competitors. (That belief was not perhaps always accurate; the environmental movement was if anything even stronger and more intrusive in many countries of Northern

Europe than in the United States; but no matter. It was enough that American businessmen felt hampered and constrained, and, they asked angrily, "For what? To preserve the snail-darter!") There was also the matter of feelings. For two generations, many businessmen, both individual entrepreneurs and corporate executives, had been convinced that the analyses and the policies of the liberal consensus did not do justice to their contribution. Now here were authoritative voices, editorial writers in famous newspapers and economics professors in great graduate schools, saying just what business wanted to hear: markets should be freed, there should be a bonfire of regulations, taxes should be cut. Go for it!

By 1980 the climate of economic thinking in the United States had changed utterly from the orthodoxy of 1965. Some of the new ideas would not survive very long. By the middle 1980s monetarism, at least in its simpler forms, was a discredited dogma. The supply-side argument for tax cuts had been called into question by the recession of 1980–1982 and by the huge federal budget deficit. Nonetheless, the whole structure of economic policy assumptions had changed decisively.

It was not an overnight emancipation for business or for tax payers. "There was no such thing as a Reagan revolution," Martin Anderson has said. "If it was a Reagan revolution, how come it happened in England, in Canada, in New Zealand, in China as well?" There was an enormous intellectual revolution, he argued. It was like a glacier. Every now and then the movement is held up by a tree or some rock. But underneath, "the intellectual change was smooth and unstoppable. Ideas do move the world."[47]

One simple measure of that change was the slow reduction of income tax.[48] The federal income tax, declared unconstitutional by the Supreme Court, was made legal by the Sixteenth Amendment, passed by Congress in 1909 and ratified by the last required state in 1913. At first it reached only 7 percent on an income of $500,000, a princely sum in those days. It was the coming of World War I in Europe that changed it into a tax on ordinary people with ordinary incomes, and a punitively redistributive tax on the rich; rates went from 7 to 77 percent. Republican administrations reduced those rates in the conservative 1920s. But the Depression made the income tax everyone's problem, and World War II brought rates as high as 94 percent for the rich. Though top rates were relaxed a little after victory in the Pacific, the Korean War sent them back up to 91 percent. The slow decline of income tax rates began not under the Republican Eisenhower, but under the Democrat Kennedy. He reduced the rate structure from 20–91 percent to 14–70 percent, and in 1969 Congress cut the top rate to 50 percent. In 1981 Congress gave President Reagan a three-year 25 percent cut, which lowered rates to a band from 11–50 percent.

Just as tax rates — the badge not only of the government's need, but also of its determination to provide services for the citizens — declined, so confidence in what government could do for society, given the resources, had been waning since its high point in the early years of the Johnson administration. That, after all, had been the essence of the liberal consensus of the postwar years: liberals, or all but a fringe to the leftward, would accept a foreign policy based on anticommunism, while conservatives, or all but extremists on the right, would settle for the main lines of an essentially liberal domestic policy. Gradually, from the late 1960s until the late 1970s, that consensus was chipped away, rather in the same way that the Roosevelt coalition in politics was hammered to pieces. Steadily, Americans lost their faith in the wisdom of government and its capacity to solve social problems. And, rather abruptly when it came to the point, many citizens decided that they no longer wanted to pay the government higher and higher taxes for services they no longer saw as being of any great use for themselves.

The will to finance government spending with taxation was ebbing away. The federal government's spending, on the other hand, showed no signs of diminishing. Indeed, expenditure, not only on the military but on various welfare programs and on subsidies for agriculture, ballooned ever higher, even under Ronald Reagan, who was committed to balancing the budget. The attempt to reverse that growth in social expenditure caused pain in the spread of inequality and poverty. But by 1980 a clear majority was spoiling for a chance to try something other than the liberal way.

In economics, as in religious and social feelings and in foreign policy, 1980 did mark the end of a cycle. Those who no longer believed in the efficacy of government or in its ability to solve pressing social problems had won the upper hand. The politicians, Democrats as well as Republicans, were beginning to sense that the voters, too, had lost confidence in government. The swift, narrow streams of conservative rebellion that had started high in the mountains, thirty-five years before, had reached the sea. A president was about to be installed in the White House who was dedicated to "getting the government off the backs of the American people." Everything was set for the Reagan revolution. But the revolution was not yet ready to happen.

The Falling Flag

Our flag was still there!
— *Francis Scott Key,*
"The Star-Spangled Banner"

ON THE EVE OF Independence Day in 1979 Jimmy Carter returned from a world economic summit in Tokyo an embattled president of a baffled, angry nation.[1] Energy was the acutest problem. All shipments of oil from Iran, the world's second-largest exporter after Saudi Arabia, had stopped the previous Christmas Day.[2] The shah, already mortally stricken with cancer, had become a wanderer on the face of the earth. His ancient enemy, the Ayatollah Ruhollah Khomeini, returned to transform Iran into a Shi'ite theocracy, bitterly hostile to the United States, which he called the "Great Satan."

Spot prices in the international oil market surged. By the end of the first quarter they had risen by 30 percent, and before the second oil shock had run its course, crude petroleum had risen from $13 a barrel — it had been $2 a barrel before the first shock of 1973 — to $34.[3]

In the early morning of March 28, a pump and then a valve failed at the nuclear generating plant at Three Mile Island, just down the Susquehanna River from Harrisburg, Pennsylvania. At the very moment when the international oil system had broken down, with nations, major oil companies, and traders desperately bidding up the price to lay their hands on any crude they could find, the only quickly available alternative to oil as a source of energy was nuclear power. Now suddenly that too seemed to have been taken away. However serious or otherwise the Three Mile Island accident turned out to be in technological terms, and it would be years before even a tentative diagnosis could be made, politically it looked as if nuclear power, as a realistic alternative to oil as a source of energy for the United States, was dead.

On June 23, the day President Carter flew to Japan for a two-day state visit before the international summit, 58 percent of the 6,286 service stations in America were closed. The next day, a Sunday, 70 percent were closed.[4] Gas lines, which had not been seen since the first oil crisis, in 1973, were back. The chairman of Exxon, offered preferential service at his home garage in suburban Connecticut, declined; he was afraid of what the people in the line might do.[5] People were angry. A national truckers' strike did more damage to the economy. It also added to the sense that things were slipping out of control. And in some ways they really were. The sharp rise in the price of oil fueled rising inflation.

President Carter's attention had been diverted from the looming crisis in Iran by the genuine progress he had made in the Camp David accords toward peace between Israel and Egypt. But the international atmosphere was sour. Jimmy Carter wrote in his diary that the first day of the Tokyo meeting was "one of the worst days of my diplomatic life."[6] He considered that Helmut Schmidt, the German chancellor, was "personally abusive." Certainly the Europeans, who had done much more than the United States to conserve energy and had North Sea oil coming strongly on stream, were disagreeably unsympathetic.

In this atmosphere Carter received a message from his chief domestic policy adviser, the normally level-headed Stu Eizenstat, who had just spent forty-five minutes sitting in a gas line at an Amoco station in suburban Washington. "Nothing else," he told the president, "has so frustrated, confused, angered the American people — or so targeted their distress at you personally." The message was spelled out by a public opinion poll from Carter's personal pollster, the youthful Pat Caddell, and by a 107-page memorandum in which Caddell interpreted the data. The American people, Caddell said, were impervious to appeals on the subject of energy. They blamed both the government and the oil companies, and saw them as incompetent or dishonest or both. And the problem transcended the immediate energy crisis, Caddell warned. Americans were losing faith in themselves and in their country. It was this broad sense of national discontent that Carter, in Caddell's opinion, ought to address.

It had been Carter's intention to go on national television and give yet another speech — it would have been his fifth — on energy. Instead, he reacted in a way that did everything to reinforce a national sense of crisis, even panic. He canceled his speech. He withdrew to Camp David. He summoned what could tactfully be called a highly personal selection of advisers to take counsel with him on the mountaintop. Lying on the floor in one of the rustic lodges, his back against a cushion, the president of the United States listened to a chorus of gloom from a congregation selected — if Carter had thought it through — by its likelihood to endorse his own tendency to cosmic self-laceration. He invited women, blacks, Hispanics, sages of many persuasions; but he pointedly refrained from asking for advice from most of his cabinet and from most of the leaders of Congress. What he heard was a sort of national prayer meeting or confessional. "We've been through a series of national crises," said one. "We have a crisis of confidence," chorused another. "In the past," said a third, "we've controlled others' lives; now OPEC controls ours." "There is a malaise," said a fourth.

So guided, or misguided, Carter went on national television on July 15. For more than a week, the press had speculated and people had genuinely worried about how bad things were. The president did not help matters by calling, in the immediate aftermath of his speech, for the resignation of his whole cabinet, a device he had foolishly adopted to make it easier for him to fire two cabinet members he wanted to get rid of. In his speech, delivered in the soulful, preacherlike manner that was his trademark, he catalogued the traumas Americans had lived through, from the assassinations of John Kennedy, Robert Kennedy, and Martin Luther King by way of the "agony" of Vietnam and the "shocks" of Watergate, inflation, and growing dependence on foreign oil. He pointed out that Americans had lost faith in their government, and he concluded that the "strength we need will not come from the White House, but from every house in America."

Carter's television sermon became known as the "national malaise" speech, though he did not use that phrase. It was earnest, high-minded, infinitely well intentioned. It was also a self-inflicted political disaster. It can be said to have ended Jimmy Carter's presidency, though much more misfortune was to be heaped on him by a cruel providence before he left office. If Carter had listened carefully to at least some of his impromptu counselors, he might have avoided his worst error. For Americans had indeed lost faith in their government. They had not lost faith in their nation, and still less in themselves. Their mood was not penitential, but frustrated, angry, even aggressive. They were getting ready to turn to another president, another, less apologetic style of leadership, and another political philosophy: conservatism.

George Shultz expressed this new, or rather rediscovered, temper. He had served in the marines as a young man before teaching economics at conservative Chicago. He had served in the Nixon administration before becoming head of Bechtel, the international engineering firm, one corporation that did not have to reproach itself with falling behind the competition. He later expressed with cold precision how wrong Jimmy Carter was. "The national mood at the end of the decade," he said, "had been captured by Jimmy Carter, unfortunately for him, in an unforgettable way. America was suffering from a bad case of 'malaise,'" he said.[7] "Americans could no longer be optimistic . . . Fear of flagging had become pervasive." And with an uncharacteristically sharp crack of the whip, revealing his own hurt and that of millions of others, Shultz cut at "Jimmy Carter's miseries, which with a weak smile he spread across the international scene."

Carter's miscalculation was disastrous for him. It led to the irrevocable judgment on the part of a large number of Americans that he was a wimp. It revealed that if some Americans wanted to chastise themselves, and search inwardly for the causes of their problems, that was definitely a minority opinion. The majority did not want to acknowledge a national malaise, still less attribute it to their own shortcomings. If anyone was to blame, it was — a growing body of opinion held — the liberals, the Democrats, and the president himself.

More than any other single event, this strange episode revealed the subterranean shift that had taken place in the national mood, and the way that mood had been misinterpreted by many politicians and most of the media. A growing number of Americans had reacted to turmoil and unfamiliar changes in society by rebelling against change. The old economic orthodoxy, Keynesianism, had been replaced by new conservative teachings in the classroom and by a populist rebellion against taxation, and by implication therefore against government, which can do little unless it can raise taxes and spend them. Such moral impulses and economic interests shook the public philosophy that had guided the country since the days of the New Deal. But what played the decisive part in bringing on the conservative victories of 1981–1985 was nationalism: a pervasive, deeply felt sense that the country was in trouble; that it was in danger of losing its reputation as well as its power in the world; and that the rot could be stopped not by government, but only by a robust reassertion of traditional American beliefs.

THAT MOOD HAD been building for a long time, both inside some of the very elites that had once cherished the liberal philosophy and in a wider public. By 1968, there was a broad national consensus that the Vietnam War was a mistake and must be ended as soon as compatible with national honor. But that consensus, as we have seen, concealed a vital distinction. Some thought that the war was immoral, even that in general it was wrong for the United States to use its military and economic power to procure desired outcomes in every last country around the world. But those who thought like that were a small minority. Far more of those who responded to pollsters' questions by saying they opposed the war did so because they thought it was, as a cynical Frenchman said of Napoleon's judicial murder of the Duc d'Enghien, "worse than a crime; it was a mistake."[8] Their opposition was practical. They did not see why the United States was sending half a million young Americans to fight and perhaps die in jungles and rice paddies in a country that meant little or nothing to them. But that did not mean they thought it shameful or wrong to want to prevent communism from taking over in South Vietnam.

So when, in 1975, after the United States had abandoned all but token support for the South Vietnamese and the communists finally took over, the predominant response in the United States was not relief but deep resentment. How deep, is suggested by the role Vietnam came to play in fiction and especially in movies. Already as early as 1978 conservative intellectuals had hailed a book by a historian, Guenter Lewy, which claimed to be the first work dealing with the Vietnam War to make use of the classified records of the army, air force, and marine corps, to which access had been allowed by the Nixon administration in 1972.[9]

Lewy's book was a summing-up for the defense. One by one, with deep (though polemical) excursions into the records, Lewy challenged the allegations made by the war's critics and largely accepted by the American public. Torture at Provincial Interrogation Centers run by the South Vietnamese but under the eyes of American advisers? "There is reason to think that, on the whole, American influence helped somewhat to mitigate the cruelties to be encountered in any civil war." Viet Cong prisoners confined in underground "tiger cages"? On the contrary, they were aboveground, ten feet high — and anyway, they'd been built by the French. Charges of genocide were "a bit grotesque," because the population of both North and South Vietnam grew during the war, and faster than that of the United States. As for the bombing of North Vietnam, Lewy found that it not only "conformed to international law," it was probably "the most restrained in modern warfare." To many Americans, Lewy summed up,

> the Vietnam War represents not only a political mistake and national defeat but also a major moral failure . . . It is the reasoned conclusion

of this book . . . that the sense of guilt created by the Vietnam War in the minds of many Americans is not warranted and that the charges of *officially condoned* illegal and grossly immoral conduct are without substance.

Like many a defense counsel before him, Lewy denied a charge that was not being made, or at least was not the main allegation. Only a handful of extreme critics of the war believed that the U.S. government "officially condoned" atrocities. The charge was, and is, that the conduct and circumstances of the war, including bombing, free-fire rules of engagement, and the whole process of interfering in a civil war whose ideological and political issues were scarcely understood in Washington, let alone by junior commanders in the field, made unnecessary suffering on a horrific scale inevitable.

Lewy's book emboldened conservative analysts. They began to poke their heads above the parapet to defend the U.S. war effort in Southeast Asia. (I remember the conservative columnist George Will pressing the book on me in 1978, arguing that one could no longer criticize the war because this scholar, Guenter Lewy, had now proved that the war was not contrary to international law!) Once again, however, the arguments of the intellectuals and the journalists reflected their perception of a changing national mood.

One indication of this was the gradual evolution of Vietnam as a subject for Hollywood, and so as a potent symbol in the American subconscious. The first response was what psychotherapists call denial. Although newspapers and television carried daily reports of the war, their impact was overwhelmingly negative. Dramatic images of the horror of war assailed the consciousness and the conscience of Americans: Morley Safer's film of a GI casually torching a Vietnamese straw hut, a Viet Cong suspect shot in the head, a naked girl, burned by napalm, running along a road.[10] Few were the images that would have reminded Americans that in a savage civil war both sides tortured, both sides killed, and both sides lied to cover up what they were doing. In addition to the sufferings they might have expected, therefore — the boredom, fear, and discomfort of a tropical war — the Americans who fought in Vietnam had to endure the suspicion that they were being hidden away as a dirty national secret because their country was ashamed of them.

Suddenly, in the late 1970s, there came a rush of books about the war[11] and then a series of powerful, troubled movies.[12] In Martin Scorsese's *Taxi Driver* (1976), Robert de Niro played a veteran returning to violence, though the fact that the origins of the central character's psychopathology lay in his service in Vietnam was only hinted at. In Michael Cimino's *The Deer Hunter* (1978), the same actor played a character who returned to Vietnam to rescue a childhood friend. In *Who'll Stop the Rain* (also 1978), Nick Nolte played a former marine who saved his friend but was killed in the effort. In *Coming Home* (1978), Bruce Dern, as a returning marine, threatened to murder a paraplegic veteran who had an affair with his wife, and then committed suicide by swimming out to sea; the wife was played by Jane Fonda, hated by conservatives for having visited Hanoi and otherwise opposed the war. In Francis Ford Coppola's *Apocalypse Now* (1979), based on Joseph Conrad's classic story *Heart of Darkness*, Martin Sheen played a veteran who returned to Vietnam to kill an American renegade standing for Kurtz, Conrad's personification of darkness and horror.

Although the plots, thrust, and underlying attitudes of these five films differed, they had many things in common. Each used the recently ended war as the setting for an adventure story with bloody killings whose central figure or figures were traumatized by their experience of Vietnam. In making their heroes, or antiheroes, both weak and complex, they followed the Westerns of the post–World War II period, which put their emphasis on the psychological disturbance of the conquering white man, and sometimes portrayed the Native American as sympathetic and historically justified. In these 1970s films, in other words, some of America's most talented young film makers accepted the peace movement's thesis that the war was evil, but focused their sympathy on the young, mostly white, mostly working-class soldiers who fought and suffered in an unjust war. (Significantly, Scorsese, Coppola, and Cimino identified with "ordinary" working-class Americans who got drafted, as opposed to graduates of elite universities who left the country, went to theological school, or otherwise avoided the draft.) The war may have been wrong. But the film makers did not imagine for a moment that the enemy was right.

Most of the action took place in the United States, Vietnam being visited either in flashback or as a sort of fugue to which characters, psychically wounded by their previous service in the war, returned. There was an absolute minimum of interest in the Vietnamese, over whose fate, after all, the war was ostensibly fought. These were films about America and about the traumas the war inflicted on individual Americans and on the collective American psyche. At the same time, these "Vietnam movies" were about a lot more than Vietnam. "We have met the enemy," they said like Pogo, "and he is us." The collective picture they painted of American society, as well as of the American psyche, was bitter, anguished, even savage. It was not just that the noble soldiers of the warrior ideal were replaced by psychopathic killing machines led by corrupt traitors. The several idealized pictures of American life — the Jeffersonian idyll of agrarian innocence, the New Deal vision of working-class solidarity, and the 1950s dream of affordable suburbs with two cars in every driveway — were replaced by Scorsese's New York, an inferno of pimps, prostitutes, and psychopaths.

It was perhaps a vision that contained a certain scalding truth about the worst dimensions of American society. But it was not in the end one that was likely to triumph in an industry devoted to mass entertainment. It was not long before others made the films people wanted to see. They did it by turning the violence safely outward. In 1973 a young California movie director, George Lucas, delighted audiences with a gently sentimental evocation of the 1950s, *American Graffiti*. In early 1977 he went out to eat with his wife at Hollywood's Hamburger Heaven; suddenly he realized that the surging crowds and traffic jams were caused by his own new release.[13] It was *Star Wars*. Lucas's own youthful movie watching, before the Flood of the 1960s, made him yearn for stories in which white Anglo-Saxon heroes wielded the sword of righteousness and — above all — won. "There's a whole generation," Lucas said later, "growing up without any kind of fairy tales." Lucas was one of the first to provide for a generation hungry for warrior dreams crowned with victory.

The American warrior legend had always owed much of its immense appeal (elsewhere in the world as well as in America) to the cunning with which it contrived to have the best of all worlds. The conquering white man won. That was not only inevitable, since history was on his side; it was reassuring. Predominantly white audiences did not want to see Indians, or for that matter Germans or Japanese or Russians, winning. At the same time, the ultimately triumphant white gunslinger must also be depicted as the underdog. Thus, war could be portrayed to adolescents of all ages not as the grimly predictable process of applying irresistible force to history's losers, but as a chivalrous adventure. Our hero triumphs over crushing odds and slays giants because his heart is pure.

Now, as the 1970s moved into the 1980s, Hollywood and those other foundries where the national culture is stamped out, the mass publishing market and the television industry, reinvented the warrior dream. Once again Americans went to war. Once again, reviving the oldest myth of a people who had once seen themselves as tiny colonies taking on the bloated might of the British Empire,[14] they did so as rebels. Lucas's *Star Wars* and its successors and imitators came to dominate the movie and even more the TV screen. Between 1978 and 1985 Kenner Products sold 250 million *Star Wars* figures, or five, on average, to every child in America. Endowed with Cold War bellicosity and *Star Wars* technology, a new generation of kids went to war again in the imagination, enacting in blissful unconsciousness the Arthurian myth of Anglo-Celtic warriors achieving purification through victory.

The warrior dream, however, was still safely distant in space and time. It took another twist to bring it back to Vietnam. Only now it was not a story of national transgression and shame like the one the peace movement had tried to tell. Nor was it a nightmare of war-induced psychopathology. The almost comically crude Rambo films gloried in war, in killing, above all in victory. The first of them, *Rambo: First Blood*, was in the tradition of films like *Taxi Driver* or *The Deer Hunter.* John Rambo destroyed an Oregon town in the course of a psycho veteran flashback. But in *Rambo: First Blood Part II*, the musclebound hero appeared in a role that was to be repeated both in later movies with Sylvester Stallone as the "pure fighting machine" and in countless imitations in movies, on TV, and in dozens of pulp cartoon books.[15] If movies and TV series watched by tens of millions of people are at once evidence of national taste and powerful shapers of national attitudes, then between 1975 and 1985, the United States experienced, in its attitudes toward war and the taste for violence, a remarkable shift from introspection and shame to unapologetic aggression. Conservatives on the whole rejoiced at this renewed national appetite for victory. They also benefited from it.

The Rambo movies, like some other movies, used a theme that generated considerable passion: the fate of American prisoners of war, of whom there were about two thousand, mostly air crews of downed bombers, and also the fate of those listed as missing in action (MIA). The fate of the POWs, which became known after they were returned to the United States in 1973, was terrible enough: many of them had been brutally tortured. But about the MIAs a mythology developed that was more than a little paranoid. There were, of course, Americans who were missing in action. The great majority of them were dead; it was just that, as in other wars, their death could not be definitely established. But the myth did not just assume that thousands of Americans were held somewhere in Vietnam in nightmarish conditions; it posited that their existence was being denied by Washington bureaucrats out of either cowardice or treason. The more the government tried to reassure people that there were no MIAs shackled in some Bluebeard's castle, the more rumors, sightings, and even bogus photographs appeared. The myth of shameful betrayal by Washington began to circulate, first in television serials and second-feature movies, then in the newsletters of the far right, feeding deep prejudices against government.

IN THE LATE 1970s, while conservative yeast was working in so many areas of American life, a comparatively trivial foreign problem revealed how strong traditional American nationalism remained in spite of all the setbacks and the questioning of the 1960s and the early 1970s. The name of the problem was Panama. It gave the conservatives a chance to turn the new mood of national frustration, the yearning for regeneration and reassertion, to their advantage. They took it with both hands.

The resentment of many Panamanians at American sovereignty over the canal that bisects their nation was first expressed in 1958. There were anti-American riots in Panama. This was a time of resurgent anti-Yanqui feeling in Latin America generally. The next year there was rioting among the Zonians (American residents in the Canal Zone) as a result of rumors that the United States might abandon sovereignty. In January 1964, again, there was evidence of how strong were the feelings of the American "colonists" (many of them Southerners by heritage) in the Canal Zone. Overpatriotic American students raised the Stars and Stripes at Balboa High School in the Canal Zone[16] and provoked several days and nights of wild rioting.

In April both countries agreed to renegotiate the three treaties by which the Republic of Panama allowed the United States to maintain armed forces and an extraterritorial presence to guard the great waterway. In June 1967 Lyndon Johnson and the president of Panama, Marco Robles, announced that agreement had been reached. But in the following year a tough military man, General Omar Torrijos, became president of Panama and immediately denounced the treaties. Johnson, now fatally embroiled in Vietnam, never dared send them to Congress.

Richard Nixon continued negotiations and in 1974 Henry Kissinger concluded them. But the agreement was immediately criticized in Congress, because it eliminated the concept of perpetual American ownership. In the fall of 1975 a resolution, introduced into the Senate, opposed any ending of U.S. sovereignty; it received thirty-eight votes, four more than would be needed to block any treaty.

In the 1976 presidential election Ronald Reagan, scenting a powerful conservative issue, began to talk about the canal. He accused the

Ford administration of a "mouselike silence" in the face of "blackmail" by a "dictator." He called Panamanian President Omar Torrijos "Castro's good friend." And he repeatedly used, with great effect, an applause line that evoked "bedlam" in an audience of retired people in Sun City, Florida and many similar places. "When it comes to the canal, we built it, we paid for it, it's ours, and we should tell Torrijos and company that we are going to keep it."[17]

In the circumstances, Jimmy Carter's absolute determination to present the Senate with new treaties that changed the canal's status by the end of the century required every ounce of the moral courage he possessed in abundance. To be sure, in the campaign Carter insisted on distinguishing between "practical control," which he would not give away, and changes, of which he did approve, that would "assuage the feelings" of the Panamanians. But less than two months after his election, he decided to do precisely what he had said in the campaign he would never contemplate. Any "eventual agreement," he concluded, "would have to include a phasing out of our absolute control of the canal, as well as the acknowledgment of Panamanian sovereignty." This was much the same conclusion Henry Kissinger had reached in 1974, but in the changing context of politics in the 1970s, it was a direct challenge to the conservatives.

Even before he was inaugurated, Carter sent the former ambassador to the OAS (and former CEO of Xerox) Sol Linowitz to Panama. His commission duly reported that renegotiating the treaties was "the most urgent issue" in Latin America, and Carter treated it as such: his very first presidential review memorandum was on Panama. The truth was that by the 1970s the canal was less vital to American interests than it had been. It was also less defensible if ever a regime in Panama were determined to close it. Carter claimed in his memoirs that "although we could not talk about it much in public," the canal was in danger of sabotage, and was not defensible unless the United States was prepared to put 100,000 men into the zone. (After the treaties finally passed, Omar Torrijos confirmed that if they had been defeated, he would have ordered his National Guard to blow up the canal.)

Commercially, the canal had been highly profitable in the 1950s and 1960s, but it experienced a sharp downturn in revenue between 1973 and 1977. The slackening of military traffic with the end of the war in Indochina and the world recession contributed to this. So did technical innovations like the invention of supertankers and the coming of the overland "minibridge" container system, which cut transit times for goods coming overland from the Orient to the East Coast by more than a week less than canal shipments. In November 1977, *Forbes* magazine summed up the business community's opinion: "From a purely economic point of view, the Panama Canal is more symbol than substance."

The interests threatened by a change in the canal's status were nevertheless far from negligible. The maritime industry was aroused by the prospect of substantial increases in the canal tolls, and so was the farm lobby. The gulf ports were especially at risk, and the State of Texas was up in arms. "Untold thousands of Texas jobs will be in jeopardy," claimed the speaker of the Texas legislature, "and the economic losses to the state could run into the billions."

The canal's status as a symbol of American patriotism was even more important. David McCullough, the historian who wrote a best-selling account of the building of the canal, well expressed its emotional power in a letter to President Carter.

> To say that the opposition [to ratification] springs from some vague or naive nostalgia for a simple past is really to miss the point. There is a grandeur about the Panama Canal ... of a kind we like to think of as peculiarly American. The Canal is a triumph of an era we remember fondly for its confidence and energy, youth and sense of purpose. The Canal is something we made and have looked after these many years; it's "ours" in that sense, which is very different from just ownership.[18]

Jimmy Carter's whole interpretation of the American predicament led him to believe that the United States could not build the relations of love and brotherhood which he craved with other countries so long as "arrogant" symbols of American domination like the canal gave the lie to his vision. With all the determination and political skill that made up the other side of his strangely contradictory personality, Carter set himself to negotiate and ratify new treaties. By September 1977, they had been signed. In January 1978 the Senate Foreign Relations Committee voted to recommend favorable consideration, and on March 16, after a highly unusual twenty-two days of debate, the Senate voted for the first treaty, which allowed the United States to use military force to defend the canal into the twenty-first century. On April 18 the Senate ratified the second, and principal, treaty, by the narrowest possible margin, after heroic arm-twisting and trading. The treaties' opponents continued the fight in the House. Only in June 1979 did the legislation finally pass, by a narrow margin, and it was not until September 27, 1979, three days before it finally came into force, that Jimmy Carter could sign what he regarded as an acceptable bill.

The politics of this surprisingly bitter struggle were complicated. Although Carter and much of the press believed that the administration succeeded in bringing public opinion round to its conviction that the treaties should be passed, a close look at the public opinion polls demonstrates that this view was an illusion. On the contrary, public opinion remained remarkably stable. Roughly 50 percent of those surveyed were against the "giveaway" of the canal, and 30 percent were in favor of the treaties.[19]

The politics of the treaties were complex. Religious groups that might have been expected to show up in the conservative column, including the Roman Catholic Church and the Southern Baptist Convention, supported the treaties, because of their concern with the possible loss of influence in Latin America if they sided with an "imperialist" position.[20] Similarly, traditional (and largely Republican) corporate business leaders lobbied for the treaties through such established bodies as the Council for the Americas and the U.S. Chambers of Commerce, while powerful business figures like David Rockefeller of the Chase Manhattan Bank, Douglas Dillon of Dillon Read, the ubiquitous moderate J. Irwin Miller of Cummins Diesel, George Shultz of Bechtel, and Robert O. Anderson of Atlantic Richfield Oil all associated themselves with a lobbying group called the Committee of Americans for the Canal Treaties.

This was, in effect, a sort of "last hurrah" for the old moderate leadership of the Republican Party. For as the moderates mustered to support the treaties that would end American sovereignty over the canal, the conservatives jumped into the breach, damning the treaties in the most emotional terms as betrayal if not treason.

The rising figures of the New Right all saw the issue's potential. "We're going to ride this hard," said Richard Viguerie. "It's a sexy issue. It's a populist issue. And here's a populist president who's going to bail out David Rockefeller." That was typical of the way the New Right interpreted Carter's desire to renegotiate the treaties — a policy he shared, after all, with Lyndon Johnson, Richard Nixon, Gerald Ford, and Henry Kissinger — none of them precisely pacifists or fellow travelers — as a "sell-out" to the Establishment. "Sixty years ago," trumpeted Patrick Buchanan in a column headlined SOLD DOWN THE CANAL AND PAYING FOR THE PRIVILEGE in the *New York Daily News*, "General Torrijos would have been lucky to make it to the foothills of the jungle before his successor was sworn in — with a Marine holding the Bible." George Will, in his *Newsweek* column, interpreted the treaty negotiation as a portent of the "vanished mastery" of the United States.

Interestingly, the patrician William F. Buckley, Jr., whether or not convinced by the Archbishop of Panama, did not join in this populist crusade. Nor did that shrewd geopolitician James D. Burnham, who argued that national security would not be served by hanging on to sovereignty over the Canal Zone. "Times change, and nations that fail to adapt to changes go under."[21] The New Right could not have disagreed more. Panama, said Howard Phillips, made conservatives want "to get revenge on those who go against us."

The treaties were seen as a litmus test. To persuade as many as possible to join their camp, conservatives poured out violent rhetoric in support of exaggerated arguments. A new version of the domino effect was invoked. "Once Panama is gone," wrote one Herman Dinsmore in *The National Educator,* "the Pandora's box would be opened for the loss of Puerto Rico and the Virgin Islands . . . and by then the irreversible process would be so familiar and Americans so conditioned to the dismemberment of their country that they would hardly care what came next — Hawaii, Alaska, Florida." It was, *The National Educator* warned, "the first step to the dismemberment of the U.S."

That moderate Republican Senator Howard Baker sagely observed that the trouble was that the people who were against the treaties were "really opposed to them, and those who are for them are just sort of." The New Right was not "just sort of."[22] Its apocalyptic language, though, was not inspired by patriotism alone. This was, the right well understood, an excellent issue on which to campaign against liberals, and they used it to deadly effect. "The Panama Canal treaties put us on the map in 1977 and 1978," said Paul Weyrich.[23] "I did a lot on TV. I wrote a lot . . . Then came the 1978 election. We backed [Roger W.] Jepsen [candidate for the Senate from Iowa], [Gordon] Humphrey in New Hampshire, [William L.] Armstrong [Colorado]. As it happens, all three of them were strong evangelicals. Had I not taken the positions I did on the Panama Canal, I might not have been able to get through to the evangelical communities." "Conservatives," said Richard Viguerie, "have one weapon the White House doesn't have — the power to punish," and went on to promise to do "an awful lot of punishing next election."[24] He and his fellow vigilantes of the New Right were as good as their word. Of the sixty-eight senators who had voted for ratification, twenty were defeated in bids for reelection in 1978 and 1980.[25] As Gary Jarman of the American Conservative Union bluntly put it, "It's a good issue for the future of the conservative movement. It's not just the issue itself we're fighting for. This is an excellent opportunity for conservatives to seize control of the Republican Party." That was exactly what they proceeded to do, under a leader, Ronald Reagan, who had been quick to grasp the strategic opportunity.

The campaign against the Panama treaties did not prove, as many conservative publicists tried to argue, that the American public was massively opposed to Jimmy Carter's attempt to improve America's standing in Latin America. Still less did it prove, as Carter himself and many of his supporters convinced themselves, that public opinion had been converted to their policy. What it did show was, first, that a massive segment of American public opinion, concentrated in, but by no means confined to, the South and Southwest, detested the idea of renegotiating the treaties. To this powerful minority, Carter's Panama policy was yet another step in a Democratic campaign of "retreat" from American "mastery." It also proved that the conservatives in general, and the New Right in particular, now knew exactly how to play on this historical world view and transform it into votes where they mattered in electoral politics. The Vietnam era was over. The Reagan era was about to begin.

CONSERVATISM IS many things, but near the heart of them was an unfeigned fear and hatred of communism. In 1976 communism and the threat it posed to America and to the world, having lain comparatively dormant for several years, suddenly reappeared as a central theme of American politics.

Even earlier, experts had been worrying about the gains the Soviet Union and its allies seemed to be making in the Third World. At the very time when Richard Nixon and Henry Kissinger were pursuing *détente* so successfully with the Soviet leadership, the Soviet Union was embarking upon what Kissinger himself later called a "geopolitical adventure."

It must be said that Soviet adventurism in the 1960s and 1970s was not particularly successful. Nikita Khrushchev's attempt to transform the strategic balance between the Soviet Union and the United States by sending nuclear warheads and their delivery systems to Cuba in 1962 had ended in a triumph for the United States. Under the so-called Brezhnev Doctrine, the Soviet Union reserved to itself the right to go to the assistance — military, if it saw fit — of revolutionary forces anywhere in the world. One of the unintended consequences of the Watergate affair was that Soviet policymakers decided the Nixon administration was so preoccupied with its own difficulties that it would allow the Soviet Union far greater leeway. With this calculation in mind, the

Soviet government sought to intervene in the Middle East war of 1973. Its bluff was called by Henry Kissinger, and the Soviet attempt to exploit perceived American weakness backfired. After the October 1973 war, President Anwar Sadat decided that the United States would be better able to help Egypt solve its domestic economic problems. He understood that the price of American alliance would be substantial concessions toward Israel. Reversing twenty years of Egyptian policy, he set out to pay that price by initiating a peace process with Israel. After five years of fluctuating and difficult negotiations first with the Ford, then with the Carter administration, this realignment was finally sealed by the Camp David accords of September 1978 and the Egyptian-Israeli peace treaty signed in Washington in March 1979.[26]

The Soviet Union had already attempted to gain a number of toeholds in Africa, first in the Congo (later Zaire), in Algeria, and in Guinea, while it did its best to help, and so if possible to influence, the African National Congress and the Pan-Africanist Congress in South Africa. In 1971 Soviet Foreign Minister Andrei Gromyko openly boasted that "there is now no question of any significance which can be decided without the Soviet Union or in opposition to it."[27] In the 1970s, Soviet aid and especially military assistance increased sharply to a number of African regimes. In Angola, in 1975–1976 and in the Horn of Africa in 1977–1978 the Soviet Union took this policy to the length of actively supporting military operations by Moscow's Cuban ally, and at their peak these Cuban operations involved the presence of thirty-six thousand Cuban troops in Angola and about twelve thousand in Ethiopia.

By 1974, experts in Washington were already concerned about the new aggressive style of Soviet interference. In June 1974 Senator Henry (Scoop) Jackson (Democrat of Washington) circulated to his Senate Subcommittee on Arms Control a critique of *détente*.

> In the present Soviet terminology, *détente* or "peaceful coexistence" denotes a strategic alternative to overt military antagonism against the so-called capitalist countries. It does not denote the abandonment by the Soviet Union or its allies of conflict with the liberal Western countries . . . Head-on conflict is to yield to indirect methods . . . [including] subversion, propaganda, political blackmail, and intelligence operations.[28]

The signatories of this paper included a number of distinguished and influential students of Soviet affairs, among them Robert Conquest, John Erickson, Joseph Godson, Bernard Lewis, Richard Pipes, Leonard

Schapiro, and Edward Shils. The paper was not only influential in the still comparatively restricted world of those in Washington and in the universities whose professional interest lay in trying to understand what the Soviet Union's intentions were, it was also an outward sign of that world's hardening attitudes toward the Soviet Union.

An important, if somewhat amorphous, part of this changing attitude to the Soviet Union was what might be called "the Israeli connection." As far back as 1969 the Nixon administration had begun to press the Soviet government, as part of its negotiations aimed at achieving detente, to allow more Soviet Jews to emigrate, and the Soviet Union had cautiously responded. By 1973 the number of Jewish emigrants had reached thirty-five thousand a year, when the Soviet authorities suddenly introduced an "exit tax" on emigrants. While Henry Kissinger tried to resolve the problem through back channels, Senator Jackson introduced an amendment that would have stopped the United States from giving "most favored nation" treatment to any nation that restricted emigration. The Jackson-Vanick Amendment, as it was known, was one of a number of factors that sharply increased suspicion and hostility to the Soviet Union in the American Jewish community.[29]

Soviet support for the Arab countries in the 1967 and 1973 wars reinforced this suspicion, as did the dawning realization that many of the few but gifted and influential Soviet dissidents were in fact Jews, and that under the Brezhnev regime anti-Semitism, if less raw and blatant than under Stalin, was still pervasive and vicious. As the dissident Soviet nuclear physicist Andrei Sakharov wrote to President Carter, "Here we have a hard, almost unbearable situation."[30] Senator Jackson's top assistant, the brilliant and persuasive Richard Perle, had strong personal commitments to Israel, and Senator Jackson soon gathered around him a number of Jewish intellectuals and foreign policy experts who were sharply critical of Soviet behavior and even more so of American indifference to it.

Growing anger among American Jews with Soviet anti-Semitism played an important part in the creation of neoconservatism and contributed to a harder attitude to the Soviet Union, at first among the foreign policy elite, journalists, politicians, and intellectuals generally, from the middle 1970s on. Norman Podhoretz has described the process that brought him to this position in his book *Breaking Ranks*. He began with a strong antipathy to what he called "the Movement," meaning the New Left of the 1960s. After the Vietnam War ended, he felt that the most important consideration was "to take a stand against the dangers of an . . . indiscriminate American withdrawal from the fight against Communism." It was for that reason, he said, that he became involved in a conservative Democratic group, the Coalition for a Democratic Majority. He did not believe that the Soviet Union was planning to launch a nuclear strike against the United States, but he did believe that it was planning to control Western Europe and that the United States must prevent this. By 1976 he was defending this position in front of the Council on Foreign Relations, and in that same year he published a number of articles in *Commentary* by Richard Pipes, Edward Luttwak, and others "demonstrating that the Soviets really were on the move." His own antipathy toward the Soviet Union, he explained, was not primarily motivated by the fact that the Russians were enemies of the State of Israel. "I loathed the Soviet Union," he wrote, "because I loathed the system of Communist totalitarianism." Still, Podhoretz and his influential circle drew from the events of the 1973 war the conclusion that the survival of Israel was inextricably bound up with American military strength.

The majority of American Jews in the 1970s still voted Democratic (and still do twenty years later). But the events of the mid-1970s did drive a number of thoughtful and influential Jews, many of whom had been strongly liberal, into a new skepticism of Soviet promises. A turning point was the notorious vote in the General Assembly of the United Nations for a resolution declaring that Zionism was a form of racism. The way the Soviet Union lobbied for this disgraceful text brought to a head the hostility of many American Jews to the Soviet Union; nor did it do wonders for the reputation in that audience of the United Nations.

There was a new mood of impatience and suspicion in superpower relations. Even more important than events in the Middle East was a new estimate of Soviet intentions in the field of strategic weaponry. No one could be indifferent if the Soviet leadership was contemplating nuclear war. And that is precisely what some influential Americans had come to believe in the middle 1970s.

In May 1976 the *New York Times* reported that "the Central Intelligence Agency has nearly doubled its estimate of how much of the Soviet economy is devoted to defense as a result of a conclusion that it has been greatly underestimating the cost of Soviet weapons production."[31] The *Times* cautiously went on to explain that the higher estimate did not reflect any growth in Soviet military strength; the agency had previously calculated that 6 to 8 percent of Soviet GNP was spent on defense. Now, according to a report sent to Director of Central Intelligence George

Bush, and made public by Senator William Proxmire (Democrat of Wisconsin), the agency calculated that defense accounted for 11 to 13 percent of GNP. There was no suggestion, in the work of the intelligence analysts, that the Soviet Union was building new bombers or missiles, or equipping new divisions to march against Europe or China; rather, "about 90 percent" of the increase was accounted for by the agency's new estimate of Soviet prices and costs.

For many years, the U.S. intelligence community had strictly separated estimates of every foreign country's military capabilities from assessments of its intentions. National intelligence estimates were prepared for each country. In 1974 the strategic expert Albert Wohlstetter at RAND wrote a series of articles, published in *Foreign Policy* magazine, arguing that the estimates for the Soviet Union were in error by increasing margins.[32] Where in earlier years, Wohlstetter revealed, the intelligence community had overestimated Soviet capabilities for taking the strategic offensive, recently these had been substantially underestimated. As a result of Wohlstetter's articles, the President's Foreign Intelligence Advisory Board, composed of veteran "wise men," urged President Ford to set up an alternative group of analysts to second-guess the CIA's estimates.

Ford agreed, and a group of experts was appointed to arrive at its own assessment of Soviet strategic defenses, missile accuracy, and strategic objectives. It was known as Team B. Headed by Richard Pipes, a professor of Russian history at Harvard, it included three retired military officers: General Daniel O. Graham, former director of the Defense Intelligence Agency, known for his concern about the "High Frontier" in space; Thomas Wolfe, once of the U.S. Air Force and currently at RAND; and General John W. Vogt, Jr., previously commander of U.S. Air Forces in Europe. It also had three civilian experts: Seymour Weiss, former head of the State Department's Bureau of Politico-Military Affairs; Professor William Van Cleave, of the University of Southern California; and Paul Wolfowitz, of the Arms Control and Disarmament Agency.

The last and perhaps the most influential member of the team was Paul H. Nitze, the former investment banker, close to the heart of strategic thinking since the days of the Berlin airlift, who had resigned from the strategic arms limitation talks delegation. Nitze was afraid that Nixon, beleaguered by the Watergate process, might make what Nitze considered damaging concessions to the Soviet Union in order to arm himself, by achieving a breakthrough in the talks, with the sort of public relations triumph he desperately needed.

By Christmas Day 1976 the *New York Times* reported that Team B had finished its report and sent it to President Carter. On page 1 of the newspaper, David Binder predicted that in the New Year the president would receive an estimate "that raises the question whether the Russians are shifting their objectives from rough parity with the United States military forces to superiority." In fact, Team B had handed in its report on December 2. It was an unnerving document. It made a number of criticisms of the way estimates of Soviet forces and the Soviet leadership's intentions were arrived at, and offered a number of recommendations, most of which were adopted over the next few years. But more alarming was Team B's conclusion that Soviet capabilities were greater than had been reported in the CIA's intelligence estimates, and that there was little evidence that Moscow shared Washington's faith in "mutually assured destruction," or MAD, which had been the central assumption of U.S. policy for many years.

On February 6 the *New York Times* published an op-ed article by John W. Finney on the Team B report, which was of course still secret.[33] Finney reported that the official National Intelligence Estimate of the strategic capabilities and intentions of the Soviet Union "or at least one version of it" asserted that it was not the case that the Soviet Union was aiming for superiority and not, as in the past, for parity. But, Finney accurately reported, an "unusual adversarial proceeding" had been adopted at the initiative of the President's Foreign Intelligence Advisory Board. Team A was composed of the professional analysts who would normally have produced the estimate, but Team B, led by Pipes, "was deliberately composed of hardliners." Finney added that "there are some indications that Team B became a runaway study group, exceeding its mandate and leaking its conclusions." He compared it with the Gaiter committee, whose "dire and ultimately unfounded warnings about the Soviet strategic threat" were leaked in 1958, leading to the bogus "missile gap," which John F. Kennedy exploited in his 1960 election campaign. Thanks to satellite reconnaissance, Finney pointed out, there was in 1976 little dispute about present Soviet capabilities, so that "the debate turned to intentions, which are notoriously hard to assess and lend themselves to worst case analysis." Not for the first time, in other words, assessments of the strategic threat posed by the Soviet Union had become entangled with politics. It goes without saying for anyone with experience of Washington reporting that the unfriendly view of Team B's work reflected by Finney's article must have been based largely on leaks by opponents, just as earlier inklings of Team B's conclusions were based on sympathetic leaks.

While this battle was being fought inside the bureaucracy, however, the issue was successfully brought to a more public stage. Shortly before the Team B report was sent to President Carter, on November 11, 1976, a number of powerful figures began to alert public opinion to their view that the Soviet Union was embarked on a dangerous new strategic policy. The move began as a typical Establishment operation, though its ripples eventually spread quite broadly.[34] Paul Nitze was deeply disillusioned with detente, and he was not alone, even in the heart of the Washington Establishment he had inhabited for a third of a century. He did what people in Washington do when they want to get something going. He had lunch with friends — with Henry H. (Joe) Fowler, a Washington lawyer and former treasury secretary under President Johnson,[35] in his office, and at the Metropolitan Club, the brownstone temple of the foreign policy Establishment, with Charls Walker, the former treasury under secretary under President Ford and lobbyist for lower taxes. These three got together with David Packard, the founder of Hewlett Packard, the computer manufacturer, and Eugene V. D. Rostow, dean of the Yale Law School.

The upshot of these discreet lobbying operations was something called the Committee on the Present Danger,[36] whose founders did a remarkable job in bringing together Democrats and Republicans, military men and intellectuals, traditionalists and neoconservatives. Besides Nitze, Fowler, Packard, Rostow, and Walker, the membership comprised Dean Rusk, secretary of state in the Kennedy and Johnson administrations; Lane Kirkland, the head of the AFL-CIO; Max Kampelman, the close associate of Vice President Hubert Humphrey and subsequently an arms control negotiator in the Reagan administration; Richard Pipes of Harvard and Team B; and the newly retired chief of naval operations, Admiral Elmo R. Zumwalt, Jr.

At first, the committee was largely ignored by the press. But over the next six months it began to attract a great deal of attention, and the tone of media coverage became more favorable. When, in the spring of 1977, the CPD published an eleven-page report called "What Is the Soviet Union Up To?" both of the major wire services ran full and friendly stories, while ABC and CBS both carried television interviews with Nitze and with Eugene Rostow. The document warned that the Soviet Union would continue its "expansionist policy" regardless of any agreements with Western powers. Nitze, one of the authors of the report, told a news conference, held to launch it, that he believed Moscow had rejected the Carter administration's arms control proposals precisely because "it is an equitable deal, and that is what they don't want."

The committee was not a partisan body. Paul Nitze estimated that 60 percent of its membership consisted of Democrats and 40 percent of Republicans. That only made it more effective. Shortly after its formation, it led the opposition to the nomination of Paul Warnke, a prominent Washington lawyer and law partner of Clark Clifford, as President Carter's chief arms control negotiator. Paul Nitze personally talked Senator John J. Sparkman, the archconservative Democrat who had succeeded the more liberal Senator J. William Fulbright as chairman of the Senate Foreign Relations Committee, into holding searching hearings into Warnke's nomination. The committee and its friends kept up a drumfire of criticism of Warnke, calling him a "dove" and naïve devotee of detente.

Bipartisan the Committee on the Present Danger may have been. But at least some of its members were getting closer to conservative anticommunist groups. In the *New York Times*, Linda Charlton reported that in May 1976 Eugene Rostow had been invited to join the National Strategic Information Center, a conservative lobbying group. The AFL-CIO financed a film, *The Price of Peace and Freedom*, produced by the Education Foundation of the American Security Council, itself a conservative organization headed by John M. Fisher, a former FBI agent. In their campaign against the Warnke nomination, former liberals and Democrats on the Committee on the Present Danger found themselves allied with such New Right organizations as Young Americans for Freedom, Paul Weyrich's Committee for the Survival of a Free Congress, and the Conservative Caucus, which, joined in an ad hoc group called the Emergency Coalition Against Unilateral Disarmament, used mailing lists supplied by Richard Viguerie.

It would be wrong, however, to exaggerate links between the neoconservative reassessment of the Soviet Union and the New Right. What was happening in the late 1970s was that concerns about Soviet adventurism in the Third World, Soviet attitudes to Jews and to Israel, and Soviet geopolitical strategy were all coming together to create a new climate of public and media opinion sharply hostile to the Soviet Union. Neoconservative, strongly anti-Soviet analyses began to be strongly expressed in many publications (including traditionally liberal ones such as the *Washington Post*, the op-ed page of the *New York Times*, *Commentary*, *The New Republic*) so as to set a new tonal background to the discussion of foreign policy. Instead of reproving what they saw as overstrong anti-Soviet positions, as these and other liberal publications had done since the 1940s, they began to stress the illiberal and totalitarian character of the Soviet regime. Where once they would have focused on the shortcomings of America's more conservative allies, such as South Africa or Latin American dictatorships like that of General Pinochet in Chile, now they focused on the Soviet Union's glaring crimes in every region of human rights. Coming into prominence was a new generation of intellectuals (for example, Elliott Abrams, Michael Ledeen), who not only attacked Soviet human rights abuses but defended conservative forces elsewhere, especially in Latin America.

On December 29, 1979, the Soviet Union invaded Afghanistan. It was one adventure too far. A Soviet expeditionary force of 100,000 troops was soon bogged down in a war that, on a smaller scale, replicated the cruel absurdities of Vietnam. It was a mistake for which the Soviet leadership was to pay dearly. The Afghan campaign, dragging on without success for ten years, was a major contributory factor in the collapse of the Soviet regime. It seemed to confirm everything conservatives and their neoconservative allies had been saying about the aggressive ambitions of the Soviet leadership. The Afghan war convinced many Americans that liberals had been hopelessly naïve all along in their attitude to the Soviet Union.

IN AN AGE of mass communications the national mood changes as a result both of slow, almost imperceptible shifts in daily life and also of dramatic events, whose impact is heightened by the full ceremonial of media treatment: the memorable visual image, the dinning repetition of images whose context is sometimes misleadingly interpreted, sometimes hardly explained at all. So the American mood changed, yet in subtle, self-contradictory ways, as a result of an accumulation of troubling events, some of them in places that had previously impinged little on the American consciousness: Saigon, Beirut, Kabul, Tehran. Nearly three quarters of a century earlier, Walter Lippmann had groped to understand the complex process by which the event, and the reporting of the event, influence public opinion. The analyst of public opinion, he said, must begin with the "triangular relationship between the scene of action, the human picture of that scene, and the human response to that picture working itself out upon the scene of the action." The event, he said, is like a play suggested to the actors by their own experience and worked out in their real lives.

The scene was the embassy of the United States in Tehran. A little over a year earlier, as the United States threw itself into the task of helping the Shah of Iran carry out an economic revolution in his country, using American know-how and buying American imports on a gigantic scale, the embassy housed fourteen hundred Americans. Now the shah had fallen. A revolution very different from the one he had planned had come, ending with the virtual apotheosis of the Ayatollah Khomeini, who saw the United States as "the great Satan." The embassy was down to little more than a skeleton crew. But there were still sixty-five Americans there when, on November 4, 1979, at 3 A.M. Eastern Standard Time a telephone rang in the operations center on the seventh floor of the State Department building in the Foggy Bottom section of Washington.[37]

The caller was the political officer Ann Swift in Tehran, reporting that a large crowd of Iranian students had broken into the embassy compound. The invaders flew a long banner, Swift reported, saying, "We do not want to inconvenience you. All we want is a sit-in." The listeners in Washington could hear Swift reproving the marine guards as they produced weapons and took up firing positions near the embassy windows, and in fact the students in the embassy compound were relatively unhostile toward their American captives, though as time went on they could sometimes be heard torturing Iranian prisoners. The U.S. ambassador, Adolf (Spike) Dubs, however, who was out of the building when the invasion took pace, was murdered.[38]

At first the assumption in Washington was that it would not be long before the Iranian government exerted its authority and rescued the American diplomats. As early as November 6, though, President Carter, who had already imposed economic sanctions on Iran and frozen Iran's very substantial assets both in the United States and in U.S.-owned banks elsewhere, heard a presentation of military options, by the Joint Chiefs of Staff, that included a mission to rescue the embassy hostages by force. As it became plain that the Iranian government had no intention of disowning the students who had taken the embassy, President Carter moved a second aircraft carrier, *Kitty Hawk*, and its attendant battlegroup of warships, aircraft, and marines to join the *Midway* battlegroup in the Persian Gulf. Jimmy Carter, who was to be castigated as a weak, near-pacifist president, had mobilized the most powerful forces ever seen in the Indian Ocean. He also warned the Iranians in no uncertain terms, both publicly and privately, of dire consequences if the embassy personnel were harmed or put on trial.[39]

From November 1979 until March 1980, President Carter and his embattled team in the White House and the State Department sought desperately, with the help of French and Argentinian intermediaries, to explore various "scenarios" whereby the hostages would be released as the culmination of an intricate minuet of "reciprocal steps." It became increasingly clear that the ayatollah did not want to dance. By early March, when it was plain even to the most dedicated optimist that the negotiations were going nowhere, Gary Sick, the naval officer who was the National Security Council's expert on Iran, recorded laconically in a memorandum that "the hawks are flying."[40] On March 22 the president was given a full briefing on a rescue plan that was certainly desperate and with hindsight can be called harebrained. On April 25 Jimmy Carter had to go on television and admit that a rescue had been attempted, but that — thanks to a spectacular illustration of the truth of Murphy's Law, that rule of human existence which decrees that whatever can go wrong, will go wrong — it had failed.[41]

That fall, negotiations began again, but were delayed by the outbreak of the Iran-Iraq war in September. They opened again in earnest, with help from an unlikely quarter, the government of Algeria, only after Jimmy Carter had been defeated by Ronald Reagan in the presidential election, which was also the first anniversary of the capture of the embassy. Those who were close to the talks insist that the Iranians were keen to conclude the negotiations before the inauguration of the new president. But even with the best will, the matters at issue, especially the disposal of the billions of dollars in Iranian assets frozen by the United States, could not be quickly unraveled. With a symbolism that was both cruel and unjust, Jimmy Carter rose early on Inauguration Day, still hopeful that he would be able to declare that the hostages were coming back on his watch; but that consolation, too, was to be denied. The president was campaigning in Chicago when Warren Christopher, the deputy secretary of state who had been in charge of the negotiations, telephoned at 3:45 A.M. on the Sunday morning to say that the Iranian parliament, the *majlis*, had voted what looked like an acceptable text of an agreement.[42] Carter flew back in the cockpit of Air Force One, watching one of the most beautiful sunsets he had ever seen. But his sun had set. When he reached Washington, he realized that he could not in honor sign the paper releasing the hostages, until further concessions had been made. The fact that, with his reelection and his own reputation so largely depending on the issue, he was still not willing to yield to the temptation to cut the last corner says much about the personal standards of a man who, among all recent presidents of the United States, has been most unjustly treated.

Over the preceding forty-eight hours, in an atmosphere of mounting national hysteria, support for Carter and the Democrats generally melted away. Carter recorded in his diary the analysis he was getting from his personal pollster, Pat Caddell. According to Caddell, more than 80 percent of respondents in his latest poll thought the hostages would not be coming back any time soon, and this

> opened up a flood of related concerns among the people that we were impotent, and reminded them of all the negative results of OPEC price increases, over which we had no control — and the hostages being seized, over which we had no control — and the Soviet's invasion of Afghanistan, the Cuban refugee situation, the high interest rates, attributable at least in part to the huge OPEC oil price increase.[43]

There was the scene, to revert to Walter Lippmann's analysis of how public opinion changes: a few dozen Americans besieged in an embassy in Tehran. There was the "human picture of that scene," a picture, for the great majority of Americans, derived from television. "Outrage was the American reaction," wrote Hal Saunders, the State Department official who was head of the government's Iran Working Group during the crisis. "Nowhere was the gulf between the Iranian and the American worlds more angrily felt than in the American living room, with fanatical Iranian faces daily screaming hatred from TV screens."[44] As to the human response to that picture, it is far from clear that Ronald Reagan, as president, would have responded in a more effective or even in a very different way.

The hard fact was that the scope of American response was limited by the unyielding realities of time and distance, as well as by profound reciprocal cultural misunderstanding between Americans and Iranians. But that emphatically was not what most Americans wanted to hear. Dismay, frustration, and finally cold anger mounted steadily. What was intolerable was the contrast between America's great ideals and great means, and its apparent impotence in the face of an impudent breach of the law of nations by a rabble of ideologically hysterical and militarily contemptible youths. In the end, as Carter wrote in his diary, the Tehran crisis reminded them of all the other frustrations they faced, foreign and domestic.[45]

Yet the historian should perhaps beware. There is very little doubt that the Carter administration's failure to bring the hostages home, one way or another, had a powerful effect on the minds of voters in the closing days of the 1980 campaign. It is plausible, too, that the hostage crisis evoked memories of other instances when governments, and especially Democratic governments, had failed to act with the vigor and success Americans expected of them: Vietnam, Panama, strategic relations with the Soviet Union, and — for older voters — Korea, Cuba, and the Cold War generally. It is hard to avoid the conclusion that these events, and the pictures of them people had in their heads, did change the national mood. They changed expectations of how the United States ought to behave in the world. They hardened voters' attitudes and strengthened the penalties for a president who incurred a charge of weakness in opposing enemies of the American way.

There is a concealed trap in this argument, though, for those who would lay too much emphasis on the Tehran hostage crisis. What if the hostages had been returned on Jimmy Carter's watch and Ronald Reagan had not won the presidency in 1980? What if Jimmy Carter had swept back to a second term? Where then would be the evidence for a deep shift toward conservative values in the 1970s?

The truth, I believe, is that there *was* such a shift, but that it was less decisive, and bit less deeply into previously unconservative territory in the spectrum of national belief, than either its supporters claimed or its opponents feared. There was a shift in attitudes to social and religious issues, of the kind that has been described in Chapter 7. There was a shift in economic thinking and in attitudes to the respective roles of government and business of the sort that is described in Chapter 8. As for the flag, it has always been a potent icon in American politics. The perception that the flag had been lowered or dishonored certainly helped to elect Reagan. But here we confront, not for the first time in this investigation, the distinction between political hegemony and ideological dominance. It is clear enough that a reaction against public perceptions of the events of the late 1960s and the 1970s provided Reagan and his conservative backers with a supreme political opportunity. The question is whether the use they made of it transformed American society and American political attitudes as the conservatives had hoped. Was there, in short, a Reagan revolution? And if there was, what was its nature?

Jimmy Carter diagnosed an American malaise. Ronald Reagan disagreed. In 1980, he recollected in his memoirs, published ten years later, there were many problems in America. He listed unemployment, an ailing economy, the "tragic neglect of our military establishment," the expansion of communism, and the taking of the hostages in Iran. But nothing, he believed, was more serious than the fact that "America had lost faith in itself." Reagan "found nothing wrong with the American people." He proposed, if elected president, to do all he could to recapture a sense of destiny and optimism. When the votes were counted in 1980, it was plain that far more Americans agreed with Ronald Reagan's diagnosis than with Jimmy Carter's. What remained to be seen was whether the majority of Americans were truly ready to accept the conservative prescription.

10

The Deep Blue Sea

*The abortive Reagan Revolution proved that the American elector-
ate wants a moderate social democracy to shield it from capitalism's
rougher edges.*
     — David Stockman, President Reagan's budget director

IN JANUARY 1981, when Ronald Reagan entered the White House,
the conservative creed seemed to have triumphed. True, the Democrats,
though they lost control of the Senate at the 1980 elections and did not
recover it — temporarily as it turned out — until 1986, still held the
House of Representatives. They would be able, if not to frustrate the
incoming Republican administration altogether, at least to exact their
price for one item on the conservative agenda after another.

In 1981, however, the initiative in Washington lay not so much with
the Republican Party as with Reagan personally and with the conservatives. They had gradually hammered out an agenda as broad as it was
revolutionary. In foreign policy, they wanted a reassertion of American
strength in the world and a showdown with the "evil empire" of the
Soviet Union. In the economy, having replaced Keynes as their guide
with Milton Friedman, they counted on new policies, some ideological,
some practical and popular — monetarism, supply-side economics, but
also tax cuts and deregulation — to unleash the frustrated energies of
American business. In the society, they dreamed of reversing what they
saw as the dire consequences of decades of permissiveness, itself the
legacy of "secular humanism," relativism, and liberal license.

For the next twelve years, Ronald Reagan and his designated successor (though hardly his ideological heir), George Bush, occupied the
White House. On March 31, 1981, less than three months into his first
term, Reagan had what turned out to be a decisive stroke of luck. A

psychologically deranged young man shot him as he left a meeting at the Washington Hilton Hotel. He might have been killed, but he was not. Before that happened, he was showing no special sign of being able to move the rusted levers of presidential power. From that moment on, he looked like the man who had found the lost key to the powerhouse.

Reagan was then nearly seventy years old, and the shooting was a grave challenge to his physical and psychological resources. He was more than equal to it. He confronted the pain and danger, as even his opponents agreed, with courage and grace, indeed with humor. "Honey," he told his wife, lifting the surgical mask from his face to speak when she first arrived at the hospital after the shooting, "I forgot to duck." It was an old Hollywood joke, but relayed to reporters by an alert press secretary, Lyn Nofziger, it sent exactly the right message. Here was a *mensch*, a human being who was tough and gutsy, and who also had a delightfully wry sense of humor.

Reagan's reward for his demeanor that day was a wave of affection and sympathy for which there is only one recent parallel: the national response to President Kennedy's assassination in 1963. There was a difference, of course. Kennedy was killed. It was Lyndon Johnson who inherited a fortune in national good will, but secondhand, as a residuary legatee. Reagan, who survived, inherited that political bonus himself. But just as that earlier trauma had endowed Johnson with the popular support he needed to press Congress into supporting a bold program of civil rights and other legislation in 1964–1965, so Reagan, in 1981, was able to profit from one of the few, brief periods in modern American political history when a president could persuade the majority of Congress to carry out his legislative program. He used it to good effect.

Even the Democratic speaker of the House of Representatives, Tip O'Neill, who once said that Reagan was the "worst" president since Harry Truman, conceded that "in 1981 Ronald Reagan enjoyed a truly remarkable rookie year . . . He pushed through the greatest increase in defense spending in American history, together with the greatest cutbacks in domestic programs and the largest tax cuts the country has ever seen."[1]

Then, by his imperious breaking of the air traffic controllers' strike in August 1983, Reagan did himself another political favor. When PATCO, the controllers' union, went on strike in spite of a commitment not to do so, the first president to have served as the head of a labor union[2] used his executive powers to fire 11,400 union members and remove the union's bargaining rights. In September 1982 Reagan asked for and received from Congress power to order 26,000 striking members of the Brotherhood of Locomotive Engineers back to work.[3] By so doing, Reagan, it can be argued, smashed the political power the labor movement had been accumulating since the 1930s. Certainly his response to the PATCO and railroad strikes sent a decisive message to union leaderships: here was a president who saw tough action against unions not as a political hazard but as a political opportunity.

Reagan's luck held. In 1984 he was opposed not by Edward Kennedy or some other political heavyweight, but by Jimmy Carter's former vice president, the worthy but uninspiring Walter F. Mondale of Minnesota, who carried all the negative baggage of the Carter administration's real and perceived failures. Reagan won by a landslide big enough to bury doubts about the solidity of his achievement.

As president, Ronald Reagan bore a strange resemblance to an inside-out sandwich. Conventional sandwiches have a slice of bread on top, a slice of bread at the bottom, and a more or less generous hunk of beef in the middle. Reagan's political profile was the opposite: a generous slice of beef on top, lots of bread in the middle, and more beef down below.

At the lower level, the level of practical politics, the beef was prime. His training as an actor, foolishly derided by liberal opponents from Governor Edmund G. (Pat) Brown onward, was ideal preparation for the daily activity of politics in a media age. At delivering a radio talk, reading a speech, entering a room, making a phone call, or simply making people feel that he appreciated them, he was superb. At his best, his set-piece speeches, like the one he made at Notre Dame University in April 1988, were delivered with an actor's perfect timing and the ability to milk the emotional response he wanted.

Above his professional competence, however, came a thick layer that was just bread, and pretty soggy bread at that. Reagan may have had sharp political antennae. But he was not hard-working. He was not well informed. Indeed, on many issues that are usually thought important for political leaders to understand, such as foreign policy, economics, the mechanics of government, he was positively ignorant. Several of those who worked for him have acknowledged with varying degrees of pain or amusement how little he knew and how little he cared that he knew so little. David Stockman, his budget director, prepped him for his campaign debate against John Anderson in 1980. "Reagan's performance," he has recorded, "was, well, miserable . . . His answers just weren't long enough. And what time he could fill, he filled with woolly platitudes."

"Reagan's body of knowledge is primarily impressionistic," Stockman said after working closely with Reagan on budget numbers. "He registers anecdotes rather than concepts." Everyone has heard the stories of his lapses: how, on a state visit to Brazil, he expressed his pleasure at being in Bolivia, and the like. Worse, he was unrepentant. In an interview, I asked him about the Reagan Doctrine (a commitment to roll back policies in the Third World, which may well have been put into his mouth by neoconservative journalists like *The New Republic*'s Charles Krauthammer).[4] Reagan's answer made it plain that he confused the Reagan Doctrine with Reaganomics. When I pressed him, he acknowledged that he knew little about such matters, and chuckled happily that he had plenty of smart people working for him who could take care of the details.

At the very highest level of politics, however, his impact was beefy indeed. Colin Powell has expressed what many intellectuals and journalists have been reluctant to concede: "He may not have commanded every detail of every policy" — he certainly did not — "but he had others to do that." The editor and author Michael Korda once wrote a perceptive definition: "great leaders are almost always great simplifiers, who cut through argument, debate, and doubt, to offer a solution everybody can understand." That description fits Ronald Reagan.[5]

"He knows so little," said one of his national security advisers, Robert C. (Bud) McFarlane, with a wondering shake of the head, "and accomplishes so much."[6] George Shultz, an almost uncritical admirer, told me he thought Reagan was "a revolutionary" who had "changed the agenda [in] the most sweeping presidency in this country since Franklin Roosevelt,"[7] but even Shultz admitted that he had "a tendency to avoid tedious detail." He maintained, and it is impossible to disagree with the judgment, that Reagan "had a strong and constructive agenda, much of it labeled impossible and unattainable in the early years . . . He changed the national and international agenda on issue after issue."[8]

Reagan had a few big ideas, deeply held, and he was brilliantly successful at communicating them. Partly, this was because he put them across simply and well. Partly, it was because millions of people shared his beliefs and his aspirations. He wanted to cut back the size of government and its effect on people's lives. He wanted to cut taxes. Most people could go along with that. He believed that if America was only strong enough, the Soviet Union must back down, and people could live their lives free from the terror of nuclear war. That explains his apparently naïve faith in the Strategic Defense Initiative: Reagan believed that literally no task was beyond American ingenuity and American optimism. This was perhaps the most strongly held of all his convictions, and one he shared with many of his fellow citizens. It was therefore the absolute core of his political appeal.

Reagan believed passionately, from the depths of his being, in the greatness, the goodness, the historical destiny, of the United States and its people. Simply put, he believed that the country had been allowed to fall from its own high standards. He wanted nothing more than that the American people should be confident once again in their strength and virtue. It is not a message that has instant appeal to the large majority of the world's population who are not Americans. Such uncomplicated faith in American exceptionalism can easily look like complacency or even arrogance. But for most Americans, especially after a decade and more of frustration and humiliation, it had for a time an irresistible magic. Few presidents have ever succeeded as Reagan did in moving both the center of gravity of political discourse and the reality of the country and the world in the direction of their own ideas as he did. President Reagan will be remembered as one of the most complex of presidents: a man who could seem idle, ignorant, even incompetent, yet was able to understand and to express as few other presidents have done the instincts, good and bad, of the American majority. That is why he succeeded, far more than is given to many of those who occupy the White House, in achieving what he most wanted to do.

Yet it was never intended, least of all by Ronald Reagan himself, that the Reagan revolution should be a period of personal rule. Instead, he presided over, and sometimes put his personal stamp on, a shift that had been prepared for him by the conservative movement, but that really took place in the court of public opinion. "By Election Day 1984," two of his severest critics have admitted, "the ideological contest was over. A combination of old- and new-style conservatives had succeeded in capturing the ideological high ground well beyond the wildest dreams of the theoreticians who had managed Reagan's electoral victories."[9]

In spite of all the optimistic predictions, though, Ronald Reagan's victory in 1980 did not lead to a conservative Golden Age. Sixteen years later, the most intensely ideological of the conservatives are the first to insist that their Golden Age is still in the future.

WAS THERE, in fact, a Reagan revolution? With a surprising degree of unanimity, the leaders of the New Right insist that there was not. Paul Weyrich was emphatic: "If you look at the domestic context, the Reagan effect is negligible. In the foreign policy, defense context, the Reagan effect is considerable." Weyrich conceded that Reagan should be given full credit for his role in ending the Soviet empire and in his vision for the future; some of his speeches, he says, were "prophetic." But domestically,

> government grew dramatically during the Reagan years. He didn't veto legislation to speak of. He didn't veto budgets. He really did not curb the growth of government. None of the agencies that he campaigned to shut down were shut down. The agencies that he despised the most, like the Legal Services Corporation, grew under his leadership. It is very hard to say what he accomplished that has had any permanent effect except that the debt grew by such an enormous proportion that the liberals today are unable to propose the kind of new spending programs that they would like.[10]

Howard Phillips of the Conservative Caucus was contemptuous when I interviewed him near the end of the Reagan administration. "I don't think there has been any president in American history who was less engaged in the conduct of affairs than Ronald Reagan since Woodrow Wilson was confined to quarters with a stroke."[11] Irving Kristol answered more in sorrow than in anger. It was, he said, "a successful presidency as a whole. He left office with the country in pretty good shape." Reagan, said Kristol, did affect American attitudes, and his armament program had a profound effect on the Soviet Union. But "there was no Reagan revolution," Kristol agreed; the most, he claimed, is that "there was a shift of emphasis."[12]

That was scarcely the new heaven and the new earth the conservatives had promised in the heady days of 1980. By 1994 one of the new model army of young conservative intellectuals, David Frum, was writing in the doom-laden tones of a Savanarola about the way conservatism had succumbed to moral and material temptation. "In retrospect," he wrote sadly, "we can see that what happened in the late 1970s was not so much a victory for conservative ideas as a collapse of liberalism." The Reagan interlude, he wrote as a still-loyal but despairing conservative, "turned our heads."

> It misled us into thinking that the American people were with us — not in a casual, happenstance sense, but deeply, even when conservative ideology might deny them some benefit out of the treasury . . .

And as we have discovered the uncomfortable truth that they are not with us, *we* have adapted to *them*.[13]

Frum had the bad luck to publish his elegant and well-documented jeremiad in 1994, just before the Republicans took over both houses of Congress for the first time in more than half a century. When his book was published, Newt Gingrich was about to emerge as the fulfillment of decades of conservative yearning, the Conservative Intellectual as Man of Power. In the next and last chapter we shall have to ask whether that victory was a decisive shift in the ideological orientation of the United States or just one more battle in a long and inconclusive war. But 1994 is a bridge too far for this chapter. At this point we are looking at the contrast between the promise and the triumphalism of 1980, and the retrospective view from 1992.

In that latter year, a Republican president managed to squander the extraordinary popularity garnered by victory in an almost bloodless war, and lost the White House to a Democrat. A new age of Republican revival seemed to have been prematurely cut short. But there was worse. For George Bush was not a conservative, not at least as the word had been used by Ronald Reagan and his entourage. He was, in fact, an updated version of the old Eastern Republican Establishment, against which the conservatives had rebelled in the first place. Patrick Buchanan, who damaged him severely in the 1992 primaries, said as much. "George Bush, if you'll pardon the expression," Buchanan told a group of fellow right-wingers as justification for his own 1992 primary run, "has come out of the closet as an Eastern Establishment liberal."[14] Bush had gone to Texas and made his fortune — with the help of a few family friends from Yale and Wall Street. But he was a Yankee. His father had represented Connecticut in the United States Senate. He himself vacationed by preference in Maine; a graduate of Andover and Yale, an internationalist, a moderate, everything that the conservatives of the movement despised and derided. He had even called supply-side theory "voodoo economics." It was hard to stomach, impossible to forgive, a man like that. "George Bush," according to Pat Buchanan's way of thinking, "has sold us down the river again and again,"[15] and on that, if on little else, most conservatives could agree.

As Bill Clinton settled into the White House, it was not only the purest of pure conservative intellectuals who felt that the Reagan revolution had been a chimera and the Reagan years a time of illusory promise and hopes betrayed.

Three strands, I have argued in the three preceding chapters, came together to weave Reagan's laurels in 1980. There was the reaction against the perceived excesses of liberalism in the social and moral domains. There was the revolution in economic thought and the turning away from public to private initiative as the provider of solutions to economic problems. And there was the frustration and anger that built up against those who had allowed American power and prestige to decline in the world. How did the conservatives' hopes fare in those three respects during the Reagan years?

The ideological "movement conservatives" had reason to feel badly treated by Reagan. He took a conscious decision, grudgingly accepted by most, that he did not owe his election to the evangelicals. Only a handful of them were given important federal jobs. Reagan and his advisers decided to give a lower priority to the "social issues" than to economics and foreign policy. From this standpoint, for all his rhetoric and that of others, he was indistinguishable from a mainstream Republican president, not a distinctively conservative one. Overall, evangelical Christians felt, and feel, badly disappointed in the Reagan administration. It was, in retrospect, perhaps naïve of them to make him, a Hollywood actor with a taste for a drink and quite a career as a ladies' man behind him, into the strong Christian leader they imagined him to be; their Reagan was made in their own image.

Still, Ralph Reed, who has moved from being an aide to Pat Robertson in 1980 to being one of the national leaders of the religious right, graphically remembered the New Right's disappointment with Reagan. Howard Phillips was mad, he says, "and in a sense he had a right to be, because the evangelicals were taken to the cleaners. They helped Reagan to get elected; then he took no notice of them."[16] And Reed recalled a vignette. "They had a meeting in the Old Executive Office Building. Pat [Robertson] flew up for it. Chase Untermeyer was the White House director of personnel. Someone said, 'Why don't you hire more evangelicals?' Chase said, 'There was an effort in the Nixon administration to hire more Jews, but you can't ask people about their beliefs.' Pat Robertson said, 'It's funny, you can count evangelicals in the election, but after it's over you can't count us anymore.'" Reed even suggested that evangelicals felt used in the same way that blacks had felt used by the Kennedy administration. Like the black leadership of the 1960s, the evangelicals had been given a lesson in political sophistication by Reagan's ingratitude. "We understand how the process works a lot better," Reed said wryly, "and we expect more; we want more before we are going to be satisfied." So much for the idea, touted in the media in 1980, that Reagan's election would install evangelicals in the seats of power.

ON THE ECONOMIC front, the Reagan administration's record is ambiguous. It began with, on the one hand, shrill claims from a small clique of publicists (and self-publicists) about the magic of supply-side economics and, on the other, a broad plan, endorsed by experienced economists. They were not conservative, in the new, exclusive sense, but came out of the Republican mainstream: Arthur Burns, Milton Friedman, Alan Greenspan, Martin Anderson, and the like. A critic has sneered that Reaganomics was "two parts supply-side economics, one part monetarism, and a generous dose of wishful thinking, which is what the administration thought 'rational expectations' meant."[17] The judgment is too harsh. Monetarism, certainly, was quietly dropped by all but its most fanatical exponents as it became harder to see what was meant by the money supply, and harder still to trace a coherent connection between it and the performance of the economy. Supply-side economics were given a rough reception by even conservative economists. "Bad talk drives out good," said Herb Stein, chairman of President Ford's Council of Economic Advisers. "It was a nonsense principle," said Robert Lucas, "that taxes are always too high." And even the august George Stigler, guardian of the flame lit at Chicago by F. A. Hayek, dismissed it as "a gimmick or, if you wish, a slogan."[18]

In truth, Reaganomics was not a carefully devised economic strategy. It was the economic wing of the politics of joy, the economic expression of the conviction that it was morning in America. The only trouble was that it was late afternoon. The revolution in economic theory, and the response of economic policy, mattered less than the fact that the Reagan administration inherited a dire economic landscape. Paul Volcker, as head of the Federal Reserve under Jimmy Carter, had decided to squeeze inflation out of the economy, and he was doing so with merciless determination. As a result, though the supply-side enthusiasts predicted that GNP, investment as a proportion of GNP, and productivity growth would all go up, in fact they all went down. Recession clouded the new administration's arrival in Washington. Shortly before the midterm elections of that year, unemployment peaked at 10.8 percent. Then came the short-lived boom that those nostalgic about the Reagan years choose to remember. In reality, it lasted for only about a year and a half, from late 1982 until the spring of 1984, with real GNP growth averaging nearly 7 percent. That was enough to set the scene for Ronald

Reagan's easy reelection in 1984. But from the second quarter of 1984 until the fourth quarter of 1986, real growth was a miserly 2.4 percent. Then came the Wall Street collapse and a new recession. The macroeconomic record of the Reagan years was patchy at best.

Much attention, at the time and subsequently, has focused on one particular aspect of the Reagan administration's economic management, the budget deficit. David Stockman, who as director of the Office of Management and Budget must bear the primary responsibility for the miscalculations involved, distanced himself from his own policy, first in a spectacular, and spectacularly ill-judged, series of interviews with the *Washington Post*'s William Greider,[19] then in a book, *The Triumph of Politics*,[20] modestly subtitled, "The Crisis in American Government and How It Affects the World." In his book Stockman argued that "politics," in the popular, pejorative sense — the tendency of elected politicians to pander to an ignorant electorate in the interests of their own careers — had triumphed over economic discipline as preached by an austere priesthood of "anti-statist conservatives who inhabit niches in the world of government, academia, business, and journalism."[21] In an interview in 1988, Stockman told me he thought "the historians will record Reaganomics as the single greatest episode of sustained economic mismanagement in the twentieth-century history of the United States."[22]

Certainly Stockman is one of those Reagan revolutionaries who insist that the Reagan revolution did not take place. Instead, before washing his hands of government and heading for Wall Street, Stockman took the almost fatalist view that the electorate is always right — even when it is wrong. "In a democracy the politicians must have the last word once it is clear that their course is consistent with the preferences of the electorate," he wrote in the closing paragraph of his long and closely argued self-justification. "The abortive Reagan revolution proved that the American electorate wants a moderate social democracy to shield it from capitalism's rougher edges."[23]

It is far from clear whether this is true: it is one of the questions we will return to in the last chapter. Stockman was reacting, however, to what became the main theme of criticism, and particularly liberal criticism, of Reaganomics. Put in very simple terms, the charge goes like this: the Reagan Administration came in politically committed to cutting taxes. On the back of a wave of congressional popularity in 1981, it enacted a substantial tax cut. The intention was to balance the budget by matching this tax cut with cuts in expenditure, specifically in entitlements (social programs such as welfare, Social Security, and the like) and in military spending. When push came to shove, however, the administration did not cut expenditure. It did not dare push through cuts in domestic entitlement programs, because it was not able or willing to pay the political price. And as for military spending, the administration increased it at the fastest pace since the crisis years of the early Cold War.

A subsidiary criticism is joined to this: the administration, it is said, was beguiled by the false hope that tax cuts would stimulate the economy to such an extent that lower tax rates would actually generate higher income. As we have seen in an earlier chapter, that charge, at least in that form, was a bum rap. While the president, in bread sandwich mode, occasionally came close to saying something of the kind, in its more formal moments the administration knew that tax cuts would not actually increase revenue in the short term. It merely counted on the resultant stimulation of the economy to minimize tax loss and make it possible to raise higher revenue from lower tax rates in the more or less distant future.[24]

Most discussion of Reaganomics ignores the context. History does not cut economic activity off short on the day a new president is inaugurated — nor does the American economy go on its way unaffected by growth or recession in the rest of the world, responsive only to what a president and his economic advisers ordain. Reagan inherited an economic situation that was already dire in several respects. His administration's attempts to improve the situation were seriously complicated by external events in the world economy, with which the United States was becoming more and more connected. Finally, neither Reagan nor any other political leader, in the United States or in any other democracy, can ignore the pressures of politics. They played their part at more than one stage of the story of Reagan's economic policy.

By 1980, inflation had settled in as an apparently permanent feature of the economic landscape. At that time, recalled Michael Boskin, of the Hoover Institution at Stanford, who served on President Bush's Council of Economic Advisers, the bulk of leading American academic economists — Boskin meant generically the leading *liberal* economists, such as Robert Solow and Paul Samuelson — were saying, in effect, "We will have to live with 12 percent inflation."[25] As a result, ordinary working Americans were seeing their standard of living sharply reduced. The two worst years for real wages since World War II were the last two years of Carter, with cuts in real wages of 7 percent. Deficit financing began under Carter.

Even before Reagan was inaugurated, the recession had bitten hard enough to make nonsense of the figures carefully calculated for him the previous fall by Alan Greenspan and his other economic advisers, figures that seemed to show that he *could* have his cake and eat it too. On Labor Day 1980, Democrats and liberal commentators thought that Reagan's reluctance to be pinned down to specifics on economic policy was handing Jimmy Carter a winning issue. John Anderson, Reagan and Carter's third party opponent, jested that the only way Reagan was going to cut taxes, increase military spending, and balance the budget was with smoke and blue mirrors.

On September 9, Reagan was scheduled to make his key economic policy speech. His advisers were desperate to come up with hard numbers to prove he could do it. Then his campaign discovered figures, from the staff of the Senate Budget Committee, which purported to show that federal tax receipts would rise faster than expected and federal expenditure would fall faster.[26] Greenspan was able to brief the traveling press corps on "deep background" that, after only two years of deficits in the $20–30 billion range, the budget could be in surplus by 1983 and in fat surplus by 1985. What blew the administration's predictions off course, and therefore saddled the country with huge, upward-spiraling deficits, was the adverse shift in economic conditions between those carefree days of fall and the inauguration.[27]

That, at least, is a sympathetic view. A more realistic one is that, desperate to acquire credibility at a crucial turning point in the campaign, the Reagan campaign committed the future president to numbers that proved wildly overoptimistic. However one interprets them, the facts are clear: in the late summer of 1980 the forecasts were for a government budget surplus by 1983. Between the fall of 1980 and the spring of 1981, the position was so different that to maintain the Reagan budget plans unchanged, let alone to cut taxes while shrinking from equivalent cuts in expenditure, condemned the country to huge and continuing deficits.

If one tries to draw up an economic balance sheet of the Reagan years, there are weighty items to be put down on the positive side of the account. Martin Anderson has made a brave attempt to describe these achievements in upbeat language. It was, he claimed, "the greatest economic expansion in history." During the five years from November 1982 to November 1987, "more wealth and services were produced than in any like period in history." (He presumably meant to add "in the United States," for of course substantially more goods and services were produced in the same period in Europe and Japan.) By the end of Reagan's second term, the economy had racked up seventy-two straight months of unbroken economic growth and a 15 percent increase in the number of jobs in the United States. Perhaps most significant, the American economy was by 1987 producing 65 percent more than in the last year of Jimmy Carter's presidency.

This was achieved, however, at the cost of serious long-term damage to the economy, damage, moreover, of a kind it is proving very difficult for the political process to remedy. Sixteen years after Reagan entered the White House, committed to a constitutional amendment to prevent budget deficits, the national debt has tripled. The Gramm-Rudman-Hollings bill, a courageously stern effort to grasp the deficit nettle, was promptly ruled unconstitutional by the Supreme Court on the grounds that it infringed the constitutional separation of powers. The judgment provided ammunition for those who argued that the rigidities of the constitutional system make it harder for the United States than for most modern countries to tackle structural problems.

The Clinton administration's energies, and those of first a Democratic, then a Republican Congress, have been consumed in trying to restrain — for there is no prospect of reversing — a series of deficits that are likely to increase. The United States has also failed to end its foreign exchange deficit. While triumphalism about the United States economic performance is de rigueur in conservative circles, the fact is that the United States is still a twin-deficit nation. Its historic position as the world's creditor, acquired by decades of successful inventing, investing, manufacturing, and marketing, was squandered in a few years. As recently as 1980, the United States lent abroad $13 billion more than it borrowed, thus accumulating not only profitable assets, which would both grow in capital value and yield growing returns, but also economic and political influence. By 1986, the United States was borrowing $144 billion more abroad than it lent. The United States easily surpassed Brazil as the most indebted nation on earth. The value of the dollar was largely in the hands of Japanese and other foreign banks, which alone had the resources to finance the federal government's spiraling deficit.[28]

Even deregulation, for which such extravagant claims were made, did not work out as its sponsors proclaimed.[29] In aviation, it led to a brief flurry of competition, followed by contraction, high fares, and some cutbacks in service.[30] In finance, it produced cowboy excesses, but left the banking system shaky and unreformed. After extravagant predictions of benefit to consumers and the economy, the results by the end of

the Reagan administration were close to the opposite of what conservative enthusiasts had promised.

Most serious of all, the chief economic consequence of the Reagan
years was a rapid growth in inequality. Reaganomics sharply increased
the share of the national wealth going to the highest tenth of the population, at the expense of everyone else. The United States had been historically a country with relatively low differentials between shop floor
workers and management. Even capital wealth and ownership were
relatively widely distributed in comparison with other nations. That was
both part of the attraction and one of the foundations of the American
dream. But after twelve years of Reaganomics, this had been largely
reversed.

The most salient fact about the economic history of the Reagan
years is that top business executives, the highest-paid professionals, and
owners of business property quickly became very much richer; everyone
else became relatively poorer, and a significant share of the population became absolutely worse off. At the same time as the situation of
the less well-off declined and the situation of many of the poor became
desperate, the welfare apparatus, painstakingly assembled over the previous fifty years, was seriously damaged. The paradox was that welfare expenditure spiraled uncontrollably upward — the neoconservatives were right about that — without providing a reliable safety net for
the unsuccessful or the unfortunate, let alone for the inadequate, in the
way that the founders of the welfare state had envisioned. The damage
done by the Reagan policies to the equality of American society and to
American productive industry may prove to be temporary. But it was
certainly substantial.

Business confidence, or at least the confidence of raiders, takeover
artists, arbitrageurs, greenmailers and suchlike financial predators, was
certainly high. For the brief period between the recessions at the beginning and the end of the 1980s, certain sectors of the economy — financial services, defense industries, real estate on the two coasts — experienced a boom. The impression of prosperity, too, was reinforced by the
fact that few industries prospered more than the media business. Columnists, commentators, film makers, and those choice spirits (in the
nature of things at the time predominantly conservatives) whose work
was funded by foundations, thrived as never before. The places where
they lived and worked — Washington and its northwestern suburbs,
midtown Manhattan, and favored locations in Connecticut and on Long
Island, the Bay Area in Northern California, Orange County in South-

ern California, and the lush suburbs of the mushrooming cities of the New South — were throwing up office buildings, restaurants, health clubs, and bookshops like the temples of a new civilization.

The real estate boom of those years was largely the consequence of tax breaks and subsidies, federal, state, and local. However fiercely anti-statist their ideology, executives of multinational corporations happily worked together with real estate developers, banks, and a "new breed of mayors" and their officials to supply the office towers, convention centers, hotels, and other facilities business needed in the rundown inner cities. "Eager to push development," two MIT scholars wrote of New York,

> city government gave tax breaks to all sorts of projects with little regard for social purpose or need for subsidy. A conspicuous example is the glittering Trump Tower on Fifth Avenue, with its million-dollar condos and peach-colored marble atrium encircled with six levels of some of the most expensive retail space in America — all subsidized with $100 million worth of tax abatements.[31]

Similar developments were using public money for private profit by transforming the centers of Atlanta, Detroit, Los Angeles, and almost every other American city, not to mention suburban areas like Bethesda, Maryland, and much of Southern California. Ironically, in an age when the conservatives were trying to get government off the backs of the people, Washington, the federal capital, experienced the biggest real estate boom of all. From Rosslyn to Alexandria, a cliff of high-rise office buildings housed the lobbyists who denounced the federal government even while they lived off it. Five other cities — New York, Boston, Chicago, Atlanta, and Los Angeles — emerged as regional capitals. Their downtown areas attracted prestige office towers for multinational corporations, and their suburbs thrived. In 1985, twenty out of the twenty-one counties in the United States with the highest per capita incomes were suburban: seven of them were in the suburbs of Washington, six in the suburbs of New York.[32]

It was natural for those who inhabited these favored places not to see what was happening elsewhere, for there was another side to the showy prosperity of the 1980s, far from evenly distributed across the country. In journeys in 1983, 1985, and again in 1988 I myself saw something of the consequences of unemployment in Houston, Birmingham, and South Bend, Indiana, not to mention the more famously deprived parts of New York, Washington, Chicago, Detroit, and Philadelphia.

Some thirty million new jobs were created in a decade or so. But too many of them were low-wage jobs with no security. Much of the increase in the working population — it is hard to quantify how much — came from women going out to work, not to celebrate their liberation, but because they were single and had no alternative, or because their partner's income was not enough to support them at the level they expected, or in some cases at any level at all. For too many others there were no jobs and no homes.

"The two most striking economic groups of 1989," wrote Kevin Phillips, the Republican analyst who had predicted the rise of the Sunbelt and the emergence of a Republican majority, "represented a stark contradiction: billionaires — and the homeless." The novel of the decade, Tom Wolfe's *Bonfire of the Vanities*,[33] was flawed by the degree to which its author seemed to share the snobbish attitudes he purported to satirize. It nevertheless captured in unforgettably pitiless images the contrast between the late Roman extravagance of the more favored neighborhoods of Manhattan and the dereliction of the South Bronx. Wolfe's Manhattan was Truman Capote's, only further corrupted by the division between desperate poverty and flamboyant wealth. The wealth seemed to be collected with absurd ease by a handful of moral imbeciles who happened to be insiders. With a cartoonist's savage skills, Wolfe contrasted the complacent "masters of the universe," terrified of losing face by walking a few blocks instead of traveling by stretch limo, with the wolf pack of "Third World people" lying in wait to devour anyone who fell off the sleigh. If anything, the harshness of the abyss between haves and have-nots was even greater in Los Angeles, where Rodeo Drive was becoming a byword for the arrogance of new wealth in the very years when deprived south-central Los Angeles, only a few short miles away, was coming to an angry boil.

Nor is this picture of a society torn by a new and rapidly widening rift between rich and poor a novelist's caricature or the invention of a politicized liberal intelligentsia. It can be solidly fleshed out with incontrovertible statistical evidence. In 1987 two writers in a Columbus, Ohio, newspaper, Ross LaRoe and John Charles Pool, using data from the nonpartisan Congressional Budget Office, showed that "since 1977, the average after-tax family income of the lowest 10 percent, in current dollars, fell from $3528 to $3157," or by 10.5 percent. "Average family income of the top 10 percent increased from $70,459 to $89,783 — up 24.4 percent." The incomes of the top 1 percent rose from $174,498 in 1977 to $303,900, or by no less than 74 percent.[34]

Republican and conservative rhetoric hammered away, attributing any criticism of this sharp increase in disparities of wealth to "the politics of envy." (If their liberal opponents had been less intimidated or coopted, they might have spoken more about the politics of greed.) They implied that the prosperity of the 1980s was evenly distributed, and that it accrued to entrepreneurs and to hard-working "regular folks," as Ronald Reagan himself put it in his 1987 State of the Union Address. Nothing could be farther from the truth. What was quite clear was that those whose income depended on wages or salaries for their work — you might call them "regular folks" — were falling behind those who owned things: businesses, stocks, real estate, property of all kinds. The average weekly wage for all workers, white collar as well as blue collar, fell from $191 a week (in 1977 dollars) to $171 in 1986. Expressed in 1987 dollars, weekly wages fell from $366 in 1972 to $312 in 1987.[35]

The Reagan years, wrote Kevin Phillips, were "a heyday for unearned income as rents, dividends, capital gains, and interest gained relative to wages and salaries as a source of wealth."[36] And in the end you couldn't fool all of the people. In 1988 a national poll found that only 38 percent rated the economy "pretty good" or "excellent," while 60 percent thought it "not so good" or "poor." Moreover, to a certain extent it could be argued that this shift of wealth from the earners to the owners was deliberate; that underlying the populist rhetoric of Reaganite conservatism was a conscious agenda of reversing decades of equalization. The effect of conservative economics was to favor those who were carefully labeled "entrepreneurs," because that suggested innovation and risk-taking. They might, however, with greater justice, since what defined them was the ownership of capital, have been called by a name with less populist resonance: capitalists.

One need hardly look further for an explanation of the tensions and resentments of American society, and the dreamlike unreality of American domestic politics in the Reagan years. Here we had an American majority being assured by their beloved president, and exhorted from every mouth of the many-headed media, that they had never had it so good. Yet the stark reality of daily life and the hard accountancy of the billfold showed that for most, things were getting, slightly but mercilessly, worse — even as they were getting better and better for those who told them how well off they were.

Why, then, was there so widespread a perception that Reagan had indeed brought back "morning in America"? His 1984 television spot commercials to that effect were skillful enough, but there was a little more to the public perception than those misty shots of white clapboard churches and sunny woodlands, so reminiscent of life insurance advertisements. Why did Reagan and Reaganism attract such an electoral following? Why, if the real economy, for so many Americans, was so disappointing, did Ronald Reagan win reelection in a landslide?

Partly, as we shall see, it resulted from perceptions and emotions that had nothing to do with economic realities and everything to do with nationalism and national self-confidence. Partly, it was because powerful messages were zapped out from the media, celebrating an aggregate prosperity that in reality enriched only a minority, albeit a minority handsomely represented in the media. (For the first time the top fifth of the American population took in over half of national income, if you include capital gains.) And partly it was because, although only a minority made solid economic gains during the Reagan years, that prosperous minority was large enough to provide Reagan with a large proportion of his electoral support.

Only 53 percent of eligible voters actually voted in 1984 and just 50 percent in 1980. Given that the top 10 percent of the population had done very well out of the Reagan years, and the next 10 percent had also done quite well, Phillips has pointed out, voters in the top 20 percent of the population by income quite likely cast over 30 percent of the votes in 1984.[37] The rich alone could not elect Ronald Reagan or any other president. But "the rich," in the sense of that top fifth of the population who had done so much better than everyone else out of the Reagan years, were so overrepresented in the electorate that they could at least give a conservative candidate an enormous advantage. Once that is understood, the mystery is at least partly explained.

There really was an entrepreneurial explosion in the 1970s and 1980s, and it did transform public attitudes. Highly educated young people were attracted to conservatism by a creed that appeared to guarantee them $80,000 a year in starting salaries and opportunities to become millionaires by the time they were thirty. The idea spread that the essence of democracy is that it allows some people to become billionaires. "What I want to see above all," said Ronald Reagan, "is that this remains a country where someone can always get rich." There were weeds in this harvest, however. As the boom swept in on either coast, industrial workers in the Middle West and the Mid-Atlantic states lost their jobs. Many family farmers — once the backbone of the Republican Party — were forced off their homesteads. In the West and the

Great Plains, dozens of whole counties were left without a single doctor. The heart of the prosperity created by the post–World War II industrial boom was ripped out as $15-an-hour workers were "downsized" from manufacturing industry. They were replaced by production facilities that had moved to unregulated plants in Mexico, or, when their multinational corporations decided to buy their hardware from Asia, to Pacific nations whose wage costs, while rising, were still a fraction of American levels.

This process of restructuring handed fortunes to corporate executives and managers, to management consultants, leveraged buyout operators, and assorted investors and professionals on Wall Street, while it sucked economic juices out of the middle-sized cities of the Midwest. It risked re-creating one of the oldest and bitterest divisions in American politics, the resentment of the back country for the Tidewater, of the Midwest for New York, and of the heartland for the coasts. The process is still increasing inequality, and thereby storing up social and ultimately political problems for the future.

ONLY IN FOREIGN policy can it be claimed that the Reagan revolution delivered more than a fraction of the achievements that were promised. And there, in spite of terrible, even scandalous, shenanigans on the way, Reagan's policies did deliver more than even their sponsors had dared to predict: the collapse of the Soviet system and the end of the Cold War. Indeed, Reagan's foreign policy showed up both the best and the worst of his political style: the soggiest bread, to pick up the sandwich metaphor once more, but also the beefiest beef.

One aspect of Reagan's personal foreign policy was a passionate and somewhat indiscriminate hostility to those he perceived as America's enemies, especially in the Third World: to terrorists, but also to radical nationalists and of course to those movements which seemed to him — with varying degrees of evidence and plausibility — to be doing the Soviet Union's work. That stance did much to restore respect for the United States as an adversary not lightly to be ignored around the world. But it also led to a number of illogical and erratic responses, to disasters and imbroglios. In the end, it came very close to derailing his whole presidency.

This is not the place to retell the entire bizarre sequence of events known as the Iran-contra affair. But it is worth highlighting certain aspects of the story, because it did reveal some glaring inconsistencies, some dangerous tendencies, not only in Ronald Reagan's foreign policy presidency, but in the attitudes of American conservatives toward the outside world. One such tendency was to ignore the context of unfavorable developments, and so to attribute to raw, gratuitous anti-American hostility actions that were in reality rooted in ancient quarrels. Often these had little to do with the United States or with the Reagan administration's obsession with communism.

In June 1985 a TWA airliner was hijacked by Shi'ite guerrillas and taken to Beirut airport, where, to emphasize their determination, they shot a U.S. Navy diver, Robert D. Stethem, and threw his body from the plane. It was a horrific and criminal murder. Led by Ronald Reagan, the government reacted as if it were also inexplicable. Reagan himself made a speech to the American Bar Association, a rather sophisticated audience, about this very incident in which he attributed Middle East terrorism to "outlaw states run by the strangest collection of misfits, Looney Tunes, and squalid criminals since the advent of the Third Reich." Within weeks he would be authorizing a secret diplomatic negotiation with the leaders of the very "outlaw state" — Islamic revolutionary Iran — which supported the Shi'ite Muslim fighters in Beirut, specifically including those responsible for Stethem's murder.

Apart from that culminating absurdity, Reagan was willfully ignoring what the Beirut highjacking was about. The highjackers, Mohammed Ali Hamadi and Hassan Ezzedine, shouted to their hostages, "Marines!" and *"New Jersey!"*[38] Those three words were the clearest indication of what was on their mind. But in case they were too cryptic, Hamadi also asked, "Did you forget the Bir-al-Abed massacre?" A civil war, raging in Lebanon since 1975, involved vicious infighting as complex as it was bloody. But in essence it was a civil war between the Lebanese Christians and the Muslims, members of both religions trapped within the rotting superstructure of a compromise state patched together after the collapse of French colonial rule.

In that conflict the United States, and specifically the Reagan administration, had intervened with overt and covert force, and intervened unambiguously on the Christian (which also happened to be the Israeli) side. Marines had been sent to Beirut to fight the Muslims, even though they were withdrawn after 241 marines were killed by a truck bomb in October 1983. (Reagan called the bombers "cowardly, skulking barbarians," though whatever else you might think of suicide bombers, they are not generally seen as cowards.) The *U.S.S. New Jersey*, one of the most powerful warships in the world, had sent hundreds of devastating sixteen-inch-high explosive shells into the Muslim villages on the slopes of the Shouf Mountains, south of Beirut, killing an unknown but surely substantial number of men, women, and children there. And Bir-al-Abed was the place where Lebanese agents, generally believed to have been working for William Casey's CIA, blew up an apartment building, killing more than eighty Muslims.

None of this justifies the highjackers' act in killing Stethem, of course. But even if Casey and the CIA were wholly innocent of the Bir-al-Abed killing, and few experts believe that they were, it certainly helps to explain why passionate young men, fanatics, if you will, might have lashed out in the only way they could think of to dramatize what they saw as American guilt. To react in that way might be criminal. But to do so you would not have to be what Reagan called, in a strangely undignified phrase, "Looney Tunes."

By reacting as he did, Reagan sent a very different message to the rest of the world from the message he wanted to send to Americans. To the folks at home, he was saying, "We are ruthless in our determination to fight terrorism." To much of the rest of the world, he seemed to be saying, "Don't bother me with the details of your quarrels; when it suits me I will send you sixteen-inch shells, and then afterward I shall forget that I shelled you, and if it suits me, I shall compare you to Hitler." By ignoring the history and context of the world his supporters expected him to dominate, he turned its complexities into a Manichean struggle between good and evil. So he confirmed a dangerous pattern of sudden, abrupt inflictions of American military force against foreign regimes that incurred his displeasure — a pattern he did not initiate, and one that was to be followed with greater or less justification by his successors, George Bush and Bill Clinton. Reagan made himself highly popular by a series of these actions against small countries — Lebanon, Libya, Grenada, Nicaragua, El Salvador — leaving a pattern for his successors' actions in Panama, the Middle East, Somalia, Haiti, and Bosnia. But he also left a divided legacy in foreign policy, not least to conservatives.

On the one hand there was always the possibility that the United States might lash out in unpredictable fashion. On the other, the president could seem cavalier in his response to allied concerns. He angered Western Europeans by trying to impose a boycott on the pipeline bringing Soviet oil to Central Europe. Then, when it turned out that several big U.S. corporations stood to profit from the pipeline, he changed his mind. He treated the United Nations with some contempt. Altogether, he expressed a conservative yearning for a United States foreign policy that would express American instincts rather than American interests; a foreign policy that would be interventionist, but not internationalist.

His indifference to the context of the angry rebellions of the Third World was clearest of all in the case of Nicaragua. In July 1979 Anastasio Somoza was overthrown by an alliance of forces, stretching politically from outright agents of Cuban communism to democratic politicians who would not have been out of place among U.S. Democrats. The Reagan administration treated these people as mere agents of Moscow and Havana, without history or context. Yet who was Anastasio Somoza DeBayle? He was a corrupt and brutal dictator whose family had been installed in power by the United States in 1927. Ever since, the Somoza dynasty had been maintained by American diplomacy, American money, and, when necessary, American marines. Who was César Sandino? Why, he was the Nicaraguan folk hero who had fought the marines and the Somoza regime and been murdered on the orders of the elder Somoza. He was widely viewed, from the Rio Grande to Tierra del Fuego, as a martyr of the struggle not against the United States, but against the corrupt dictatorships the United States has too often supported in Latin America, as if in so many fits of forgetfulness of its own values.

Reagan had appointed as director of Central Intelligence William Casey, an ultraconservative New York lawyer who had learned his international politics, gun in hand, as an OSS agent in Europe in World War II. In December 1981 Casey proposed covert paramilitary action against the Cuban advisers who were helping the Sandinistas.[39] Armed with an executive order from the president authorizing action against the "Cuban-Sandinista" support system, Casey and his men began to wage secret war in Central America. Specifically, they backed the contras, a counterrevolutionary guerrilla group, largely made up of former Somocistas. This put the United States on the side of the bad old regime against the new, which was hugely popular, even if it did contain elements that were trying to make a Cuban-style revolution. Anticommunism, for Casey and those who thought like him, took clear precedence over the notion of replacing dictatorship with democracy.

Casey's secret war was repugnant to the Democrats, who controlled the House of Representatives. In 1982 the latter succeeded in adding to a CIA authorization bill, and to a military appropriation, an amendment, known from its sponsor as the Boland Amendment.[40] In early 1984 the Republican-controlled Senate Intelligence Committee, chaired by no less a conservative than Barry Goldwater, discovered that Casey's operatives were secretly mining Nicaraguan harbors, in flat defiance of Congress. Goldwater was furious, and sent Casey a bluntly worded note: "This is no way to run a railroad. I am pissed off."[41]

The Casey view appears to have been that the security of the United States itself was gravely threatened by a Cuban-led revolutionary uprising in Central America, of which the Sandinista victory in Nicaragua was only one prong. This view, which ignored the realities of politics, economics, military power, and geography, was enthusiastically adopted by a clique of gung-ho conservative officials in the State Department, led by Assistant Secretary Elliott Abrams, and in the president's own National Security Council staff, led by Bud McFarlane, a marine colonel, but epitomized by an engagingly boyish fanatic, Marine Lieutenant Colonel Oliver North.

This view was also unquestioningly embraced by the president himself. On May 9, 1984, he attacked congressional critics of covert action by the contras and others in Central America as "new isolationists." He denounced the Sandinista government as "a communist reign of terror." A little less than a year later he told his speechwriter Peggy Noonan to call the contras "the moral equivalent of our Founding Fathers." (Among those he honored with this comparison was one Adolfo Calero, a former manager of Coca-Cola in Nicaragua, who ended up as the beneficiary of several million dollars, some of it diverted from the Kingdom of Saudi Arabia.) And in March 1986 Reagan appeared on television once again with a map that displayed the red tide of communism lapping all the way up from Central America to the borders of Texas and California.

In spite of these efforts, the fanatics in the Reagan administration despaired of persuading Congress to change its mind and authorize funds for covert military action against the communist menace in Central America. (Ironically, in 1985 and 1986 Congress did relent and provide substantial sums for that very purpose. By that time whole herds of horses had bolted the stable door.) Central America appeared to Reagan's loyalists as a sort of return match, an opportunity to erase the Vietnam War from the mind of America by a resounding victory over creeping communism south of the border.

In the summer of 1985, however, this game of red dominoes became fatefully intertwined with the essentially unrelated fate of the Western (and especially American) hostages taken by Iran-backed — and, incidentally, anticommunist — terrorists in Beirut. At the same time, U.S. policy also became commingled with the foreign policy of Israel, which was understandably eager to improve relations with Iran. Israel had been selling arms to Iran at least since 1980, its strategic objective being to offset the threat from Iraq and other Arab nations. On July 18, 1985, the die was cast. National Security Adviser Bud McFarlane visited the president in Bethesda Naval Hospital, where he was having a growth removed from his intestine, and proposed establishing political contact with Iran through Israeli good offices. Precisely what Reagan knew — and when he knew it — about the connection between Israeli relations with Iran, the improvement of U.S. relations with imaginary "moderates" in the Iranian regime, arms sales, and bargaining for Iranian help in recovering the American hostages from Beirut is still a matter of angry assertion and outraged denial. It is plain that Reagan knew much more than he admitted when the scandal broke.

The details are intricate and do not matter. In 1985 and 1986, with vague cover from the president but without the knowledge of the secretaries of state and defense, rogue officials on the National Security staff, at State, and in the Central Intelligence Agency created a kind of "right-wing international," a web of unofficial conduits to barter arms for the hostages, to raise money for the contras (some of it begged from foreign rulers, of whom the king of Saudi Arabia said yes while the almost equally wealthy sultan of Brunei said no), and to supply them with arms.

The tale had its moments of drama. A shot from a hand-held surface-to-air missile launcher brought down a transport bearing illegal arms to the contras. All of the men were veterans of earlier operations with the CIA's clandestine Air America. Only one survived. As his parachute fluttered to the ground, he introduced himself as Eugene Hasenfus from Marinette, Wisconsin. The rabbit was out of the hat. Even stranger was the revelation, due in the first place to a tip from an obscure radical weekly in Beirut, *Al Shiraa*, that the president's national security adviser, accompanied by a crew of unlikely desperadoes — including a senior Israeli intelligence officer masquerading as an American — carrying fake Irish passports, pistols, and suicide pills, had arrived in Tehran in search of "moderates." If they could find any, they hoped to woo them with a chocolate layer cake in the shape of a key. Some of this activity was motivated by high-minded anticommunist passion, some by mere greed. Some of it was unofficial, some official. All of it was illegal and — worse than illegal — insanely unwise, illogical, counterproductive, and profoundly damaging to the reputation and long-term interests of the United States. It was also clear that Ronald Reagan approved of whatever he learned of the plan and that conservatives in general were thrilled by such uninhibited and red-blooded anticommunist activism.

Several members of this comically inept conservative conspiracy were subsequently convicted of criminal offenses. The president of the United States told one of them, Lieutenant Colonel North, to his face, that he was "a national hero." He added, "This is going to make a great movie one day." The movie is still unmade. But Colonel North, testifying in full uniform to a congressional committee, and making it plain that he cared little for Congress-made law when it came into conflict with the higher law of the conservative dispensation, did become a national hero. Indeed, he came close to parlaying his parody of the gung-ho military man, blundering through the political jungles, into the United States Senate.

Compared with Watergate, the Iran-contra affair certainly bears out Karl Marx's often-quoted dictum that history repeats itself, the first time as tragedy, the second time as farce: first Karl, then Groucho. Of course the Iran and Nicaragua affairs were in reality quite separate and ought to have been treated as such. Egged on by conservative wild men he should have controlled, Reagan blundered, and then blundered again when he tried to cover up the degree of his knowledge and involvement. Unlike Nixon, he got away with it. He did not resign, nor in the end was he ever seriously in danger of impeachment. This was not, however, because some mysterious political chemistry made him a Teflon president, as Representative Pat Schroeder complained. He was protected by his great personal popularity and also perhaps by the very fact that Nixon, only a dozen years earlier, had been forced from office. There were many, in the media and in Congress, who felt that the country could not stand another crisis like that.

THERE WAS, however, more to it than that. In his last two years, after the wretched muddles and prevarications of Iran-contra, there was evident another side of Reagan's policy, which reflected all that was best in his political instincts and his remarkable patience and determination. That was his management, in the end brilliantly successful, of America's relationship with the Soviet Union.

He began as an unreconstructed, even a simplistic anticommunist. In his election campaign he had promised to go right over and tell whoever was running the Soviet Union *nyet*, on first principles. In his first press conference he said that, so far, detente had been a one-way street and that the Soviet leadership reserved to itself "the right to commit any crime, to lie, to cheat."[42] Two years later he called the Soviet Union an "evil empire." Yet by 1988 he had created better relations with the Soviet Union than any president since Franklin D. Roosevelt, more than forty years earlier. His relations with the Soviet leader, Mikhail Sergeyevitch Gorbachev, were so close that Reagan himself discovered with apparent surprise that he and the first secretary of the Communist Party of the Soviet Union had "a chemistry . . . that produced something very close to a friendship."[43]

Many factors, of course, went into that rather spectacular transformation. The most important, no doubt, was the crisis in the Soviet Union itself, a crisis of the economy and also of the spirit. It is a mistake to exaggerate the role of American policy, or any outside force, in producing that crisis. The slow working of years of undisclosed outrage at the squalor and brutality of the regime's behavior; the mounting frustration that years of effort and sacrifice had built a giant military power, but had not been able to improve the daily lives of ordinary Soviet citizens; the strengthening perception even inside the Soviet elite that Soviet communism was not a future that would work, but a towering intellectual error: all of this convinced Mikhail Gorbachev, as the chosen representative of the party itself, that his government was hurtling out of control along a track that must end in the abyss. Essentially, Ronald Reagan was able to reach agreements with the Soviet Union because its leaders had thrown in the towel. In the end — and the end came suddenly — these leaders realized that they could no longer compete. They could no longer afford to treat the United States as an enemy. They even had to hope that the United States would be their rescuer.

Reagan's attitude, too, was changed by a number of outside influences. He appears to have been greatly influenced by his conversations with a woman, a Russian-language teacher at Hunter College in New York City, who got in touch with him and, in a number of face-to-face meetings, taught him to draw a distinction between the hateful Russian regime and the lovable Russian people.[44] He may also have been influenced by his wife's steely ambition on his behalf. Nancy Reagan did her best to arrange with his staff that important events be scheduled for days her astrologer thought propitious.[45] She also claimed in her memoirs to have done her best to encourage him to consider a more conciliatory relationship with the Soviet Union. For years, she wrote in her memoirs, it had troubled her that her husband was portrayed as a warmonger. She also felt "that us calling the Soviet Union an evil empire was not particularly helpful." She confirmed that she argued that he tone down his tough rhetoric.[46] And she claimed credit for pushing Reagan into meeting Gorbachev as soon as possible.[47]

That last statement is certainly not true. Neither the slow conjunction of forces in Moscow nor the persuasiveness of a wife or a new acquaintance could have made Ronald Reagan take a line in his dealings with the Soviet Union that was not traced by his deepest instincts and strongest convictions. Hard as it seems for many knowledgeable and sophisticated people to recognize, Ronald Reagan was successful in his dealings because he was right all along; and the experts, those who knew infinitely more than he did about Russia and the Soviet system, were wrong. It was Reagan's conviction, his living faith, that the United States was a great society and must prevail. He believed that if the United States put forth its strength — military, material, and moral — the Soviet Union could not live with it. And he was right.

His policy had an almost guileless simplicity. First, he was determined to increase military spending to a level where, if the Soviet Union tried to stay in contention, it would shake its ramshackle economy to pieces. Then, he insisted that negotiations, on arms control and arms reductions, must be conducted on American terms. That meant abandoning the bad habit, which had grown especially in the long years when Dr. Henry Kissinger was the engineer of American policy, of offering concessions and compromises, so that American responses showed a steady tendency to move closer to Soviet demands. Finally, when the more visionary of the scientists claimed that American technology could perform the miracle of creating an impassable shield against missile attack, Reagan did not allow himself to be put off by the (all too plausible) doubts about whether such a concept could ever work, but seized on it. He convinced all but the most recalcitrant of the Soviet leadership that the cost of keeping up with the Americans would inflict such damage on the Soviet economy that the regime itself would be in danger.

In the end, after Reagan left the White House, his policy was crowned with success beyond even his dreams. The Soviet leaders abandoned their objections to arms reduction proposals one by one. They accepted agreements to reduce arms, then discovered they could not afford even the lower levels of armaments they had negotiated. They abandoned the regime and the party. They gave up Marxism-Leninism, and at last the Soviet Union itself split apart, until only Russia, its neighbors and former subjects, and its long-suffering people were left. Looking at the turmoil and potentially dangerous chaos that has taken the place of the Soviet order, it is hard not to flirt, at least for a moment, with the idea that Ronald Reagan's dealings with the Soviet Union confirm the old saying that we should be careful what we want, because we may end up getting it.

The conventional wisdom is that Reagan began as the hardest of hardliners in his first term, then miraculously converted to negotiation. If we look at the sequence of Reagan's dealings with the Soviet Union, that is not what happened. It is clear that Reagan was intent on successful negotiations from the start, but he did not believe that an excessively conciliatory stance would make them come about. During the 1980 campaign he was in close touch with Eugene Rostow, Paul Nitze, and the hardline group associated with the Committee on the Present Danger. Once in the White House, Reagan put Rostow in charge of his arms control team, and in mid-1981 Rostow invited Nitze to be the head of the negotiating team. As early as September 1981, Reagan's first secretary of state, General Alexander Haig, was already talking about strategic arms *reduction*, not arms *limitation*, and before the end of his first year in the White House the president himself was offering to forgo deployment of the controversial Pershing II and ground-launched cruise missiles if the Russians would reduce their intermediate-range missiles in what became known as the "zero-zero option." In the summer of 1982 Paul Nitze came close to persuading his Soviet opposite number, Kvitsinskii, to agree to a dramatic arms reduction deal in the course of their bizarre "walk in the woods" in the Jura Mountains above Geneva.

That November Leonid Brezhnev died, and power in the Soviet Union lay in the shaking fingers of two other old men — Yuri Andropov, then Konstantin Chernenko — until, in March 1985, Reagan found himself confronted by a young, vigorous, and highly intelligent Soviet leader who understood that something urgently needed to be done to relieve a faltering economy of the impossible burden of trying to compete with the United States.

Mikhail Gorbachev was indeed, in Margaret Thatcher's words, "a man we can do business with." But before Ronald Reagan could do business with him, a certain number of obstacles had to be cleared away. On March 8, 1983, Ronald Reagan made a speech that appeared to confirm the worst fears of those who thought he was locked in the simplicities of the early Cold War years. When the communists, he said, "preach the supremacy of the state, declare its omnipotence over individual man, and predict its eventual domination of all peoples on the Earth, they are the focus of evil in the modern world."[48]

That was the soundbite that went round the world. Ronald Reagan had called the Soviet Union an evil empire. The world could prepare for a long cold winter. It was the turn of Reagan's critics to ignore the context of what he was saying. For Reagan was talking to an audience of

Southern evangelicals, and he was not only talking politics; he was talking church politics. He was declaring his support for the conservative evangelical churches, specifically in contradistinction to the Northern leadership of the predominantly liberal "mainstream" Protestant denominations.[49] That was what he meant when he urged his evangelical supporters "in your discussion of the nuclear freeze proposals . . . to beware the temptation of pride — the temptation of blithely declaring yourselves above it all and label both sides equally at fault, to ignore the facts of history *and the aggressive impulses of an evil empire.*" That was why he told reporters at a press conference three weeks later, "No, I didn't think there were many polemics in that particular message."[50] And that was why, shortly after *that*, he told Henry Brandon of the London *Sunday Times*, who asked him about the speech, "I have stated, very frankly, what I believe the differences are, but at the same time, I have expressed my determination and my belief that peace is at hand."[51]

Ronald Reagan was not merely sounding off like a primitive, belching out his gut hostility to communism. He was engaged in a delicate political operation to bring his conservative supporters along with him on a journey that would offend their deepest instincts. He knew it would, because he shared those instincts. But he was president, and they were not. It was up to him to find common ground even with those who had rationalized and defended the *gulag*, who had lied and prevaricated for decades in all their dealings with the United States, and who had most recently invaded Afghanistan and declared their willingness to do the same wherever the Brezhnev Doctrine told them their ideology was engaged.

Reagan was not, however, willing to let the search for that common ground endanger the great nation entrusted to his care. That is the explanation of the second, more serious obstacle he threw in the way of successful negotiations with the Soviet Union on the traditional pattern, that of so-called detente. The evolution of his thinking will always elude those who think of strategic policy as a conflict between "hawks" and "doves," an oversimple metaphor that has done much to confuse discussion of United States foreign policy. In the same month, March 1983, in which he made the "evil empire" speech, Reagan astonished the world with what became known as the Star Wars speech. "The final fact," he said, "is that the Soviet Union is acquiring what can only be considered an offensive military force." Then, with the deceptive simplicity that was the hallmark of his best speeches, he dropped his own intellectual bombshell. "Wouldn't it be better," he asked, "to save lives than to avenge them? . . . What if free people could live secure in the knowledge that their security did not rest upon the threat of instant retaliation to deter a Soviet attack, that we could intercept and destroy strategic ballistic missiles before they reached our soil or that of our allies?"

What Reagan was proposing was what he called a "strategic defense initiative" and the media swiftly dubbed "Star Wars," after the vastly successful film series of that name. Nowhere was the sounding of dropping jaws louder than in his own administration. Neither the secretary of state nor the secretary of defense knew that his president was about to spring this surprise. Both George Shultz and Caspar Weinberger were angry. "A speech like this by the president will unilaterally destroy the foundation of the Western alliance," said one high official at the State Department, Richard Burt. "The president seems to be proposing an updated version of the Maginot Line," sneered another, Laurence Eagleburger. [52] It was widely assumed that the president had seized on a stray idea served up to him by Edward Teller, usually known as the "father of the H-bomb" but also one of the godfathers of the original atomic bomb. Teller, in 1983 a seventy-five-year-old retired professor at the University of California, had been widely demonized as a man who was prepared to confront the nuclear realities in too cavalier a manner.

Teller was indeed in the plot. But the story went farther back than the horrified media assumed after the Stars Wars speech. Early in the 1960s United States intelligence learned that the Soviet Union was building two antiballistic missile (ABM) complexes, and in the middle 1960s Congress "virtually forced" appropriations for the United States to follow suit.[53] Two ABM complexes were duly built by each side, one protecting each national capital and one a "field" of intercontinental ballistic missiles. ABM construction was frozen by the treaty negotiated by Henry Kissinger in 1972.[54] By 1975 the U.S. ABM site near Grand Forks, North Dakota, had been torn down.[55] The military establishment, in the Carter years, was cool to the very idea that antiballistic missile defense was a possibility. But the thought that it would be better to shoot down incoming Soviet missiles rather than rely on deterrence had not been eradicated.

In the late 1970s U.S. Air Force General Daniel O. Graham (another Committee on the Present Danger member) had been working to interest the Pentagon, the armed forces, the strategic community in the academic world, and members of Congress in what he called the "High Frontier" concept of strategic missile defense. Senator Malcolm Wallop, of Wyoming, was one of several Westerners in Congress who were attracted to it. And so were some of Ronald Reagan's oldest friends, the "kitchen cabinet" who had backed him in his early forays into California politics, including Karl Bendetsen, a former high official in the Pentagon under President Truman, and the Colorado brewer Joseph Coors, whose money had bankrolled so many earlier conservative institutions, including the Heritage Foundation.[56] The first White House meeting to discuss strategic missile defense took place as early as September 1981. The idea continued to be pressed by Edward Teller, General Graham, and President Reagan's science adviser, George A. Keyworth. So when President Reagan went public with it, what was surprising to insiders was not that he wanted to do so, but that he had persisted in the teeth of the bureaucracy's resistance.

A strategic defense initiative office had been set up in the Pentagon by early 1984. More than a decade later, no one really knows whether Reagan's concept would have worked. He seemed to have in mind some kind of high technology dome over the territory of the United States and — perhaps — of some of its allies. No one knows how expensive would have been a system effective enough to deter potential attackers, whether enemy states or nuclear terrorists. Enthusiasts spoke in visionary terms of layered defense, tackling incoming missiles at each successive stage of their flight, of mirrors and high-powered lasers, of nuclear warheads in space, of computers of amazing power tracking all the thousands of incoming, multiple, independently targeted warheads the Soviet Union could throw in a desperate spasm of aggression. Others scoffed. The technology was unproven, perhaps impossible, the cost prohibitive: the administration spoke of $26 billion; others predicted that a full antiballistic umbrella would cost a cool trillion.

The risk of nuclear explosions in space was unimaginable. Strategy pundits predicted that SDI would trigger a new and perilous round of the arms race. Lawyers tangled over whether what Reagan proposed would be in breach of the ABM treaty or not; and strategic experts wondered whether the United States was accusing the Soviet Union of violating the ABM treaty at least partly in the hope of being free of the treaty's limitations so that it could press on with the SDI. Allies feared that the Americans, retreating behind their cosmic Plexiglas, would abandon them to their fate. And the Soviet Union, issuing solemn (if somewhat hypocritical) warnings against the "militarization of space," argued that SDI would make a nuclear first strike more likely.[57]

In the event, all of these arguments were beside the point. For the Soviet response made it plain that, whether the United States could have built a strategic missile defense on these lines, the Soviet leadership simply did not mean to wait around to find out. Gorbachev's whole conduct of arms control and arms reduction negotiations, from the Geneva "fireside summit" of November 1985 on, makes sense only on one assumption: that the Soviet leaders desperately wanted to get rid of an American strategic defense initiative because they knew that the Soviet economy could not stand the diversion of resources of all kinds that would be needed to make an effective strategic missile defense. The evidence is that Reagan was perfectly aware of this. At the beginning of 1986, he wrote in his memoirs, "We were getting more and more indications that the Soviet economy was in dire shape. It made me believe that, if nothing else, the Soviet economic tailspin would force Mikhail Gorbachev to come around on an arms reduction agreement we both could live with."

That January, Gorbachev offered to go to zero in all nuclear weapons and in the ballistic missiles to deliver them. The Russian had picked up an unguarded remark by the American president in Geneva, George Shultz revealed: if there was no need for nuclear missiles, Reagan had said, then there was no need for defense against nuclear missiles.[58] Gorbachev was so desperate to avoid having to build defense against nuclear missiles that he was prepared to throw away the whole arsenal the Soviet Union had built up at a fearful cost over a third of a century.

Gorbachev's obsession with eliminating SDI was the hinge of Reagan's apparent failure at the Reykjavik summit in October 1986, actually his decisive success. On the first day, Gorbachev accepted in principle the U.S. proposal for eliminating all nuclear missiles from Europe. Then he agreed to eliminate all ballistic missiles everywhere in ten years. Reagan himself described graphically what happened, as it seemed to him:

> Then, after everything had been decided, or so I thought, Gorbachev threw us a curve. With a smile on his face, he said: "This all depends, of course, on your giving up SDI." I couldn't believe it and blew my top.

Throughout 1987 Gorbachev made it plain that the ending of SDI was the essential condition, the *sine qua non*, of strategic arms reductions, and Reagan made it equally clear that he was not budging. Only when the game was truly up, when the Soviet empire in Eastern Europe was on the point of breaking away, and when the Soviet Union itself was in danger of collapse, did Gorbachev abandon his steely determination to disarm Reagan of the weapon that the Soviet Union could not match, the one that gave him his decisive edge.

RONALD REAGAN was a man who came to politics with great personal abilities, with a mishmash of personal prejudices and misconceptions, and with a handful of big ideas. One of those had been dear to the hearts of conservatives since the days when the young Bill Buckley was encouraging James Burnham to ask why the United States could not confront communism and roll back its pretensions. It was the idea that if the United States committed its resources of economic power, scientific know-how, and political will, the Soviet Union — in Dean Rusk's famous phrase, uttered at the tensest moment of the Cuban missile crisis — would blink first. As Reagan, with earnest modesty, expounded his political philosophy to the highly educated students of Moscow State University in May 1988, he may have been thinking of his own experience more than they could have suspected. Freedom, he said, was the right to question established ways of doing things. It was the continuing revolution of the marketplace. Then he added, "It is the right to put forth an idea, scoffed at by the experts, and watch it catch fire." Was he thinking of his own idea that preventing nuclear war might be better than avenging it? Perhaps. Certainly Reagan's dealings with the Soviet Union proved him right and many of his most sophisticated critics wrong. This was not triumphalism. This was triumph.

When Richard Nixon climbed into a helicopter to leave the White House on his way to California in 1974, a conservative revolution had been aborted, and by its parents' own folly. When Reagan set out on that same journey fourteen years later, he had not succeeded in transforming the country, even if he had changed it. But he had succeeded in changing its situation in the world. It is time now to pull back the focus from Ronald Reagan, the man who was chosen to carry through the conservative program, and see how the program itself has fared since his departure.

11

Full Circle

Great God! That's it! They're all Southern! The whole United
States is *Southern!*
                        — *Douglas Kiker, 1968*

IN FEBRUARY 1994 Republican members of the House of Representatives met at a conference in Salisbury, Maryland.¹ They there asserted five principles they called their "basic philosophy of American
civilization": individual liberty, economic opportunity, limited government, personal responsibility, and security at home and abroad.

For good reasons, the Republican congressmen did not call them
conservative principles. For one thing, they did not want to risk alienat-
ing any remnant within their own ranks who might have difficulty with
that adjective. More to the point, they were eager to reach out to the
largest possible swathe of American voters. Still, the five Salisbury principles, broad enough to be subscribed to by a great majority of Americans, were subsequently converted, under the political leadership of the
then minority leader of the House, Representative Newt Gingrich of
Georgia, into a document he called *The Contract with America.*

The contract was nothing less than a manifesto reaffirming the principles of the new populist conservatism and locking into place Republican, and conservative, control of Congress. Ultimately, the Gingrich
conservatives hoped to take over government in the United States at the
federal, state, and local levels. That truly would have fulfilled the Reagan revolution.

Skillfully taking advantage of the anger and cynicism in the country
directed against Congress itself and a series of recent "inside the Belt-
way" scandals, the contract began by pledging action to clean up Congress's act, making it more democratically accountable. Then it moved

on to what was unmistakably a project for conservative legislation and eventually for conservative government. A fiscal responsibility act, with the aim of balancing the budget and providing incentives to small business, such as cuts in the capital gains tax, would, it said, revivify the economy. A tough anticrime package, including "effective death penalty provisions," legislation intended to discourage illegitimacy and teenage pregnancy, and a basket of tax credits for parents and families, all addressed themselves to popular, and populist, concerns about supposed national moral decline. Widespread disillusion with the United Nations, strengthened by the UN's miserable performance in Somalia the previous year, was the context for the demand that no American troops serve under UN command. A number of measures were designed to gain support from older voters. Law reforms would "stem the endless tide of litigation"; term limits would "replace career politicians with citizen legislators."

Many of the provisions of *The Contract with America* have about them the unmistakable reek of political demagoguery. To call a modest measure of middle-class tax relief the "American Dream Restoration Act," for example, smacked of propaganda going on hype. The strategy nonetheless got off to a highly successful start. On September 27 more than three hundred Republican candidates for the House of Representatives stood in front of the west front of the Capitol and signed the contract.[2] A week later, at similar ceremonies in state capitals, Republican candidates for state legislatures made a similar pledge; and a week later local candidates did much the same in front of city halls and county courthouses.

On November 8, 1994, the Republicans won a smashing victory at the midterm elections. They got control of both houses of Congress, breaking decades of Democratic dominance. For the first time in history an incumbent speaker of the House, Tom Foley of Washington, was defeated. Not a single Republican candidate for senator, congressman, or governor was beaten, while Republicans won control of seventeen additional state legislatures and, for the first time in twenty years, of a majority of governorships. The new speaker, Newt Gingrich, was quick to claim that credit for this impressive electoral sweep belonged to his *Contract with America*. It was, he said, "the most shatteringly one-sided Republican victory since 1946." He could with truth have made an even larger claim: that the Republicans had ended a Democratic hegemony in American politics that had lasted, with only brief and partial interruptions, since the Great Depression.

That was 1994. Fifty years had passed since Friedrich Hayek had

uttered, in *The Road to Serfdom*, his vatic warning against the consequences of turning to the state to solve the problems of society. Now, the
conservatives could be forgiven for feeling they had won the intellectual
as well as the political battle. Decisively, they had converted the majority
of the American people to the conservative philosophy.

Or had they?

By the beginning of another election year, as the front-end–loaded
1996 primary season began, President Bill Clinton seemed to have at
least a 50 percent chance of yet another comeback. In a November
budget shootout, Speaker Gingrich overplayed his hand. By a margin of
two to one, Americans told pollsters they blamed Gingrich and his
take-no-prisoners Republican freshmen for the shutdown of government. Gingrich upstaged the Republican Senate majority leader and
probable candidate, Robert Dole, on every TV appearance, then made
himself look foolish by going public with complaints about how the
president had treated him on the flight to the funeral of Israeli Prime
Minister Yitzhak Rabin. Magic, for sure, had departed. Now, Gingrich
and many of his conservative colleagues seemed more concerned with
the good opinion of those they could count on — the professional conservative politicians and activists — than with that of those they would
need if the Republicans were to recapture the presidency: the ordinary
Americans who might sympathize with some conservative instincts, but
dreaded the loss of Medicare, Social Security, jobs, and other benefits.
President Clinton, who had thrown it in George Bush's teeth as a kind of
insult that he was a "foreign policy president," made the best of his
office's potential for international leadership. He offered himself as the
peacemaker in Bosnia, the Middle East, Ireland. Suddenly he looked
more and more credible as a second-term president — something few
would have been willing to bet on even as little as six months earlier.
Presidential politics, in fact, were as volatile as ever. A Republican might
or might not be inaugurated president in January 1997, but no one could
any longer cite the midterm elections of 1994 as evidence of conservative dominance of the political scene.

Ronald Reagan's last years were bathed in a golden light by his
successful arms control negotiations and, in retrospect, by the collapse
of the Soviet Union. His moments of triumph in Moscow hid the fact
that, from 1986 on, his presidency was nearly derailed by the Iran-contra affair. Even earlier, the Reagan administration had run out of steam
as an engine of conservative transformation. There was no Reagan revolution. After a flurry of successes, when he took advantage of his per-

sonal popularity to pass a surprising part of his legislative program in the first half of his first term, Reagan won reelection by an impressive margin. He owed his victory to his ability to convince the voters that, however little their own personal situation had improved, it was "morning in America." In international affairs, his second term was a time of high ambitions and high risk, of embarrassing failure and authentic triumph. But domestically, the late 1980s were a time of frustration. The stock market fell sharply in the fall of 1987. The economy was headed for the second recession within a decade. And then came Bush.

George Bush was not a conservative — at least not in the judgment of conservatives. He did not conceal his dislike for the conservative gurus and their intellectual jungle gym. He called supply-side theory "voodoo economics," and the conservatives never let him forget it. His personal style and instincts were not theirs. Under a veneer of Texas conservatism he was, in the literal senses of the two words, an "Eastern internationalist," and he behaved like one.

In 1990, Bush's already frayed political fortunes were patched up by his victory in the Gulf War. With commendable decisiveness, he threw the whole weight of the United States' commitment behind his determination that the Iraqi invasion of Kuwait "will not stand." With real skill, he put together an alliance broad enough to make a substantial contribution — militarily and, even more, financially — to victory. For the first time, American forces were being paid like mercenaries to fight the international community's battles. Still, Bush presided with nerve and excellent judgment over the buildup of forces, the air war, and the final triumph.

Such an overwhelming victory might have been expected to make him an outstandingly popular president. It did not. For one thing, few Americans identified strongly with the causes of the war. To have fought to preserve Israel might perhaps have been popular. To have fought to protect Western oil might also have engaged U.S. public opinion. But this was presented as a war to protect Kuwait, an unappealing authoritarian monarchy, and to maintain the integrity of the international system at a time and in a place where few Americans thought their own interests were seriously threatened. Then, having won an impressive victory with a military performance of which all Americans could be proud, President Bush switched off his war. Geopolitical *coitus interruptus* took place. Saddam Hussein was not the kind of man to waste too much energy regretting his humiliation by the United States and the international community. As soon as he saw that the United States had withdrawn into its shell, he went back to massacring the Kurds in the

north and the Shi'ites in the south of Iraq, and to torturing opponents in
the remaining, central third of the country. He lost the Mother of All
Battles. But he won the war.

Within two years, George Bush was back in Kennebunkport, but
Saddam Hussein was still in power in Baghdad. The war and the reason for the United States' involvement in it had not been thoroughly
thought through. Nor had the fact, only too apparent with the approach
of a presidential election year, that it was easier to commit massive forces
to a war in the Middle East than to end up with a desirable situation
there. George Bush's approval rating in the Gallup Poll, which had
skirted an all-time high for postwar presidents at nearly 80 percent in
1991, fell like a stone. By mid-1992 it stood at 25 percent — close to an
all-time low. The war, it became plain, was far less important to a broad
stripe of the American electorate than their domestic economic woes.

For them the issue was, to borrow a phrase from candidate Clinton,
"the economy, stupid." If, after almost a dozen years of Republican
control of the White House, the economy was still a dangerously negative factor for a Republican president, that did not speak volumes for the
effectiveness of Reaganomics. One element of the new conservative
economic wisdom, monetarism, had in fact almost disappeared from
view by the time Bush became president. The emphasis on strengthening the supply side of the economy, while still part of the Republican
agenda in theory, had failed in practice to perform as its boosters had
claimed it would. While Republican publicists vigorously maintained
that they were unimportant, the twin deficits seemed to hobble the
American economy. And the persistence of huge budget deficits was not
just a drag on the economy and a gigantic national liability; it was the
embodiment of a serious question about the truth of the conservatives'
claim to have converted the American majority to their doctrines. The
persisting budget deficit was direct evidence of how little the very politicians who talked most about getting government off the people's backs
really dared to cut government spending.

Sixteen years after Ronald Reagan's triumph in 1980 first turned the
American political world "right side up," in fact, anyone who wanted to
evaluate the impact of the new conservatism on American life had to
answer two questions: What did really change? And what changes are
likely to be permanent?

FOR ONE THING, conservatives, and more especially neoconservatives,
did take over the intellectual initiative in Washington and in other key
nodes of intellectual influence in America, including many influential

media institutions and certain famous graduate schools. It ceased to be fashionable to advocate government action as the answer to every social question. Instead, it became fashionable to treat government as if it were, not the legitimate instrument of American democracy, but a trick played on gullible citizens.

The conversion of many intellectuals is both less parochial and more important than it may sound, because of the links that exist between "pure" scholarship and journalism through a newly created middle ground of ideological public relations. The neoconservatives, the Heritage Foundation, the Christian Right, and the rest have built a network of funding foundations, fund-raising bodies, direct mail operators, journals, and channels of communication to mass media to disseminate their interpretation of the world and their policy prescriptions. In the process, by the 1990s they had gone a long way toward marginalizing all who disagreed with their ideas.

A typical neoconservative operation would begin with an article by a reputable social scientist in a journal such as *The Public Interest.* (The authors, even when on the payroll of avowedly conservative research institutions, are always referred to as "scholars," a term that suggests objectivity. In fact, while many of these neoconservative social scientists have the highest possible qualifications and reputations, for these purposes they often write not in their capacity as scholars but as practitioners of that very "advocacy journalism" conservatives used to denounce so fiercely in liberals. Readers of Charles Murray's work, for example, will not easily be convinced that he comes to his views about the underclass driven by the pure light of social science alone, unguided by political preconceptions.) These "new" ideas would then be discovered, commended, circulated in a host of other publications, all ultimately supported by the same ring of half a dozen foundations committed to conservative ideology. Conferences would be organized. Speakers would be carefully and selectively invited. The right (and right) journalists would be invited to attend. The favored ideas would duly circulate through media more and more closely approaching the objective mainstream until they had received the widest possible exposure and, it was hoped, acceptance. Thus the trail from the avowedly partisan conservative fringe to the op-ed columns of major newspapers could be blazed by patient, dedicated conservative scouts. If necessary, an incipient counterattack could be beaten off, sometimes with surprising *ad hominem* acerbity. Throughout, it would have been made unambiguously clear that the glittering prizes of career advancement, research posts, research assistance, publication, and promotion awaited those, and only those, who hewed close to the ideological line. Such skillful use of the carrot and the stick has succeeded in creating, in the Washington think tanks, in some newspapers and magazines, and in some university departments, a sort of conservative *nomenclatura;* and this careful process has enabled the conservatives, to a remarkable degree, to drown out discordant voices.

In this, it could be said, the conservatives have done little more than mainstream Cold War liberals did between the censure of Senator Joe McCarthy, in 1955, and Richard Nixon's inauguration, in 1969. But to dominate the intellectual horizon as the liberals once did is in itself no negligible achievement. It must also have had a substantial effect, through the mass media, on wider public opinion. Certainly, many of the themes public opinion has sounded most strongly in the last dozen years are the very ones the neoconservatives have played: bitter, theological hostility to liberals and all their works; much rhetoric (often with unmistakable racial undertones) about the "underclass" and social dysfunction; emotive defense of "quality," often a euphemism for traditionalism, if not elitism, in education; a fairly strident nationalism, often extending to calls for a crusade to spread "the American ideology of democratic capitalism" (in Michael Novak's phrase) to the whole world.

There is no question that the contested ground of American policy debate has shifted visibly to the right. In late 1995 Senator Daniel Patrick Moynihan pointed out one example that will stand for many. When congressional Republicans proposed welfare reforms that amounted to repealing Title IV–A of the Social Security Act of 1935, the title that had established Aid for Families with Dependent Children, Democrats scarcely bothered to fight. Moynihan quoted with approval the judgment of a reporter in the *Washington Post*, Malcolm Gladwell, that the "[liberal] defenders of the old activism toward the poor surrendered willingly, with the shrugs and indifference of those who no longer believed in what they stood for." Moynihan commented that if liberalism continues to fail to take the same account of the complexities of real life as conservatives do, "then the current revival of liberalism will be brief and inconsequential."[3]

Many of the shibboleths of liberal policy from the New Deal, Fair Deal, and Great Society years have indeed been tacitly abandoned. Industrial unionism is a shadow of the social democratic dream that animated Philip Murray of the CIO in the 1940s and Walter Reuther of the UAW in the 1950s. Progressive ideas in education are widely regarded as obsolete. There has been widespread rejection of the notion that punishment should be rehabilitative, evidenced by the reintroduction of the death penalty and the imposition of life imprisonment for third-felony offenders. State intervention in the economy and in social policy are seen as both undesirable and futile, though all but the most austere libertarians wink at various abundant subsidies for corporate business and for the real estate industry. Quintessentially, there has been a massive rejection of the idea of positive discrimination.

Most influential of all has been the widespread shift of assumptions about the role of government. In spite of the fact that government is legitimated, however remotely or even dubiously, by the electorate, the idea has become current that almost everyone else — businessmen, banks, real estate developers, private universities, research companies, and privately funded foundations, for example — is more qualified to make decisions about the future of society and the fortunes of individuals. This suspicion of government — now often and rather tendentiously called "the State" — has its roots deep in American history. But over the past twenty years it has made notable advances. The liberal instinct, when confronted with any social or economic problem, was to set up a government program to deal with it. That instinct has now been replaced as the ruling orthodoxy by a presumption, nourished and spread by conservatives, that government is bad and its interventions generally harmful.

Liberalism, in short, has become a dirty word for many Americans. Survey evidence reveals a steady growth in the proportion of respondents who identified themselves as conservatives, a steady decline in the number of those calling themselves liberals. One survey, for example, showed that in 1970 34 percent called themselves liberal, but by 1980 only 20 percent did so, and the trend has continued.

To attribute this shift exclusively to the admittedly mighty labors of the conservative "scholars," journalists, and foundation executives, however, may be to give them more than their due. Tens of millions of Americans have reacted angrily against what they saw, and what they were incessantly told, were the *excesses* of liberalism. But there are also awkward indications, both from surveys and from elections, that people have not so much shifted from a liberal agenda to a conservative one as they have decided that it would be nice to enjoy the best of both political philosophies: the benefits of liberal spending without the burden of liberal taxation.

There is abundant evidence, from the whole period of 1981 to 1994, that Americans, in large majorities, wanted *both* lower taxes *and* higher benefits. They wanted their country, a "gentler America," to enjoy the "peace dividend"; at the same time, they wanted it to be feared and respected for its military strength. Those whose jobs depended on the vast gamut of military industries understandably did not want to lose them. The supermarket view of politics has ousted the politics of principle as relentlessly as mom-and-pop shops have given ground to shopping malls. A range of policies is on offer. The voter-shopper is free to fill his or her basket with whatever policies and programs are best packaged and most attractively presented, while deferring to the end of the month the need to pay for them.

When conservatives pointed to their success at persuading the voters to agree with them that taxes should be lower and government smaller, they did not face the fact that the majority of Americans also insisted that government continue to provide the services those taxes paid for. The persistent budget deficits of the Reagan years, as David Stockman pointed out in his memoir from the heart of the Reagan White House, was the institutionalization of this indecision on the part of the electorate — and of the politicians' unwillingness to cut the knot. The "failure" of the Reagan revolution, as Stockman put it, "represents the triumph of politics over a particular doctrine of economic governance" — that is, the conservative doctrine.

> Its implications [he went on] are deeply pessimistic only for the small and politically insignificant set of anti-statist conservatives who inhabit niches in the world of government, academia, business, and journalism . . . The Reagan Revolution amounted to the clearest test of doctrine ever likely to occur in a heterogenous democracy like our own. And the anti-statist position was utterly repudiated by the combined forces of the politicians — Republican and Democrat, those in the executive branch as well as in the legislative.[1]

The election of 1992, therefore, represented a strange, transitional moment in American politics. Excluded — temporarily, they hoped — from influence over presidential politics, and still denied control of Congress, conservatives were uncertain and divided. It was conservative thinkers in 1992–1993 who insisted most emphatically that there had been no Reagan revolution, that all was still to fight for. Some obeyed the advice of Ralph Reed, of the Christian Coalition, to leave national politics alone and concentrate on building strength in local politics. Others wasted their energies on internal quarrels of surprising venom, between neoconservatives and what were now called "paleoconservatives," for example. Some remarkably vicious disputes of this kind absorbed much conservative energy in 1991 and 1992.

Candidates, announced and unannounced, for the presidential nomination in 1992, in succession to George Bush, were already beginning to maneuver. Finally, the resignation of Speaker of the House Jim Wright (Democrat of Texas), after allegations of corruption, and similar allegations against other powerful Democratic congressional leaders, such as Dan Rostenkowski of Illinois, chairman of the Ways and Means Committee, and Tony Coelho, the Democratic whip from California, coming on top of tawdry revelations about abuse of the House of Representatives "bank," whipped up to frenzy the campaign against "Washington." That, in turn, opened the way for the bizarre, off-and-on-again, but extremely significant campaign of one of the strongest third-party presidential candidates in history, the self-made billionaire Ross Perot. It was Perot who, by winning 19 percent of the vote, defeated George Bush and made possible the election of the Democratic candidate, Bill Clinton of Arkansas. By the time of Clinton's inauguration in January 1993, in fact, with the Democrats still in control of both houses of Congress, it was hard for conservatives to look back over the previous dozen years and claim that there had been any such thing as a conservative revolution.

That was why the "Gingrich revolution" of November 1994 had such an impact on onlookers and especially on the media. Here, it seemed, at long last was evidence that the country truly had shifted to the right. Yet even those Republican victories in the midterm elections of 1994 did not look decisive. They did not wholly chase away the suspicion that conservatism had still not yet captured the mind of Middle America quite as its prophets had hoped. Much of the steam behind the Republican victories came not from converts to conservative ideas, but from those who wanted to punish insiders and Washington politicians generally.

Has nothing, then, changed since the apparent conservative triumph of 1980, even after the new speaker leaped onto the stage, brandishing his *Contract with America*? As I write in early 1996, President Clinton's chances of reelection in November 1996 look fairly good, and Speaker Gingrich seems only to have damaged Republican chances by appealing to convinced conservatives rather than to a larger audience of Americans who, while sympathetic to some aspects of conservatism, remain stubbornly reluctant to buy the whole package.

To the question, though, "Has nothing changed, after a decade and a half of the Reagan revolution?" the honest answer has to be "Yes, much has changed." The center line of American politics has shifted a long way to the right. Not only has the word "liberal" become unpopular; so too have essential components of the liberal philosophy itself.

The old liberal instinct was to identify a problem, target it with a program of government action, entrust the program to a public agency, and so create a constituency to conserve the program and its funding in perpetuity. That instinct is now dormant. Bureaucracy has been demonized. (The public now assumes the worst of the bureaucracy of government agencies; for some reason the bureaucracy of insurance companies, banks, and private hospitals, not to mention foundations, usually escapes criticism.) Instead, the study of issues of public policy has been jobbed out to a swarm of private consultants, research companies, and think tanks, each with as good reason as the next always to come down on the side of the private as opposed to the public solution.

There is this major difference between the heyday of liberal ideology in the 1960s and that of the conservatives in the 1980s. Democratic administrations and their liberal advisers in the earlier period had to work against the grain of a corporate culture that retained enormous power over many areas of American life and remained essentially conservative, in the old mainstream Republican sense. To be sure, liberal ideas about economics had begun to make their appearance in corporate hierarchies in the 1960s. So, too, however timidly, in the more sensitive corporations, had liberal fashions in such fields of social policy as nondiscriminatory hiring of women and minorities. But liberals had to come to terms in one way or another with a business culture that was unmistakably not their own patch. Conservative ideologues in the 1980s, on the contrary, found themselves working with the grain of many traditional corporate attitudes and with many managerial instincts, not least with the old suspicion of, and the new contempt for, labor.

So much the more striking, therefore, was the substantial failure of the conservatives in the 1980s to wean large groups in the American public away from the essential liberal promise of a welfare state. The American economy responded more successfully than the economies of Europe to the hard times of the late 1980s and the early 1990s. It did not deliver any significant increase in real incomes after taxes and inflation. But it did at least create a large number of new jobs. No doubt many of these were both less secure and not as well paid as most of the jobs being destroyed by recession, foreign competition, restructuring, and "downsizing." But at least they were jobs. Many of them were flexible jobs, which suited women and young people rather well.

Meanwhile, behind the screen of this change in the job market, American manufacturing and service industry were carrying out a far-reaching transformation. As the traditional wealth-producing industries of the Northeast and Midwest experienced a frightening crisis, American management imposed a tough new regime. The power of labor unions was all but broken. Work forces were ruthlessly pruned. A tidal wave of mergers and acquisitions shook up managerial structures and attitudes. New managements invested in labor-saving production equipment. The American computer industry, and especially the software sector, took a grip on world markets comparable to that which American automobiles and machinery had once enjoyed but then lost to European and Japanese competitors. But other manufacturers shed workers until whole communities, even whole states, were devastated.

It was a period of uneven wealth creation and uneven wealth distribution. It was a period when "liberal" ideas of public provision were eclipsed by a new faith in private enterprise. But that did not mean that the American public as a whole was ready to trust to, or able to rely on, the free market for health care, for retirement income, or for its children's education. Up until the midterm elections of 1994, at least, in spite of all the conservative gains and liberal losses, the central conflict for the ideological allegiance of the American electorate remained what it had been essentially since 1980: a standoff. On the eve of another presidential election, the prevailing pattern of American politics confirms that conservatives have captured the strategic advantage; it does not yet prove that conservative ideas will monopolize the American future.

Presidential elections serve two functions. They elect presidents and vice presidents and thousands of other holders of specific offices. They are also a kind of national stock-taking — or psychoanalysis or referendum — a time, that is, when with the help of the news media Americans reassess how, as a nation, they think they are doing, and what their priorities for future effort and action are. Not the least important function of the 1996 election will be trying to resolve the question: Do Americans really want less government, as the conservatives say they do? Or do they want the best of both worlds?

Large numbers of Americans certainly want both lower taxes and higher benefits. They want the country to be "a gentler nation" *and* to be feared for its military strength. They want a return to old-time religion, the nuclear family, and traditional schooling; they also want to "have fun," to experience personal freedom, and to grow up free from oppressive authority figures and strict rules. When the Japanese threaten their jobs, or Saddam Hussein threatens their oil, or the Mississippi overflows its levees, or California runs short of water, or the Gulf Coast is ravaged by hurricanes, they want the government to step in and help. Yet quite genuinely they dislike "Washington," to the point that political figures who have been wholly created by Washington (Bob Dole, Newt Gingrich, Patrick Buchanan, even Ross Perot) cheerfully, if a little absurdly, campaign against the place that has been the origin of their political and financial fortunes.

There is nothing unusual about this wish to have the national cake and eat it too. Most people, after all, want to do just that most of the time, in America and elsewhere, in politics and in their private lives. But as long as so many Americans continue to have that ambiguous attitude to government, then however much they may applaud conservative politicians who say they want to "get government off your back," they can hardly be said to have wholeheartedly adopted the conservative creed.

AFTER THE PUBLICATION of Kevin Phillips's perceptive and influential 1969 book, *The Emerging Republican Majority,*[5] it became received journalistic wisdom that the poor old Rust Belt of the Northeast and the Midwest was in decline, while it was all "go! go!" in the conservative Sunbelt. The section of the nation that was on the rise, demographically, economically, and politically, could be defined by its sunshine, but it could also be defined in another way. The Sunbelt was also the South. To be more precise, the rising section included both the South and those parts of the Southwest, especially Southern California, which have inherited what is in many ways a Southern conservative political culture.

Many of the roots of the conservative conquest of America, only partial though we have seen it to be, go back to the troubled years of the 1960s and in particular to the belated but still massive attempt of the Kennedy and Johnson administrations to make the South more like the rest of the United States. By a complex series of historical and political ironies, it was this most ambitious of liberal thrusts that turned out to have the most lasting, profound, and, on balance, conservative effects on the political system.

The South, said the bumper stickers at the time, SAYS, HELL, NO!

More than thirty-five years later, not only is a large part of the South still saying "hell, no!" to liberalism; it has persuaded a good part of the rest of the country to say "hell, no!" too. Even in 1968, the eleven states of the former Confederacy carried 20 percent of the popular vote. By the 1990s, the South and border together carried close to one third of the population of the United States. Moreover, where it had once been demographically and economically stagnant, the South was now growing faster in both respects than any part of the country except California, and Texas and Florida had passed New York to become the second and third most populous states. In 1968 the television reporter Douglas Kiker, a Southerner who was covering the George Wallace campaign, put the matter more bluntly:

> It was as if somewhere, sometime a while back, George Wallace had been awakened by a white, blinding vision: they all hate black people, all of them. They're all afraid, all of them. Great God! That's it! They're all Southern! The whole United States is *Southern!*[6]

At the time of the civil rights movement, in the 1950s and early 1960s, the assumption of Northern liberals and the national news media was that the differentness of the South was residual. The task of the civil rights movement, it was taken for granted, was to welcome the South home and make it more like the North. In some respects, that is precisely what happened. But the political consequences have been very different from what anyone foresaw at the time. And in the process the rest of the country, in crucial respects, has become more like the South.

The South has indeed become more like the rest of the country in certain important respects. That is not surprising, considering how very different the South was as late as the 1940s.[7] In 1940, when Franklin D. Roosevelt set up a commission to report on the condition of the South, its average income was not much more than half that of the country as a whole. In every index of poverty, deprivation, or underdevelopment, the eleven states of the old Confederacy led the nation, or came close to leading it. In Arkansas, in those days, they used to say, "Thank God for Mississippi!"

The South was a developing country inside the frontiers of the most developed country in the world — except that it was developing slowly. The South in 1940 was what we would call now a Third World country. In many ways, as late as the 1930s, it was in a colonial relationship to the North, and Southern politics reflected that underlying economic and emotional truth. Discriminatory railroad tariffs were only one of the devices by which New York, Chicago, and Philadelphia flooded the South with Northern manufactures, while making it hard for Southern products to gain more than a toe-hold in Northern markets. Southern labor, its wages kept down by competition from quasi-peonage and by the often brutal repression of union organizers, worked for sharply lower wages than were paid up North. As a result, the South did not fully share in what was the greatest single innovation of the United States economy in the half century before World War II, the discovery that you could make higher profits by selling to very large numbers of consumers even if the markup on each item was perilously low, so that it made sense for industrial society collectively to pay good wages to work-ers who were also potential consumers. As for capital, a Southern bank, in those far-off days, was an institution that borrowed money in New York and lent it for a point or two of added interest to Southern borrow-ers. Educational standards were low for whites and pitifully low for blacks. In health, in transportation, in every department of life that needed investment, the South lagged far behind.

The South has now become richer, more urban, more industrial, less rural, less parochial, less agrarian, less absorbed in its own tragic history. It has also become more diverse ethnically. Fifty years ago the over-whelming majority of its inhabitants were descended either from early Anglo-Celtic settlers — English, Scots, Welsh, and Irish (often what is called Scotch-Irish, that is, Protestants from the Scots settlements in Ulster) — or from African slaves. Tiny communities of other back-grounds could be found, such as the German liberals in the Texas hill country, Cajuns and Italians in New Orleans. But only in enclaves such as Miami Beach or the bigger Texas cities was the diversity of ethnic origin commonplace in Northern cities to be found. Now, partly as a result of the military, disproportionately encamped across the South as a result of Southern dominance on congressional committees, partly as a result of industry's movement toward union-free locations, not to men-tion the *douce* attractions of the Southern climate and lifestyle, much of the region approaches the diversity of the Middle West, if not yet that of New York or California.

What is even more significant, the South has become much like the rest of the country politically. It is no longer ruled by a distinctive one-party political system based on its peculiar history. Until the 1970s, Southern politics were dominated by the Democratic Party, essentially for the simple reason that it was the Republicans who had fought the Confederacy and won, emancipated the four million slaves in whom

Southerners, with disastrous economic as well as moral consequences, had overinvested, and then imposed Reconstruction, gun in hand, upon the outraged Southern whites.

The political consequences of the fact that for the best part of a hundred years a dozen states were to all intents and purposes one-party fiefs are often forgotten. For the South, one-party rule meant fiercely tribal politics from which blacks were virtually excluded. It would be foolish to generalize about a class of Southern politics that included such various talents as those of Lyndon B. Johnson of Texas, Richard B. Russell of Georgia, and J. William Fulbright of Arkansas. It was a rich political fauna that embraced the Longs of Louisiana, the Gores of Tennessee, Judge Stennis of Mississippi and the Armed Services Committee, and Judge Howard Smith of Virginia and the House Rules Committee, not to mention politicians of almost every conceivable species imaginable, from the loftiest patrician to the crassest populist, and from the most high-minded liberal to the crudest racist.

Yet some statements can be made. Most Southern Democratic politicians from the 1930s to the 1970s, in Washington and in the state capitals, were intensely nationalist, even nativist. They were unconditional supporters of the military and "internationalist" in the sense of being strongly anticommunist and instinctively in favor of assertions of American power in support of American principles and interests abroad. Yet most of them also usually believed in free trade. They were social conservatives, ultracautious about any change, especially in the status and rights of African Americans, to whom, until well into the 1960s, many of them habitually referred, as if to a nonhuman species, as "the Negro." With the exception of a handful of patricians (many of them, incidentally, patricians by education rather than by lineage), they were robust populists, reflexively on the side of "the little man," whether — like George Wallace — they had really emerged from the ranks of the plain people or, like Wallace's predecessor as governor of Alabama[8] and many, many other Southern politicians of the time, they chose to present themselves as more barefoot in their origins than they really were.

Strong supporters of the farmer and the small-town businessman, most of them also endorsed the New Deal and its successor programs, because they understood that for most of their constituents it had been a welcome lifeline in a desperate time. They knew all too well that to come out against support prices or such forms of federal assistance was to invite a challenge from some less scrupulous would-be statesman.

("My daddy planted cotton," one Mississippi planter once memorably told me. "I plow the corridors of Washington.") Few had much time for labor unions. Some were more or less avowedly in the pocket of powerful interests like the oil and gas industry, the power and light companies, and the various farm lobbies.

Yet as a group, except where the South's traditional concern with race was touched on, they had a strong sense of the national, as opposed to the local or even the sectional, interest. This vision — it may be too much to call it statesmanlike except in individual cases (Johnson, Russell, Fulbright, a few others) — was nevertheless marked in all of them, helped no doubt by the extreme political longevity of their terms in Washington. Coming from one-party states, Southern senators and representatives had time to acquire seniority in the committee system. They had every interest in defending a system which guaranteed that a majority of the powerful committee and subcommittee chairmanships would be theirs.

In the Congress that confronted Lyndon Johnson's civil rights legislation in 1964, there were still almost a hundred safe Democratic conservative votes in the House and around twenty in the Senate. As a consequence, Congress, in its various guises during the 1960s, though nominally controlled by large Democratic majorities, was in reality in the hands of what was known at the time as the "conservative coalition." These Southern Democrats (all men), and their Republican counterparts from the Middle West and West, were by no means conservatives in the sense that the word would be used by the New Right of the 1970s or by a follower of Newt Gingrich today. Nonetheless, they instinctively mistrusted liberal projects for government-led reform, except where they judged that such projects were either unavoidable or likely to produce economic benefits for their states, their supporters, or for themselves.

The swift changes of the late 1960s and the early 1970s swept away this time-honored Southern Democratic monopoly of power. Back in their states and districts, the members of the Southern club in Congress were caught between the political upheaval consequent upon the Voting Rights Act of 1965 and highly successful minority voter registration drives, and on the other the steady advance of the Republicans. From 1969 on, the Southern strategy was successfully led, with President Nixon's approval, by the likes of Harry Dent in South Carolina. In Washington, the Southern oligarchs were bewildered by puzzling changes in the political culture. There was impatience with the seniority system that had enabled the South, with less than a third of the country's population, to dominate Congress. This new mood was marked by the gradual and eventually successful pressure for political reform, especially from the Northern Democrats led by the Democratic Study Group. Beginning in 1969, the DSG succeeded in transforming the House Democratic caucus, which had been a powerless grouping of all Democratic members of the House for fifty years, into an effective and sometimes aggressive instrument for political reform. In 1970 the caucus set up a committee, under Representative Julia Butler Hansen, of the State of Washington, to study the seniority system, and by 1975 the seniority system was essentially dead. The Democrats also modified the "closed rule" procedure, which had given the Committee on Ways and Means and its chairman, Wilbur Mills of Arkansas, awesome practical power by protecting money bills from amendment on the floor of the House. The caucus broke the power of the Rules Committee, which under its chairman, Judge Howard Smith of Virginia, had played a scandalous role in blocking civil rights legislation by allowing the speaker to nominate all Democratic members of the Rules Committee, subject to ratification by the caucus as a whole. The Senate, which had always been a more open place than the House, with power more evenly distributed, adopted similar reforms in the early and mid-1970s.

The new mood was also exemplified by a number of cases — not without their comic side, except for the protagonists — in which the alcoholic and sexual indiscretions of leading Southern politicians were pitilessly exposed. Wilbur Mills, all-powerful chairman of Ways and Means, survived the revelation that he had frolicked in a Washington fountain with an Argentinian striptease dancer called Fanne Foxe, but when he got up on the stage to congratulate Ms. Foxe in a Boston burlesque house, he had to resign and was later treated for alcoholism. Speaker Carl Albert called him "one of the greatest congressmen of his generation" but added that Mills was "a sick man." Two years later a limousine containing Speaker Albert and a lady of the town drove through the front window of an elegant Georgetown dining room. Albert, too, resigned for reasons of health. These were only two of the saltiest of a whole string of ethics cases involving the old Southern congressional leadership. A political caste, already facing expropriation, seemed to be committing suicide.

For the Southern Democrats, the consequences of the passing of the Solid South were obvious. Men, and they were almost all men, who had held on to power for decades by promising their white constituents that

never would they bow the knee to Northern assaults on white supremacy, now found themselves explaining to voters, a growing proportion of
whom were black, why they had supported positions that were against
the law. Meanwhile, in many districts a new breed of Republicans was
outbidding them by taking even more conservative positions, but in a
language usually free from traditional Southern racial code language.
Their bewilderment and desperation at this new situation goes a long
way to explain why so many of them seriously contemplated crossing the
floor of Congress to become Republicans themselves in the winter of
1972–1973. The Democrat Party is by no means extinct in the South,
even a quarter of a century later, but it is losing its traditional voter base
among white males and is becoming a party of black and a few white
liberal voters. Its long-term prospects are not promising.

The consequences of this silent revolution in the South for the
national Democratic Party are even more grave. The party of the
Roosevelt coalition was forged by an alliance between traditional conservative white Democrats in the South and working-class people —
some of them black, most of them white, many of them Roman Catholics and Jews, with a sprinkling of intellectuals — in the North. While
some of these traditional Northern Democrats were peeling away from
the party allegiance anyway (in some cases because of their distaste for
what they perceived as excessive sympathy on the part of the Democrats
for African Americans), what was happening in the South condemned
the national Democratic Party to trade nickels for dimes.

It would gain the great majority of the new black voters, but in a
political game that was still racially polarized, albeit in a more genteel
way than in the past, it would lose the votes of a larger number of whites.
In 1976 and again in 1992 the Democrats won the presidency when they
nominated a Southern candidate, and the feeling grew among professional politicians that the Democrats could win *only* by choosing a
Southerner. But throughout the whole period from the middle 1970s
to the middle 1990s, the Democratic Party was being steadily maneu-
vered away from the commanding central high ground of American
politics, and ever more remorselessly faced with the prospect of becoming a "rainbow coalition" of minorities. Democratic pundits like Lyndon
Johnson's former speechwriter Horace Busby never ceased to warn their
fellow Democrats of the danger of losing the votes of white males,
especially suburban white males. A whole section of the party's office
holders, under the banner of the "moderates" of the Democratic Leadership Council, strove to recapture the middle ground and its predomi-

nantly white male occupants. Bill Clinton, once a chairman of the DLC, actually succeeded in riding "New Democrat" ideas into the White House. Admittedly, he might not have been able to do so except in a year, like 1992, when there was an exceptionally strong third-party candidate in Ross Perot. No one could say that the Democratic Party was dead. But it was being jockeyed into the dangerous position of being perceived as the liberal party, confronting the conservative Republicans, and at a time when, as we have seen, a majority of the American people declared themselves to be conservatives.

Awkward for the Democrats, the consequences of the political revolution in the South, however, were most dramatic of all for the Republicans. Up until the 1970s, after all, the Republicans, already essentially a conservative party, had been fenced off from something like half the country's most promising hunting territory for conservatives. That quirk of history, going back to the Civil War and Reconstruction, can even be said to be *the* single reason why successive more or less liberal Democrats (Roosevelt, Truman, Kennedy, Johnson) occupied the White House, and that Democrats, many of them far from liberal, dominated Capitol Hill for even longer. It was important that Republicans in the North and West converted so many people to their conservative views. It was even more important that from the 1970s on Republicans were able to acquire, ready made, so to speak, the votes of tens of millions of white Southerners who had always been conservatives and were now becoming Republicans, as well.

In this new, increasingly Southern, unmistakably conservative Republican Party there was no longer any room for the rump of the Eastern moderate wing. Comparatively few in number, the Rockefeller wing of the Republican Party continued to act as a brake on the national party's steady drift to the right for some years after Nelson Rockefeller's defeat in 1968. The growing weight of the Southern Republicans put an end to that. The last, tenuous link with the abolitionist traditions of the party of Lincoln was broken. The party of Gingrich would be something else.

It is tempting to play with superficial cultural examples: the national acceptance of once regional country and Western music, the folk poetry of the South, for example, or the Northern adoption of something of the religious fervor of Southern attitudes to sports. In religion, the Southern confessional traditions — evangelical, fundamentalist, Pentecostal — continued to expand, winning adherents, while the denominations of the Northern business elites, Episcopalian, Presbyterian, Methodist, lost communicants and influence. A new, overt, emotional patriotism, a political faith that wore its heart on its sleeve in a Southern, definitely not a Yankee style, was part of the political elixir of the Reagan presidency. A certain militarism, arguably, marched out of the South into regions once immune to the Southern love of soldiers, uniforms, generals, guns, drums, and uphill charges. With *Top Gun* and *A Few Good Men*, Hollywood discovered the military virtues, and the nation rediscovered the thrill of victory.

These are all wispy speculations in fields where it is hard to prove a point conclusively one way or another. In two areas, though, the rest of the country has indisputably become more like the South: in race relations and in politics. Racially, the United States has evolved since the 1960s in ways that can only be called both contradictory and paradoxical. The contradiction is that, although by some measures the rigid separation between whites and blacks, especially in the South, has been largely removed, by other tests the gap between white people and black people has actually widened. The paradox is that, though open racism of the kind that was widespread forty years ago is both illegal and socially unacceptable in all but comparatively unimportant corners of American life, both white and nonwhite Americans show strong signs of moving toward a kind of voluntary apartheid.

Sudden, only partially explicable outbursts of intense media obsession with race — the Willie Horton ad that helped George Bush to win the 1988 election, the Rodney King beating and subsequent Los Angeles riots, the O. J. Simpson trial — all hint at banked fires of racial suspicion, stereotyping, fear, and plain reciprocal dislike. The Million Man March organized by the Reverend Louis Farrakhan, like Farrakhan's startling popularity in African American circles that would once have utterly repudiated his call to separatism, suggests that many black people reject assimilation with what they see as an obdurately unfriendly white majority. Many more African Americans are wearying of the dream of acceptance. The tight security of middle-class apartments, three decades of white flight to the suburbs, and the overt separatism of some white housing developments behind the protection of walls, checkpoints, and armed guards — these and many other social innovations suggest an impulse toward partial resegregation among at least some white people.

No longer do even the most conservative Southerners openly defend in public the "agrarian tradition," the "peculiar institution" and — most durable of these euphemisms — the "Southern way of life." Such phrases revealed how carefully Southerners avoided confronting, or admitting to others, the ugly realities of plantation, slavery, and sectional resentment over Reconstruction. For generations of Southerners this language papered over the fact that Southern life was permeated by arrangements for more or less acknowledged racial segregation and racial subordination. Race had been at the heart of Southern political discourse for generations.

Now it is plain that national politics, too, are to a considerable extent about race. Racial assumptions, racial stereotypes, racial fears, lurk behind many painful national political issues from Boston to California: drugs, crime, law and order, education, cities, welfare, "welfare mothers," and so on. It is not that there are no real issues to be confronted and no real problems to be solved. American cities do need reinvigoration, investment, government reform. But too often that is not what people mean when they decry the state of the "cities." It is impossible to talk about crime and drugs without every participant in the discussion, white and black, being subliminally aware that a disproportionate number of criminals and drug dealers are black, *and* that most white people assume the disproportion is even greater than it actually is. In discussion of welfare reform and the underclass, there is much code language. This too, it seems to me, is very "Southern." A verbal culture of euphemism inhibits discussion of issues, while at the same time conservatives have launched a spectacularly successful campaign to ridicule what they dub "political correctness."

This has become a joke. But it was originally a scent by which conservative bloodhounds sniffed out latent liberalism. Originally, liberals took care to avoid language demeaning to women, blacks and other minorities, the handicapped. No doubt, given the overtender consciences of those in the liberal tradition, some of these periphrases were oversensitive to the point of self-abasement. Linguistic absurdities were bred of the desire of professionally sensitive persons — interest group careerists, minority leaders, journalists, timid academics, and the like — to avoid giving offense. Gleefully, conservatives poked fun at this namby-pambyism. In a stroke of public relations genius, some inspired polemicist of the devil-may-care right dubbed this nonsense "politically correct." Hooting and slapping their thighs, popular fellows in country club and law school alike fell over themselves to poke fun at the despised liberals, inventing such masterpieces of cant as "vertically challenged" for "short." In the ensuing gusts of contemptuous laughter, it was forgotten that political correctness was not an arrogant attempt on the part of liberals to tell Americans how they could talk; it was a conservative caricature of what was at bottom a decent and democratic instinct. Now that conservatives have laughed political correctness out of court, the way is more open for a return to polite conversation of the old, dirty fighting words: for "dago" and "guinea," "dyke" and "fairy," "kike" and "nigger." As Michael Lind has written, some targets of the politically correct really *are* racists.[9]

Even more dangerous is the abrupt revival in the 1990s, in some conservative circles, of more or less openly racist hereditarian pseudosociology of the *Bell Curve* school. There is nothing new about hereditarian explanations of differences of class and caste. A Frenchman, Alfred Binet, devised intelligence tests a hundred years ago. An English psychologist, Charles Spearman, invented the concept of g, a supposedly inherited genetic factor relating to general intelligence, in 1904. In 1969 the American social scientist Arthur Jensen dared to suggest that "genetic factors" might play a part in inequalities of achievement in school and afterward: for his pains, Students for a Democratic Society, in those bad old days, marched round campus, chanting, "Fight racism! Fire Jensen!" In 1971 Richard Herrnstein wrote his famous article in *The Atlantic Monthly*, raising for the first time for the educated lay public the possibility of a hereditary connection between race and intelligence. As a Harvard colleague wrote, Herrnstein "challenged the traditional liberal idea that stupidity results from the inheritance of poverty, contending instead that poverty results from the inheritance of stupidity."[10]

By 1973 a controversy was raging about education, intelligence, race, and IQ.[11] Charles Murray's own earlier book, *Losing Ground*, was published in 1984. So there was nothing especially new about the idea that performance in education and life might be determined, at least in part, by genetic factors, and that there might be some correlation between inherited intelligence and race.

Yet in 1994 a new book by Richard Herrnstein (who died shortly before it appeared) and Charles Murray had an extraordinary impact. It was a publishing and media event, for one thing, comparable with that attendant a year or so later on Colin Powell's memoirs.[12] And it divided the American intelligentsia, including the conservative intelligentsia, as few books have done for decades.[13] *Newsweek* called it "frightening stuff," and accused its authors of playing to "public anxieties over crime, illegitimacy, welfare dependency, and racial friction." *New York* magazine saw it as "grist for racism," but *National Review* called it "magisterial," and the *Wall Street Journal* denounced the liberal media for denouncing it.

The Bell Curve is indeed a strange book.[14] Over eight hundred pages long, with all the apparatus of a work of scholarship, it argued in what seemed superficially to be a scientific way that class differences are largely caused by genetic differences. Yet numerous scholars pointed out that its ostensibly scientific method conceals breathtaking manipulation of the evidence. Richard Nisbett, after noting how the study manipulates away crucial evidence suggesting that the gap in the performance of blacks and whites in the United States in IQ tests may be rapidly shrinking, commented that "for the question of genetic contribution to the IQ gap almost all the direct evidence has been left out" and the other evidence was selectively treated.[15] On the question of what can be done to diminish racial differences, Nisbett added, "Most of the relevant evidence has not been presented." He went so far as to hope that it would be recognized by the scientific community that the Murray-Herrnstein treatment of the issues could not be published "in any respectable peer-reviewed journal." Two editors at *The New Republic*, by no means the knee-jerk liberal journal it once was, dismissed the book as "a chilly synthesis of the work of disreputable race theorists and eccentric eugenicists." It was not an original or provocative book, they said, as Murray claimed, but "the work of a controversialist and popularizer of ideas from the fringe of the academy."[16] It was also tricky, in that again and again the authors offered a glimpse of a thought that they hastened to assure the reader they would not dream of harboring themselves. In a popular British television series, there was a devious and unscrupulous politician whose trademark was to say to reporters, "I couldn't possibly comment — but you might think that . . ." This was the Murray method, too. He speculated, without quite committing himself to the idea, that American society, increasingly divided by genetically inevitable inequality, was headed toward a "custodial state," which would be "a high-tech and more lavish version of the Indian reservation for some substantial minority of the nation's population, while the rest of America tries to go about its business." A *custodial* Indian reservation, indeed! Perhaps what Murray really had in mind was a plantation. With a third of black males between the ages of eighteen and thirty involved in one way or another (awaiting trial, in jail, or on parole), and with several states reintroducing the chain gang, not exclusively but in large majority for black prisoners, the image is not so preposterous as it may sound.

The interesting question is why *The Bell Curve* — long, dull, scientifically dubious, and far from original — should have had such an explosive impact in the United States in 1994. Stephen Jay Gould, the Harvard professor of geology and author of an earlier rebuttal of hereditarian theory, *The Mismeasure of Man*, explained its success as reflecting "a historical moment of unprecedented ungenerosity, when a mood for slashing social programs can be powerfully abetted by an argument that beneficiaries cannot be helped, owing to inborn cognitive limits expressed as low IQ scores."[17]

His phrase uncannily echoes pollster Mervyn Field's judgment on the *Bakke* case, that "it has become much more acceptable to be less generous." Michael Lind saw its impact as evidence not of the triumph of conservatism, but of its divisions.[18] As David Frum pointed out in an article in *The American Spectator*, some conservatives, led by Jack Kemp, pinned their hopes on such government interventions in the free market as enterprise zones or sales of public housing. Others, following William Bennett, secretary of education in the second Reagan term, called for efforts to change the "culture of poverty." Both accepted, as most conservatives had for decades, that the causes of poverty were essentially environmental; both turned to some kind of government action for solutions. Charles Murray's appeal to conservatives, Lind and Gould suggested, had something to do with conservative aversion to public action and with conservative reluctance to advocate public spending. But Lind added another explanation. He saw the appeal based on a transformation of the American conservative movement itself; in effect, in its "Southernization." "In a remarkably short period of time the broadly based, optimistic conservatism of the Reagan years, with its focus on the economy and foreign policy, has given way to a new 'culture war' conservatism, obsessed with immigration, race, and sex." In this transformation, he added, "the growing importance, within the Republican Party, of the Deep South no doubt also plays a role . . . Sunbelt conservatism is being rewritten Southern Gothic style. Race, sex, breeding, class — these are the classic themes of Tidewater reaction."[19]

There is a sense in which American public life *is* being Southernized. But the popularity of Charles Murray's theories about the genetic inferiority of African Americans does not need to be traced to the Great Dismal Swamp. It springs from sights all too close at hand: from the commuters' daily sight of the doughnut of blighted real estate that separates the gilded kernel of great American cities from their secluded suburbs. It is the stubborn social pathology of the inner city, and of what Murray termed "the underclass," that seems to call for explanation. Murray offered a tempting excuse to do what many conservatives want to do anyway: turn away from the expensive, frustrating, and unrewarding pursuit of equality.

* * *

IT IS NOT only in a racial context that under conservative leadership America has become a significantly less equal society. There is no need to repeat the devastating evidence recited in Chapter 9 for that proposition. A simple table makes the point with devastating implications. Between 1973 and 1993 the share of the national income received by the poorest fifth of the population fell from 5.5 percent to 4.6 percent, while the share received by the highest fifth rose by 3.5 percent, from 41.1 percent to 44.6 percent. The income of the bottom 60 percent of Americans fell by 3.2 percent, from 34.9 percent to 31.7. Three percent, 3.5 percent, sound like small numbers. But 3 percent of the United States national income is not a trivial amount. We are talking about something like $200 billion a year that used to go to the worst-off three-fifths of the population, and now goes to the best-off fifth.

The 3.5 percent rise in the income share of the richest 20 percent of the population was an 8.5 percent increase in their share, while the share of the poorest three-fifths fell by just over 9 percent. Moreover, the richest 1 or 2 percent were pocketing by far the largest share of the gains made by the richest 20 percent.

A simple argument illustrates the reality behind these small proportional shifts. Over the whole period since the late 1970s, the United States economy has grown substantially in real terms. Over the same period, the real income of the average American has hardly grown; only in the late 1980s did it climb back to its 1973 level. Yet we know that *some* Americans have become vastly wealthier over that period. The evidence is everywhere: in glistening condos and mellow suburban living; in college tuition fees for good universities as high as the national average income; in Manhattan and Rodeo Drive prices; in multimillion-dollar salaries and in the steady growth of the billionaire baronage. Well, if the average income has increased scarcely, if at all, over a period when arbitrageurs, real estate developers, Wall Street lawyers, investment bankers, chief executives, and celebrities in every branch of show business have been making so much money, then it follows arithmetically that the average American is worse off during this conservative age of inequality and excess. After decades in which Americans' incomes were becoming more equal, suddenly the numbers are moving quite sharply in the opposite direction.

A number of comments should be made. The first is that while the reversal of the long-term trend toward greater inequality in American life seems to have started before the Reagan administration, it intensified after the triumph of conservatism in the national political arena.

(From 1969 to 1976, too, the United States was governed by conservative Republican administrations.) The impact of the economic policies of the Reagan administration, especially deregulation, was in the direction of greater inequality. And to the extent that the Reagan and Bush administrations had any intentions in the matter of equality, it is plain that they were happy to see growing inequality, even if they saw it as no more than the price they would have to pay for "putting things right."

The policies of government were probably even less determinant of economic outcomes during the Reagan and Bush years than in earlier periods. Officials in those administrations, conservatives, were less inclined than their predecessors to pursue social and economic outcomes (such as greater equality or greater inequality) by their economic strategies. The transformation of the American economy and of American society over the past fifteen years was not primarily the work of Republican presidents and their officials. The political rhetoric reflected new realities in the world of business.

The stagnation of American incomes, and the growth of inequality, were essentially the consequences of the actions of corporate management, both directly in industrial corporations and indirectly as a result of policies pursued and intellectual fashions embraced in the financial sector. Political deregulation freed managers' elbows. A political climate encouraged them to take less account of noneconomic considerations. Business culture itself changed. Corporate business imposed greater inequality. Conservative doctrine rationalized it.

There are many alternative theories about exactly what happened. The most plausible interprets the change in corporate management's behavior in defensive terms. In the 1970s American managers confronted a profit squeeze of potentially disastrous dimensions because of global competition and declining American competitiveness. They could have sought to restore profitability through a "creative" strategy of high investment in new product development, product engineering, and improved productivity enhancement, to restore competitiveness. Some, to their credit, did. Most managements instead, under the lash of Wall Street corporate raiders, chose to cut costs, especially labor costs.

Pro-business governments are the default in American political history. At regular intervals, roughly every twenty to thirty years, business and its friends in government make such a mess of things that business government is swept away by a coalition of the disenchanted. Thus, in 1912 a coalition of those who were shocked by what business government had done to the ethics of American life, to the cities, and to the condition of a largely immigrant working class, voted for Progressive reform. In 1932, business government had allowed the economic system itself to come within an inch of collapse. In 1960 millions of Americans felt that government had been conducted in the interests of corporate business to the point where it was utterly out of touch with new issues and with new groups — blacks, women, young people — who were demanding to be heard. In the 1970s, as we have seen in detail, the rhythm of this political pendulum was disrupted by external events, among them unsuccessful war, near-insurrectionary movements at home, and a series of economic shocks.

The mere predestined swing of a pendulum, though, does not explain what was happening in the 1980s. Supply-side business policies, including deregulation, may have restored profits for corporate business and helped to trigger the wild, short-lived boom of the middle 1980s, but corporate profits conspicuously failed to "trickle down" to workers, as conservative theory promised they would. The boom was not only brief, it was largely confined to favored parts of the East and West Coasts. Its impact even there was selective. There is legitimate room for argument about precisely what happened. Some blame deindustrialization. Others claim that wage rates were depressed by the bulge in those coming into the labor market because of the post–World War II baby boom. Others blame attacks, including those by government, on labor unions, and others again point the finger at foreign competition and at "outsourcing" abroad by multinationals.

On two conclusions there can be no serious argument. The whole process was good for profits and bad for workers, as contrasted to owners and top management. Of course it is true that, through pension funds, personal savings, and life insurance, many workers are also to some degree owners. Indeed, that very fact was one of the explanations of how it was possible to take the "class struggle" element out of American labor relations and American politics in the twenty-five years after World War II. But it was one thing for industrial workers with stable jobs to see the shared interest between themselves, management, and democratically dispersed ownership. It was quite another to tell men and women who had lost stable jobs or were afraid of losing them that they were in the same boat with arbitrageurs, mergers and acquisitions men, greenmailers, and golden parachutists who were juggling with billions and paying themselves tens of millions. The American economy in the 1950s and 1960s was the envy of the world because of its capacity to function as a machine for enhancing equality by distributing higher real incomes for almost all. Now the great equality machine seemed to have gone into reverse. It had become an inequality machine.

In short, the blue-collar workers who voted for Reagan in 1980 and 1984 (and they included more than 40 percent of the traditionally radical UAW, for example) did not get the paradise of workers' capitalism they were promised. By turning the clock back to a new Gilded Age for the bankers and brokers whom Tom Wolfe, in the novel that seemed to sum up a decade,[20] called the Masters of the Universe, while simultaneously reviving the hard times of the Depression for the excluded, the conservatives succeeded in bringing back to American life not only greater economic inequality, but also something many thought even longer dead: the politics of class.

Why, then, did the desperate and the disappointed not flock back into the arms of a radicalized Democratic Party? Why did they not rush to support new populist movements? One of the most puzzling questions about American politics in the 1990s is precisely why issues of economic inequality and social class feature so *little*. It is not, after all, as though there were no tradition of class politics in America. Successive waves of social protest politics have broken on the rock of business government ever since the United States took its modern form as an urbanized, industrial nation of immigrants more than a century ago. Why has no such wave swelled among those who have been the losers over these last conservative years?

The answer lies, I believe, in two closely related characteristics of contemporary American conservatism. The first is in the conservatives' ability to articulate an idea so deeply embedded in the American political consciousness that it actually underlies both American liberalism and American conservatism: this is the deep, unquestioning belief of the American majority in what is called American *exceptionalism*. The second, closely allied to the first, is the extent to which conservatism is populist.

Exceptionalism is not just nationalism. This is not the quasi-tribal national loyalty for which people will kill and be killed almost anywhere: certainly, as we have seen, in Cambodia and Kashmir, Chechnya and western Slavonia. It is not even the assumption of universality that so many great and successful political societies have made from time to time in the past.[21] It is nationalism elevated to the status of an ideology: Americanism striving on equal terms with socialism or fascism. What is distinctive about American exceptionalism, awesome in its universal implications and almost endearing in its simplicity, is the idea that the United States, that "shining city set upon a hill," that "last best hope of mankind," that "first new nation,"[22] is a *better* country than any other, a society unique in its moral nature.

This is not, of course, an idea likely to commend itself to more than a minority of the rest of the world's population, however much they may admire the United States. But in America it is not held only by American conservatives. American liberals, too, have often shared the world view, called Wilsonian when held by Democrats, that it is the high duty of the United States to share its particular forms of democracy, and of capitalism, with the other peoples of the world.[23] One of the keys to Ronald Reagan's triumph was that, whatever they thought of his policies, tens of millions of Americans, and especially the working-class "Reagan Democrats" who gave him the margin of political victory, felt that he articulated their deepest convictions about the moral nature, the destiny, and promise of America.

When Reagan said, for example, that it was "morning in America," he may have meant that he hoped the economy would improve and individual Americans would be better off. But the political resonance of what, on the face of it, was a fairly vapid slogan came from the idea that, now morning had broken, Americans would *stop criticizing* their country. In 1982, when the conservative journalist Burton Yale Pines wanted to sum up how conservatism, which he called "traditionalism," was sweeping America, he emphasized that "ideological rebelliousness is over; so is the wholesale assault on authority and the massive rejection of the United States, its civilization, and its history." Students, in particular, he asserted, were far less critical of America.

It is part of the thesis of this book that one of the main sources of conservatism was a reaction against liberalism. One of the things that most deeply offended many Americans about the liberals is that they seemed always to be running down America. The paradox is that never has American exceptionalism been more energetically asserted than at a time when the United States, in terms of economic power and social cohesion, is less exceptional than ever. When Irving Kristol joined the editorial staff of *Commentary* magazine in 1947, for example, or William F. Buckley, Jr., went to Yale, the United States really did tower like a giant over the world. In 1950 the United States produced roughly half the world's economic product. Today, it produces roughly a fifth. That share is falling and must fall further. It was plausible in the 1950s that

America could lead a crusade to make the world more like itself. Now the Soviet empire has collapsed, but not even the Russians imagine that the United States can or will do for them, let alone for all of the world's other unhappy peoples, what America did for Europe in the 1940s. Newt Gingrich says he has only one prescription for American foreign policy in the twenty-first century: "The United States must lead. Period." The alternative? "A dark and bloody planet." Immense applause.

Modern conservatives are not isolationists in the sense in which that word was used between World Wars I and II. Apart from anything else, the United States is far too involved in, and dependent on, the rest of the world, in trade, investment, and a dozen other ways, to have the luxury of withdrawing from it even if it chose to. To be sure, the conservative instinct in foreign policy is to shun the United Nations, to avoid collective action, to cut foreign aid. The United States, to the conservative mind, ought not to entangle itself with foreigners, tainted, as they are all too likely to be with dubious motives and equivocal values.

What united conservatives of all kinds with neoconservative policy intellectuals and with tens of millions of other Americans was a fierce resentment of any movement, any trend, any individual that seemed to cast doubt, not on the superiority of America, but on its perfectibility. Conservatives can be surprisingly pessimistic in the short term. The worst is always about to happen. Our schools, our streets, our businesses, politics, religion, the institution of the family, are always on the verge of collapse. But conservatives do not give up. Their faith in American exceptionalism means that in the end society can be perfected, but only by following the American Way.

IN MODERN CONSERVATISM, unlike the wing-collar-and-black-tie conservatism of the 1920s, nationalism goes hand in hand with populism. Perversely, conservatives often identify liberalism with class privilege. Senator Joseph McCarthy did just that in his speeches:

> It has not been the less fortunate or members of minority groups who have been selling this nation out, but rather those who have had all the benefits . . . the finest homes, the finest college education . . . the bright young men who are born with silver spoons in their mouths are the ones who have been worst.[24]

Reagan's favorite speechwriter, Peggy Noonan, described in her memoirs how she rediscovered this same emotion when she encountered student protest.

What am I doing with these intellectuals or whatever they are, what
am I doing with this contemptuous elite? As far as I was concerned
they were encouraging the real bastards of the world . . . That was
the moment it changed for me.[25]

Never again, she went on, did she respect the people who went on
TV or wrote for the papers.[26] Alan Crawford accused the New Right
of "deliberately exploiting social protest and encouraging class hostility by trying to fuel the hostilities of lower-middle-class Americans
against those above and below them on the economic ladder."[27] Richard
Viguerie is only one of the New Right leaders to inveigh constantly
against "the Establishment," and several leading New Right and conservative spokesmen openly call themselves radicals, like Paul Weyrich,
who said, "We are different from previous generations of conservatives
. . . We are radicals working to overthrow the present power structure in
this country."[28] What was distinctive about the new conservatism was
precisely its radicalism.

The *New Republic* editor John Judis has shrewdly suggested that
when conservatives use populist rhetoric, they do so not because their
views are really so very different from those of traditional conservatives,
but only as a new way to market their beliefs. But even if all populist
conservatism were no more than sugar to coat the pill of vested economic interest — and that is clearly an overstatement — the very fact
that conservatives began to phrase their appeal in populist language
transformed the nature of American politics. The appeal of the new
conservatism was that it denied liberalism because liberalism in turn
seemed to deny the unique promise of American life. "At the political
level, conservatives are bound together for the most part by negative
response to liberalism," wrote William F. Buckley, with characteristic
perceptiveness,[29] in *Up from Liberalism* as long ago as 1960. (He went on
to add that this was not necessarily a bad thing.) What conservatives in
the Reagan decade were able to offer was a philosophy that appealed to
American pride, that claimed to be more American than the views it
opposed, and presented itself in the language of populism and popular
belief. In Ronald Reagan's mouth, it was an irresistible formula. But how
lasting a transformation of American life can it be expected to achieve?

One traditionally important element in the appeal of conservatism
was called into question by the collapse of communism, at least in Eastern Europe and the former Soviet Union. For almost fifty years — for
as long, that is, as the new conservatism discussed in this book has

been alive — there lay at the heart of its creed the struggle against communism. Traditional conservatives and libertarians, business spokesmen and Christians, neoconservatives and old believers, all could unite against the communist threat. Then, suddenly, the communist threat was not there anymore. Francis Fukuyama's prediction of *The End of History*, which was in fact more accurately a prediction of the end of one particular school of historiography, known as historicism, now looks considerably less relevant than Oswald Spengler's *Decline of the West*, written seventy-five years earlier. Take down those four books, once more, that helped to launch the long march of conservatism: Nock and Kirk, Rand and Hayek. Do they speak to a new generation, as they did when it was thrillingly shocking to read a denunciation of equality, a celebration of Toryism, a clarion call for selfishness, or an assertion that the welfare state was the road to serfdom? Not really. The paradox is that, by succeeding, they failed.

Once communism had disappeared, there was a certain scurrying search for alternative external enemies against whom Americans might rally. The most popular candidate seemed to be Islam, in one form or another. Professor Samuel P. Huntington of Harvard predicted a "clash of civilizations," preeminently but not exclusively between the West and Islam. To the extent that the threat of communism, perceived as real, imminent, and potentially catastrophic, was the cement that held conservatives together, it could have been predicted on theoretical grounds that conservatives would begin to fall out among themselves. And that is exactly what seems to be happening.

The conservative movement is divided. This is not just a matter of spectacularly shrill and abusive catfights among grant hunters in New York and Washington, though there are plenty of entertaining tales to be told of these "conservative wars."[30] There are serious philosophical divisions among conservatives. Two of them are sufficiently deep to raise doubts, absent a new "fusion" like that brokered by William F. Buckley and Frank S. Meyer in the 1950s, about predictions of a lasting conservative hegemony.

The first is that there is a deep cleft within the conservative movement, as it has emerged, between neoconservatives and paleoconservatives. On the one side are those neoconservatives, many of them walk-in recruits from liberalism, who want above all to occupy power. They are prepared to compromise with the state, and even with welfare state policies, in order to do so. They say they want to cut back the size and the pretensions of the federal government; yet they have no objection to accepting a job as a staffer, a speechwriter, or an official with the federal government, or, better still, as the holder of a permanent place with a research foundation funded by a mixture of direct federal appropriations and federal tax breaks for rich individuals. Their ultimate aim seems to be nationalist; everything, even strong government, is justified in the name of making the United States, and themselves along with it, richer, stronger, more admired, and more feared.

On the other side are the paleoconservatives, whose creed is rooted in religious belief, in respect for peculiarity and particularity, for locality and tradition. Their suspicion of the state is genuine. They see no contradiction between conservative politics and religious belief. They say that the American belief in individualism and liberty is not only compatible with, but actually springs from, the Judeo-Christian tradition. Theirs is a persuasive view for those whose perspective is the history of ideas. But there still seems to be a certain conflict between those who want to weaken government and those who want it to operate a six-hundred-ship navy. Nor is belief in traditional sources of authority such as the Sermon on the Mount easily reconcilable with doing the things that have to be done to elect conservative candidates to public office.

The other split is between authoritarians and libertarians; between those whose conservatism is rooted in a commitment to traditional values and those who put personal freedom above all other values in society. Traditionalists value religion, the family, personal restraint. They tend to subordinate personal fulfillment and economic success to "higher" or at least external sources of ethical authority. Conservative libertarians brush aside such transcendental values. They set the highest value on personal and economic freedom. In many cases, indeed, conservative libertarians seem almost unable to distinguish between personal and economic freedom.

Many do not see any incompatibility between traditional and libertarian values. They try to suggest that, in calling for unregulated free enterprise, conservatives are merely smashing constraints on personal freedom imposed by liberalism. They seem to assume that libertarian values *are* traditional. This position has become increasingly untenable in practice in the last fifteen years. For one thing, the conflicts between unregulated capitalism and the moral order are more troubling. The difficulties of maximizing corporate profit and protecting the environment are an obvious example, but not an easy one for conservative dogmatists to brush away.

Many of the most serious threats to the value system the traditionalist conservatives cherish are actually encouraged by a prevailing culture of permissiveness that is intimately bound up with market capitalism. Sexual libertinism? The breakdown of the family? Crime? Violence? Hedonism? Conservatives have tried to blame all of these pathologies on liberal doctrine and liberal policies. This is not plausible. It is clear that to a substantial degree the blame for them lies much more with unrestrained commercialism, or — to put it another way — with unregulated free markets.

Few traditionalist conservatives, for example, can now credibly argue that the widespread commercial availability of pornography — in books and magazines, in popular music lyrics, on television, and in advertising — has *nothing* to do with the spread of casual attitudes to sexual ethics. It is hard to absolve Hollywood, the gun lobby, the marketers of rap music, or for that matter income inequality, of all responsibility for the rise in crimes of violence. If the American family is under pressure, can this have nothing whatever to do with the fact that from the age of ten or younger most American children are exposed to an unremitting barrage from TV and the music industry, mocking parents, family, authority, discipline, and all forms of self-restraint? Or if parents find it hard to keep the traditional family together, is that unaffected by the fact that the hugely powerful fast-food industry has been using its advertising for years to dismantle the idea of a shared family meal? Does the culture of advertising, of debt, of consumerism, have nothing to do with the prevalence of greed?

Greed, say the bolder champions of unregulated free market capitalism, is good. "Is it really and always so good?" ask many instinctive conservatives. Nor are these just disagreements for idle debate. With growing urgency they push their way into the arena of practical politics, for just this conflict between traditional and libertarian values underlies some of the hottest political issues of the 1990s. What else is the division between pro-life and pro-choice on abortion? Again, how can one reconcile a belief in the ultimate primacy of personal freedom with a public policy that aims to protect property by depriving hundreds of thousands of Americans of their freedom in the most literal manner, by sending them to jail? (Almost 2 percent of the labor force is incarcerated, enough to make a substantial difference to the unemployment rate.) How does one strike the balance between the environment and the rights of the logger, the real estate developer, and the tourism industry? The rights of the doctor-entrepreneur and those of the patient? How does one stamp out drugs without stamping on the rights of individuals?[31]

How does one free the entrepreneur to operate savings and loan businesses in the most efficient way while protecting the small investor's savings? How does one deregulate airlines so as to take full advantage of the market's power to allocate resources — but without sacrificing service to passengers, let alone air safety? How much should one protect the institutional integrity of local, city, and state governments, of the federal government itself, and their various rights to tax, regulate, investigate, and legislate in the public interest, against the almost unlimited claims made by the spokesmen of free enterprise and free markets? How does one, in short, "get government off the backs of the people," and still allow government to perform the functions the people expect of it? The chasm between the values of traditionalist-authoritarians and libertarian-capitalists reaches into almost every corner of American politics because it is to be found in every corner of American life.

There are profound contradictions between the conservatism of Viscount Falkland, who believed that "where it is not necessary to change, it is necessary not to change," and the conservatism of Roger Jepsen, the Iowa senator who is a conservative because he believes in change. What does it mean to say that Ray Kroc, the founder of McDonald's, who was the biggest single contributor to the Nixon campaign in 1968, is a *conservative?* He and his colleagues want to put their golden arches in front of every beautiful building in the world, and they are willing to chop down as much of the world's rain forest as it will take to convert the world's population to eating beef patties. That is what Ayn Rand meant by conservatism. It is probably not what Friedrich Hayek meant by liberalism, though if he were alive he might stiffen his chin and defend to the death the right of McDonald's to spoil the cityscapes of Europe and the forests of Latin America. But it certainly is *not* what either Russell Kirk or Albert Jay Nock meant by conservatism.

To deny the fundamental conflicts between capitalism and conservatism is to ignore the immensely powerful and often beneficent engine for change and innovation that is the capitalist system. It is also to pretend that change and innovation are not in conflict with those strands of the conservative philosophy which emphasize order, authority, religion, family, and tradition. If conservatism is to become, or to remain, the public philosophy of the United States, those conflicts will have to be resolved. So far, there is little sign of any serious attempt to reconcile the libertarian and traditionalist creeds now that anticommunism is no longer there to act as the fig leaf for fusionism.

So when one asks, what has changed since the late 1970s, one true, if flippant, answer is that now the conservatives no longer agree with one another on what the problems are, or what the solutions are, or even on who is now a conservative.

More seriously, modern conservatism has come full circle. It began as a fragile movement of rebellion against the prevailing liberal orthodoxy, that is, against what can be called the Great Deal. Under the terms of that unspoken compact, the older conservatives, demoralized by their inability to recover from their rout at the hands of Franklin D. Roosevelt, agreed to go along with significant elements of the welfare state domestically, in return for the Cold War liberals' support for their anticommunism. What liberals did not fully understand is that, though ostensibly conservative anticommunism looked overseas, it had vital domestic implications as well. The grand consensus of the 1950s was about preventing the communists from crossing the Elbe and the Yalu: it was also about industrial unionism in Detroit and the ideological content of Hollywood movies.

At first the new conservatism genuinely was a radical movement. It was an assault by a band of outlaws on the citadels of privilege, and the new conservatives found it exhilarating. They did not identify with circles of power and influence in business, in universities, and law firms. They saw themselves not as the heirs of the old conservatives, but as their nemesis. They wanted to tear down the hierarchies they saw as having betrayed the true faith.

Gradually and skillfully the conservatives took advantage of the contingencies and the changing perceptions of three decades. Four widespread perceptions in particular offered favorable opportunities for them. One was the Cold War itself: liberals could never outbid the new conservatives in an anticommunist auction. Then there was widespread anger that the United States had been allowed to decline, both morally and in its power and influence in the world; and conservatives were successful in convincing many that this was the fault of the liberals. There was the conviction that the liberal attack on fundamental social and racial inequality not only had been a failure, but was fundamentally misconceived. Lastly, there was a surprising degree of popular acceptance of the tempting, if ill-founded, idea that liberalism was the creed of an overprivileged elite, out of touch with people's real needs and wishes.

So, as we have seen, the time came when the conservatives flourished at the expense of their liberal antagonists. Conservative politicians were elected to public office, to Congress, even in the shape of Ronald Reagan to the presidency. Conservative intellectuals felt they

had won the argument. Certainly by the 1990s they had all but monop-
olized the rewards of a fast-growing corporate intelligentsia: chairs,
research grants, book contracts, fame, and fortune. In Sidney Blumenthal's phrase, they became the "counterestablishment."[32] Conservative
businessmen flourished most of all. While the incomes of the many
stagnated, the incomes of the few exploded.

By the 1990s conservatives had become once again what they were in
the 1880s and again in the 1920s and the 1950s, the spokesmen of
business interests, business ideology, a business elite. They had genuinely believed that their ideas were liberating, that all Americans would
benefit from a bonfire of regulations, controls, bureaucracies. They had
honestly seen themselves as the populist champions of the plain people's
best interests. But in reality, they began to look more and more like the
old Republican conservatives they had set out to replace.

The idea that liberalism is peculiarly the doctrine of a political elite
may have a superficial plausibility. But it does not stand close inspection.
The majority of the economic elite does not favor radical social change.
Not even a majority of the elite's most neurotic and dissatisfied children
are to be found on the left. For every investment banker's or corporate
lawyer's child who took to radical politics, there were hundreds who
turned to drugs or alcohol to assuage the misery of being rich. No doubt
if there was one thing the new conservatives of the 1950s, the 1960s, and
the 1970s wanted above all, it was to be something more than the mere
defenders of suburban economic privilege. By the 1990s, the wheel had
come full circle. Whether they liked it or not, that was just what they
were defending.

It had been an inspiring and in many ways a noble movement. It
sought to roll up together the dreams of an America older and stronger
than the great federal state of the New Deal and the Cold War. It
offered those dreams of freedom as an invigorating alternative to regi-
mentation and dependency. From their new-old philosophy, the conservatives hoped, there would come renewed abundance, social regeneration, national restoration.

Many streams flowed into the conservative delta. One of the strongest was the determination to put freedom, political and economic, as the
first of priorities. At least as strong was hatred of that priggish, queru-
lous side of liberalism which seemed to deny the exceptional moral
nature of American society and the promise of American life. As the
1990s flowed back into the past and the millennium approached, the
contradictions between some of the impulses of conservatism began to
look more ominous. It was one thing to want to restore the old ways,

another to reconcile that nostalgia with the imperatives of economic freedom; one thing to share a vision of an ordered, God-fearing society, another to unleash the creative impatience of America.

What was certain, as the political gladiators stripped to descend again into the electoral arena, was that the conservative movement had transformed America. For millions, it had restored confidence, rekindled creativity, made pride possible once more. Yet for as many other millions, it seemed to have become only a narrow and exclusive interpretation of what America has meant and could mean again. Marching under the banner of freedom, conservatives seemed to have diminished equality and too often denied fraternity altogether. A philosophy that demeaned and rejected the state risked forgetting, and so forfeiting, the great capacity of American society for collective, public action.

Individuals may have built America, but not in isolation from one another. The great achievements, the great conquests, the political and moral illuminations of America, from the making of the Constitution to the victorious wars of the twentieth century, were public, not private achievements. Many of them, indeed, were achievements of the American state. It was not by stinting on taxes or on collective effort that Americans won their independence, restored the Union, emancipated the slaves, built the railroads and the universities. The atom bomb, the California water projects, the interstate highways and aviation networks and the space probes were not private ventures. The Internet was created by the Pentagon's Advanced Projects Research Agency. Nor certainly was it by discouraging immigrants or by excluding groups of Americans from full citizenship that the United States earned the admiration of the world. If the conservatives persisted in interpreting the spirit of America too narrowly, they would only have turned the world upside down for a time.

Only if they could see beyond their obsession with liberal shortcomings, and expand their views to a more generous vision of the promise of American life for all, might their promise be kept. Only if they could offer a vision that transcended the narrow interests of the economically advantaged, and faced up to the interdependence of the individual and society; if they could offer a model of political freedom that would protect the citizen against blind, impersonal economic forces, in which one man's freedom would not be another's subjection; only, in fact, if they could steal the fire of idealism that once gave the liberals their conquering morale, might the conservatives truly be able to claim that they had turned the world right side up.

Notes

1. The World Turned Right Side Up

1. Interview quoted in Alan Crawford, *Thunder on the Right*, p. 275.
2. Barbara Tuchman has cast some doubt on whether this is in fact so. She writes, "The words occur" in one of many versions sung to the popular tune "Derry Down." Best known of these was the ballad "The King Enjoys His Own Again." Another version, entitled "The Old Woman Taught Wisdom," or "When the World Turned Upside Down," contained these lines of notably uninspired poetry: "If buttercups buzz'd after the bee, / If boats were on land, churches on sea, / If ponies rode men and if grass ate the cows, / If summer were spring and the other way 'round, / Then all the world would be upside down!" She concludes that "the tune played by the capitulators at Yorktown, like what song the sirens sang, is historically obscure." Barbara Tuchman, *The First Salute*, pp. 288–289.
3. Congressional Quarterly, Inc., *Congress and the Nation*, Vol. V, 1977–1980, p. 22 ff.
4. Morton Kondracke, *New Republic*, May 17, 1980.
5. Jerome L. Himmelstein, *To the Right*, p. 94.
6. *Ibid.*
7. Burton Yale Pines, *Back to Basics: The Traditionalist Movement That Is Sweeping Grass-Roots America*, New York, 1982, p. 13.
8. Rowland Evans and Robert Novak, *The Reagan Revolution: An Inside Look at the Transformation of the U.S. Government*, New York, 1981, p. xiv.
9. Walter Dean Burnham, the leading authority on realignments in American politics, was at first reluctant to accredit 1980 as one. "The 1980 election," he wrote, "was a landslide vote of no confidence in an incumbent administration" but did not mean "the arrival of critical realignment." A similar view was expressed by James L. Sundquist and Richard M. Scammon, "The 1980 Election: Profile and Historical Perspective," in Ellis Sandoz and Cecil V. Crabbe, Jr., eds., *A Tide of Discontent: The 1980 Elections and Their Meaning*, Washington, DC, 1981, pp. 19–44. In the 1980s, some political scientists developed a new theory, called "dealignment," to explain what came to be called "divided government," that is, when the Congress was controlled by the Democrats and the presidency occupied by a Republican. See, e.g., Everett Carl Ladd, "On Mandates, Re-alignments and the 1980 Presidential Election," *Political Science Quarterly*, 100, no. 1 (spring 1985). See also Theodore J. Lowi, *The End of the Republican Era*, Nor-

man, Oklahoma, 1995, p. 90. Scarcely was the ink dry on the dealignment theory, however, when government ceased to be divided in 1992. And almost before political scientists could formulate a new interpretation, divided government was back — only the other way round, with Democrats in the White House and the Republicans in control of both houses of Congress.

10. George Gilder, *Wealth and Poverty*, p. 3 (first page of book).
11. Interestingly, those — mostly "Anglo-Saxon" — countries that embraced something similar to the Reagan policies, such as Britain, Canada, Australia, and New Zealand, now seem to be having second thoughts about the experiment. In Britain, the Conservative Party currently attracts little more than a quarter of the electorate in opinion polls, while in Canada the conservatives were for a time virtually eliminated from national politics. Countries that did retain a strong state sector, such as France and Sweden, seem to be having second thoughts of their own in the opposite sense.
12. TRB, *New Republic*, December 6, 1980.
13. Hedrick Smith, *New York Times*, January 21, 1981, Section II, p. 2, col 1.
14. Gallup Poll, reported in *New York Times*, March 18, 1981, p. 22.
15. Hinckley, son of a wealthy Denver Republican family, was apparently under the impression that his act would endear him to the actress Jodie Foster. She had played the girlfriend of the hero in Martin Scorsese's film *Taxi Driver* who also tried to murder a politician.
16. Congressional Quarterly, Inc., *Congress and the Nation*, Vol. VI, 1981–1984, p. 3.
17. Hedrick Smith, *New York Times*, July 30, 1981, p. 1.
18. *Time*, July 1981.
19. John Chubb and Paul Peterson, *The New Directions in American Politics*, Brookings Institute, Washington, DC, p. 1.
20. Martin Anderson, *Revolution: The Reagan Legacy*, p. xv.
21. *Ibid.*, p. 7.
22. Martin Anderson, interview with author, April 9, 1995.
23. Richard M. Weaver, *Ideas Have Consequences*, Chicago, 1948. For Weaver, see George H. Nash, *The Conservative Intellectual Movement in America Since 1945*, New York, 1976, pp. 36–43.
24. The new party names came into use soon after Andrew Jackson's inauguration as president in 1829. The Jacksonians came to be called Democrats. See Hugh Brogan, *History of the United States of America*, pp. 281–282; Robert A. Rutland, *The Democrats from Jefferson to Carter*, pp. 53, 55.
25. An entertaining account is to be found in Matthew Josephson, *The Politicos*, New York, 1938.
26. See in particular the essays by Sir Isaiah Berlin, Ronald M. Dworkin, Robert Nozick, Michael Oakeshott, and John Rawls in Michael Sandel (ed.), *Liberalism and Its Critics*, New York, 1984. See also John A. Hall, *Liberalism: Politics, Ideology and the Market*, Chapel Hill, NC, 1988. Needless to say, the interpretation in this chapter is my own.
27. See F. A. Hayek, "Why I Am Not a Conservative," in *The Constitution of Liberty*, p. 397.
28. See Nelson Lichtenstein, *The Most Dangerous Man in Detroit: Walter Reuther and the Fate of American Labor*, New York, 1995, *passim*, but especially pp. 122–131.
29. J. K. Galbraith, *A Life in Our Times*, p. 277.

30. Nicholas Comfort, *Brewer's Politics*, p. 336.
31. Lord Hugh Cecil, *Conservatism*, London, 1912. Lord Hugh was later created Lord Quickswood.
32. We call it the French Revolution, but in fact it spread, or threatened to spread, to virtually every country in Europe. See, for example, E. J. Hobsbawm, *The Age of Revolution*, p. 78. "In a very broad sense virtually every person of education, talent and enlightenment sympathized with the Revolution." See also R. R. Palmer, *The Age of Revolutions, passim*.
33. Robert Nisbet, *Conservatism: Dream and Reality*, Minneapolis, 1986, p. 1
34. Samuel P. Huntington, "Conservatism as an Ideology," *American Political Science Review*, 51, no. 2, June 1957, p. 45.
35. See C. B. Macpherson, *Burke*, Oxford, 1980; Conor Cruise O'Brien, *The Great Melody*, London, 1992.
36. John Hampden, killed at the battle of Chalgrove Field in 1641, was one of the leaders of the Parliamentary Party. Algernon Sidney, executed in 1683 for his alleged part in the Rye House plot, was a leading Whig in the reign of Charles II. *Dictionary of National Biography*, vol. XVIII, p. 208.
37. Burke's chief patron was the Marquis of Rockingham, who owned vast estates in Yorkshire, Leicestershire, and Ireland.
38. These three are taken, slightly modified, from the interesting essay "Conservatism," by Jeremy A. Rabkin, in Joel Krieger (ed.), *The Oxford Companion to Politics*, New York-Oxford, 1993.
39. Quentin Hogg, *The Case for Conservatism*, London, 1947.
40. Robert Nesbit, *op. cit.*, p. 63.
41. Michael Kazin, *The Populist Persuasion: An American History*, New York, 1995.
42. Kazin, *op. cit.*, p. 1.
43. Lewis Chester, Bruce Page, and Godfrey Hodgson, *An American Melodrama*, pp. 280–281.
44. There have been some signs in recent decades that European conservatism too is embracing these same largely incompatible ideologies, and therefore that European conservatism too faces the consequences. The British Conservative Party, in particular, since Margaret Thatcher became its leader in 1979, has been split between the traditional and the entrepreneurial wings, known in Thatcher's own terminology as "wets" and "dries." In Germany, for example, the Christian Democratic Party (Christlicher Demokratische Union) now embraces both Catholic traditionalists and big business.
45. My formulation of these alternatives owes much to the definitions of my friend Simon Blackburn, in his magisterial *Oxford Dictionary of Philosophy*, Oxford, 1995, p. 78. See the entry "conservatism."
46. Edmund Burke, *Reflections on the Revolution in France*, London, 1790.
47. There is an alternative, left-libertarian, anarchist tradition.
48. Robert Nisbet, *op. cit.*

2. Headwaters

1. He was born Friedrich August von Hayek, but after his move to England preferred to be called F. A. Hayek.

2. George H. Nash, *The Conservative Intellectual Movement in America Since 1945*, pp. 9–13.
3. Ludwig von Mises, *Omnipotent Government*, p. 48.
4. George H. Nash, *op. cit.*, pp. 36–49.
5. This phrase comes from Weaver's doctoral dissertation, "The Confederate South, 1865–1910: A Study in the Survival of a Mind and Culture," published in 1968, after Weaver's death as: George Core and M. E. Bradford (eds.), *The Southern Tradition at Bay: A History of Postbellum Thought*, New Rochelle, NY, 1968. The phrase quoted appears on p. 391 of the published text.
6. Richard M. Weaver, *Ideas Have Consequences*, Chicago, 1948, p. 3.
7. This account of Nock is based largely on Nock's own *Memoirs of a Superfluous Man* and on Robert M. Crunden, *The Mind and Art of Albert Jay Nock*, Chicago 1964.
8. Nock, *Memoirs*, p. 137.
9. *Ibid.*
10. *Ibid.*, p. 7.
11. *Ibid.*, p. 54.
12. *Ibid.*, p. 75.
13. *Ibid.*, p. 147.
14. Ralph M. Crunden, *The Mind and Art of Albert Jay Nock*, p. 14.
15. Barbara Branden, *The Passion of Ayn Rand*, New York, 1986.
16. *Ibid.*, p. 27.
17. *Ibid.*, pp. 12–13.
18. *Ibid.*, p. 21.
19. *Ibid.*
20. *Ibid.*, pp. 44–45.
21. *Ibid.*, p. 55.
22. *Ibid.*, p. 63.
23. *Ibid.*, p. 71.
24. *Ibid.*, pp. 73–79,
25. *Ibid.*, p. 106.
26. *Ibid.*, p. 127.
27. *Ibid.*, pp. 175–181.
28. Ayn Rand, *The Fountainhead*, New York, 1943.
29. For this sketch of what was happening in Vienna around the time of Hayek's birth, I have drawn on Carl E. Schorske, *Fin-de-Siècle Vienna*, New York, 1961.
30. I have taken this biographical sketch of Hayek's early career from Fritz Machlup (ed.), *Essays on Hayek*, 1976.
31. J. R. Hicks, *Critical Essays in Monetary Theory*, p. 203.
32. It is widely believed, especially in the United States, that the London School of Economics was a hotbed of left-wingers. This mistaken belief was partly caused by the prominence there of Harold Laski, who certainly was the epitome of the Fabian socialist. But the School had no distinctive tradition, and its conservatives, Graham Wallas, Lionel Robbins, Karl Popper, and Michael Oakeshott among them, were at least as influential as its radicals.
33. F. A. Hayek, *The Road to Serfdom*, London, 1944. The book was finished in December 1943 and published in 1944.
34. *Vide*, Marie-Claire Bancqart (ed.), *Anatole France*, Paris, 1994, p. 14. "La ma-

jesteuse égalité des lois, qui interdit au riche comme au pauvre de coucher sous les ponts."

35. Hayek, *Road to Serfdom*, p. 19.

36. *Ibid.*, p. 18.

37. *Ibid.*, p. 102.

38. *Ibid.*, p. 105.

39. *Ibid.*, p. 61.

40. *Ibid.*, p. 106.

41. "Liberalism" came to be used in the United States in the 1920s thereafter as a euphemism for "radical" or "socialist." In Europe it denotes a champion of economic freedom, or what is known in Britain as a "Manchester liberal." In Britain the Liberal Party is theoretically divided from the Labour Party by its traditional support for economic liberty, but in practice has opposed the Conservative Party for so long that it has come to embrace something like American liberalism. The distinction has been neatly put by Fritz Machlup: "The classical liberal wants the individual to be free from coercive interference, especially from interventions from the state, whereas the American liberal wants the state to intervene in all sorts of situations and restrict the individual's freedom of action in a variety of ways for a variety of objectives."

42. Hayek, *Road to Serfdom*, p. 13, p. 153.

43. See Fritz Machlup (ed.), *Essays on Hayek*, based on the papers of a conference at Hillsdale College, Hillsdale, Michigan, 1976.

44. Temporarily: In 1962 he returned to Europe to teach first at the University of Freiburg, in the Black Forest, and then as an honorary professor at Salzburg, in his native Austria. Hayek remained a bilingual scholar: of his 131 articles in learned journals, 83 were written in English and 41 in German.

45. Russell Kirk, *The Conservative Mind: From Burke to Santayana*, Chicago, 1953.

46. These biographical notes on Kirk are taken from Nash, *op. cit.*, pp. 69–72.

47. Interestingly, in 1976, at the time of the Bicentennial, Richard Nixon maintained explicitly that the American Revolution "was not a revolution."

48. Russell Kirk, *op. cit.*, p. 113.

49. *Ibid.*, pp. 364–375.

50. *Ibid.*, pp. 375–384.

51. *Ibid.*, p. 412.

52. *Ibid.*, p. 398.

53. *Ibid.*, p. 423.

54. The publisher was Henry Regnery, the well-known conservative publisher. His remark appeared in "A Conservative Publisher in a Liberal World," *The Alternative 5*, October 1971, p. 15, quoted in Nash, *op. cit.*, p. 73.

55. F. A. Hayek, *The Constitution of Liberty*, London, 1960, paperback edition, Routledge, 1990, pp. 397–411.

56. *Ibid.*, p. 397.

3. Mainstream: the 1950s

1. James T. Patterson, *Mr. Republican*, p. 270.

2. See, for example, Dean G. Acheson, *Present at the Creation*, p. 105: "He is a

dapper little man . . . He might be a dentist in Eldora, Iowa. But he isn't." Acheson also quoted with approval the anonymous judgment that if Truman "was not a great man, he was the greatest little man the author of the statement knew anything about." Acheson, who came to have immense appreciation of Truman's character, called him "the captain with the mighty heart."

3. I have been criticized for using the expression "the liberal consensus" in my earlier book, *America in Our Time*, for example by Jerome L. Himmelstein in his 1990 book *To the Right: The Transformation of American Conservatism*. I am not aware, however, of any other phrase that better describes the truce between liberalism and traditional conservatism that lasted until 1968. The essence of the bargain underlying that truce, I have argued elsewhere, was that from 1946–1947 onward orthodox Cold War liberals accepted an essentially conservative foreign policy ground in anticommunism and interventionism, while conservatives did not challenge the essence of New Deal welfare policies, however much they may have disliked them.

4. The word itself is said to have been "invented" by President Harding when he misread the word "normality" in a speech written for him.

5. See James T. Patterson, *Mr. Republican*, p. 419.

6. James T. Patterson, *Mr. Republican*, p. 422.

7. *Ibid.*, p. 78.

8. *Ibid.*, p. 288.

9. *Ibid.*, p. 424.

10. There is a vast literature on McCarthy and McCarthysim. Besides the works specifically referred to in endnotes, I have found particularly useful: Edwin R. Bayley, *Joe McCarthy and the Press*, Madison, WI, 1981; David Caute, *The Great Fear: The Anti-Communist Purge under Truman and Eisenhower*, London, 1978; Griffin Fariello, *Red Scare: An Oral History of the American Inquisition*, New York, 1995; Richard M. Fried, *Men Against McCarthy*, New York, 1976; William B. Hixson, Jr., *Search for the American Right Wing: An Analysis of the Social Science Record*, Princeton, NJ, 1992; Michael Kazin, *The Populist Persuasion*, New York, 1995; Thomas C. Reeves, *The Life and Times of Joe McCarthy* (British edition), London, 1982; Michael Paul Rogin, *The Intellectuals and McCarthy: The Radical Specter*, Cambridge, MA, 1967; Richard H. Rovere, *Senator Joe McCarthy*, New York, 1959.

11. David McCullough, *Truman*, p. 766.

12. Richard M. Fried, *Nightmare in Red*, p. 60.

13. Arthur M. Schlesinger, *The Vital Center*, New York, 1949.

14. The different interpretations of McCarthyism are analyzed with great clarity by Nelson W. Polsby, "Towards an Explanation of McCarthyism," *Political Studies*, Vol. 8, 1960, pp. 250–271.

15. Theodor W. Adorno, Else Frenkel-Brunswick, Daniel J. Levinson, R. Nevitt Sanford, *The Authoritarian Personality*, New York, 1950.

16. Samuel J. Lubell, *The Future of American Politics*, New York, 1952.

17. Daniel Bell (ed.), *The New American Right*, New York, 1955. See also Daniel Bell (ed.), *The Radical Right*, 1963, a partial recantation of the views in the earlier volume.

18. Nelson W. Polsby, *op. cit.*

19. This account of Robert Welch's life is based on Alan Crawford, *Thunder on the*

Right, pp. 94–97; Arnold Forster and Benjamin R. Epstein, *Danger on the Right*, New York, 1964, pp. 17 ff; William B. Hixson, Jr., *Search for the American Right Wing: An Analysis of the Social Science Record 1955–1987*, Princeton, NJ, 1992, pp. 75–95; David W. Reinhard, *The Republican Right Since 1945*, Lexington, KY, 1983.

20. Forster and Epstein, *op. cit.*, p. 11.
21. *Ibid.*, p. xx.
22. Nelson Lichtenstein, *The Most Dangerous Man in Detroit: Walter Reuther and the Fate of American Labor, passim*, but especially pp. 59–66 and pp. 179–193.
23. The classic account of these early "fascist" movements is in Morris R. Schonbach, *Native American Fascism during the 1930s and 1940s: A Study of Its Roots, Its Growth and Its Decline*, Ph.D. dissertation 1958, published New York, 1985. But his interpretation has been challenged by Alan Brinkley, *Voices of Protest: Huey Long, Father Coughlin and the Great Depression*, New York, 1982. See also William B. Hixson, Jr., *Search for the American Right Wing*, p. xi.
24. Richard Hofstadter, *The Paranoid Tradition in American Politics*, claimed that no single member of the Illuminati is known to have set foot in the United States.

4. Watersmeet

1. See Michael Emery and Edwin Emery, *The Press and America: An Interpretive History of the Mass Media*, Englewood Cliffs, NJ, 1992, pp. 333–335, 584–585.
2. *World Almanac*, 1953, p. 570.
3. For an entertaining sketch of Time Inc. at a slightly earlier period, including a vignette of Jackson and his emollient prose, see J. K. Galbraith, *A Life in Our Times*, pp. 258–269.
4. John B. Judis, *William F. Buckley, Jr: Patron Saint of the Conservatives*, New York, 1988; George H. Nash, *The Conservative Intellectual Movement in America since 1945*, pp. 145–147.
5. This whole chapter draws heavily on Judis, *op. cit.*, as well as on Buckley's own work, on an interview with Buckley by the author, and on the files of *National Review*.
6. William F. Buckley, Jr., *God and Man at Yale*, Chicago, 1951.
7. I owe this formulation, and much else, to John B. Judis's fine 1988 biography of William F. Buckley, Jr.
8. See, *inter alia*, Lewis H. Lapham, *Money and Class in America*, pp. 122–24. Of the vast literature on the Kennedys, three books free from the usual enveloping obsequiousness are Joan and Clay Blair, Jr., *The Search for J.F.K.*; Nigel Hamilton, *JFK: Life and Death of an American President*, pp. 53–55, p. 229; Richard J. Whalen, *The Founding Father*, New York, 1964.
9. Judis, *op. cit.*, pp. 29–32.
10. *Ibid.*, p. 32.
11. *Ibid.*, p. 33.
12. *Ibid.*, p. 22.
13. *Ibid.*, pp. 45–46.
14. *Ibid.*, p. 27 and note.

15. Buckley, *op. cit.*

16. *Ibid.*, p. 8.

17. *Ibid.*, p. 14.

18. *Ibid.*

19. *Ibid.*, p. 46.

20. *Ibid.*, p. 113.

21. Buckley himself, as chairman of the *Yale Daily News*, had been involved in an unpleasant controversy about an FBI investigation of faculty members. Buckley's role, interestingly, was to decline to publish in the *News* a *Harvard Crimson* story that the FBI had informed against Yale faculty with communist connections. L. B. Nichols wrote to Clyde Tolson, assistant (and lover) of FBI director J. Edgar Hoover, that he was "very much impressed with William Buckley . . . I have a very definite feeling that we will hear from this young man in years to come. I would say very definitely that he is pro-FBI." Judis, *op. cit.*, pp. 72–74.

22. Buckley, *op. cit.*, p. 190.

23. *Ibid.*, p. 197.

24. Bundy, of course, went on to a distinguished career as national security adviser to Presidents Kennedy and Johnson. At this stage of his career, however, he made something of a profession of being the Establishment's ghostwriter. He largely wrote the autobiography of his father's friend and boss, Secretary of State and Secretary of War Henry L. Stimson. Henry L. Stimson and McGeorge Bundy, *On Active Service in Peace and War*, New York, 1948.

25. McGeorge Bundy, "The Attack on Yale," *Atlantic Monthly* 188, November 1951, p. 51.

26. Editorial in *Life*, "God, Socialism and Yale," quoted in Judis, *op. cit.*, p. 94.

27. Author of *The Revolt of Mamie Stover, The Americanization of Emily*, and other fictions of a sardonically subversive character and also of some fine magazine reporting.

28. William F. Buckley, Jr., and L. Brent Bozell, *McCarthy and His Enemies*, Chicago, 1954.

29. Judis, *op. cit.*, p. 108.

30. Buckley and Bozell, *op. cit.*

31. *Ibid.*, p. 331.

32. *Ibid.*, p. 252.

33. *Ibid.*

34. *National Review*, December 1, 1956, pp. 15–16.

35. *Ibid.*, November 19, 1955.

36. *Ibid.*

37. Judis, *op. cit.*, pp. 120–121.

38. George H. Nash, *op. cit.*, pp. 147–153.

39. *National Review*, December 28, 1955.

40. Though Revilo P. Oliver, long a regular contributor, did eventually come out with unconcealed anti-Semitic sentiments. Decades later, in 1985–86, Buckley was embarrassed by the anti-Semitic language used by a *National Review* contributor, Joe Sobran, whom he liked. Eventually, after heated correspondence with Midge Decter (wife of *Commentary* editor Norman Podhoretz) and others, Buckley wrote a long note in *NR*. In it he denied that Sobran was an anti-Semite, but acknowledged that he had violated "the prevailing taboos respecting Israel

and the Jews." Somewhat surprisingly, Midge Decter accepted this. Notwithstanding this faintly equivocal handling of an unpleasant controversy brought on by a young colleague he respected, it is plain that Buckley, brought up in an anti-Semitic atmosphere, has decisively put anti-Semitism behind him, and one of the great virtues of *NR* was that, unlike most conservative journals up to the time it was launched, it was indeed virtually free from anti-Semitism.

41. *National Review, passim,* but cf. October 20, 1956, January 15, 1957.

42. *National Review,* Frank S. Meyer, February 2, 1957.

43. Nash, *op. cit.,* pp. 256–270, deals with the whole controversy among conservatives about how to meet the communist challenge in the aftermath of the Soviet invasion of Hungary. For Schlamm's departure, see Judis, *op. cit.,* p. 157.

44. Whittaker Chambers, *Witness,* New York, p. 52.

45. Garry Wills, *Confessions of a Conservative,* New York, 1979.

46. *"Grau, teurer Freund, ist alle Theorie,"* Goethe, *Faust, Studierzimmer.*

47. See Chapter III.

48. On Bell, see Nash, *op. cit., Conservative Intellectual Movement,* pp. 46–48. President of Bard College, where he was a close friend of Albert Jay Nock, Canon Bell was a sharp critic of John Dewey's theories of education. Bernard Iddings Bell, *Education in Crisis,* New York, 1950.

49. On Murray Rothbard, see Nash, *op. cit.,* pp. 313–318.

50. Murray Rothbard, "Confessions of a Right-Wing Liberal," *Ramparts* 6, June 1968, pp. 47–52.

51. F. A. Hayek, *The Constitution of Liberty,* Chicago, 1960.

52. William Buckley, in an appendix to *God and Man at Yale,* listed "at least" 159 colleges where Samuelson's *Economics: An Introductory Analysis* had been adopted. It is to be taken with a pinch of salt, since it lists Cambridge University among the offending institutions; Cambridge University has never "adopted" any textbook in any subject. Such assignments as were made would have been made by individual tutors in independent colleges. Samuelson's book would have been read only among other texts at Cambridge. Yet it remains true that from the 1950s until the 1970s, Keynesian economics predominated on most U.S. college campuses, and Samuelson's textbook (admittedly made more politically correct in successive editions) was very widely used as a basic text.

53. *National Review,* August 26, 1961.

54. Personal conversation with the author, August 1993.

55. Samuel P. Huntington, "Conservatism as an Ideology," *American Political Science Review* 51, June 1957, p. 445.

56. Even a partial list of publications on this subject in those years makes the point. Peter Viereck, *Conservatism Revisited: The Revolt Against Revolt,* New York 1949, and *The Glory and Shame of the Intellectuals,* Boston, 1953; Clinton Rossiter, *Conservatism in America,* New York, 1955; Arthur M. Schlesinger, Jr., "Conservative v. Liberal: A Debate," *New York Times Magazine,* March 4, 1956.

57. William F. Buckley, Jr., *Up from Liberalism!,* New York, 1959, p. 161.

58. *Ibid.,* p. 222.

59. Nash, *op. cit.,* pp. 155–156.

60. Frank S. Meyer, "In Defense of John Stuart Mill," *National Review,* March 26, 1956.

61. Frank S. Meyer, "The Separation of Powers," *National Review,* p. 59.

62. Frank S. Meyer, *In Defense of Freedom: A Conservative Credo*, Chicago, 1962.
63. Frank S. Meyer, "Freedom, Tradition, Conservatism," *Modern Age* 4, Fall 1960, pp. 355–363.
64. Frank S. Meyer (ed.), *What Is Conservatism?* New York, 1964.
65. F. A. Hayek, "Why I Am Not a Conservative," in *The Constitution of Liberty*, pp. 397–411.
66. Frank S. Meyer (ed.), *What Is Conservatism?* pp. 229–332.

5. Broken Levees and Horseshoe Lakes: 1963–1973

1. Author's personal reminiscence. I covered the 1964 Republican convention for *The London Observer.*
2. William A. Rusher, *The Making of the New Majority Party*, New York, 1975, pp. 39–41.
3. *Ibid.*, p. 42.
4. George H. Nash, *The Conservative Intellectual Movement in America*, pp. 30–31.
5. An eminent British conservative once remarked about ex-communists that he did not like to eat regurgitated matter which he would not have ingested in the first place.
6. William F. Buckley, Jr., interview with the author, August 16, 1993.
7. Interview with author, August 27, 1993.
8. Jack Bell, *Mr. Conservative: Barry Goldwater*, Garden City, N.Y., 1962, pp. 96–98.
9. Stephen Shadegg, *What Happened to Goldwater?* New York, 1965, p. 21.
10. *Ibid.*, p. 27.
11. *Ibid.*, p. 30.
12. F. Clifton White, *Suite 3505*, Ashland, OH, 1992 (previously published New York, 1967).
13. Shadegg, *op. cit.*, p. 42.
14. White, *Suite 3505*, p. 23.
15. The reader will not have failed to notice the repeated and important connections between Goldwater, the fresh face from the West, and the conservative intellectuals associated with William Buckley and *National Review.*
16. F. Clifton White, *op. cit.*
17. *Ibid.*, p. 43.
18. *Ibid.*, p. 44.
19. *Ibid.*, p. 67.
20. *Ibid.*, pp. 92–93.
21. *Ibid.*, p. 90.
22. *Ibid.*, p. 105.
23. *Ibid.*, p. 115.
24. In 1884 General William Tecumseh Sherman, when offered the Republican presidential nomination, replied, "If nominated, I will not run, and if elected I will not serve." So much has it become a convention of American politics that candidates should appear to be reluctant that anything short of a "Sherman declaration" is disbelieved, or at least scrutinized for the faintest hint of ambiguity.

25. White, *op. cit.*, pp. 164–171.

26. *Ibid.*, p. 214.

27. *Ibid.*, p. 232.

28. Electoral statistics from Congressional Quarterly Inc., *Congress and the Nation*, Vol. I, 1945–1964, pp. 8–9.

29. George H. Mayer, *The Republican Party 1854–66*, second edition, New York, 1967, Chapter XIV ("The Amateur Hour and After") and pp. 528–558.

30. *Ibid.*, p. 557.

31. *Congress and the Nation*, Vol. I, p. 10.

32. David S. Broder, *Changing of the Guard*, New York, 1980, p. 374.

33. *Ibid.*, p. 376.

34. *Ibid.*, p. 175.

35. White, *op. cit.*, p. 250.

36. For Reagan, GE, and "the Speech," see Ronald Reagan, *An American Life*, pp. 126–143; and Garry Wills, *Reagan's America: Innocents at Home*, pp. 279–288.

37. Reagan, *op. cit.*, p. 140.

38. Interview with Richard Viguerie, August 27, 1993.

39. See Alan Crawford, *Thunder on the Right*, pp. 43–77. I have also interviewed Richard Viguerie on several occasions.

40. See Congressional Quarterly, *Congress and the Nation*, Vol. III, pp. 397–99, and *Congress and the Nation*, Vol. IV, 1973–76, pp. 988–1007. Briefly, the first act was a response to the cost of campaigning, and especially to the rapid increase in the cost of political advertising on TV, which had risen from $9.8 million in 1956 to $59.6 million in 1970. The amendments passed in 1974, influenced by concern over the Watergate scandal, which in part involved campaign fund-raising, limited campaign expenditure, provided matching public funds for candidates, and tightened disclosure regulations. However, conservative direct mail fund raising and political action committees (PACs) soon offered loopholes to the legislation. A third piece of legislation, passed in 1976, was required because the Supreme Court's decision in *Buckley* v. *Valeo* (an action brought by Bill Buckley's brother James Buckley as well as by former Senator Eugene J. McCarthy and other plaintiffs) struck down the Federal Election Commission established by the 1974 act and certain other provisions as unconstitutional breaches of the separation of powers.

41. Lines carved by the Marquis of Montrose with the diamond in his signet ring on the window of his prison in Edinburgh the night before he was hanged for rebellion.

42. Karl Hess, *op. cit.*, p. 37.

43. Stephen Shadegg, *What Happened to Goldwater?* New York, 1965, p. 10.

44. Few best sellers became obsolete quicker than Charles Reich's *The Greening of America*, published in 1972.

   If I may inscribe a personal benchmark, I covered the Berkeley student dissent of 1964–1968, and then found myself teaching at Berkeley in 1973. The campus might have been a different place, so much had student attitudes changed.

45. Congressional Quarterly, *Congress and the Nation*, Vol. II, 1965–68, p. 8.

46. See Henry Brandon, *The Retreat of American Power*, London, 1973. This book,

by the long-serving Washington correspondent of the London *Sunday Times*, a close friend of Henry Kissinger's, gives an interesting account of how the Nixon Doctrine seemed to its only begetter — Kissinger.

47. See Lewis Chester, Godfrey Hodgson, and Bruce Page, *An American Melodrama*, pp. 427–499, for a fuller account of the origins of the Southern strategy in the exigencies of the 1968 campaign.

48. Jonathan Aitken, *Nixon: A Life*, p. 391. The author, a British Conservative member of Parliament and government minister, interviewed Nixon for more than sixty hours and knew him well.

49. "De Gaulle approached the microphone, breathed in, like a diver before his brief effort, and declared, in two stages separated by a slight pause, '*Je vous ai* [three words that are inaudible] *compris*. There was stupefied silence for two or three seconds, followed by a yell of collective joy." Jean Lacouture, *De Gaulle: The Ruler 1945–1970*, English trans., Harvill, London, 1991.

50. This was not, however, of the Nixon administration's doing; it resulted from the working through the pipeline of judicial decisions consequent to *Brown*.

51. For example, see Rusher, *The Making of the New Majority*. Rusher quotes a May 1974 Gallup Poll as showing that if there were a liberal and a conservative party, instead of a Democratic and a Republican Party, 26 percent would vote liberal, 38 percent would vote conservative, and 36 percent would be undecided; so that of those expressing an opinion, 59 percent were inclined to vote conservative, as against only 41 percent inclined to vote liberal; whereas in another Gallup Poll published two months later 44 percent said they were Democrats, 33 percent were Independents, and only 23 percent Republicans. One flaw in this argument, as Rusher notes, is that the interviews took place at the nadir of President Nixon's Watergate troubles, scarcely a propitious moment for finding Republican Party loyalty.

52. Barbara Mikulski, representative and later senator from Maryland, chaired the first, and Senator George McGovern (Dem. South Dakota) chaired the second of the party reform commissions designed to increase representation of women, blacks, and other minorities and young people in delegations to the national convention.

53. The following account of the negotiations is based on an interview with a prominent conservative politician who took part in them, and has been confirmed by other interviews.

54. This account is based on interviews with a number of conservatives involved in the negotiations.

6. Out of the Alcove

1. Nathan Glazer and Daniel Patrick Moynihan, *Beyond the Melting Pot*, New York, 1963.

2. Nathan Glazer, "On Being Deradicalized," *Commentary*, October 1970, pp. 74–80.

3. *The Public Interest*, published by National Affairs Inc., quarterly, 1965—.

4. *The Public Interest*, Number 41, Fall 1975, "The American Commonwealth — 1976–", tenth anniversary issue.

5. Alexander Bloom, *Prodigal Sons, The New York Intellectuals and Their World*, p. 372.

6. Unlike Harvard, Columbia, and other Ivy League and elite colleges in the late 1930s, City College did not operate a *numerus clausus* or quota for Jewish students. See Alexander Bloom, *Prodigal Sons*, pp. 28–31. Bloom explains that while in the early years of the century and even after World War I many Jewish students graduated from Harvard (Felix Frankfurter, Walter Lippmann), Columbia (Lionel Trilling), and Radcliffe (Diana Trilling), "many private schools began to perceive what began to be known euphemistically as the Jewish problem." "During the middle 1920s, the lines of ethnic discrimination were drawn firmly across American higher education. . . City College remained the one major New York school that freely admitted Jews." John Kenneth Galbraith describes in his memoirs (J. K. Galbraith, *A Life in Our Times*, Boston, 1981) how he himself was called upon, when a tutor at Winthrop House, Harvard College, in the middle 1930s, to operate a quota system to limit Jewish applicants.

7. The alcoves are remembered in Alexander Bloom, *op. cit*, pp. 39–40.

8. Godfrey Hodgson, Bruce Page, and Charles Raw, *Do You Sincerely Want to Be Rich?*, New York, 1971, p. 22.

9. Interview with author.

10. The following passages come from Peter Steinfels, *Neo-conservatives: The Men Who Are Changing America*, pp. 83–85. "The American Committee for Cultural Freedom was affiliated to the international Congress for Cultural Freedom founded in 1950 — probably with CIA support from the start and, in case, with a CIA agent, Michael Josselson, as executive director." Proposals were developed for an English-language journal. "The first issue of *Encounter* appeared in October 1953, edited by [Stephen] Spender and Kristol in London . . ." In 1966 an article in the *New York Times* reported the CIA support of the Congress and its magazines, thereby initiating a period of evasive "denials" from Spender, Kristol, Melvin J. Lasky (who had succeeded Kristol as editor of *Encounter* in 1958) . . . A year later, however, *Ramparts* magazine's exposé of CIA manipulation of the National Students Association reopened the whole file. In *The Saturday Evening Post*, former CIA official Thomas W. Braden . . . announced his pride in the CIA's "immoral" cultural activities. What follows paraphrases Steinfels's argument: Braden went on to say that one of the editors was an "agent." Melvin Lasky very probably was a CIA agent, but the services performed by Braden's "agent" happened long before Lasky came over from Germany to London. No one seriously supposed the antiwar poet Stephen Spender was an American agent. Therefore the finger points at Kristol, who sued Braden for saying he was a CIA agent, then dropped his suit. My own conclusion is that Kristol, whom I first met in the 1960s, when he was the New York correspondent and I the Washington correspondent of the London *Observer*, very probably was a conscious agent of the CIA, something he would have regarded at the time and probably still regards as a matter for pride rather than shame, though he would have been aware, especially at the time of the revelations in the 1960s of his behavior in the 1950s, that it would have been prudent to keep the official sponsorship of his activities unknown. CIA funding of *Encounter* while Kristol was editor is confirmed by Peter Grose, *Gentleman Spy*,

New York, 1994, p. 321, citing Peter Coleman, *The Liberal Conspiracy*, New York, 1989, pp. 40 ff.

11. "There is no question that *Encounter* had a distinct political mission, not only to be anti-Communist, but, if one might exploit the revealing weakness of the period for piling up negatives, to be *anti-anti-American*, that is, to root out, smother over, or absorb whatever might provoke thoroughgoing opposition to the United States." Steinfels, *op. cit.*, p. 85.

12. This idea came to be called "American exceptionalism," and it is significant that Bell, the least complacent and most "left-wing" of the group, should have published an essay called "The End of American Exceptionalism" (*The Public Interest*, Fall 1975, the Bicentennial issue). On inspection, however, Bell's essay, while it does say "The American Century lasted scarcely 30 years. It foundered on the shoals of Vietnam" and again, "We are a nation like all other nations," is a lamentation for the passing of American exceptionalism. It is not so much a criticism of what he also calls, apparently almost synonymously, "Americanism," as a worried inquiry into how much of that faith can be preserved in a changing world. "Do most Americans today believe in 'Americanism'? Do people identify the doctrine of achievement and equality with pride in nation or patriotism? It is an open question." The unspoken assumption that there is something distinctly American about "pride in nation" is one that would strike, say, a Frenchman or a Japanese, let alone a Chinese, with astonishment.

13. A good example among many is Lewis H. Lapham, author of *Money and Class in America*, a Savonarolan jeremiad about the almost total corruption of American society written by a man, educated at Hotchkiss and Yale, whose family comes of old American stock and whose grandfather and great-grandfather were respectively mayor of San Francisco and one of the founders of the Texas Oil Company.

14. Bloom, *op. cit.*, p. 25.

15. Quoted *ibid.*, p. 21. Norman Podhoretz, too, has written that he was ashamed of his mother when he contrasted her with a "patrician" high school teacher. (Podhoretz, *Making It*, p. 14.)

16. Max Brod (ed.), *The Diaries of Franz Kafka*, p. 174. Kafka appears to have found this couplet in Pines, *Histoire de la Littérature Judéo-Allemande*.

17. Bloom, *op. cit*, p. 23.

18. The title of the first volume of Norman Podhoretz's autobiography is *Making It*. The term is ambiguous: it can mean "getting by," or it can mean "being impressively successful." Podhoretz uses it about himself in the second sense.

19. "Our Country and Our Culture: A Symposium," *Commentary*, May–June 1952, pp. 282–284.

20. Alexander Bloom points out (*op. cit.* p. 311) that such was the need for teachers in the postwar boom in higher education, and such the esteem in which intellectuals were now held, that several of the New York intellectuals became professors without the normally requisite Ph.D. Irving Howe, Alfred Kazin, and William Phillips all became professors without a Ph.D. At Columbia, Daniel Bell and Nathan Glazer were awarded Ph.D.'s, after they had been employed, on the basis of earlier published work. And Philip Rahv became a professor without even a bachelor's degree.

21. David J. Potter, *People of Plenty*, Chicago, 1954.

22. See essay on Hofstadter by Arthur M. Schlesinger, Jr., in Marcus Cunliffe and Robin W. Winks, *Pastmasters*, New York, 1969.

23. Seymour Martin Lipset, The First New Nation, pp. 125–133.

24. Daniel Bell, *The End of Ideology*, New York, 1962. See also Chaim Waxman (ed.), *The End of Ideology Debate*. I have discussed the origins and meaning of the "end of ideology" in Godfrey Hodgson, *American in Our Time*, New York, 1976, p. 75.

25. By Peter Steinfels, *The Neo-conservatives*, p. 47.

26. It is striking how many liberal or left-leaning intellectuals worked for *Fortune* magazine at one time or another, including James Burnham, Daniel Bell, John Chamberlain, Whittaker Chambers, John Kenneth Galbraith, Willmoore Kendall, Willy Schramm, and many others. It is even more striking how many of them subsequently moved to the right. Was there something in the air of the *Fortune* offices that predisposed such changes of mind? Or was it rather that, when an intellectual of the left felt doubts about his Marxist faith creeping upon him, he would say to himself, "What the hell, I might as well take Harry Luce's dollar"? Nor should the sheer length of the articles *Fortune* ran, the opulence of the format and layout, not to mention the size of the circulation, be entirely discounted. Intellectuals like to see due honor paid to their ideas.

27. Published as *The Negro Family: The Case for National Action*, Washington, DC, 1965, as an official publication of the Office of Planning and Research in the US Department of Labor, where Moynihan was a senior official at the time it was published.

28. As Nathan Glazer has put it: "The demand for economic equality is now not the demand for equal opportunities for the equally qualified; it is now the demand for equality of economic results."

29. See Lee Rainwater and William L. Yancey, *The Moynihan Report and the Politics of Controversy*, Cambridge (Mass.), 1967, p. 24.

30. George Wallace, cited in Lewis Chester, Bruce Page, and Godfrey Hodgson, *An American Melodrama*, New York, 1969, p. 280.

31. *Ibid.*, p. 288.

32. Congressional Quarterly, *Congress and the Nation*, Washington, DC, 1965, Vol. I, 1945–64, p. 48. Purists might argue that Indiana has always had a Southern tinge — it was one of the strongest recruiting grounds of the second Klan in the 1920s — and that Maryland was Southern in the sense that it was a slaveholding state. That hardly diminishes the magnitude of Wallace's achievement or the surprise it caused to most commentators.

33. Later, in 1968, Wallace claimed that he was not a racist. But in 1963–1964 he continued to proclaim "segregation forever!"

34. The future President Gerald Ford, then the Republican minority leader in the House, was one of those who predicted to me in a personal interview at the time that Wallace would force the election into the House. Wallace himself indicated that he expected the election to be resolved in the Electoral College, but he hoped that his supporters would hold the balance of power in the college so that he would be able to exact concessions in return for supporting the ultimate winner. *Congress and the Nation*, Vol. II, p. 21.

35. *Ibid.*, p. 23.

36. Strictly, "helped to found," with his wife, Barbara, among others. But Epstein was the driving figure. His falling-out with the future neoconservatives, and

especially with Norman Podhoretz, is an important subplot in the history of New York intellectual life in general, and in the progression of a substantial fraction of the New York intelligentsia toward the right.

37. Of course by no means all the teachers, even in the Ocean Hill–Brownsville schools, were Jewish. Still less is it true that Jews in New York became then, or have even become twenty-five and more years later, a conservative group. Still, it is true that the close alliance between many Jewish liberal politicians and intellectuals and the black leadership in New York has not recovered from the stresses of Ocean Hill–Brownsville and similar clashes in the late 1960s.

38. Nathan Glazer and Daniel P. Moynihan, *Beyond the Melting Pot*, second edition, Cambridge, 1970, Introduction, p. xxvi–xxvii.

39. Alfred Kazin, *On Native Grounds*.

40. Irving Howe, *World of Our Fathers*, New York, 1976. Paperback ed., p. 132.

41. Maurice R. Berube and Marilyn Gittell (eds.), *Confrontation at Ocean Hill-Brownsville: The New York School Strikes of 1969*, New York, 1969.

42. *Ibid.*, chronology, pp. 335–340.

43. See Jason Epstein, "The Brooklyn Dodgers," *New York Review of Books*, October 10, 1968.

44. Berube and Gittell, *op. cit. passim*.

45. Jonathan Rieder, *Canarsie: The Jews and Italians of Brooklyn against Liberalism*.

46. *Ibid.*, p. 206.

47. *Ibid.*, p. 114, quoting Alan Erlichman, *Fatal Affliction*. Erlichman was the leader of anti-black agitation in Canarsie.

48. Michael Novak, *The Rise of the Unmeltable Ethnics*, New York, 1971.

49. Rieder, *op. cit.*, p. 220.

50. J. Anthony Lukas, *Common Ground*, pp. 25 ff. I am indebted to this magnificent book not only for much detail but for a deepened understanding of the evolving attitudes of all parties to the inner city conflicts of the 1960s and 1970s.

51. Judge Garrity's first plan actually reduced the number of children to be bused from 17,000 to 14,900, but his final decision increased the number sharply. Lukas, *op. cit.*, pp. 249–251.

52. Neoconservatives have set themselves against two weapons, believed to be in the new class: sentimental humanism and guilt. The chief defense against the first is the *theory of unanticipated consequences*. By insisting on the layers of complexity that divide any policy from its ultimate effect, neoconservatives warn their audience to restrain its sympathetic impulses. Steinfels, *op. cit.*, p. 65.

53. The following account of the background to the *DeFunis* and *Bakke* cases relies heavily on Robert C. Berring (ed.), *The Bakke Case*, three volumes, Harvard Law School; Joel Dreyfuss and Charles Lawrence III, *The Bakke Case: The Politics of Inequality*; and Allan P. Sindler, *Bakke, DeFunis and Minority Admissions*, New York, 1978.

54. Sindler, *op. cit.*, p. 38.

55. His action reached the U.S. Supreme Court as *DeFunis* v. *Odegaard* 416 U.S. 312 (1974).

56. See notably the article by Professor Ronald M. Dworkin of Oxford and New York Universities, "The Bakke Decision. Did It Decide Anything?" *New York Review of Books*, August 17, 1978.

57. Sindler, *op. cit.*, p. 55.

58. In 1970 14.7 percent of the population of California were Spanish-speaking or had "Spanish" surnames; 7 percent were black; 2.65 percent were Asian-Americans (then taken to mean persons of Chinese, Japanese, or Filipino origin); and 0.5 percent were Native Americans. Sindler, *op. cit.*, p. 55.
59. Colvin was president of Temple Emanu-el, the leading synagogue in the city and president of the local branch of the American Jewish Committee. He also held what was known as the "Jewish seat" (itself arguably an example of a benign quota?) on the San Francisco Board of Education. The "zero quota" case Colvin won was *Anderson v. San Francisco Unified School District* (1971).
60. See John H. Bunzel, "Bakke vs. University of California," *Commentary*, March 1977, pp 59–64.
61. See analysis in Dworkin, "The Bakke Decision. Did It Decide Anything?" cited in introduction to Robert C. Berring (ed.), *The Bakke Case*.
62. Alexander M. Bickel, *The Morality of Consent*, p. 87.
63. Nathan Glazer, *Affirmative Discrimination*, New York, 1975, pp. 75–76.
64. Dreyfuss and Lawrence, *The Bakke Case*, p. 227.

7. Tributaries: The River of Jordan

1. Christiano, *op. cit.*, p. 1540.
2. Corwin Smidt, professor of political science at Calvin College in Michigan, a student of the political culture of evangelicalism, has supplied a succinct definition: "Evangelicals are defined," he wrote, "as those Protestants who emphasize that conversion is the first step in the Christian life (that is, that salvation is obtained through confession of faith in Jesus Christ) and who regard the Bible as the basis of religious authority." Smidt concedes, however, that there are those who argue that some Roman Catholics can be classified as evangelicals. However, Smidt classified as evangelical those respondents to surveys who (1) responded affirmatively to the question whether they had been "born again"; (2) stated that the Bible was the word of God; *and* (3) reported having tried to encourage someone else to believe in Jesus Christ. Italics in original.
3. See definition in James Davison Hunter, *American Evangelism*, New Brunswick, NJ, 1983, p.7: "At the doctrinal core, contemporary Evangelicals can be identified by their adherence to (1) the belief that the Bible is the inerrant word of God, (2) the belief in the divinity of Christ, and (3) the belief in the efficacy of Christ's life, death, and physical resurrection for the salvation of the human soul. Behaviorally, Evangelicals are typically characterized by an individuated and experiential orientation toward spiritual salvation and religiosity in general and by the conviction of the necessity of actively attempting to proselytize all nonbelievers to the tenets of the Evangelical belief system."
4. *Ibid.*, pp. 79–89.
5. This is the *glossolalia* described in the Acts of the Apostles, Chapter X, verse 44, and referred to in I Corinthians, Chapter 12. The believer, in the grip of strong religious emotion, "speaks" words either of no known language or of a language known, but not to him or her. This is interpreted as the Holy Spirit working within the believer.

6. See Anson Shupe and John Heinerman, "Mormonism and the New Christian Right: An Emerging Coalition?" *Review of Religious Research*, Vol. 27, No. 2, December 1985, pp. 145 ff.

7. James Davison Hunter, *op. cit.*, p. 24.

8. A. James Reichley, *Religion in American Public Life*, p. 192.

9. Dan Morgan, *Rising in the West*, New York, 1992.

10. Andrew Greeley, *Religious Change in America*, Cambridge, Mass., 1989.

11. Theodore Caplow *et al.*, *All Faithful People: Change and Continuity in Middletown's Religion*, Minneapolis, 1983.

12. Martin E. Marty, "Rediscovery: Discerning Religious America," in Marty (ed.), *Religion and Republic: The American Circumstance*, Boston, 1987, p. 22.

13. Quoted without citation in Kevin J. Christiano, "Contemporary Developments in American Religion," in Godfrey Hodgson (ed.), *Handbooks to the Modern World: The United States*, Vol. 3, p. 1526, New York and Oxford, 1992.

14. Stephen Bates, *Battleground*, p. 61.

15. Will Herberg, *Protestant — Catholic — Jew: An Essay in American Religious Sociology*, Garden City, NY, 1955.

16. Kevin Christiano, *op. cit.*, quoting Father Andrew Greeley.

17. See Dean R. Hoge and David A. Roozen (eds.), *Understanding Church Growth and Decline*, New York, 1979; Dean M. Kelley, *Why Conservative Churches Are Growing*, San Francisco, 1977; *Yearbook of American and Canadian Churches*, Nashville, annual.

18. Kelley, *op. cit.*. p. 21.

19. Bates, *op. cit.*, p. 51.

20. Moran, *op. cit*, p. 228.

21. Bruce, *op. cit.*, p. 48.

22. Later renamed the Criswell School of Theology.

23. James Davison Hunter, *Evangelism*, quoted in Steve Bruce, *The Rise and Fall of the New Christian Right*, p. 41.

24. J. Haddon and C. E. Swann, *Prime Time Preachers: The Rising Power of Televangelism*, Reading, Mass., 1981.

25. Alan Crawford, *Thunder on the Right*, p. 150.

26. *Ibid.*, p. 152.

27. Paul Gottfried, *The Conservative Movement*, pp. 105–106.

28. Peter Skerry, *op. cit.*, p. 31.

29. Interview with author, 1993.

30. Paul Gottfried, *The Conservative Movement*, p. 99. Viguerie, of course, is a Catholic.

31. Richard V. Pierard, "Reagan and the Evangelicals: The Making of a Love Affair," *Christian Century*, December 21–28 1983.

32. Also known as the "Christian Church." A pietist denomination, strong in Illinois in the early years of the twentieth century, the Disciples were strongly anti-Catholic, strongly pro-temperance. Carrie Nation was a Disciple, as was President Garfield. The denomination resulted from a merging of the Stoneites who derived from Barton Stone and the Great Revival in Kentucky, and from the Campbellites, founded by Alexander Campbell, an Ulster Scot. Garry Wills, *Reagan's America: Innocents at Home*, pp. 22–25.

33. Peele, *op. cit.*, p. 107.
34. I am indebted to Dr. Gillian Peele of Lady Margaret Hall, Oxford University, for her account of some of these links. Peele, *Revival and Reaction*, pp. 106–116.
35. Robert Billings was one of the few evangelicals rewarded with jobs in the Reagan administration. He was appointed assistant secretary of education for nonpublic schools, but because of objections from Catholic organizations, he was removed.
36. Peele, *op. cit.*, p. 110.
37. Jerry Falwell, *Listen America*, p. 6.
38. Carol Flake, *Redemptorama: Culture, Politics, and the New Evangelicalism*, Garden City, N.Y., 1984, p. 118.
39. For an interesting interview with Beverly LaHaye, see Stephen Bates, *Battleground*, pp. 100–105.
40. *Ibid.*, p.103.
41. *Ibid.*, p. 105.
42. E. J. Dionne, *Why Americans Hate Politics*, p. 211.
43. Result from *Congress and the Nation*, Vol. V, Washington DC, 1981, pp.26–27.
44. In the following analysis I have followed quite closely Corwin Smidt, "Evangelical Voting Patterns 1976–1988," in Michael Cromartie (ed.), *No Longer Exiles: The Religious Right in American Politics*, Washington DC, 1993, pp. 85–106.
45. Smidt, *op. cit.*, p. 96.

8. The Strange Death of John Maynard Keynes

1. Burton Yale Pines, *Back to Basics*, p. 94.
2. Daniel Yergin, *The Prize*, New York, 1991 (paperback edition, 1993), p. 567.
3. Alan S. Blinder, *Hard Heads, Soft Hearts*, New York, 1987, p. 40.
4. The discussion of corporate strategies to deal with the profit squeeze owes a great deal to the lucid account in Bennett Harrison and Barry Bluestone, *The Great U-Turn: Corporate Restructuring and the Polarizing of America*, New York, Basic Books, 1988, paperback edition, 1991. I have drawn greedily on it for examples and illustrations. See also the account by Lester Thurow, *The Zero-Sum Solution*, New York, Simon & Schuster, 1985.
5. Charles Sabel, unpublished MS, "The Re-emergence of Regional Economies: Changes in the Scale of Production," Social Science Research Council, 1987, cited in Harrison and Bluestone, *op. cit.*
6. Numbers from Council of Economic Advisers, *Economic Report of the President 1986*, Washington DC, 1986; Council of Economic Advisers, "Economic Indicators," September 1986; U.S. Department of Commerce, *Survey of Current Business* 67, No. 4 (April 1987), cited in Harrison and Bluestone, *op. cit.*
7. Samuel Bowles, David Gordon, and Thomas Weiskopf, "Power and Profits: The Social Structure of Accumulation and the Profitability of the Postwar U.S. Economy," *Review of Radical Political Economics*, 18, Nos. 1 and 2.
8. Robert B. Reich and John D. Donahue, *New Deals: The Chrysler Revival and the American System*, New York, 1986, p. 219.
9. Bennet Harrison and Barry Bluestone, *op. cit.*, p. 25.
10. *Ibid.*, p. 14.

11. For example, by Robert J. Samuelson, *Newsweek*, February 23, 1987, "The Great American Job Machine," who argued that "the low-wage explosion is mostly a statistical illusion"; and, more robustly, by Warren Brookes, of the conservative Heritage Foundation, who called the Joint Economic Committee's finding that many of the new jobs were of low quality "the Big Lie."

12. Nelson Lichtenstein, *The Most Dangerous Man in Detroit: Walter Reuther and the Fate of American Labor*, New York, 1995, p. 439.

13. Charles Raw, Bruce Page, and Godfrey Hodgson, *Do You Sincerely Want to Be Rich?* New York, 1971, pp. 38–39.

14. *Wall Street Journal*, March 31, 1989.

15. The three examples that follow are taken from Martin Anderson, *Revolution: The Reagan Legacy*, p. 147.

16. *Ibid.*

17. The Phillips curve was made public in A. W. Phillips, "The Relationship between Unemployment and the Rate of Change of Money Wage Rates in the United Kingdom, 1861–1957," *Economica*, November 1958, pp. 283–299.

18. Michael Boskin, in interview with the author, April 7, 1995.

19. Telephone interview with the author, April 8, 1995.

20. Milton Friedman, 1976 Nobel lecture, reprinted in Kurt R. Leube (ed.), *The Essence of Friedman*, Stanford, CA, 1987, p. 366.

21. A particularly interesting example is his paper on "Capitalism and the Jews," first read as a presidential lecture to the Mont Pelerin Society in 1972, in which he argued that the great virtue of capitalism was its freedom of entry, and that Jews historically had flourished, or otherwise, in particular circumstances according to how free the entry to particular activities was.

22. This account owes a great deal to the summary of Professor Friedman's work by his colleague Anna Schwartz in Introduction, *The Essence of Friedman. op. cit.* pp. xxii–xxvii.

23. He even went so far as to hint that all would have been different but for the early death in 1928 of Benjamin Strong, the first chairman of the Federal Reserve Bank of New York, whom Friedman admired. Milton Friedman, "Monetary Policy for the 1980s," in John H. Moor (ed.), *To Promote Prosperity: U.S. Domestic Policy in the Mid-1980s*, Stanford, CA, 1984.

24. The two key references are: Milton Friedman, "The Role of Monetary Policy," the presidential address delivered at the 80th annual meeting of the American Economic Association, Washington DC, December 29, 1967, reprinted in *American Economic Review* 58, No. 1, March 1968, pp. 1–17; and E. S. Phelps, "Phillips Curve, Expectations of Inflation and Optimal Unemployment Over Time," *Economica* 34, August 1967, pp. 254–281.

25. Interview with Michael Boskin, April 7, 1995.

26. Leube (ed.), *The Essence of Friedman*, pp. 393–396.

27. Milton Friedman and Anna Jacobson Schwartz, *A Monetary History of the United States 1867–1960*, Princeton, NJ, 1963.

28. Milton Friedman with David Mieselman, "The Relative Stability of Monetary Velocity and the Investment Multiplier in the United States, 1897–1952", in *Stabilization Policies*, Englewood, New Jersey, 1963, pp. 165–268.

29. Milton Friedman, "Quantity Theory of Money," in John Eatwell, Murray Mill-

gate, and Peter Newman (eds.), *The New Palgrave: A Dictionary of Economics*, 4 vols. London, 1987, cited in Kurt R. Leube (ed.), *The Essence of Friedman*, p. 377. See also Alan S. Blinder, *op. cit.*, p. 76.

30. John F. Muth, "Rational Expectations and the Theory of Price Movements," *Econometrica*, July 1961, reprinted in Robert E. Lucas and Thomas J. Sargent (eds.), *Rational Expectations and Economic Practice*, Vols. 1 and 2, Minneapolis, 1981. See also account by Milton Friedman, "Quantity Theory of Money," in Eatwell, Millgate and Newman, *op. cit.*, adapted in Leube (ed.), *The Essence of Friedman*, pp. 371–372.

31. Milton Friedman came close to saying this in so many words in his seminal 1967 presidential lecture to the American Economic Association. "Today," he said, "primacy is assigned to the promotion of full employment, with the prevention of inflation a continuing but definitely secondary objective." But now — he was writing in 1967 — things were changing. There was a "revival of belief in the potency of monetary policy." Hardly an economist now accepted views — of the unimportance of monetary policy — that were near-universal twenty years earlier. The pendulum has swung far since then, if not all the way to the position of the 1920s, at least much closer to that position than to the position of 1945.

32. Quoted in Blinder, p. 50.

33. Robert Kuttner, *Revolt of the Haves*, 1980, quoting a study by Steven Lile. He also quoted a study by Professor Donald Phares of the University of Missouri, St. Louis, which found that the total burden of state and local taxation was highly regressive in every state, with the lowest-income class paying a far higher rate than the highest.

34. Kuttner, *op. cit.*, p. 34.

35. *Ibid.*, p. 39.

36. Robert E. Hall and Alvin Rabushka, *The Flat Tax*, Palo Alto, CA, 1985, p. 30.

37. William E. Simon, *A Time for Truth*, New York, 1978.

38. See Sidney Blumenthal, *The Rise of the Counter-Establishment*, pp. 65 ff.

39. Kuttner, *op. cit.*, p. 238.

40. Blumenthal, *op. cit.*, p. 80.

41. Congressional Quarterly, *Congress and the Nation*, Vol. V, pp. 238–244.

42. Alan Crawford, *Thunder on the Right*, p. 95.

43. Blumenthal, *op. cit.*, p. 185.

44. Martin Anderson, *Revolution: The Reagan Legacy*, p. 161.

45. Martin Anderson, *The Power of Ideas in the Making of Economic Policy*, Hoover Institue, Stanford, CA, 1987.

46. George Shultz, *Triumph and Turmoil*, p. 8; Martin Anderson, *Revolution*, p. 168.

47. Martin Anderson, interview with the author, April 7, 1995.

48. For the following account, see Robert E. Hall and Alvin Rabushka, *The Flat Tax*.

9. The Falling Flag

1. Jimmy Carter, *Keeping Faith: Memoirs of a President*, pp. 111–121.

2. Daniel Yergin, *The Prize*, p. 681.

3. *Ibid.*, p. 685.

4. *Ibid.*, p. 694.
5. *Ibid.*, p. 692.
6. Carter, *op. cit.*, p. 111.
7. Not in so many words in his speech, but the word was on everyone's lips.
8. The Frenchman was Boulay de la Meurthe. The Duc d'Enghien was a member of the royal family whom Napoleon had shot as a traitor. By doing so he prevented reconciliation with the old nobility and the royalists, who as French nationalists might have been drawn back to Napoleon's side by the threat of foreign nations to France.
9. Guenter Lewy, *America in Vietnam*, New York, 1978.
10. Many years later it transpired that the girl, though seriously burned, had grown up, gone to medical school, become a doctor, and even had children of her own. In the new climate this was somehow seen as suggesting that it was OK to napalm children.
11. For example, Michael Herr's *Dispatches* (1977), Gloria Emerson, *Winners and Losers* (1978).
12. For movies and Vietnam and the return of "victory culture" and "war culture," see Tom Engelhardt, *The End of Victory Culture.*
13. *Ibid.*, p. 263.
14. Theodore Draper, *A Struggle for Power*, argues that the patriotic mythology of the Revolution misrepresents reality. According to Draper, the American colonies were rich and getting richer. So far from being an imperial Goliath oppressing the colonial David, the British governors in North America were dependent on colonial assemblies for their salaries. There were (before the Seven Years' War) only four understrength battalions in all the colonies. And the colonists were far more lightly taxed than were George III's other subjects.
15. Englehardt, *op. cit.*, pp. 187–193.
16. Jimmy Carter, *op. cit.*, p. 153.
17. George D. Moffett III, *The Limits of Victory: The Ratification of the Panama Canal Treaties*, Ithaca and London, 1985, p. 45.
18. David McCullough to President Jimmy Carter, October 21, 1977, quoted in Moffett, *op. cit.*, p. 134.
19. *Ibid.*, pp. 112–137, and Appendix A.
20. It may also be relevant that both Catholic and Protestant decision makers in the United States were aware of the keen anxiety of their own allies in Latin America on this point. An important individual role was played by the archbishop of Panama, Marcos G. McGrath, born in Panama of American parents, who in earlier pastoral roles had identified strongly with his impoverished, Spanish-speaking flock. McGrath threw himself into persuading the U.S. Bishops Conference to take a position in favor of the treaties; he played the leading role in bringing the church's influence to bear at the United Nations when the Security Council debated Panama in 1975; and converted William F. Buckley, Jr., to his view after inviting him to visit Panama and observe the situation in 1977. Buckley even debated Ronald Reagan on the issue on television.
21. James D. Burnham, "Panama or Taiwan," *National Review*, September 16, 1977.
22. Moffett, *op. cit.*, p. 180.
23. Interview with the author.

24. Moffett, *op. cit.*, p. 176.

25. *Ibid.*

26. See William B. Quandt, "U.S.–Soviet Rivalry in the Middle East," in Marshall D. Shulman (ed.), *East-West Tensions in the Third World*, pp. 33–34.

27. David E. Albright, "East-West Tensions in Africa," in Marshall D. Shulman, *op. cit.*

28. Henry Kissinger, *Diplomacy*, New York, 1994, p. 746.

29. "The congressional stand on the Jewish emigration issue resulted from an unusual coalition of interest among hard-line anti-Communist conservatives, humanitarian liberals and members with large Jewish constituencies." Congressional Quarterly Inc., *Congress and the Nation*, Vol. IV, 1973–1976, Washington DC, 1977, p. 133.

30. *New York Times*, January 29, 1977.

31. *New York Times*, May 19, p. 4.

32. Paul H. Nitze, *From Hiroshima to Glasnost: At the Center of Decision: A Memoir*, New York, 1989, p. 351.

33. *New York Times*, February 6, 1977, Section IV, p. 1.

34. Nitze, *op. cit.*, p. 353.

35. Henry H. Fowler, Democrat of Virginia, appointed July 1, 1965.

36. The name harked back to the early days of the Cold War. In 1950 James Bryant Conant, president of Harvard University, Tracy Voorhees of the CIA, and Robert Patterson, a New York lawyer and former secretary of war, had formed a Committee on the Present Danger to mobilize public support for the Korean War.

37. Harold H. Saunders, "The Crisis Begins," in Warren Christopher (ed.), *American Hostage in Iran*, Council on Foreign Relations, New York, 1985, p. 35.

38. Christopher, *op. cit.*, p. 37.

39. Gary Sick, "Military Options and Constraints," in Christopher (ed.) *American Hostages in Iran*, p. 153.

40. *Ibid.*, p. 147.

41. *Ibid.*, p. 159.

42. Jimmy Carter, *op. cit.*, p. 366.

43. *Ibid.*, p. 568.

44. Harold H. Saunders in Christopher, *op. cit.*, p. 47.

45. Jimmy Carter, *op. cit.*, p. 568.

10. The Deep Blue Sea

1. Quoted in Richard Nathan, "Institutional Change under Reagan," in John Palmer (ed.), *Perspectives on the Reagan Years*, Washington, DC, 1986, pp. 127, 341. See also David Mervin, "Ronald Reagan's Place in History," paper delivered at the British Association of American Studies, 1988.

2. Reagan was president of the Screen Actors Guild in Hollywood from 1945 to 1950.

3. Congressional Quarterly, *Congress and the Nation*, Vol. VI (1981–84), p. 290.

4. Sidney Blumenthal, "The Conservative Crackup," in *Our Long National Day-*

dream, p. 317. Aid to the contras loomed larger than ever as a conservative imperative and was cast as an element in the world historical march of a new doctrine: the Reagan Doctrine. This doctrine was never proclaimed by the president but was discovered by a number of columnists. One of them, Charles Krauthammer, wrote in the April 1, 1985, issue of *Time:* "Ronald Reagan is the master of the new idea . . . He has produced the Reagan Doctrine."

5. Colin L. Powell (with Joseph Persico), *My American Journey*, 1995, p. 395.
6. George Shultz, *Turmoil and Triumph*, p. 1134.
7. Shultz interview with author.
8. Shultz, *op. cit.*, p. 1135.
9. Bennett Harrison and Barry Bluestone, *The Great U-Turn*, New York, paperback edition, 1990, p. 77.
10. Paul Weyrich, interview with author. 1993.
11. Howard Phillips, interview with author. 1988.
12. Irving Kristol, interview with author. 1993.
13. David Frum, *Dead Right*, p. 204.
14. Peter Goldman, Thomas DeFrank, *et al.*, *The Question for the Presidency*, College Station, Texas, 1994, chapter 15.
15. Goldman, DeFrank, *et al.*, *Ibid.*, chapter 15.
16. Interview with Ralph Reed, 1993.
17. Alan S. Blinder, *Hard Heads, Soft Hearts*, p. 90.
18. *Ibid.*, p. 89.
19. Published as William Greider, "The Education of David Stockman," *Atlantic Monthly*, 248, no. 6, December 1981.
20. David Stockman, *The Triumph of Politics: The Crisis in American Government and How It Affects the World*, New York, 1986.
21. *Ibid.*, p. 418.
22. Interview with the author for the television series *Reagan on Reagan*, Channel Four TV, London.
23. Stockman, *op. cit.*, p. 422.
24. In his book *Revolution*, Martin Anderson has gone to some lengths to pin down what he calls the "myth" that Reagan and his advisers thought large tax cuts would produce more revenue. The closest anyone involved came to saying that, Anderson finds, was in 1976, at the height of the presidential campaign between Jimmy Carter and President Gerald Ford. In a national newspaper column on October 8, 1976, Reagan wrote that both Warren Harding and John Kennedy had cut the income tax, and in both cases federal revenues went up. And he asked, "Who's to say it couldn't work again?"
25. Michael Boskin interview with author, 1995.
26. Martin Anderson, *op. cit.*, p. 130.
27. *Ibid.*, pp. 122–139, confirmed in interview with the author. This is of course a sympathetic account of what some regard as a manipulation of data that were in any case soon rendered out of date.
28. Alan S. Blinder, *op. cit.*
29. "Deregulating America," *Business Week*, November 28, 1983, pp. 80–96.
30. Bennett Harrison and Barry Bluestone, *op. cit.*, p. 160. "The effect of the de-regulation of airlines on the quality of service is now well known. The combination of delayed flights, canceled flights, lost baggage, and an increase in the

number of reported 'near-misses' — a strange term for barely avoided midair collisions — resulted in a soaring number of complaints to the Department of Transportation." Morever, there is a good deal of evidence that deregulation actually produces *less* true competition — at least, after markets have "settled down" — than before. In the rather understated words of Alfred Kahn, an economist at Cornell University and one of the original architects of airline deregulation: "When you have the same six carriers meeting each other in market after market, there is danger of softer competition." See also Kevin Phillips, *op. cit.*, p. 99. Phillips points out that "during the four years following deregulation in 1978, weekly departures from large cities had risen 5 percent. Weekly departures from small towns, by contrast, had dropped 12 percent. By 1988 approximately 140 small towns had lost all their air service, and in 190 others large airlines had handed over responsibility to smaller commuter carriers lacking comparable comfort, convenience and safety."

31. Bernard Frieden and Lynn Sagalyn, *Behind the New Downtowns: Politics, Money, and Marketplaces*, Cambridge, Mass., 1988.

32. Kevin Phillips, *op. cit.*, pp. 197–198. The seven Washington counties were Falls Church, Arlington, Alexandria, Fairfax, and Fairfax City, all in Virginia, and Montgomery and Howard in Maryland.

33. Tom Wolfe, *The Bonfire of the Vanities*, New York, 1987.

34. Ross LaRoe and John Charles Pool, "Gap Grows between Rich and Poor," *Columbus Dispatch*, July 16, 1988, cited in Kevin L. Phillips, *op. cit.*, p. 14.

35. *Ibid.*, pp. 15, 18.

36. *Ibid.*, p. 11.

37. *Ibid.*, p. 25.

38. Jane Mayer and Doyle McManus, *Landslide*, Boston, Houghton Mifflin, 1988, p. 92.

39. *Ibid.*, p. 71.

40. Congressional Quarterly, Inc., *Congress and the Nation*, Vol. VI, 1981–1984, *passim.*

41. Mayer and McManus, *op. cit.*, p. 74.

42. *Public Papers of the Presidents: Ronald Reagan: 1981*, p. 57.

43. Ronald Reagan, *An American Life*, p. 707.

44. *New York Times*, April 4, 1977.

45. Donald T. Regan, *For the Record*, pp. 3–5, 300–301, 366–370 *etc.*; Nancy Reagan, *My Turn*, pp. 46–54. Mrs. Reagan acknowledges that she did consult an astrologer, Joan Quigley, about the president's schedule, but she insists (italics in original) that *"Joan's recommendations had nothing to do with policy or politics — ever. Her advice was confined to timing — to Ronnie's schedule, and to what days were good or bad, especially with regard to his out-of-town trips."*

46. Nancy Reagan, *op. cit.*, pp. 63–64.

47. *Ibid.*, pp. 336–337. "With the world so dangerous, I felt it was ridiculous for these two heavily armed superpowers to be sitting there and not talking to each other. I encouraged Ronnie to meet with Gorbachev as soon as possible, especially when I realized that some people in the administration did not favor any real talks. So yes, I did push Ronnie a little. But he would never have met Gorbachev if he hadn't wanted to."

48. *The Public Papers of the Presidents: Ronald Reagan: 1983*, Vol. 1, pp. 363–364.

Speech of the president to the Annual Convention of the National Association of Evangelicals at Orlando, Florida, March 8, 1983.

49. See Chapter 7 *passim*, esp. p. 32.

50. *Public Papers, op. cit.*, p. 416.

51. *Ibid.*, p. 464.

52. Richard Burt was assistant secretary of state for European affairs. Lawrence Eagleburger was under secretary of state for political affairs.

53. Henry A. Kissinger, *White House Years*, p. 205.

54. *Ibid., passim*, especially p. 1244; the text of the White House fact sheet, released March 26, 1972, is to be found in Congressional Quarterly, Inc., *Congress and the Nation*, Vol. III, 1969–1972, p. 895.

55. Martin Anderson, *op. cit.*, p. 93.

56. *Ibid., op. cit.*, p. 92.

57. See good summary of the arguments in Congressional Quarterly, *Congress and the Nation*, Vol. VI, p. 253.

58. Shultz, *op. cit.*, p. 699.

11. Full Circle

1. *Contract with America: The Bold Plan by Representative Newt Gingrich, Representative Dick Armey, and the House Republicans to Change the Nation*, ed. by Ed Gillespie and Bob Schellhas, New York, 1994, p. 4.

2. *Ibid.*, p. 6.

3. Senator Daniel Patrick Moynihan, speech in the Senate reported in *Congressional Record*, December 12, 1995, reprinted as "Congress Builds a Coffin," *The New York Review of Books*, January 11, 1996.

4. David Stockman, *The Triumph of Politics*, p. 418.

5. Kevin P. Phillips, *The Emerging Republican Majority*, New Rochelle, NY, 1969.

6. Lewis Chester, Bruce Page, and Godfrey Hodgson, *An American Melodrama*, p. 652.

7. For these differences, see Howard W. Odum, *Southern Regions*, Chapel Hill, NC, 1936.

8. "Kissin' Jim" Folsom, Governor of Alabama 1946–50 and 1954–58. Folsom's social advantages were only relative. See Donald S. Strong, "Alabama: Tradition and Alienation" in William C. Harvard, *The Changing Politics of the South*, Baton Rouge, 1972.

9. Michael Lind, "Brave New Right," *The Bell Curve Wars*, ed. Steven Fraser, New York, 1995, p. 173, an expanded version of an article that appeared in *The New Republic*, October 31, 1994.

10. The Harvard social scientist was David K. Cohen, writing in *Commentary*. See Godfrey Hodgson, "Do Schools Make a Difference?" *Atlantic Monthly*, March 1973.

11. Godfrey Hodgson, "Do Schools Make a Difference?"

12. Colin L. Powell (with Joseph E. Persico), *My American Journey*, New York, 1995.

13. The following account owes much to a volume edited by my editor, Steve

Fraser, *The Bell Curve Wars*, containing essays by, among others, Stephen Jay Gould, Richard Nisbett, and Michael Lind, cited here.

14. Richard J. Herrnstein and Charles Murray, *The Bell Curve: Intelligence and Class Structure in American Life*, New York, 1994.

15. Richard Nisbett, "Race, IQ, and Scientism," in Steven Fraser (ed.), *The Bell Curve Wars*, p. 53.

16. Jeffrey Rosen and Charles Lane in Fraser (ed.), *op. cit.*, p. 61.

17. *Ibid.*, p. 11. Professor Gould also states his opinion that *The Bell Curve* is not an academic treatise but "a manifesto of conservative ideology."

18. *Ibid.*, pp. 172–178.

19. *Ibid.*, p. 173.

20. Tom Wolfe, *The Bonfire of the Vanities*.

21. America is by no means the first nation to believe in its universal destiny. The Romans and at least five European nations — Spanish, French, British, German, and Russian — have believed at some point or another in their history that they had a universal, God-given mission of one sort or another. Both Chinese and Japanese have held similar beliefs, and so too have several other Asian peoples, including Egyptians and Iranians. For a long time the Chinese emperors found it hard to understand the concept of an ambassador from another power, since by definition the whole world was already under their empire! See Alain Peyrefitte, *The Collision of Two Civilizations*, London, 1993, pp. 552–553.

22. The title of a book by the social scientist Seymour Martin Lipset.

23. Daniel Bell, *The End of American Exceptionalism*, turns out to be an expression of regret for the passing of this, to Bell, desirable belief.

24. Senator Joseph McCarthy, speech in Wisconsin, July 1950.

25. Peggy Noonan, *What I Saw at the Revolution: A Political Life in the Reagan Era*, p. 14.

26. *Ibid.*

27. Alan Crawford, *Thunder on the Right*, p. 5.

28. Paul Weyrich, quoted in John S. Saloma, *Ominous Politics: The New Conservative Labyrinth*, p. 49.

29. It is only fair to add that Buckley went on to say, "But altogether too much is made of that fact. Negative action is not necessarily of negative value." Buckley, *Up from Liberalism*, p. 219.

30. See, for example, Paul Gottfried, *The Conservative Movement*, New York, 1993; note his account of the "meetings and informal sessions" in 1990, such as the Union League Club meeting on January 22, attended by Richard John Neuhaus, William F. Buckley, Irving Kristol, and Norman Podhoretz. Gottfried also described the many charges and countercharges of anti-Semitism in conservative circles from 1989 on.

31. David Frum has a good example of this particular dilemma in *Dead Right*, p. 105. Under the Constitution, forfeiture of property may not be enforced as a penalty for high treason. But when a police dog sniffed cocaine on three one-dollar bills in the till of a Chaldean merchant in Detroit, meaning that he might have sold a bottle of beer to a drug user, police confiscated all the cash on the premises: more than $4,000. And the Feds instituted forfeiture proceedings on Robert

Machin, a Harvard dropout living in Vermont, because twelve marijuana plants had been seen growing on his farm.

32. Sidney Blumenthal, *The Rise of the Counter-Establishment*, New York, 1986. "To counteract this Liberal Establishment, which conservatives believe encompasses both political parties, they deliberately created the Counter-Establishment . . . Through the making of a far-flung network they attempted to conquer political society. Their factories of ideology — think tanks, institutes, and journals — would win legitimacy for notions that would be translated into policy. The Counter-Establishment was a political elite aspiring to become a governing elite."

Select Bibliography

The literature relevant to an understanding of the rise and prospects of American conservatism between the 1940s and the 1990s is as voluminous as the sands of the sea. Even on quite small specific areas crucial to understanding the development of conservative thought and conservative political strength, such as McCarthyism, the religious right, or the attack on Keynesian orthodoxy, it is considerable. The bibliography that follows does not exhaust even this particular hard-pressed author's reading, let alone the subject. It is offered in the hope that it may give readers some ideas for further reading and for investigating aspects of the subject.

Abel, Lionel. *The Intellectual Follies: A Memoir of the Literary Venture in New York and Paris.* New York, 1984.

Adonis, Andrew, and Tim Hames, eds. *A Conservative Revolution?* Manchester, 1994.

Anderson, Martin. *Revolution.* New York, 1988.

——. *The Power of Ideas in the Making of Economic Policy.* Palo Alto, Cal., 1987.

Bakke v. Regents of the University of California. 438 US 265 (1978).

Banfield, Edward C. *The Unheavenly City.* Boston, 1970.

Bates, Stephen. *Battleground.* New York, 1993.

Bell, Daniel, ed. *The Radical Right.* Freeport, N.Y., 1971.

Berube, Maurice R., and Marilyn Gittell, eds. *Confrontation at Ocean Hill–Brownsville: The New York School Strikes of 1968.* New York, 1969.

Binder, David. "New CIA Estimate Finds Soviet Seeks Superiority in Arms." *New York Times,* December 26, 1976.

Blinder, Alan S. *Hard Heads, Soft Hearts: Tough-Minded Economics for a Just Society.* Reading, Mass., 1987.

Bloom, Alexander. *Prodigal Sons: The New York Intellectuals and Their World.* New York and Oxford, 1986.

Blumenthal, Sidney. "The Conservative Elite." Series of four articles, *Washington Post*, September 22–25, 1985.

———. *The Rise of the Counter-Establishment: From Conservative Ideology to Political Power.* New York, 1986.

———. *Our Long National Daydream.* New York, 1990.

"Born Again!" *Newsweek*, October 25, 1976.

Brady, David W., John E. Cogan, and Douglas Rivers. *How the Republicans Captured the House: An Assessment of the 1994 Midterm Elections.* Palo Alto, Cal., 1995.

Branden, Barbara. *The Passion of Ayn Rand.* New York, 1986.

Brinkley, Alan. *Voices of Protest: Huey Long, Father Coughlin and the Great Depression.* New York, 1982.

Bruce, Steve. *The Rise and Fall of the New Christian Right.* New York and Oxford, 1988.

Buckley, William F., Jr. *God and Man at Yale.* Chicago, 1951.

———. *Up from Liberalism.* New York, 1965.

———. *Happy Days Were Here Again: Reflections of a Libertarian Journalist.* New York, 1993.

Buckley, William F., Jr., ed. *Did You Ever See a Dream Walking?* New York, 1970.

Buckley, William F., with L. Brent Bozell. *McCarthy and His Enemies.* Chicago, 1954.

Bunzel, John H. "Bakke vs. University of California." *Commentary*, March 1977.

Cannon, Lou. *Reagan.* New York, 1982.

Carlson, Jody. *George C. Wallace and the Politics of Powerlessness.* New Brunswick, N.J., and London, 1981.

Carter, Jimmy. *Keeping Faith: Memoirs of a President.* New York, 1982.

Chambers, Whittaker. *Witness.* New York, 1952.

Christiano, Kevin J. "Contemporary Developments in American Religion." In Godfrey Hodgson, ed., *Handbooks to the Modern World: The United States.* New York, 1992.

Clendinen, Dudley. "'Christian New Right's Rush to Power." *New York Times*, August 18, 1980, p. B7.

Cox, Michael. *U.S. Foreign Policy after the Cold War: Superpower Without a Mission.* London, 1995.

Craig, Barbara Hinkson, and David O'Brien. *Abortion and American Politics*, Chatham, N.J., 1993.

Crawford, Alan. *Thunder on the Right: The "New Right" and the Politics of Resentment.* New York, 1980.

Cromartie, Michael, ed. *No Longer Exiles.* Washington, D.C., 1993.

———. *Disciples and Democracy: Religious Conservatives and the Future of American Politics.* Washington, D.C., 1994.

Crunden, Robert M. *The Mind and Art of Albert Jay Nock.* New York, 1964.

Danzig, David. "The Radical Right and the Rise of The Fundamentalist Minority." *Commentary*, April 1962, pp. 291–98.

Danziger, Sheldon, and Peter Gottschalk, eds. *Uneven Tides: Rising Inequality in America.* New York, 1992.

Dionne, E. J., Jr. *Why Americans Hate Politics.* New York, 1991.

———. *They Only Look Dead: Why Progressives Will Dominate the Next Political Era.* New York, 1996.

Dreyfuss, Joel, and Charles Lawrence III. *The Bakke Case: The Politics of Inequality*. New York, 1979.

D'Souza, Dinesh. *Illiberal Education: The Politics of Race and Sex on Campus*. New York, 1991.

Dworkin, Ronald M. "The Bakke Case: Did It Decide Anything?" *New York Review of Books*, August 17, 1978.

———. *Life's Dominion*. New York, 1993.

Edsall, Thomas Byrne. *The New Politics of Inequality*. New York, 1984.

Engelhardt, Tom. *The End of Victory Culture*. New York, 1994.

Evans, M. Stanton. *The Future of Conservatism*. New York, 1968.

Evans, Rowland, and Robert Novak. *The Reagan Revolution*. New York, 1981.

Ferguson, Thomas, and Joel Rogers, eds. *The Hidden Election: Politics and Economics in the 1980 Presidential Campaign*. New York, 1981.

Feulner, Edwin J., Jr. "Waging and Winning the War of Ideas." Address to the Public Relations Society of America, 39th national conference. Washington, D.C., November 12, 1986.

———. "Building the New Establishment." Interviewed by Adam Meyerson. Heritage Foundation, *Policy Review*, Fall 1991.

Finney, John W. "Assessing Soviet Strength Is a Team Task." *New York Times*, February 6, 1977.

Forster, Arnold, and Benjamin R. Epstein. *Danger on the Right*. New York, 1964.

Fossedal, Gregory A., and Dinesh D'Souza. "Dartmouth's Restoration." *National Review*, September 1981.

Frank, Robert H., and Philip J. Cook. *The Winner-Take-All Society*. New York, 1995.

Fraser, Steven, ed. *The Bell Curve Wars*. New York, 1994.

Friedman, Milton. *Capitalism and Freedom*. Chicago, 1962.

———. "The Role of Monetary Policy." Presidential address to the 80th annual general meeting of the American Economic Association. *American Economic Review* 58, 1 (March 1968), pp. 1–17.

Friedman, Milton, and Anna Jacobson Schwartz. *A Monetary History of the United States, 1867–1960*. Princeton, N.J., 1963.

Friedman, Murray. "Is White Racism the Problem?" *Commentary*, January 1969.

Frum, David. *Dead Right*. New York, 1994.

Gilder, George. *Wealth and Poverty*. New York, 1981.

Gillespie, Ed, and Bob Schellhas, eds. *Contract with America*. New York, 1994.

Glad, Betty. *Jimmy Carter: In Search of the Great White House*. New York, 1980.

Glazer, Nathan. *Remembering the Answers: Essays on the American Student Revolt*. New York, 1970.

———. "On Being Deradicalized." *Commentary*, October 1970.

———. "The Limits of Social Policy." *Commentary*, September 1971.

———. *Affirmative Discrimination: Ethnic Inequality and Public Policy*. New York, 1983.

Gottfried, Paul. *The Conservative Movement*. New York, 1993.

Hall, Robert E., and Alvin Rabushka. *The Flat Tax*. Palo Alto, Cal., 1985.

Harrison, Bennett, and Barry Bluestone. *The Great U-Turn: Corporate Restructuring and the Polarizing of America*. New York, 1988; new ed., 1990.

Hayek, F. A. *The Road to Serfdom*. London, 1944.

————. *The Constitution of Liberty*. Chicago, 1960.

Herrnstein, Richard J., and Charles Murray. *The Bell Curve: Intelligence and Class Structure in American Life*. New York, 1994.

Himmelstein, Jerome L. *To the Right: The Transformation of American Conservatism*. Berkeley, Cal., 1989.

Hixson, William B., Jr. *Search for the American Right Wing*, Princeton, N.J., 1992.

Hofstadter, Richard. *The Paranoid Tradition in American Politics*. New York, 1965.

Hollenweger, Walter J. *The Pentecostals*. London, 1972.

Howe, Irving. *World of Our Fathers*. New York, 1983.

Judis, John B. *William F. Buckley, Jr.* New York, 1988.

————. "The Conservative Crackup." *The American Prospect*, Fall 1990.

Kazin, Michael. *The Populist Persuasion*. New York, 1994.

Kelley, Dean. *Why Conservative Churches Are Growing*. New York, 1972.

Kirk, Russell. *The Conservative Mind*. New York, 1953.

Kotz, Nick. "King Midas of the 'New Right.'" *Atlantic Monthly*, November 1978.

Kristol, Irving. "Why Jews Turn Conservative." *Wall Street Journal*, September 14, 1972.

————. "The Battle for Reagan's Soul." *Wall Street Journal*, May 16, 1980.

————. *Reflections of a Neoconservative*. New York, 1983.

Kuttner, Robert. *Revolt of the Haves*. New York, 1980.

Lacey, Michael J., ed. *Religion and Twentieth-Century American Intellectual Life*. Cambridge, England, 1989.

Leube, Kurt R., ed. *The Essence of Friedman*. Palo Alto, Cal., 1987.

Lewy, Guenter. *America in Vietnam*. New York, 1978.

Lichtenstein, Nelson. *The Most Dangerous Man in Detroit: Walter Reuther and the Fate of American Labor*. New York, 1995.

Limbaugh, Rush. *The Way Things Ought to Be*. New York, 1992.

Lind, Michael. *The Next American Nation*. New York, 1995.

Lowi, Theodore J. *The End of the Republican Era*. Norman, Okla., 1995.

Lukas, J. Anthony. *Common Ground*. New York, 1978.

Mack, Bob. "The Boys Who Would Be Buckley." *Spy*, July 1989.

Mervin, David. *Ronald Reagan and the American Presidency*. New York, 1990.

Meyer, Frank S., ed. *What Is Conservatism?* New York, 1964.

Miles, Michael W. *The Odyssey of the American Right*. New York, 1980.

Moffett, George D., III. *The Limits of Victory: The Ratification of the Panama Treaties*. Ithaca, N.Y., 1985.

Morgan, Dan. *Rising in the West*. New York, 1992.

Murray, Charles. *Losing Ground: American Social Policy, 1950–1980*. New York, 1984.

Nash, George H. *The Conservative Intellectual Movement in America Since 1945*. New York, 1976.

National Review. Files, 1955 to 1980, on microfilm.

Neuhaus, Richard J. *The Naked Public Square*. Grand Rapids, Mich., 1984.

Neuhaus, Richard J., and Michael Cromartie, eds. *Piety and Politics: Evangelicals and Fundamentalists Confront the World*. Washington, D.C., 1987.

Nisbet, Robert. *Conservatism*. Minneapolis, 1986.

Nitze, Paul L. *From Hiroshima to Glasnost: At the Center of Decision*. New York, 1989.

Noonan, Peggy. *What I Saw at the Revolution: A Political Life in the Reagan Era*. New York, 1990.

Novak, Michael. *The Rise of the Unmeltable Ethnics.* New York, 1971.

Peele, Gillian. *Revival and Reaction: The Right in Contemporary America.* Oxford, 1984.

Phelps, E. S. "Phillips Curve, Expectations of Inflation and Optimal Unemployment over Time." *Economica* 34 (August 1967), pp. 254–281.

Phillips, A. W. "The Relationship Between Unemployment and the Rate of Change of Money Wage Rates in the United Kingdom." *Economica,* November 1958, pp. 283–299.

Phillips, Kevin L. *The Emerging Republican Majority.* New York, 1968.

———. *The Politics of Rich and Poor.* New York, 1990.

Pierard, Richard V. "Reagan and the Evangelicals." *Christian Century,* December 21–28, 1983.

Pines, Burton Yale. *Back to Basics: The Traditionalist Movement That Is Sweeping Grass-Roots America.* New York, 1982.

Pipes, Richard. "Why the Soviet Union Thinks It Could Fight and Win a Nuclear War." *Commentary,* July 1977.

Podhoretz, Norman. *Breaking Ranks: A Political Memoir.* New York, 1979.

———. "The New American Majority." *Commentary,* January 1981.

———. "Why Reagan and Koch Are the Most Popular Politicians in America." *New York,* April 6, 1981.

Polsby, Nelson W. "Towards an Explanation of McCarthyism." *Political Studies* 8 (1960), pp. 250–271.

Powell, Colin. *A Soldier's Way.* London, 1995.

Public Interest, The. 1966–.

Rand, Ayn. *The Fountainhead.* New York, 1943.

———. *Atlas Shrugged.* New York, 1957.

Reagan, Ronald W. *An American Life.* New York, 1990.

Reinhard, David W. *The Republican Right Since 1945.* Lexington, Ky., 1983.

Rieder, Jonathan. *Canarsie: The Jews and Italians of Brooklyn Against Liberalism.* Cambridge, Mass., 1985.

Rifkin, Jeremy, and Ted Howard. "Second Reformation Ahead." *Raleigh News and Observer,* October 7, 1979.

Rogin, Michael P. *The Intellectuals and McCarthy.* Cambridge, Mass., 1967.

Rogin, Michael Paul, and John L. Shover. *Political Change in California.* Westport, Conn., 1970.

Rothmyer, Karen. "Citizen Scaife." *Columbia Journalism Review,* July/August 1981.

Rusher, William. *The Making of the New Majority Party.* New York, 1975.

Rutland, Robert A. *The Democrats: From Jefferson to Carter.* Baton Rouge and London, 1979.

Sallis, Jim, and Wesley Michaelson. "The Plan to Save America." *Sojourners,* April 1976.

Sandel, Michael, ed. *Liberalism and Its Critics.* New York, 1984.

Sandoz, Ellis. *A Tide of Discontent: The 1980 Elections and Their Meaning.* New York, 1981.

Schuck, Peter H. "Can 'Neoconservatives' Do More Than Oppose?" *Wall Street Journal,* July 3, 1979.

Shadegg, Stephen. *What Happened to Goldwater?* New York, 1965.

Shultz, George P. *Turmoil and Triumph.* New York, 1993.

Shupe, Anson, and John Heinerman. "Mormonism and the New Christian Right: An Emerging Coalition." *Review of Religious Research*, Vol. 27, no. 2, December 1985.

Sindler, Allan P. *Bakke, DeFunis and Minority Admissions*. New York, 1989.

Skerry, Peter. "Christian Schools versus the IRS." *The Public Interest* 61–64, 1980–81.

Smith, Hedrick, et al. *Reagan, the Man, the President*. New York, 1980.

Stein, Herbert. *Presidential Economics: The Making of Economic Policy from Roosevelt to Reagan and Beyond*. Washington, D.C., 1988.

Steinfels, Peter. *Neo-Conservatives: The Men Who Are Changing American Politics*. New York, 1980.

Stockman, David. *The Triumph of Politics*. New York, 1986.

Strauss, Leo. *Liberalism Ancient and Modern*, New York and London, 1968.

———. *Natural Right and History*, Chicago, 1953.

Tuchman, Barbara. *The First Salute*. London, 1989.

Viereck, Peter. *The Unadjusted Man*. Boston, 1956.

Viguerie, Richard A. *The New Right: We're Ready to Lead*. Falls Church, Va., 1980.

———. *The Establishment vs. The People: Is a New Populist Revolt on the Way?* Chicago, 1983.

Wanniski, Jude. *The Way the World Works: How Economies Fail — and Succeed*. New York, 1978.

Warner, Judith, and Max Berley. *Newt Gingrich: Speaker to America*. New York, 1995.

Weisberg, Jacob. "Hunter Gatherers." *New Republic*, September 2, 1991.

"What Is a Liberal — Who Is a Conservative?" Symposium in *Commentary*, September 1976.

Wills, Garry. *Reagan's America: Innocents at Home*. Garden City, N.Y., 1985.

White, F. Clifton, with William J. Gill. *Suite 3505: The Story of the Goldwater Movement*. Ashland, Ohio, 1992.

Zwier, Robert, and Richard Smith. "Christian Politics and the New Right." *Christian Century* 97 (October 8, 1980), pp. 937–941.

Index